I'M TEMPTED TO STOP ACTING RANDOMLY

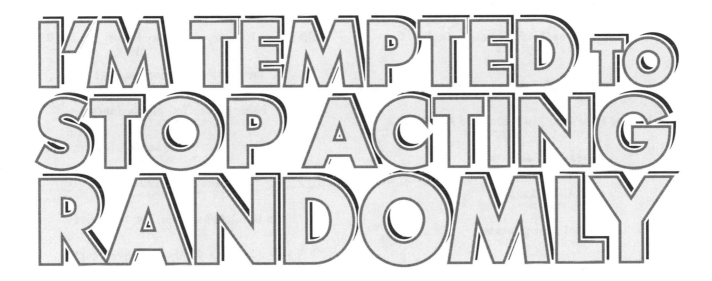

Other DILBERT® books from Andrews McMeel Publishing

Problem Identified
ISBN: 978-7407-8534-4

14 Years of Loyal Service in a Fabric-Covered Box
ISBN: 978-0-7407-7365-5

Freedom's Just Another Word for People Finding Out You're Useless
ISBN: 978-0-7407-7815-5

Dilbert 2.0: 20 Years of Dilbert
ISBN: 978-0-7407-7735-6

This Is the Part Where You Pretend to Add Value
ISBN: 978-0-7407-7227-6

Cubes and Punishment
ISBN: 978-0-7407-6837-8

Positive Attitude
ISBN: 978-0-7407-6379-3

Try Rebooting Yourself
ISBN: 978-0-7407-6190-4

What Would Wally Do?
ISBN: 978-0-7407-5769-3

Thriving on Vague Objectives
ISBN: 978-0-7407-5533-0

The Fluorescent Light Glistens Off Your Head
ISBN: 978-0-7407-5113-4

It's Not Funny If I Have to Explain It
ISBN: 978-0-7407-4658-1

Don't Stand Where the Comet Is Assumed to Strike Oil
ISBN: 978-0-7407-4539-3

Words You Don't Want to Hear During Your Annual Performance Review
ISBN: 978-0-7407-3805-0

When Body Language Goes Bad
ISBN: 978-0-7407-3298-0

What Do You Call a Sociopath in a Cubicle? Answer: A Coworker
ISBN: 978-0-7407-2663-7

Another Day in Cubicle Paradise
ISBN: 978-0-7407-2194-6

When Did Ignorance Become a Point of View?
ISBN: 978-0-7407-1839-7

Excuse Me While I Wag
ISBN: 978-0-7407-1390-3

Dilbert—A Treasury of Sunday Strips: Version 00
ISBN: 978-0-7407-0531-1

Random Acts of Management
ISBN: 978-0-7407-0453-6

Dilbert Gives You the Business
ISBN: 978-0-7407-0003-3

Don't Step in the Leadership
ISBN: 978-0-8362-7844-6

Journey to Cubeville
ISBN: 978-0-8362-6745-7

I'm Not Anti-Business, I'm Anti-Idiot
ISBN: 978-0-8362-5182-1

Seven Years of Highly Defective People
ISBN: 978-0-8362-3668-2

Casual Day Has Gone Too Far
ISBN: 978-0-8362-2899-1

Fugitive from the Cubicle Police
ISBN: 978-0-8362-2119-0

It's Obvious You Won't Survive by Your Wits Alone
ISBN: 978-0-8362-0415-5

Still Pumped from Using the Mouse
ISBN: 978-0-8362-1026-2

Bring Me the Head of Willy the Mailboy!
ISBN: 978-0-8362-1779-7

Shave the Whales
ISBN: 978-0-8362-1740-7

Dogbert's Clues for the Clueless
ISBN: 978-0-8362-1737-7

Always Postpone Meetings with Time-Wasting Morons
ISBN: 978-0-8362-1758-2

Build a Better Life by Stealing Office Supplies
ISBN: 978-0-8362-1757-5

For ordering information, call 1-800-223-2336.

I'M TEMPTED TO STOP ACTING RANDOMLY

DILBERT

by SCOTT ADAMS

Andrews McMeel
Publishing, LLC

Kansas City • Sydney • London

10 11 12 13 14 RR2 10 9 8 7 6 5 4 3 2 1

ISBN: 978-0-7407-7806-3

Library of Congress Control Number: 2010924494

www.andrewsmcmeel.com

www.dilbert.com

——— **ATTENTION: SCHOOLS AND BUSINESSES** ———

Andrews McMeel books are available at quantity discounts with bulk purchase for educational, business, or sales promotional use. For information, please write to: Special Sales Department, Andrews McMeel Publishing, LLC, 1130 Walnut Street, Kansas City, Missouri 64106.

For Shelly

Introduction

I know an engineer who figured out a clever way to improve his company's product to the point where it suddenly leapfrogged the competition. As a result of his excellent work, the sales guys became millionaires. It turns out that there were no caps on commissions, and management didn't raise the sales quotas to account for the fact that the improved product would practically sell itself. The moral of the story is that it's great to be a technical genius, but it's even better to be lucky.

There was a time when I believed that my rewards were related to my actions. Eventually I discovered that my rewards were more related to the actions of strangers. For example, you're only reading this book because there weren't any strangers creating their own popular office-based comic strip when Dilbert was new. You can't get the benefit of going first unless all of the other people in the world decide to do something else. Thank you for that.

Recently, a yogurt shop with a great concept opened in my town. Customers can serve themselves from a variety of flavors, add their own toppings, and pay based on weight. Unfortunately for the owner, two more yogurt shops with the same concept popped up nearby within months. That means all three owners were probably working on the same secret idea at about the same time. I'm guessing that none of the yogurt shops is doing well after splitting the market three ways. This is yet another example where acting randomly would have been equal to, or better than, executing a great idea.

Woody Allen famously said that ninety percent of life is just showing up. But that doesn't give enough credit to all of the people who decide to be somewhere else and stay out of your way. And how do you know where you should show up? Success is more random than we like to believe.

The good news is that you can read this book with a clean conscience because whatever you were going to do otherwise is probably just as worthless. And if you have any good workplace stories of random behavior being rewarded, I'd love to hear them. Send me an e-mail if you get a chance.

S. Adams

DilbertCartoonist@gmail.com

HOW MUCH WILL IT COST TO DEVELOP OUR NEXT GENERATION PRODUCT?
IT WILL COST WHATEVER YOU PUT IN THE BUDGET.
HOW MUCH SHOULD I PUT IN THE BUDGET?
ASK FOR THE BIGGEST NUMBER YOU THINK WILL GET APPROVED.
IF WE GET A LOT OF MONEY WE CAN BUILD SOMETHING GREAT.
IF WE DON'T GET MUCH MONEY WE CAN BUILD SOMETHING LAME, AND COMPENSATE FOR THE LACK OF QUALITY BY LYING MORE VIGOROUSLY THAN USUAL.
I'LL AIM LOW SO I DON'T GET YELLED AT DURING THE EXECUTIVE BUDGET MEETING.
I REMEMBER A TIME WHEN THIS SORT OF THING WOULD HAUNT ME.
©2009 Scott Adams, Inc./Dist. by UFS, Inc.
7-26-09

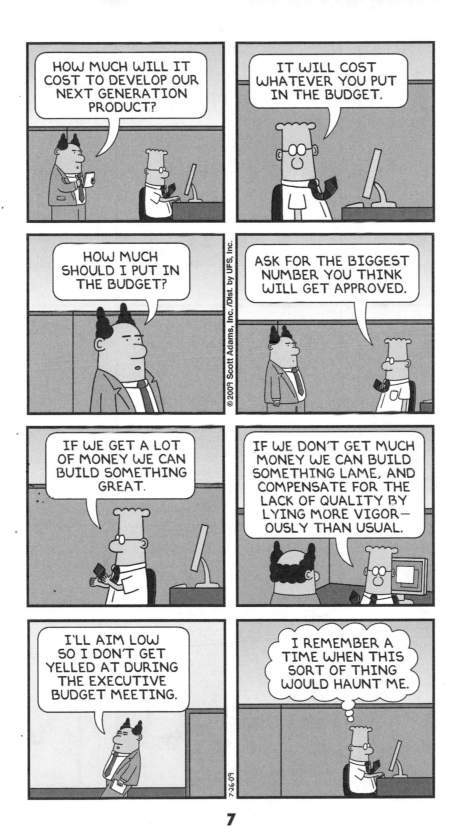

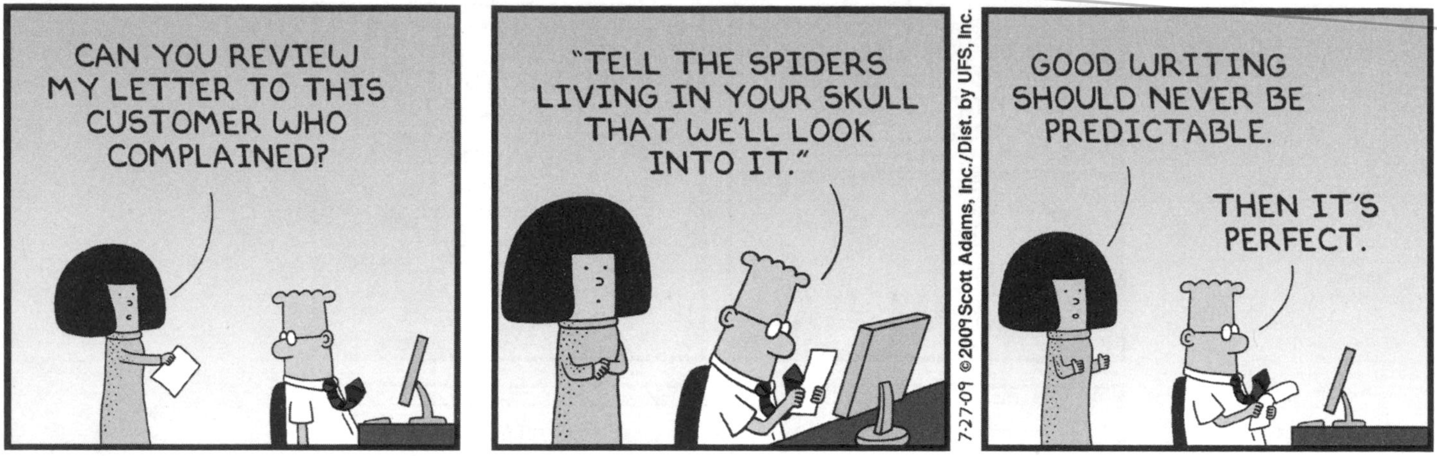
CAN YOU REVIEW MY LETTER TO THIS CUSTOMER WHO COMPLAINED?
"TELL THE SPIDERS LIVING IN YOUR SKULL THAT WE'LL LOOK INTO IT."
7-27-09 © 2009 Scott Adams, Inc./Dist. by UFS, Inc.
GOOD WRITING SHOULD NEVER BE PREDICTABLE.
THEN IT'S PERFECT.

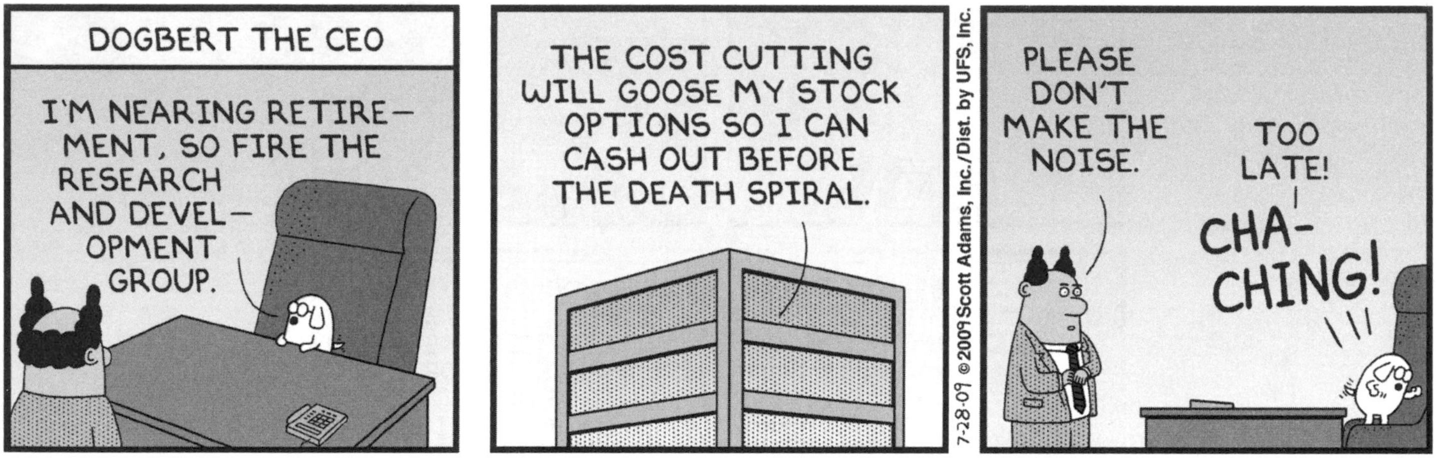
DOGBERT THE CEO
I'M NEARING RETIRE-MENT, SO FIRE THE RESEARCH AND DEVEL-OPMENT GROUP.
THE COST CUTTING WILL GOOSE MY STOCK OPTIONS SO I CAN CASH OUT BEFORE THE DEATH SPIRAL.
7-28-09 © 2009 Scott Adams, Inc./Dist. by UFS, Inc.
PLEASE DON'T MAKE THE NOISE.
TOO LATE!
CHA-CHING!

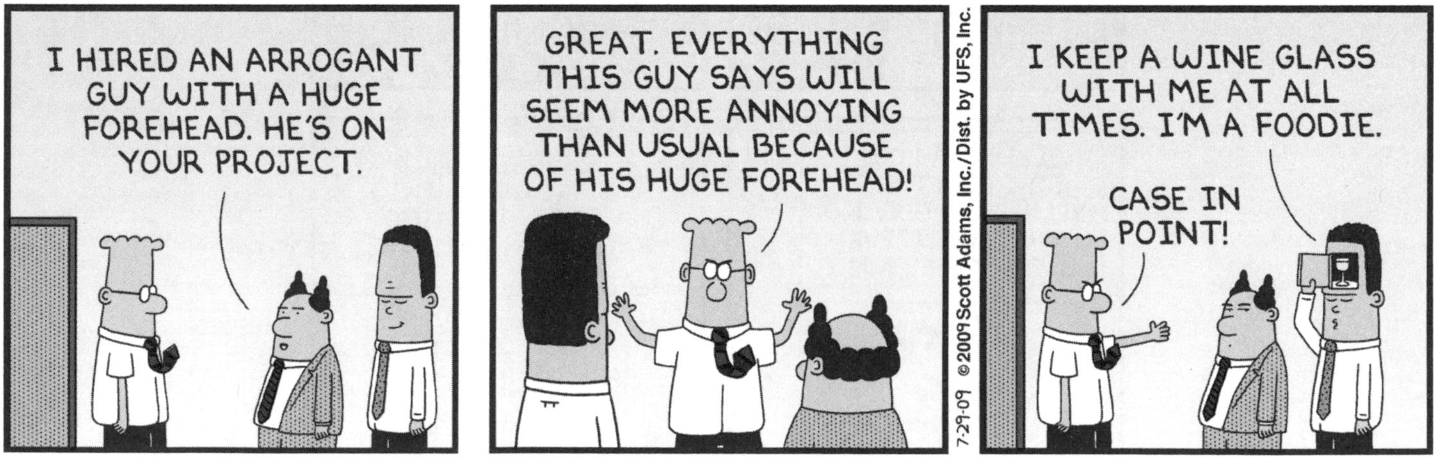
I HIRED AN ARROGANT GUY WITH A HUGE FOREHEAD. HE'S ON YOUR PROJECT.
GREAT. EVERYTHING THIS GUY SAYS WILL SEEM MORE ANNOYING THAN USUAL BECAUSE OF HIS HUGE FOREHEAD!
7-29-09 © 2009 Scott Adams, Inc./Dist. by UFS, Inc.
I KEEP A WINE GLASS WITH ME AT ALL TIMES. I'M A FOODIE.
CASE IN POINT!

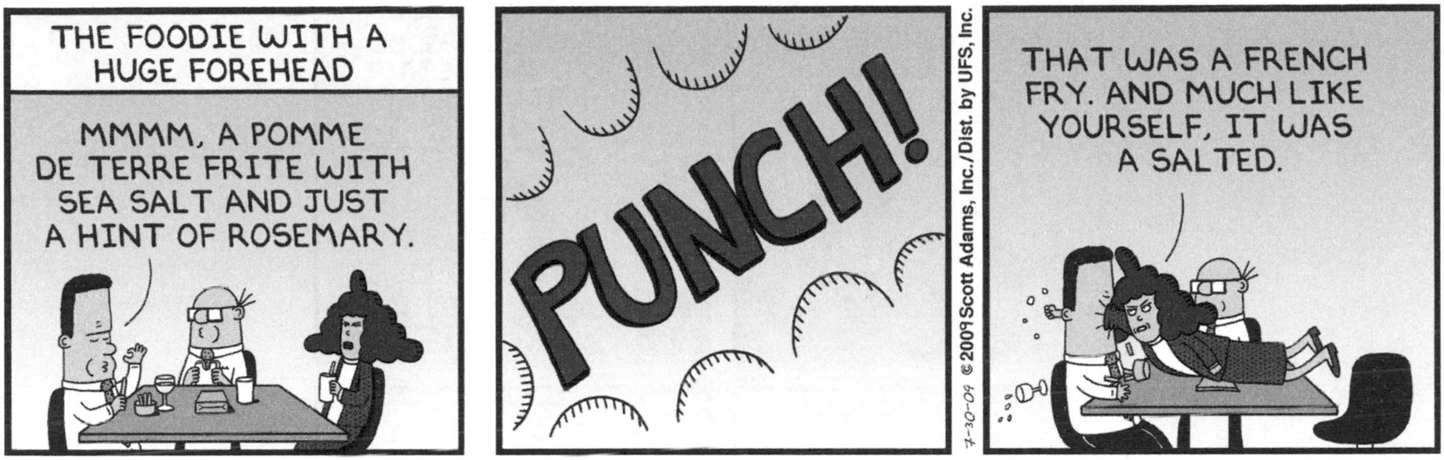
THE FOODIE WITH A HUGE FOREHEAD
MMMM, A POMME DE TERRE FRITE WITH SEA SALT AND JUST A HINT OF ROSEMARY.
PUNCH!
©2009 Scott Adams, Inc./Dist. by UFS, Inc.
7-30-09
THAT WAS A FRENCH FRY. AND MUCH LIKE YOURSELF, IT WAS A SALTED.

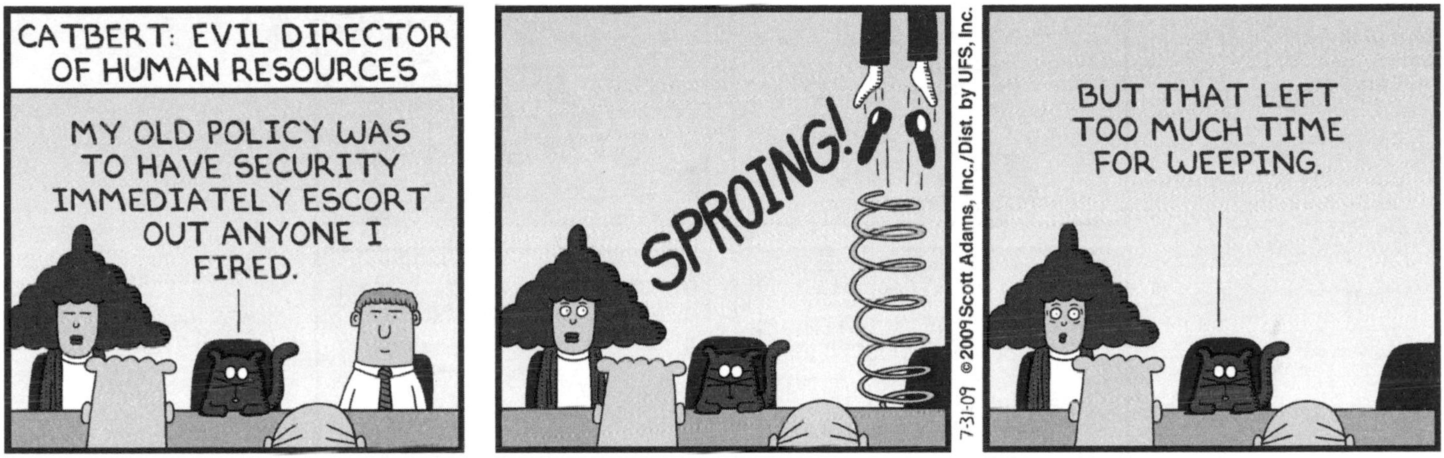
CATBERT: EVIL DIRECTOR OF HUMAN RESOURCES
MY OLD POLICY WAS TO HAVE SECURITY IMMEDIATELY ESCORT OUT ANYONE I FIRED.
SPROING!
©2009 Scott Adams, Inc./Dist. by UFS, Inc.
7-31-09
BUT THAT LEFT TOO MUCH TIME FOR WEEPING.

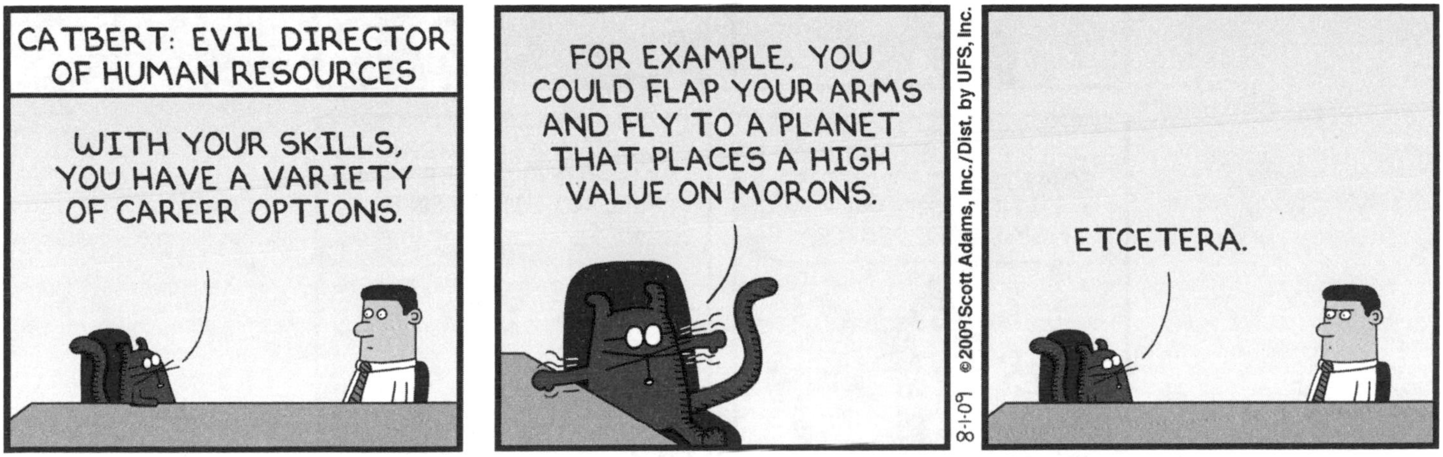
CATBERT: EVIL DIRECTOR OF HUMAN RESOURCES
WITH YOUR SKILLS, YOU HAVE A VARIETY OF CAREER OPTIONS.
FOR EXAMPLE, YOU COULD FLAP YOUR ARMS AND FLY TO A PLANET THAT PLACES A HIGH VALUE ON MORONS.
©2009 Scott Adams, Inc./Dist. by UFS, Inc.
8-1-09
ETCETERA.

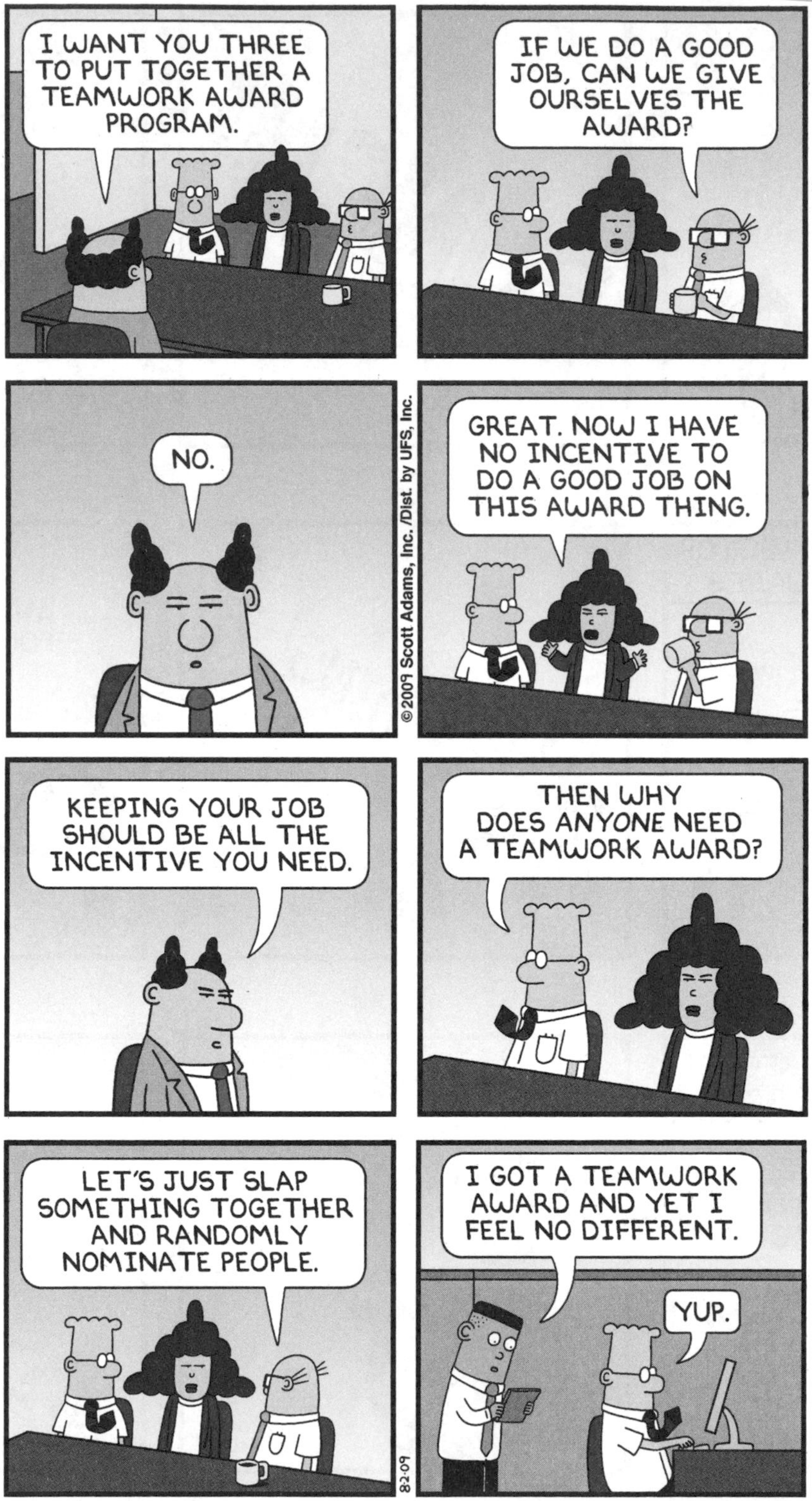
I WANT YOU THREE TO PUT TOGETHER A TEAMWORK AWARD PROGRAM.
IF WE DO A GOOD JOB, CAN WE GIVE OURSELVES THE AWARD?
NO.
GREAT. NOW I HAVE NO INCENTIVE TO DO A GOOD JOB ON THIS AWARD THING.
KEEPING YOUR JOB SHOULD BE ALL THE INCENTIVE YOU NEED.
THEN WHY DOES *ANYONE* NEED A TEAMWORK AWARD?
LET'S JUST SLAP SOMETHING TOGETHER AND RANDOMLY NOMINATE PEOPLE.
I GOT A TEAMWORK AWARD AND YET I FEEL NO DIFFERENT.
YUP.
©2009 Scott Adams, Inc./Dist. by UFS, Inc.
8-2-09

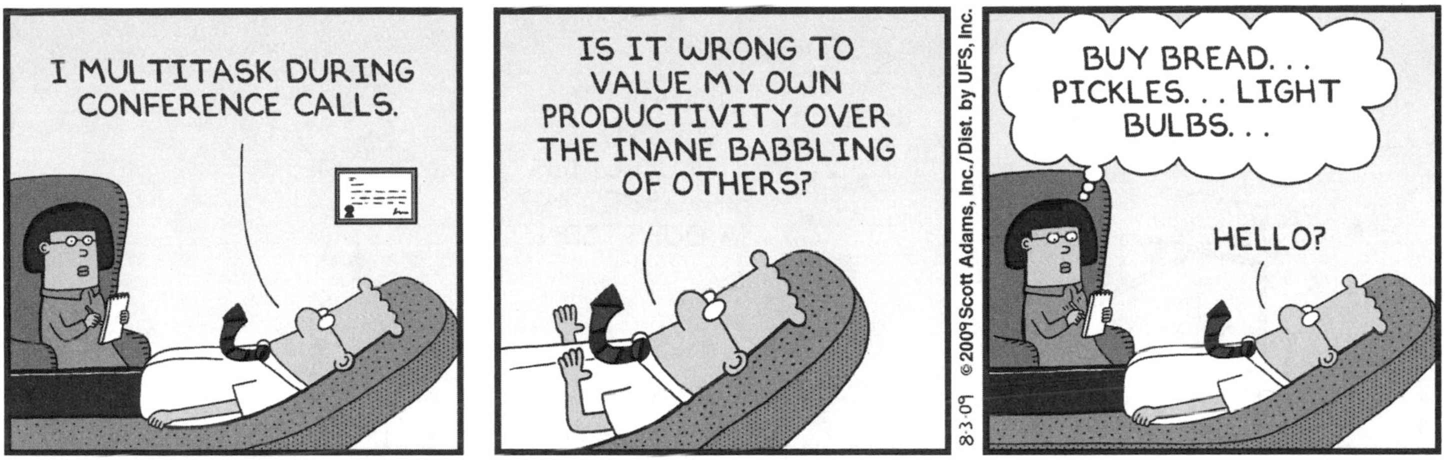
I MULTITASK DURING CONFERENCE CALLS.
IS IT WRONG TO VALUE MY OWN PRODUCTIVITY OVER THE INANE BABBLING OF OTHERS?
8-3-09 ©2009 Scott Adams, Inc./Dist. by UFS, Inc.
BUY BREAD. . . PICKLES. . . LIGHT BULBS. . .
HELLO?

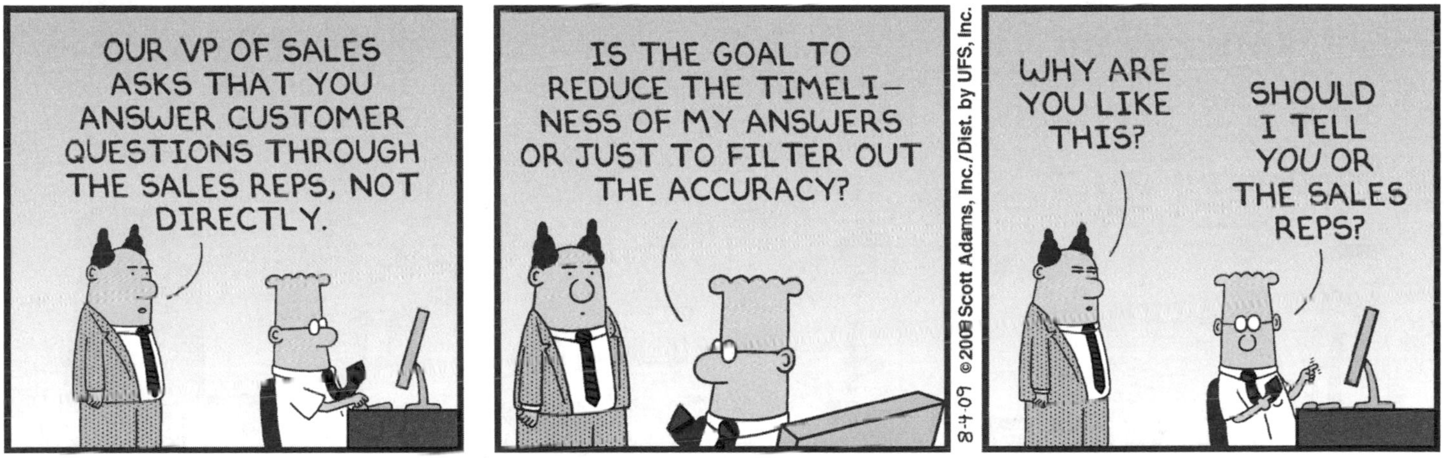
OUR VP OF SALES ASKS THAT YOU ANSWER CUSTOMER QUESTIONS THROUGH THE SALES REPS, NOT DIRECTLY.
IS THE GOAL TO REDUCE THE TIMELI-NESS OF MY ANSWERS OR JUST TO FILTER OUT THE ACCURACY?
8-4-09 ©2009 Scott Adams, Inc./Dist. by UFS, Inc.
WHY ARE YOU LIKE THIS?
SHOULD I TELL *YOU* OR THE SALES REPS?

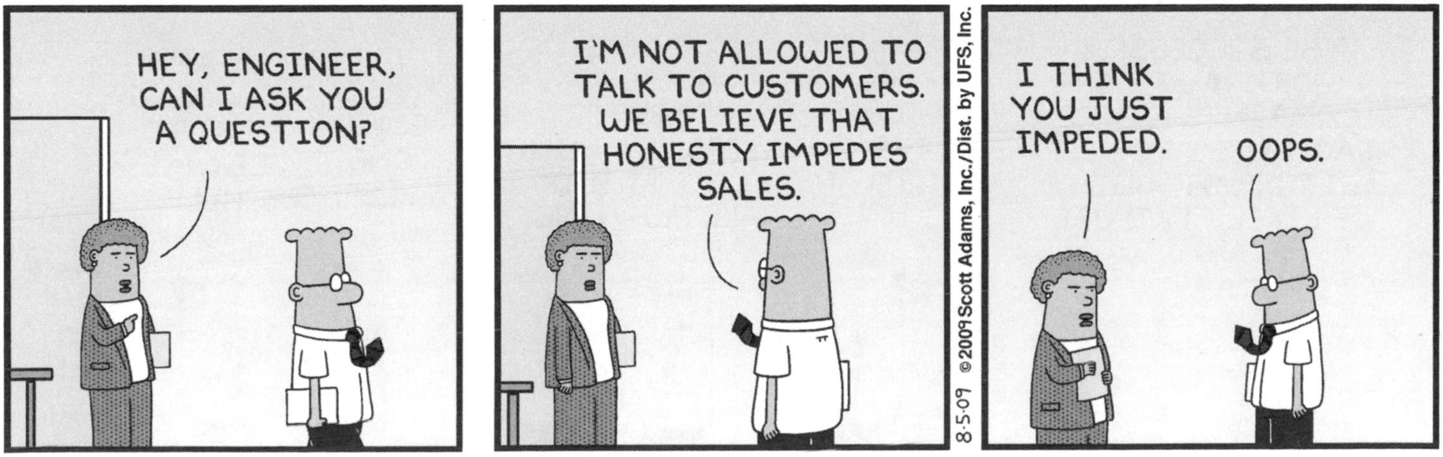
HEY, ENGINEER, CAN I ASK YOU A QUESTION?
I'M NOT ALLOWED TO TALK TO CUSTOMERS. WE BELIEVE THAT HONESTY IMPEDES SALES.
8-5-09 ©2009 Scott Adams, Inc./Dist. by UFS, Inc.
I THINK YOU JUST IMPEDED.
OOPS.

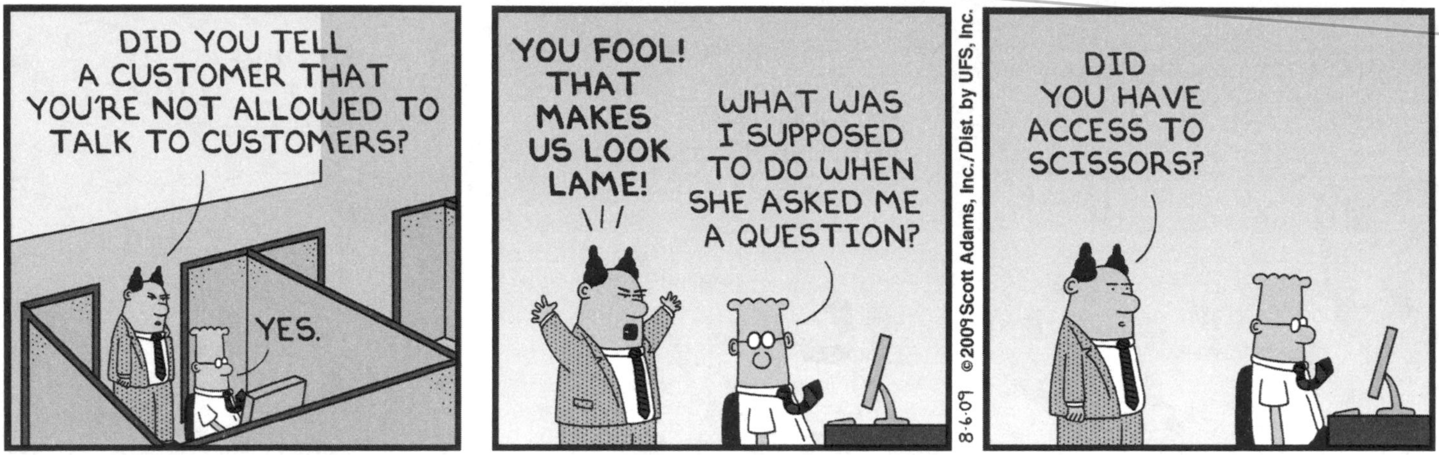
DID YOU TELL A CUSTOMER THAT YOU'RE NOT ALLOWED TO TALK TO CUSTOMERS?
YES.
YOU FOOL! THAT MAKES US LOOK LAME!
WHAT WAS I SUPPOSED TO DO WHEN SHE ASKED ME A QUESTION?
8-6-09 © 2009 Scott Adams, Inc./Dist. by UFS, Inc.
DID YOU HAVE ACCESS TO SCISSORS?

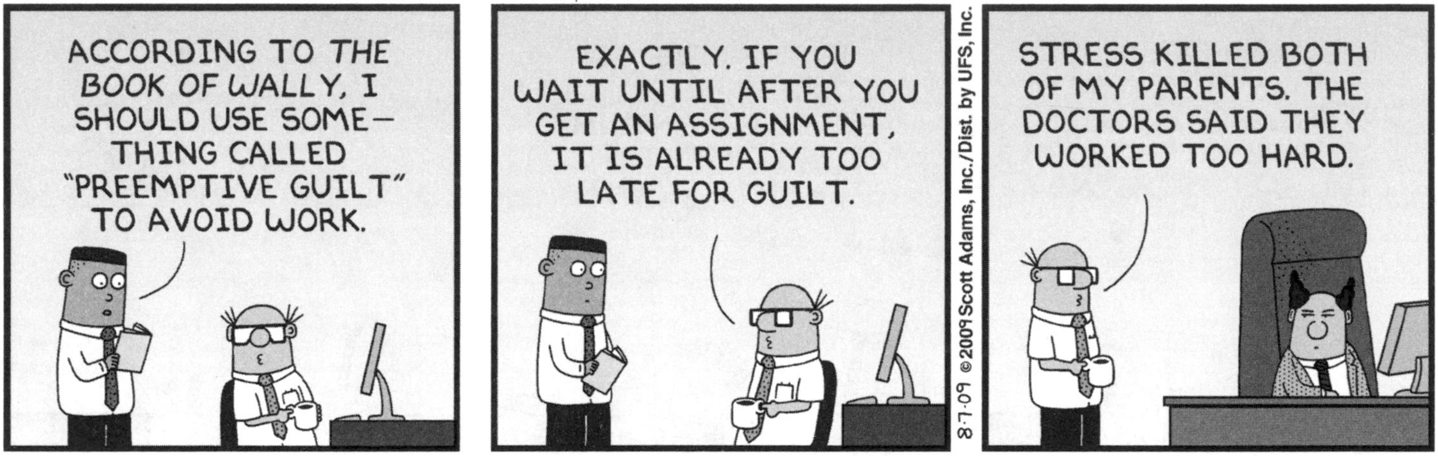
ACCORDING TO *THE BOOK OF WALLY*, I SHOULD USE SOME-THING CALLED "PREEMPTIVE GUILT" TO AVOID WORK.
EXACTLY. IF YOU WAIT UNTIL AFTER YOU GET AN ASSIGNMENT, IT IS ALREADY TOO LATE FOR GUILT.
8-7-09 © 2009 Scott Adams, Inc./Dist. by UFS, Inc.
STRESS KILLED BOTH OF MY PARENTS. THE DOCTORS SAID THEY WORKED TOO HARD.

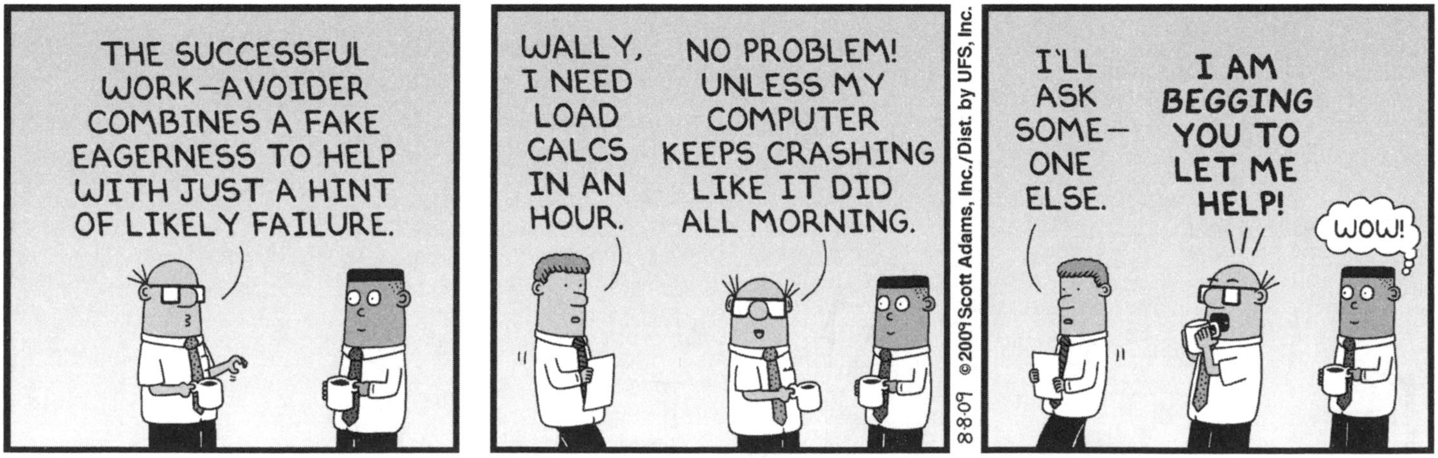
THE SUCCESSFUL WORK-AVOIDER COMBINES A FAKE EAGERNESS TO HELP WITH JUST A HINT OF LIKELY FAILURE.
WALLY, I NEED LOAD CALCS IN AN HOUR.
NO PROBLEM! UNLESS MY COMPUTER KEEPS CRASHING LIKE IT DID ALL MORNING.
8-8-09 © 2009 Scott Adams, Inc./Dist. by UFS, Inc.
I'LL ASK SOME-ONE ELSE.
I AM BEGGING YOU TO LET ME HELP!
WOW!

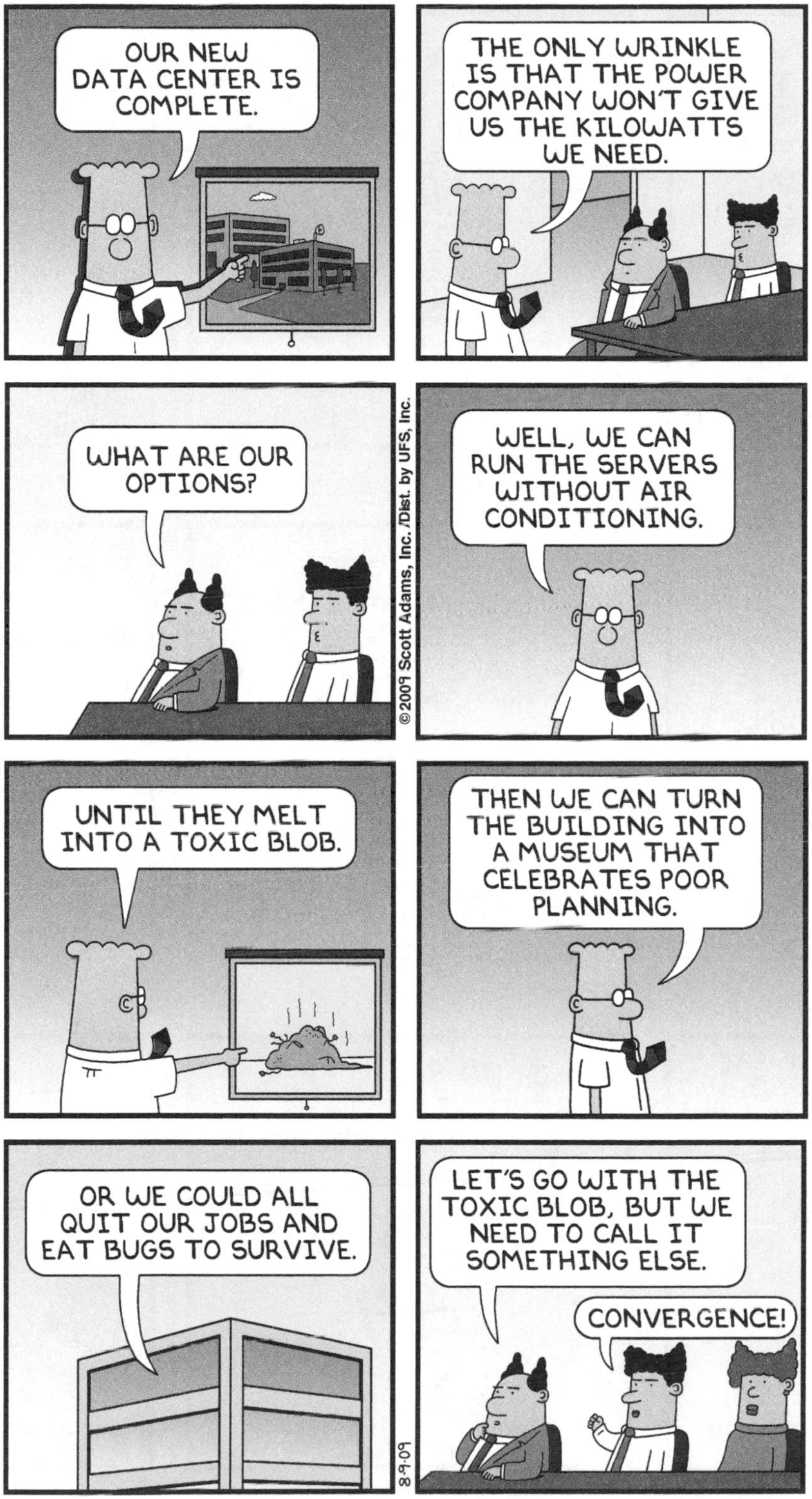
OUR NEW DATA CENTER IS COMPLETE.
THE ONLY WRINKLE IS THAT THE POWER COMPANY WON'T GIVE US THE KILOWATTS WE NEED.
WHAT ARE OUR OPTIONS?
WELL, WE CAN RUN THE SERVERS WITHOUT AIR CONDITIONING.
UNTIL THEY MELT INTO A TOXIC BLOB.
THEN WE CAN TURN THE BUILDING INTO A MUSEUM THAT CELEBRATES POOR PLANNING.
OR WE COULD ALL QUIT OUR JOBS AND EAT BUGS TO SURVIVE.
LET'S GO WITH THE TOXIC BLOB, BUT WE NEED TO CALL IT SOMETHING ELSE.
CONVERGENCE!
©2009 Scott Adams, Inc./Dist. by UFS, Inc.
8-9-09

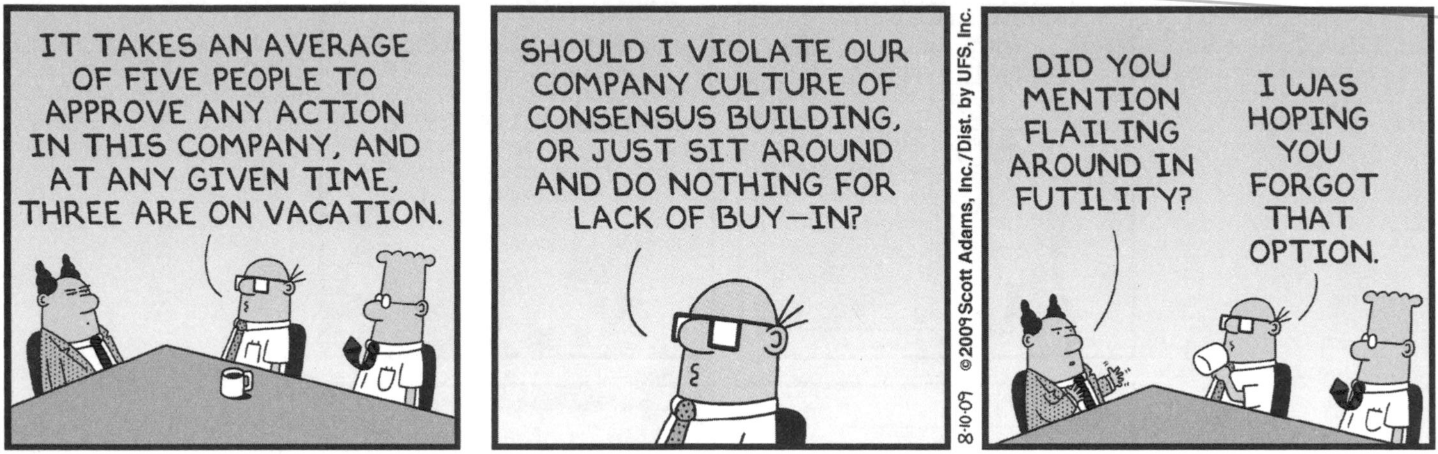
IT TAKES AN AVERAGE OF FIVE PEOPLE TO APPROVE ANY ACTION IN THIS COMPANY, AND AT ANY GIVEN TIME, THREE ARE ON VACATION.
SHOULD I VIOLATE OUR COMPANY CULTURE OF CONSENSUS BUILDING, OR JUST SIT AROUND AND DO NOTHING FOR LACK OF BUY-IN?
8-10-09 ©2009 Scott Adams, Inc./Dist. by UFS, Inc.
DID YOU MENTION FLAILING AROUND IN FUTILITY?
I WAS HOPING YOU FORGOT THAT OPTION.

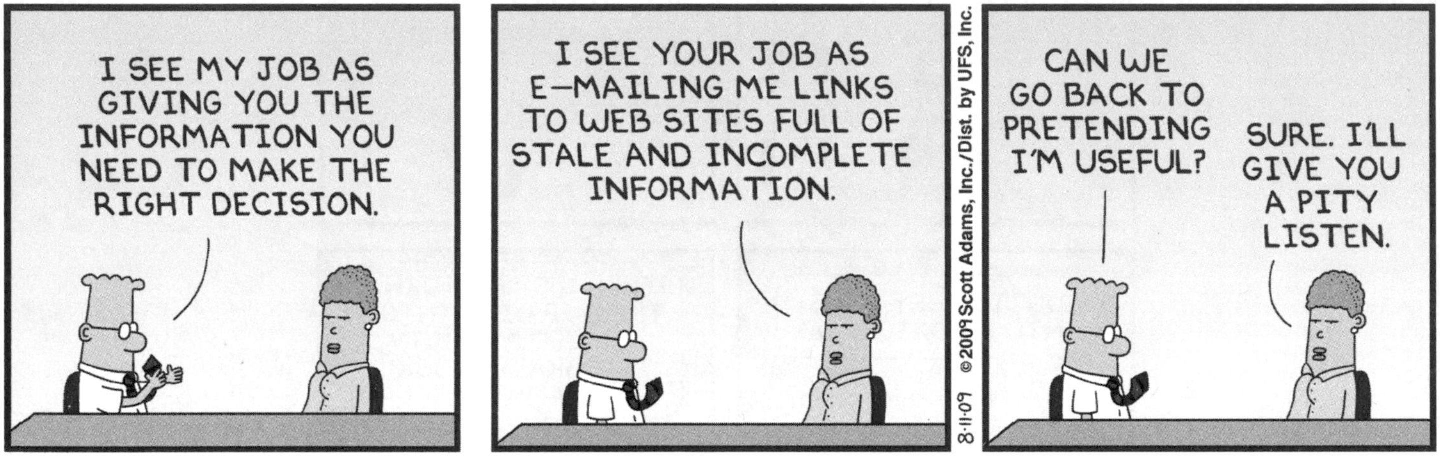
I SEE MY JOB AS GIVING YOU THE INFORMATION YOU NEED TO MAKE THE RIGHT DECISION.
I SEE YOUR JOB AS E-MAILING ME LINKS TO WEB SITES FULL OF STALE AND INCOMPLETE INFORMATION.
8-11-09 ©2009 Scott Adams, Inc./Dist. by UFS, Inc.
CAN WE GO BACK TO PRETENDING I'M USEFUL?
SURE. I'LL GIVE YOU A PITY LISTEN.

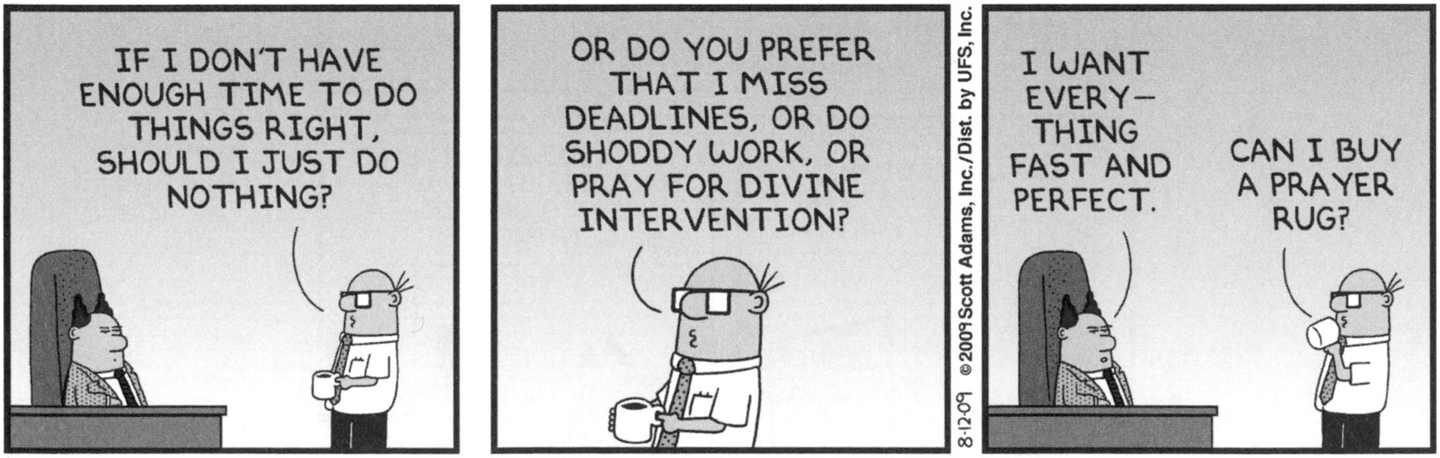
IF I DON'T HAVE ENOUGH TIME TO DO THINGS RIGHT, SHOULD I JUST DO NOTHING?
OR DO YOU PREFER THAT I MISS DEADLINES, OR DO SHODDY WORK, OR PRAY FOR DIVINE INTERVENTION?
8-12-09 ©2009 Scott Adams, Inc./Dist. by UFS, Inc.
I WANT EVERY-THING FAST AND PERFECT.
CAN I BUY A PRAYER RUG?

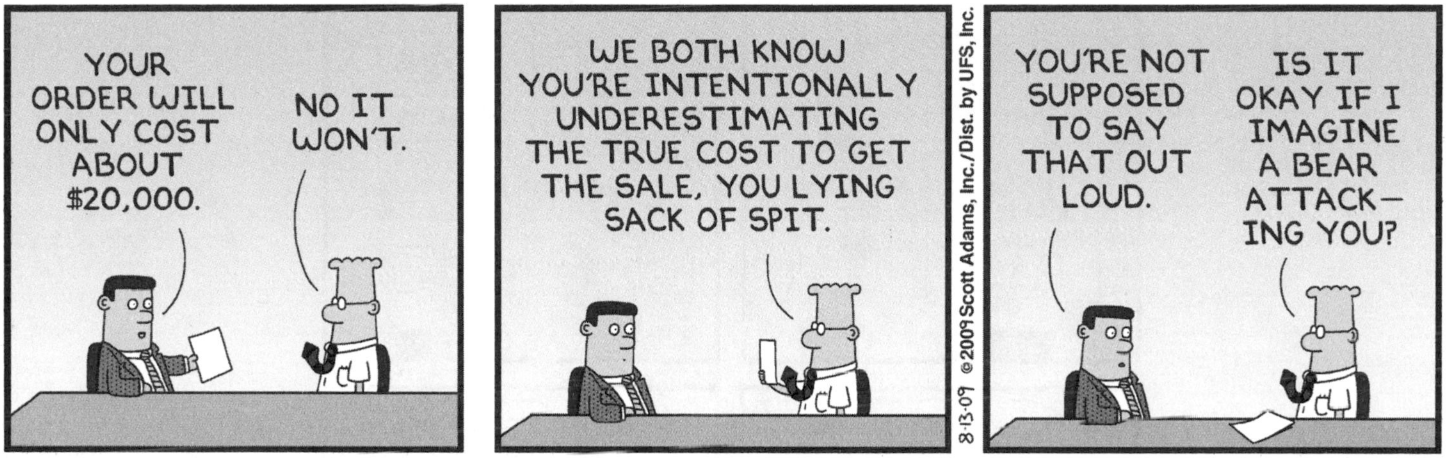
YOUR ORDER WILL ONLY COST ABOUT $20,000.
NO IT WON'T.
WE BOTH KNOW YOU'RE INTENTIONALLY UNDERESTIMATING THE TRUE COST TO GET THE SALE, YOU LYING SACK OF SPIT.
8-13-09 ©2009 Scott Adams, Inc./Dist. by UFS, Inc.
YOU'RE NOT SUPPOSED TO SAY THAT OUT LOUD.
IS IT OKAY IF I IMAGINE A BEAR ATTACKING YOU?

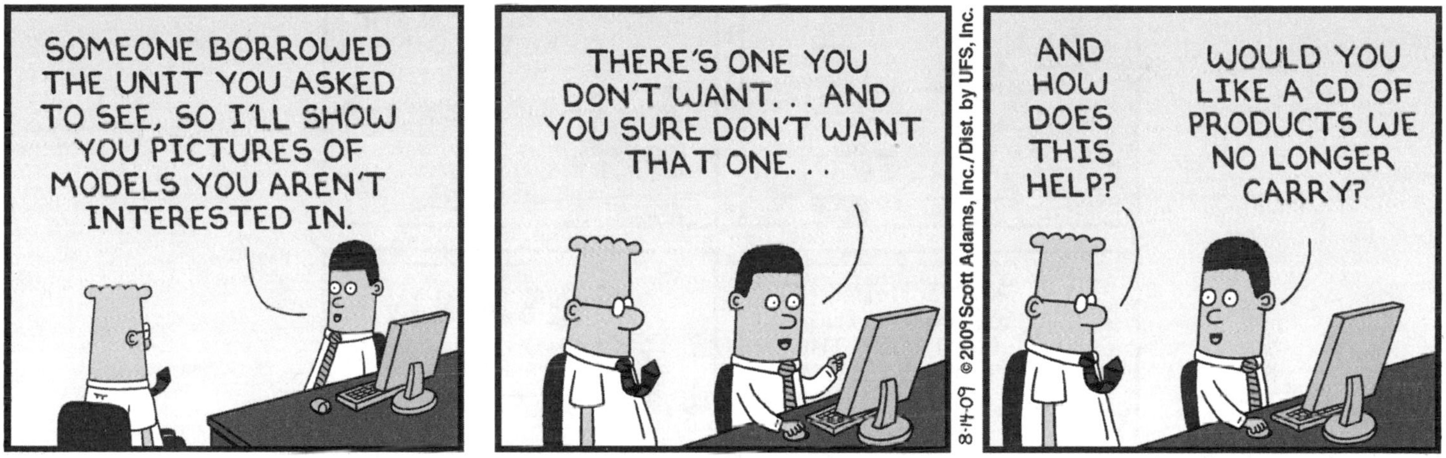
SOMEONE BORROWED THE UNIT YOU ASKED TO SEE, SO I'LL SHOW YOU PICTURES OF MODELS YOU AREN'T INTERESTED IN.
THERE'S ONE YOU DON'T WANT. . . AND YOU SURE DON'T WANT THAT ONE. . .
8-14-09 ©2009 Scott Adams, Inc./Dist. by UFS, Inc.
AND HOW DOES THIS HELP?
WOULD YOU LIKE A CD OF PRODUCTS WE NO LONGER CARRY?

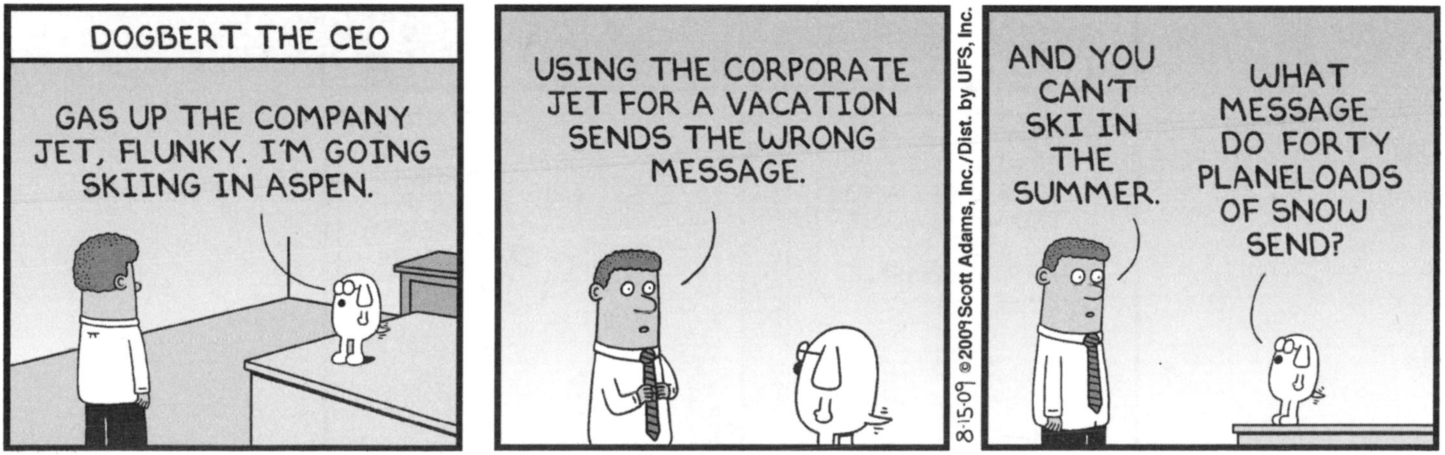
DOGBERT THE CEO
GAS UP THE COMPANY JET, FLUNKY. I'M GOING SKIING IN ASPEN.
USING THE CORPORATE JET FOR A VACATION SENDS THE WRONG MESSAGE.
8-15-09 ©2009 Scott Adams, Inc./Dist. by UFS, Inc.
AND YOU CAN'T SKI IN THE SUMMER.
WHAT MESSAGE DO FORTY PLANELOADS OF SNOW SEND?

IT'S TIME TO STIR THE SOUP.
I THINK TED IS STEALING.
YOU KNOW HOW SOMETIMES YOU CAN'T FIND THINGS IN YOUR OFFICE?
UM. . . YES.
THAT ONLY HAPPENS ON DAYS WHEN TED HAS BEEN IN THE BUILDING.
AND I THINK HE WAS WEARING A NEW SOCK THE OTHER DAY. HAVE YOU EVER LOST A SOCK?
HE'S BEEN IN MY HOUSE?!
EITHER THAT OR YOUR WIFE AND TED HAVE SOME SORT OF ARRANGEMENT.
TED. . .
IT MAKES MY LACK OF ACCOMP– LISHMENTS SEEM UNIM– PORTANT.
©2009 Scott Adams, Inc./Dist. by UFS, Inc.
8-16-09

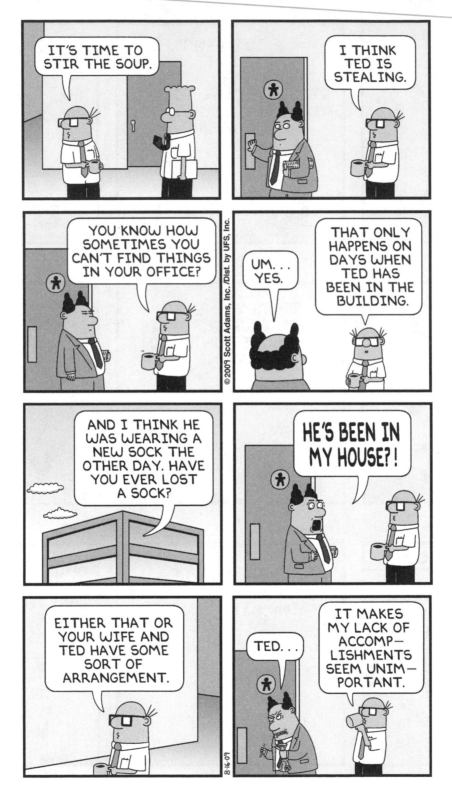

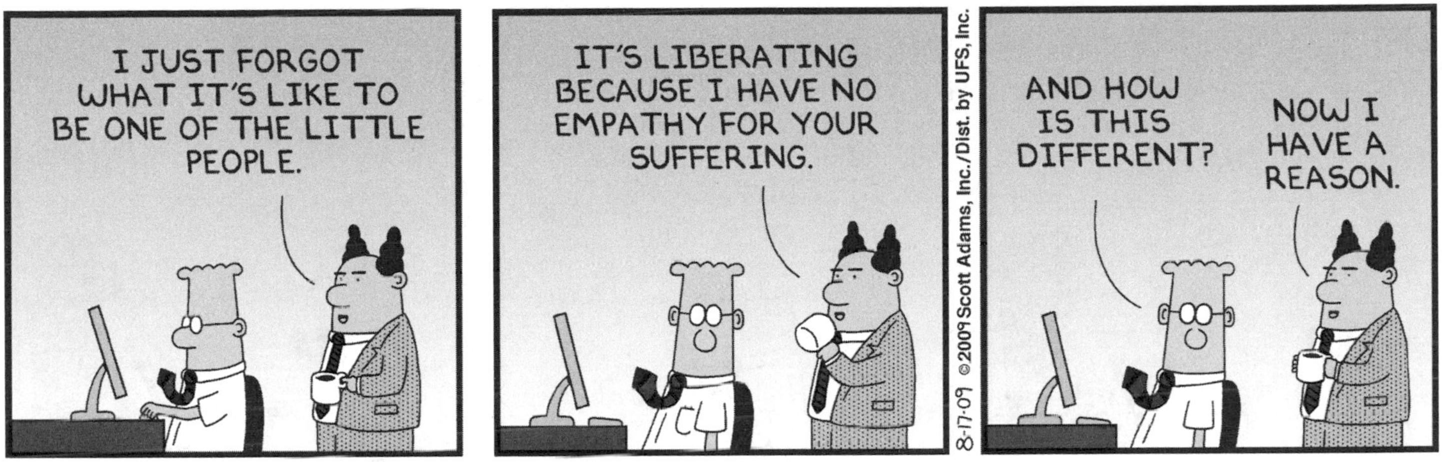
I JUST FORGOT WHAT IT'S LIKE TO BE ONE OF THE LITTLE PEOPLE.
IT'S LIBERATING BECAUSE I HAVE NO EMPATHY FOR YOUR SUFFERING.
8-17-09 © 2009 Scott Adams, Inc./Dist. by UFS, Inc.
AND HOW IS THIS DIFFERENT?
NOW I HAVE A REASON.

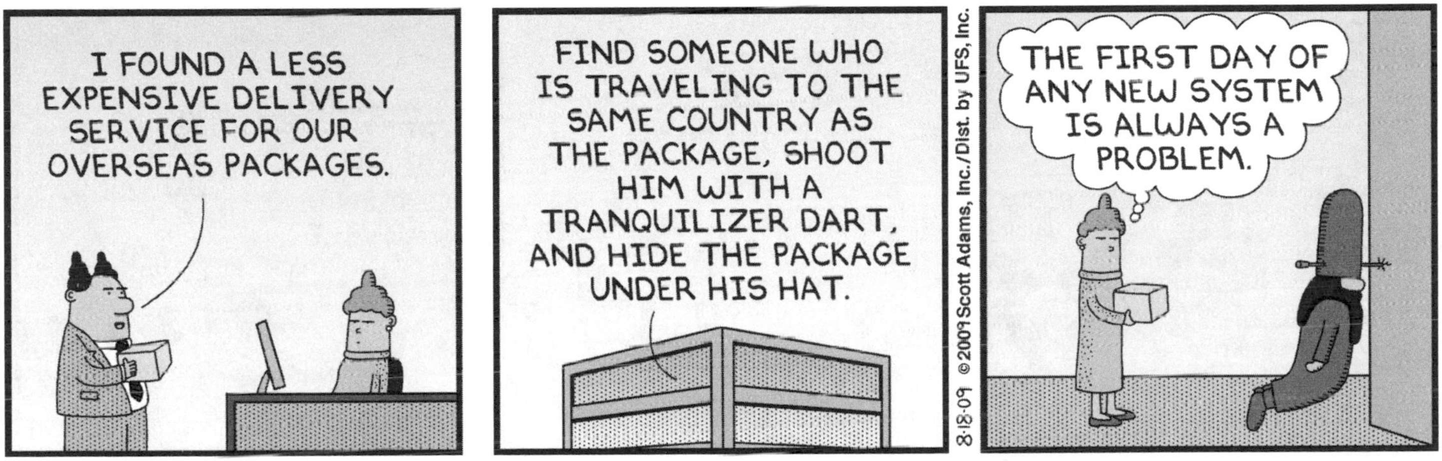
I FOUND A LESS EXPENSIVE DELIVERY SERVICE FOR OUR OVERSEAS PACKAGES.
FIND SOMEONE WHO IS TRAVELING TO THE SAME COUNTRY AS THE PACKAGE, SHOOT HIM WITH A TRANQUILIZER DART, AND HIDE THE PACKAGE UNDER HIS HAT.
8-18-09 © 2009 Scott Adams, Inc./Dist. by UFS, Inc.
THE FIRST DAY OF ANY NEW SYSTEM IS ALWAYS A PROBLEM.

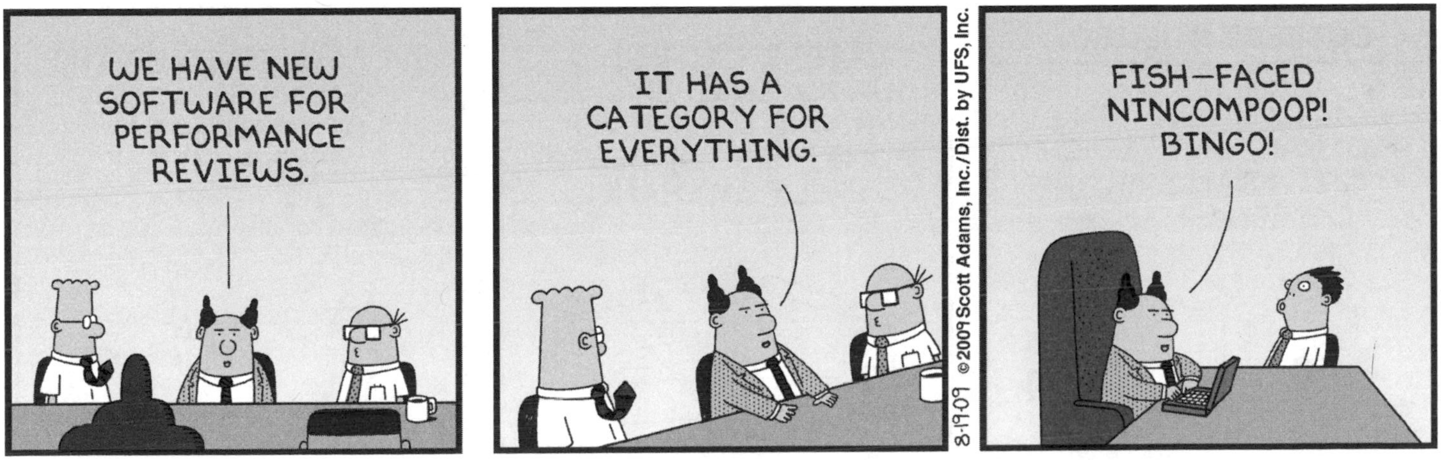
WE HAVE NEW SOFTWARE FOR PERFORMANCE REVIEWS.
IT HAS A CATEGORY FOR EVERYTHING.
8-19-09 © 2009 Scott Adams, Inc./Dist. by UFS, Inc.
FISH-FACED NINCOMPOOP! BINGO!

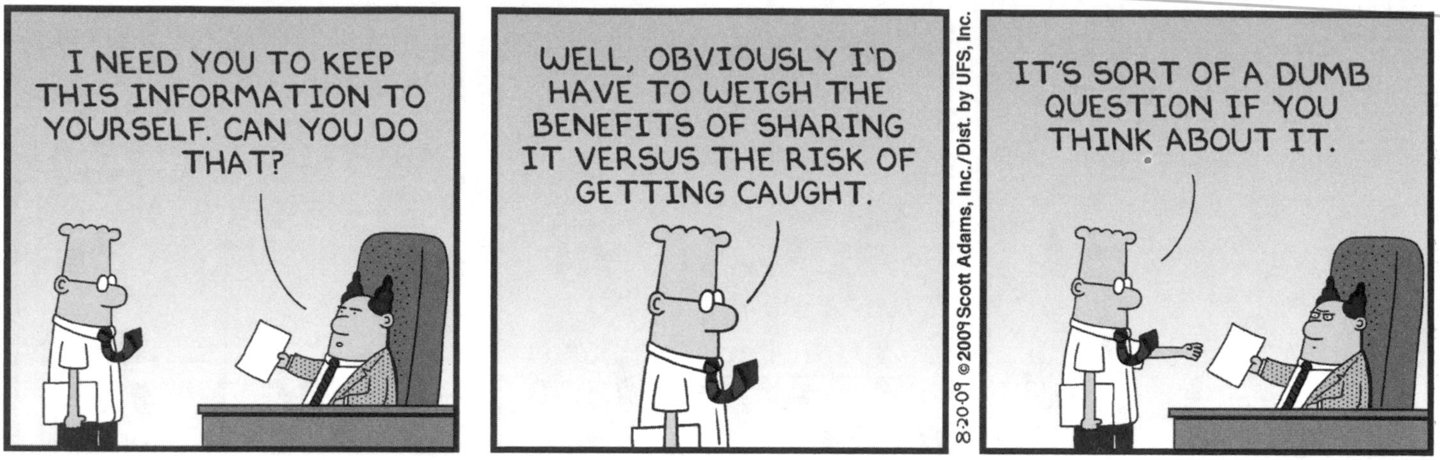
I NEED YOU TO KEEP THIS INFORMATION TO YOURSELF. CAN YOU DO THAT?
WELL, OBVIOUSLY I'D HAVE TO WEIGH THE BENEFITS OF SHARING IT VERSUS THE RISK OF GETTING CAUGHT.
8-20-09 ©2009 Scott Adams, Inc./Dist. by UFS, Inc.
IT'S SORT OF A DUMB QUESTION IF YOU THINK ABOUT IT.

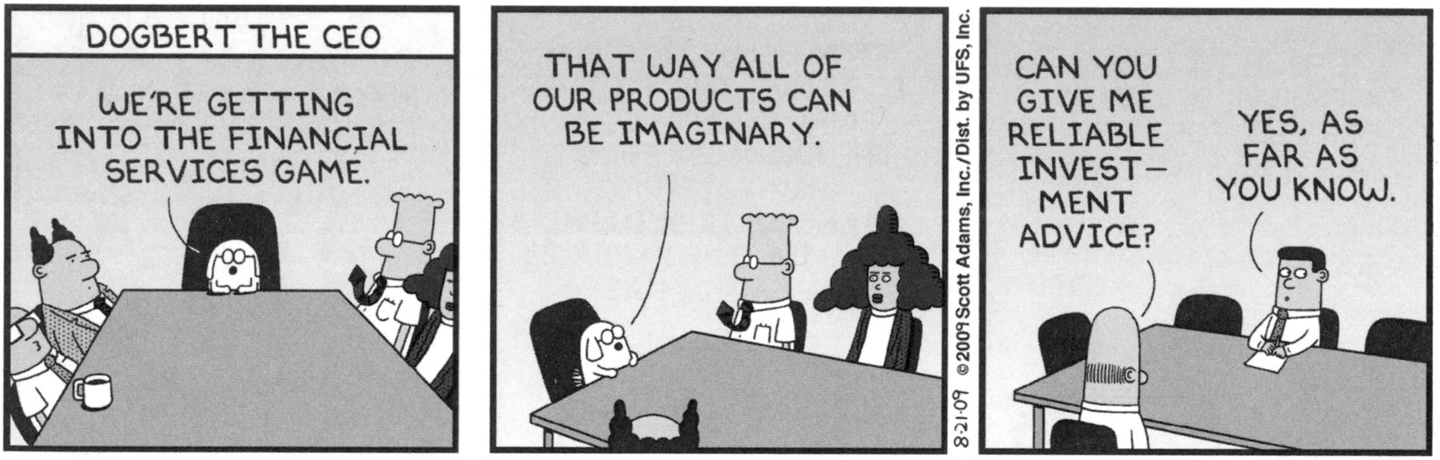
DOGBERT THE CEO
WE'RE GETTING INTO THE FINANCIAL SERVICES GAME.
THAT WAY ALL OF OUR PRODUCTS CAN BE IMAGINARY.
8-21-09 ©2009 Scott Adams, Inc./Dist. by UFS, Inc.
CAN YOU GIVE ME RELIABLE INVEST-MENT ADVICE?
YES, AS FAR AS YOU KNOW.

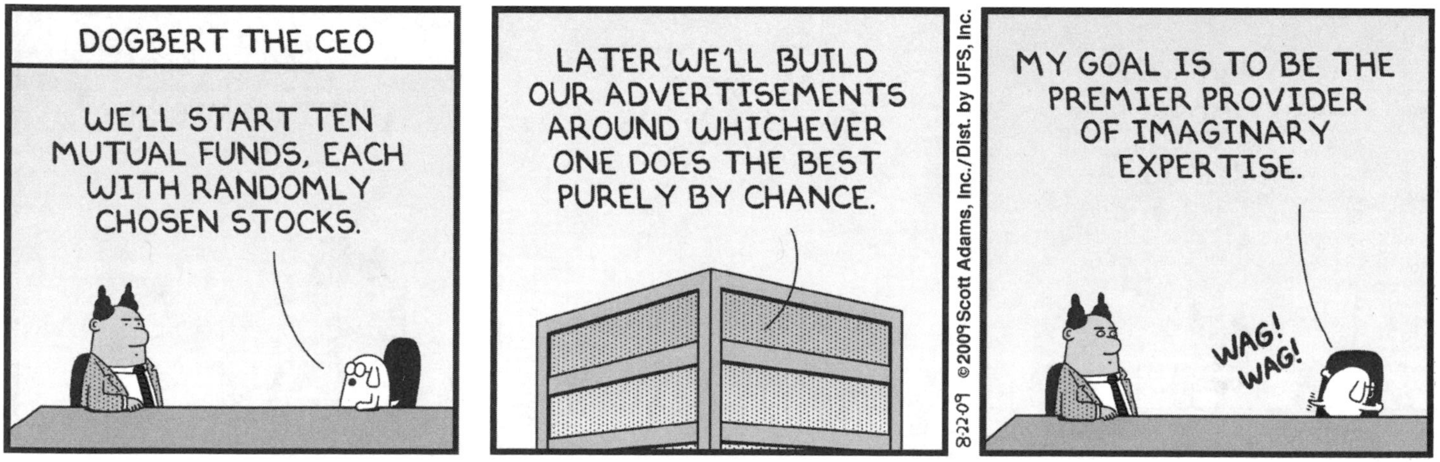
DOGBERT THE CEO
WE'LL START TEN MUTUAL FUNDS, EACH WITH RANDOMLY CHOSEN STOCKS.
LATER WE'LL BUILD OUR ADVERTISEMENTS AROUND WHICHEVER ONE DOES THE BEST PURELY BY CHANCE.
8-22-09 ©2009 Scott Adams, Inc./Dist. by UFS, Inc.
MY GOAL IS TO BE THE PREMIER PROVIDER OF IMAGINARY EXPERTISE.
WAG! WAG!

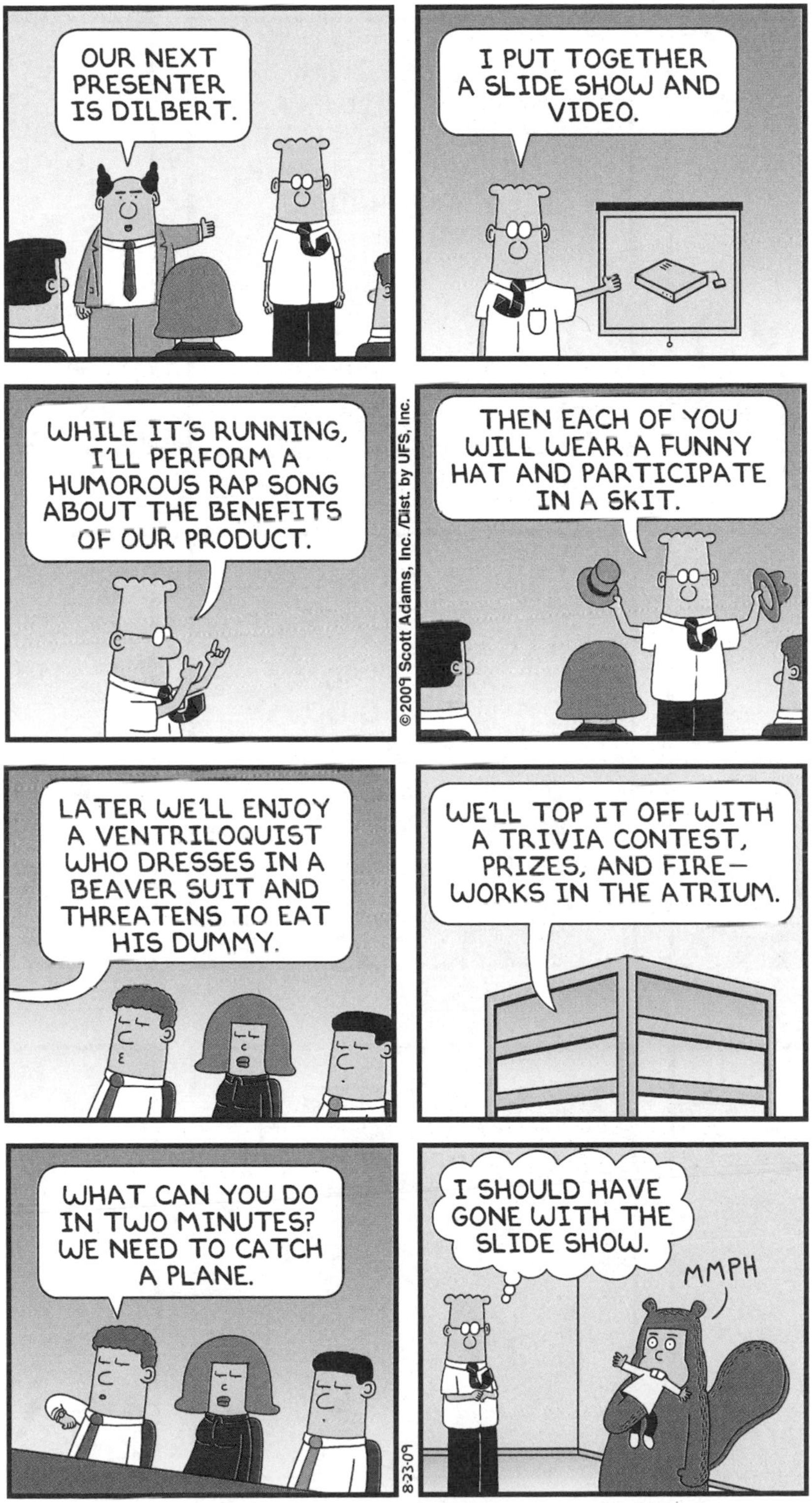
OUR NEXT PRESENTER IS DILBERT.
I PUT TOGETHER A SLIDE SHOW AND VIDEO.
WHILE IT'S RUNNING, I'LL PERFORM A HUMOROUS RAP SONG ABOUT THE BENEFITS OF OUR PRODUCT.
©2009 Scott Adams, Inc./Dist. by UFS, Inc.
THEN EACH OF YOU WILL WEAR A FUNNY HAT AND PARTICIPATE IN A SKIT.
LATER WE'LL ENJOY A VENTRILOQUIST WHO DRESSES IN A BEAVER SUIT AND THREATENS TO EAT HIS DUMMY.
WE'LL TOP IT OFF WITH A TRIVIA CONTEST, PRIZES, AND FIRE-WORKS IN THE ATRIUM.
WHAT CAN YOU DO IN TWO MINUTES? WE NEED TO CATCH A PLANE.
8-23-09
I SHOULD HAVE GONE WITH THE SLIDE SHOW.
MMPH

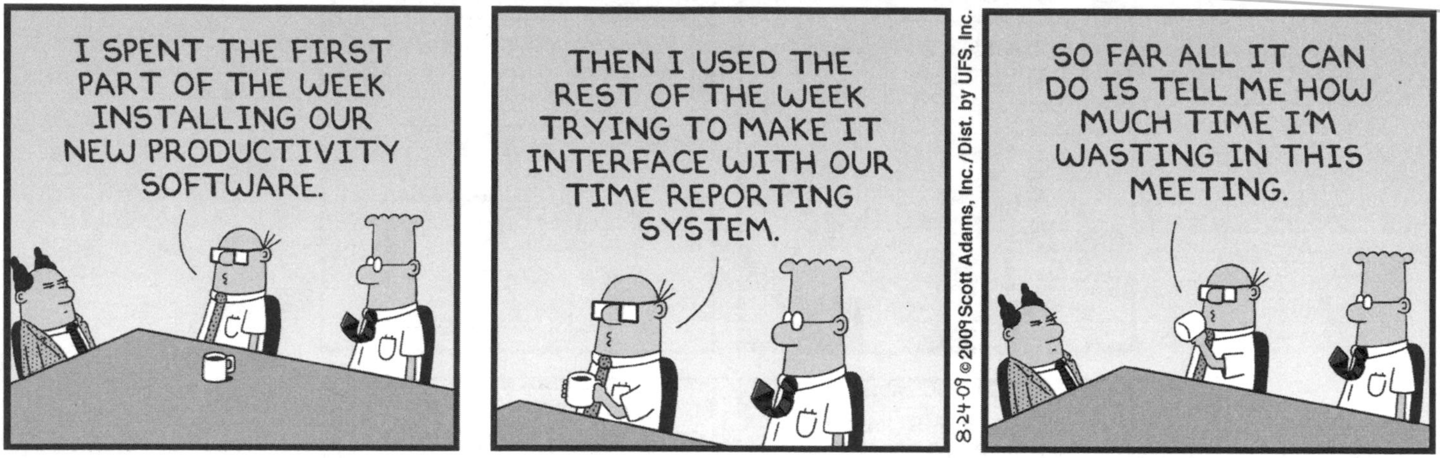
I SPENT THE FIRST PART OF THE WEEK INSTALLING OUR NEW PRODUCTIVITY SOFTWARE.
THEN I USED THE REST OF THE WEEK TRYING TO MAKE IT INTERFACE WITH OUR TIME REPORTING SYSTEM.
8-24-09 ©2009 Scott Adams, Inc./Dist. by UFS, Inc.
SO FAR ALL IT CAN DO IS TELL ME HOW MUCH TIME I'M WASTING IN THIS MEETING.

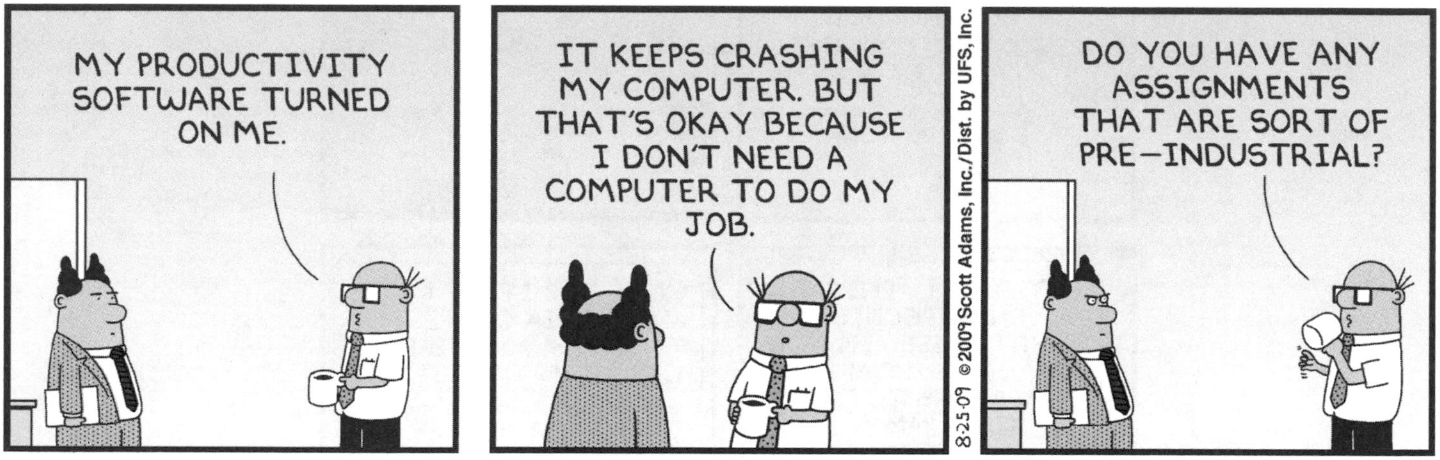
MY PRODUCTIVITY SOFTWARE TURNED ON ME.
IT KEEPS CRASHING MY COMPUTER. BUT THAT'S OKAY BECAUSE I DON'T NEED A COMPUTER TO DO MY JOB.
8-25-09 ©2009 Scott Adams, Inc./Dist. by UFS, Inc.
DO YOU HAVE ANY ASSIGNMENTS THAT ARE SORT OF PRE-INDUSTRIAL?

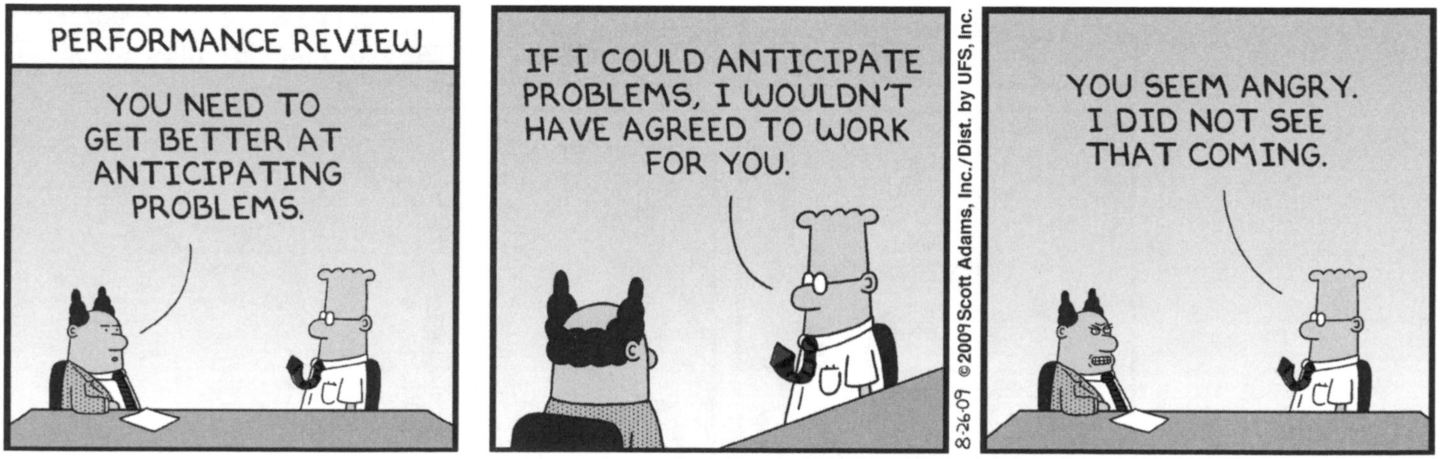
PERFORMANCE REVIEW
YOU NEED TO GET BETTER AT ANTICIPATING PROBLEMS.
IF I COULD ANTICIPATE PROBLEMS, I WOULDN'T HAVE AGREED TO WORK FOR YOU.
8-26-09 ©2009 Scott Adams, Inc./Dist. by UFS, Inc.
YOU SEEM ANGRY. I DID NOT SEE THAT COMING.

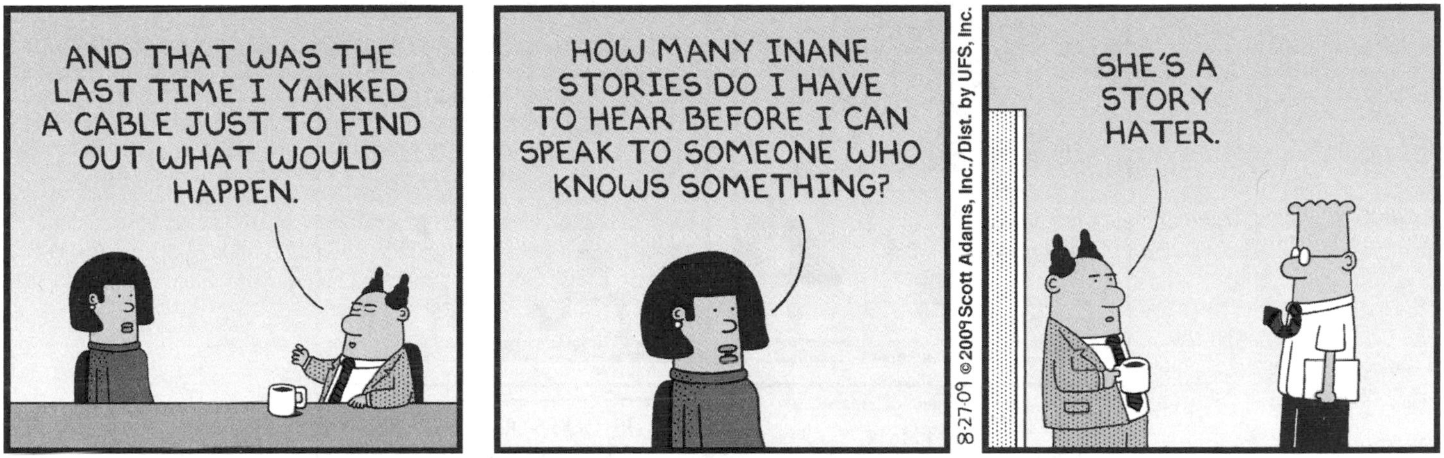
AND THAT WAS THE LAST TIME I YANKED A CABLE JUST TO FIND OUT WHAT WOULD HAPPEN.
HOW MANY INANE STORIES DO I HAVE TO HEAR BEFORE I CAN SPEAK TO SOMEONE WHO KNOWS SOMETHING?
8-27-09 © 2009 Scott Adams, Inc./Dist. by UFS, Inc.
SHE'S A STORY HATER.

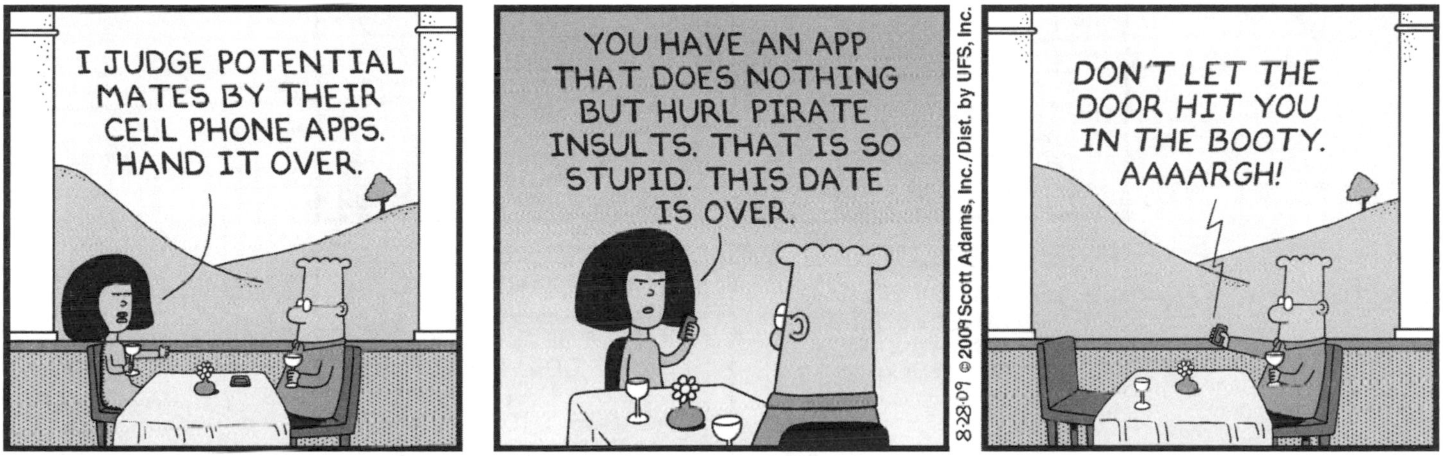
I JUDGE POTENTIAL MATES BY THEIR CELL PHONE APPS. HAND IT OVER.
YOU HAVE AN APP THAT DOES NOTHING BUT HURL PIRATE INSULTS. THAT IS SO STUPID. THIS DATE IS OVER.
8-28-09 © 2009 Scott Adams, Inc./Dist. by UFS, Inc.
DON'T LET THE DOOR HIT YOU IN THE BOOTY. AAAARGH!

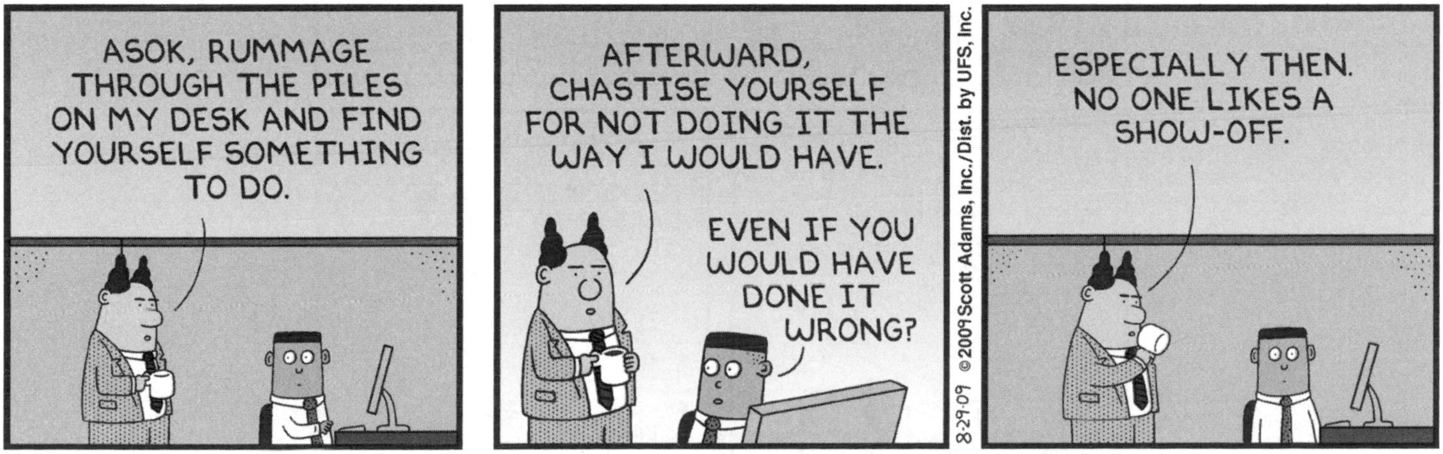
ASOK, RUMMAGE THROUGH THE PILES ON MY DESK AND FIND YOURSELF SOMETHING TO DO.
AFTERWARD, CHASTISE YOURSELF FOR NOT DOING IT THE WAY I WOULD HAVE.
EVEN IF YOU WOULD HAVE DONE IT WRONG?
8-29-09 © 2009 Scott Adams, Inc./Dist. by UFS, Inc.
ESPECIALLY THEN. NO ONE LIKES A SHOW-OFF.

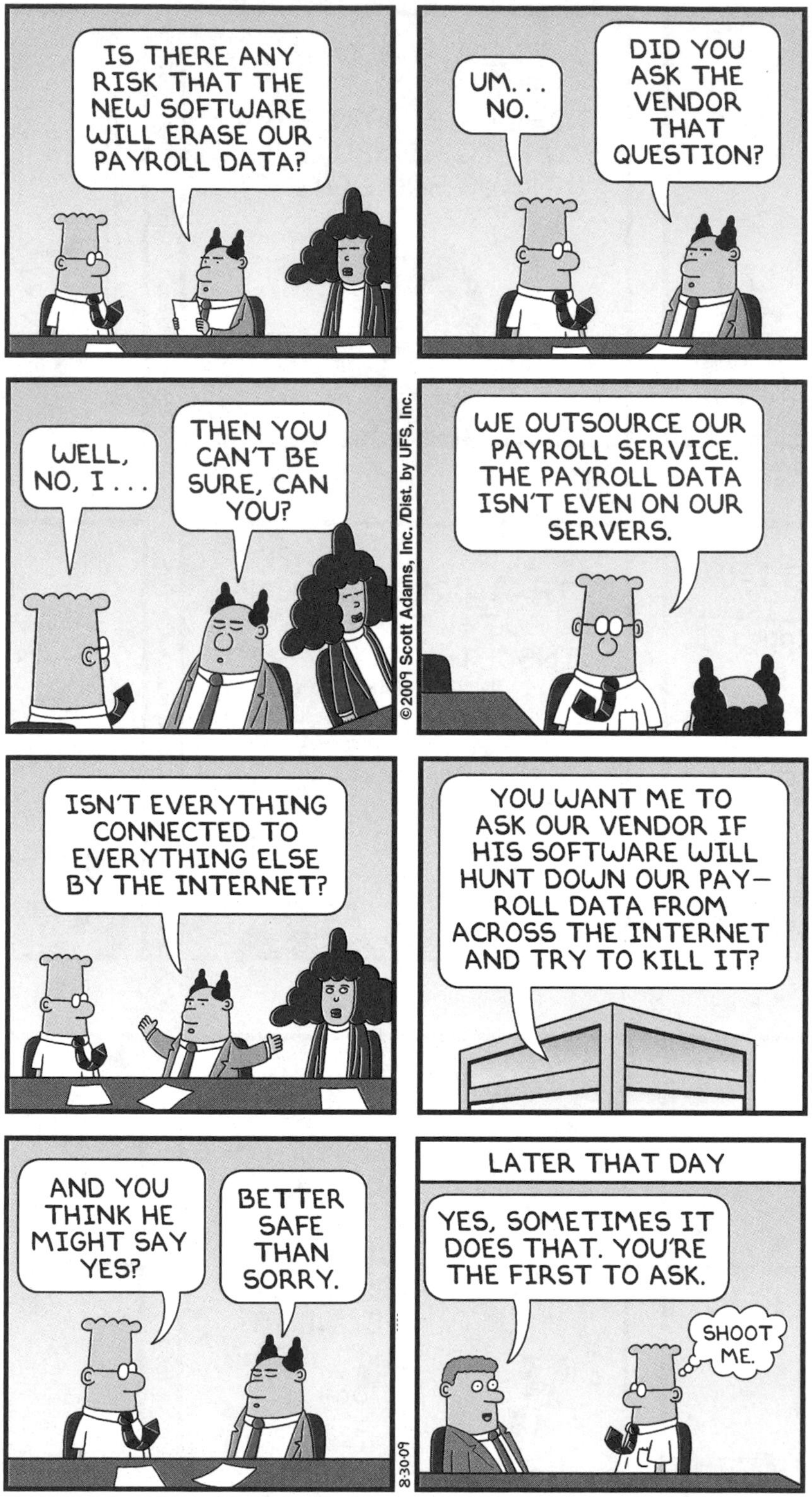

IS THERE ANY RISK THAT THE NEW SOFTWARE WILL ERASE OUR PAYROLL DATA?
UM... NO.
DID YOU ASK THE VENDOR THAT QUESTION?
WELL, NO, I...
THEN YOU CAN'T BE SURE, CAN YOU?
©2009 Scott Adams, Inc./Dist. by UFS, Inc.
WE OUTSOURCE OUR PAYROLL SERVICE. THE PAYROLL DATA ISN'T EVEN ON OUR SERVERS.
ISN'T EVERYTHING CONNECTED TO EVERYTHING ELSE BY THE INTERNET?
YOU WANT ME TO ASK OUR VENDOR IF HIS SOFTWARE WILL HUNT DOWN OUR PAY-ROLL DATA FROM ACROSS THE INTERNET AND TRY TO KILL IT?
AND YOU THINK HE MIGHT SAY YES?
BETTER SAFE THAN SORRY.
8-30-09
LATER THAT DAY
YES, SOMETIMES IT DOES THAT. YOU'RE THE FIRST TO ASK.
SHOOT ME.

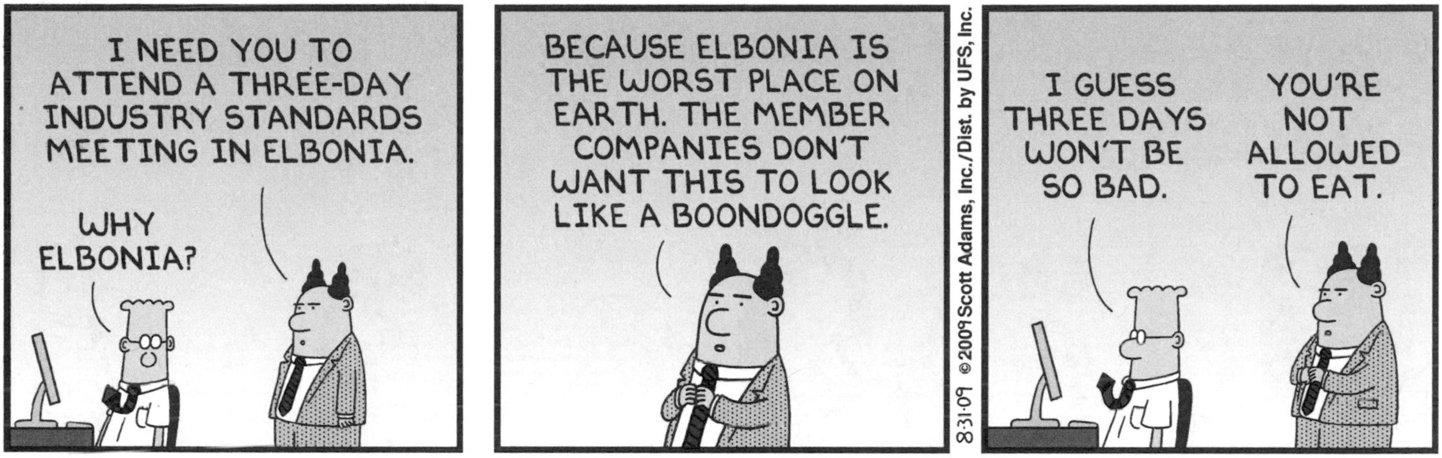
I NEED YOU TO ATTEND A THREE-DAY INDUSTRY STANDARDS MEETING IN ELBONIA.
WHY ELBONIA?
BECAUSE ELBONIA IS THE WORST PLACE ON EARTH. THE MEMBER COMPANIES DON'T WANT THIS TO LOOK LIKE A BOONDOGGLE.
8-31-09 ©2009 Scott Adams, Inc./Dist. by UFS, Inc.
I GUESS THREE DAYS WON'T BE SO BAD.
YOU'RE NOT ALLOWED TO EAT.

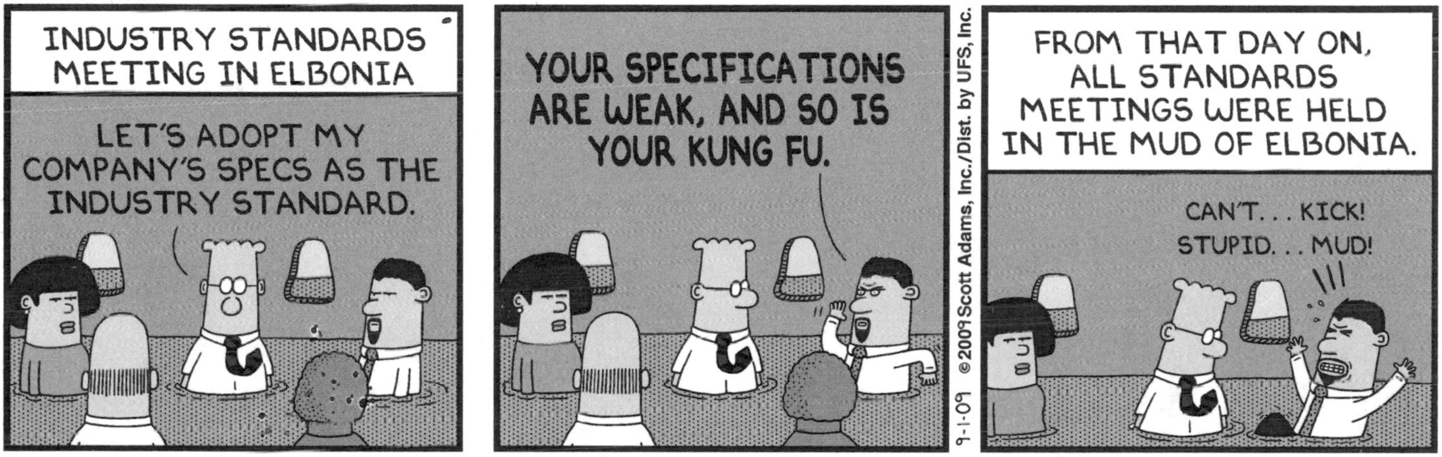
INDUSTRY STANDARDS MEETING IN ELBONIA
LET'S ADOPT MY COMPANY'S SPECS AS THE INDUSTRY STANDARD.
YOUR SPECIFICATIONS ARE WEAK, AND SO IS YOUR KUNG FU.
9-1-09 ©2009 Scott Adams, Inc./Dist. by UFS, Inc.
FROM THAT DAY ON, ALL STANDARDS MEETINGS WERE HELD IN THE MUD OF ELBONIA.
CAN'T... KICK!
STUPID... MUD!

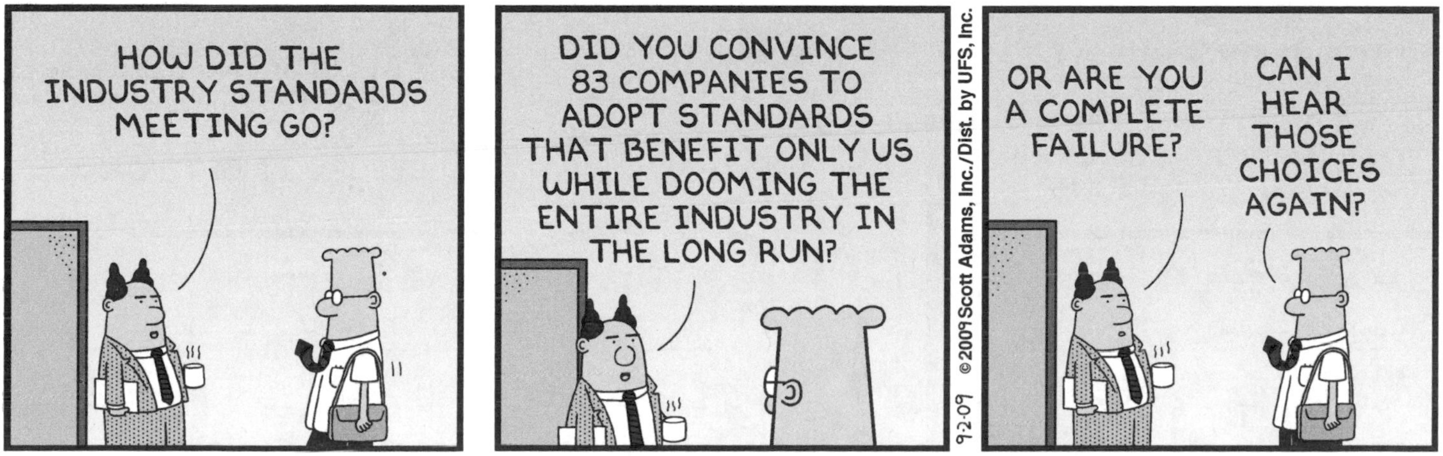
HOW DID THE INDUSTRY STANDARDS MEETING GO?
DID YOU CONVINCE 83 COMPANIES TO ADOPT STANDARDS THAT BENEFIT ONLY US WHILE DOOMING THE ENTIRE INDUSTRY IN THE LONG RUN?
9-2-09 ©2009 Scott Adams, Inc./Dist. by UFS, Inc.
OR ARE YOU A COMPLETE FAILURE?
CAN I HEAR THOSE CHOICES AGAIN?

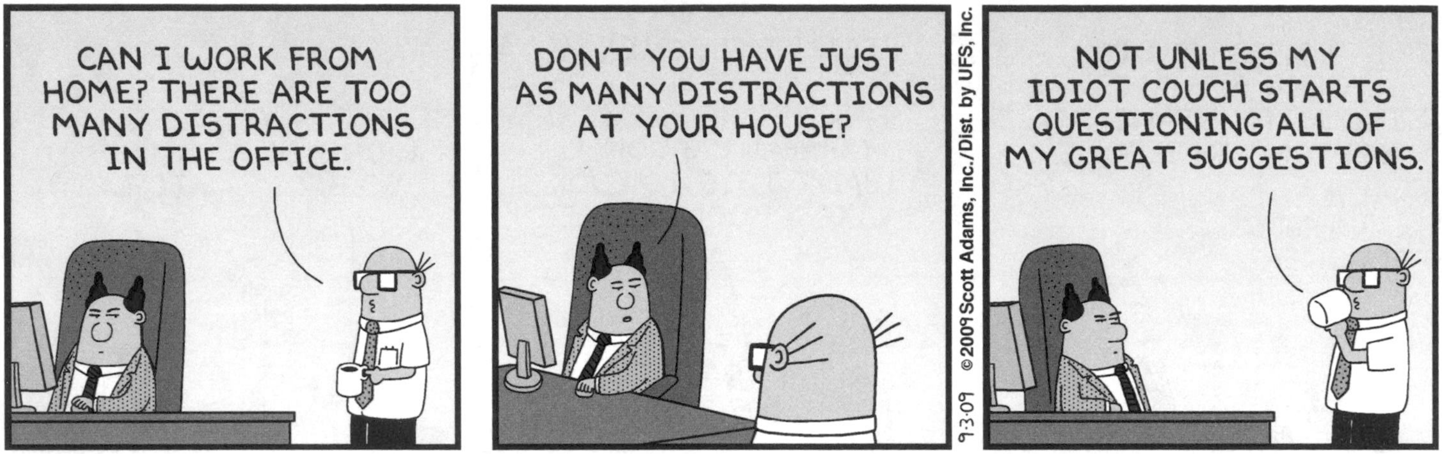
CAN I WORK FROM HOME? THERE ARE TOO MANY DISTRACTIONS IN THE OFFICE.
DON'T YOU HAVE JUST AS MANY DISTRACTIONS AT YOUR HOUSE?
NOT UNLESS MY IDIOT COUCH STARTS QUESTIONING ALL OF MY GREAT SUGGESTIONS.
9-3-09 © 2009 Scott Adams, Inc./Dist. by UFS, Inc.

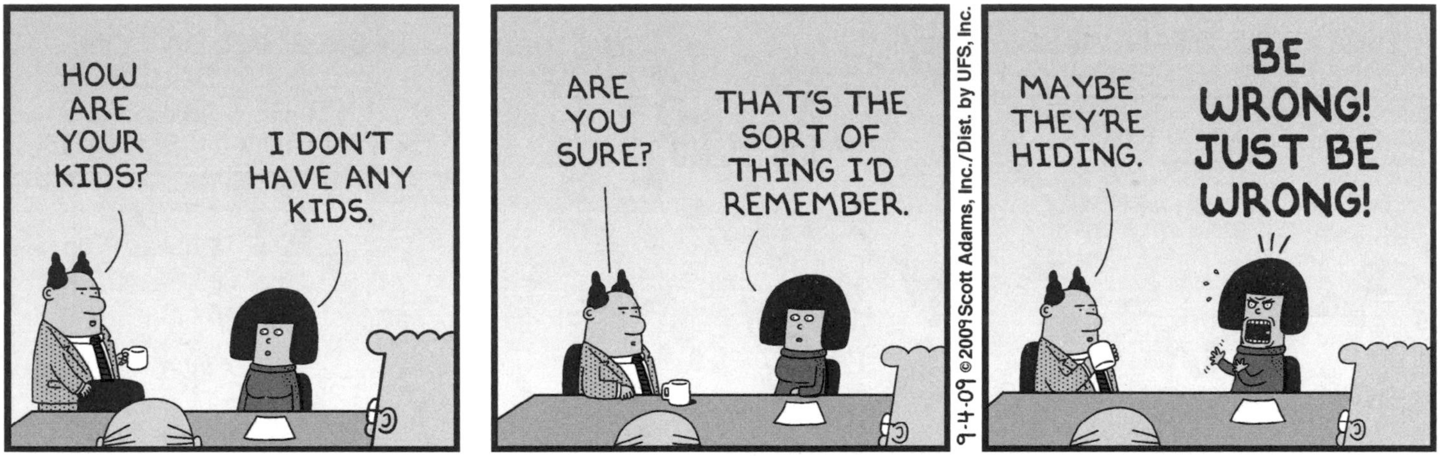
HOW ARE YOUR KIDS?
I DON'T HAVE ANY KIDS.
ARE YOU SURE?
THAT'S THE SORT OF THING I'D REMEMBER.
MAYBE THEY'RE HIDING.
BE WRONG! JUST BE WRONG!
9-4-09 © 2009 Scott Adams, Inc./Dist. by UFS, Inc.

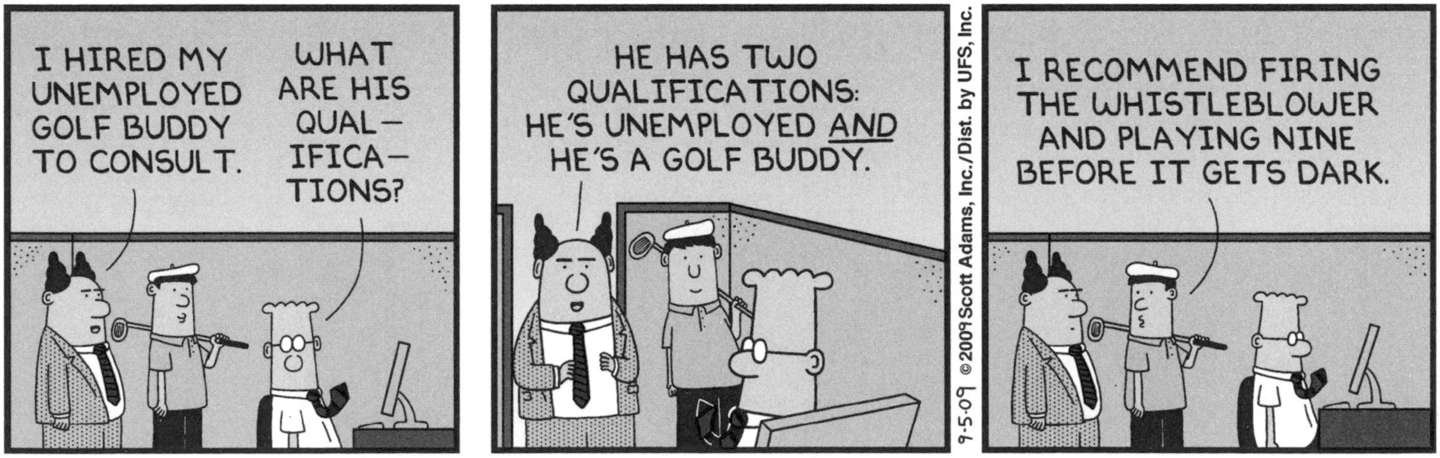
I HIRED MY UNEMPLOYED GOLF BUDDY TO CONSULT.
WHAT ARE HIS QUAL-IFICA-TIONS?
HE HAS TWO QUALIFICATIONS: HE'S UNEMPLOYED AND HE'S A GOLF BUDDY.
I RECOMMEND FIRING THE WHISTLEBLOWER AND PLAYING NINE BEFORE IT GETS DARK.
9-5-09 © 2009 Scott Adams, Inc./Dist. by UFS, Inc.

CAN YOU APPROVE THIS CHANGE?
I'LL HAVE TO RUN IT BY MY CORPORATE OFFICE.
AND WE'RE IN MERGER TALKS, SO THEY'LL NEED TO CLEAR IT WITH OUR FUTURE OWNERS.
NO ONE WILL KNOW WHO SHOULD MAKE THE DECISION OR WHAT THE RIGHT DECISION IS.
WHEN DO YOU THINK YOU'LL HAVE AN ANSWER?
SOMETIME BETWEEN NEXT WEEK AND WHENEVER THE EARTH IS DEVOURED BY A GRAVITATIONAL SINGULARITY.
MEANWHILE I WILL AVOID YOUR CALLS AND E-MAILS BY BECOMING A VAPOR.
YOU FORGOT THE APPROVAL FORM.
©2009 Scott Adams, Inc./Dist. by UFS, Inc.
9-6-09

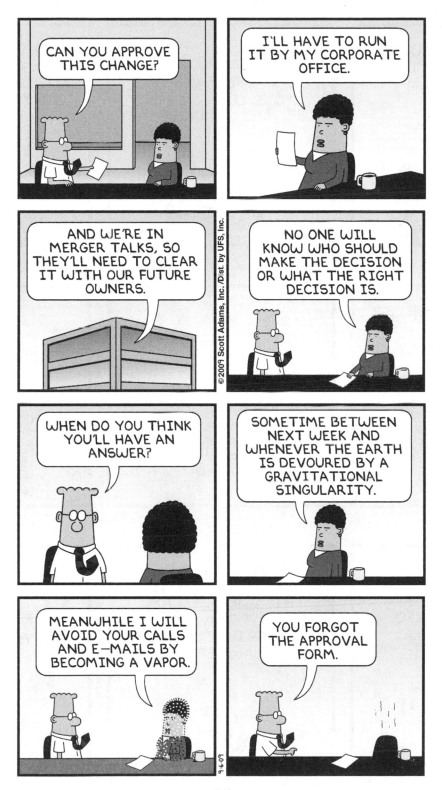

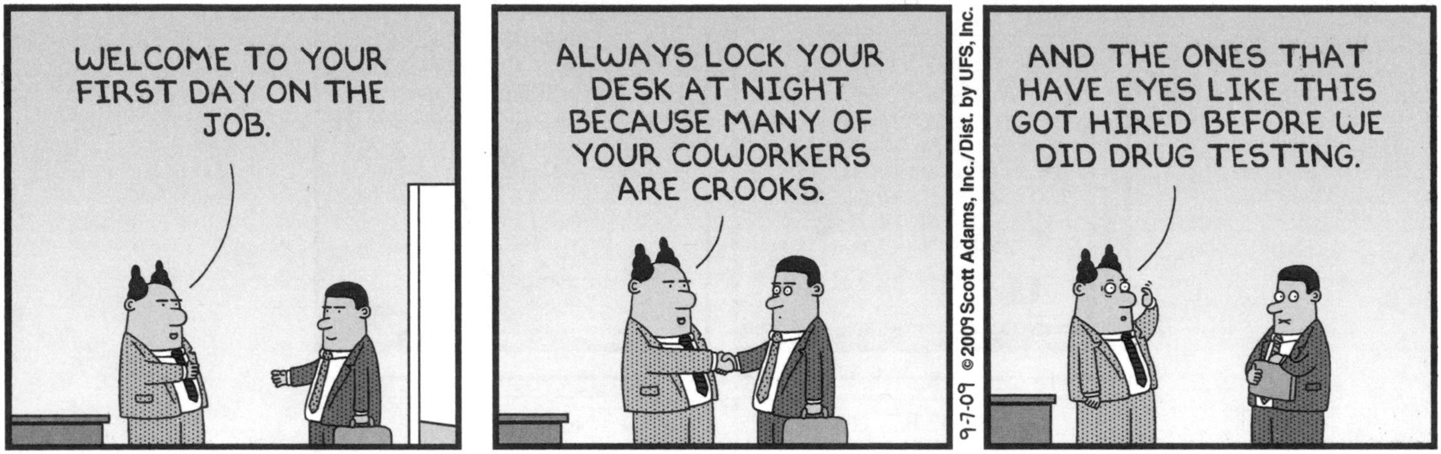
WELCOME TO YOUR FIRST DAY ON THE JOB.
ALWAYS LOCK YOUR DESK AT NIGHT BECAUSE MANY OF YOUR COWORKERS ARE CROOKS.
AND THE ONES THAT HAVE EYES LIKE THIS GOT HIRED BEFORE WE DID DRUG TESTING.
9-7-09 © 2009 Scott Adams, Inc./Dist. by UFS, Inc.

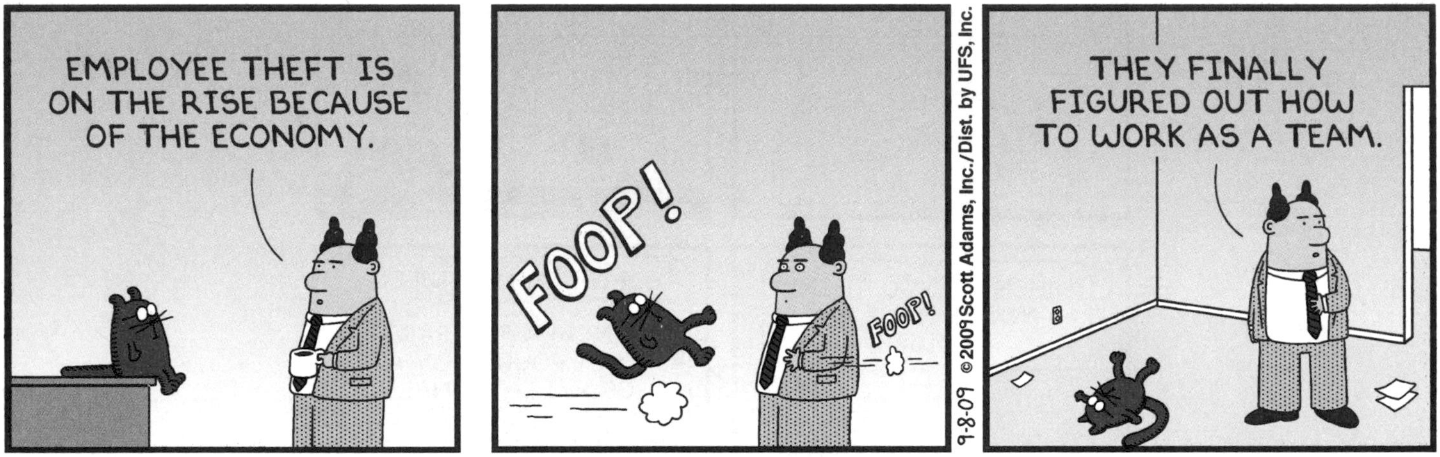
EMPLOYEE THEFT IS ON THE RISE BECAUSE OF THE ECONOMY.
FOOP!
FOOP!
THEY FINALLY FIGURED OUT HOW TO WORK AS A TEAM.
9-8-09 © 2009 Scott Adams, Inc./Dist. by UFS, Inc.

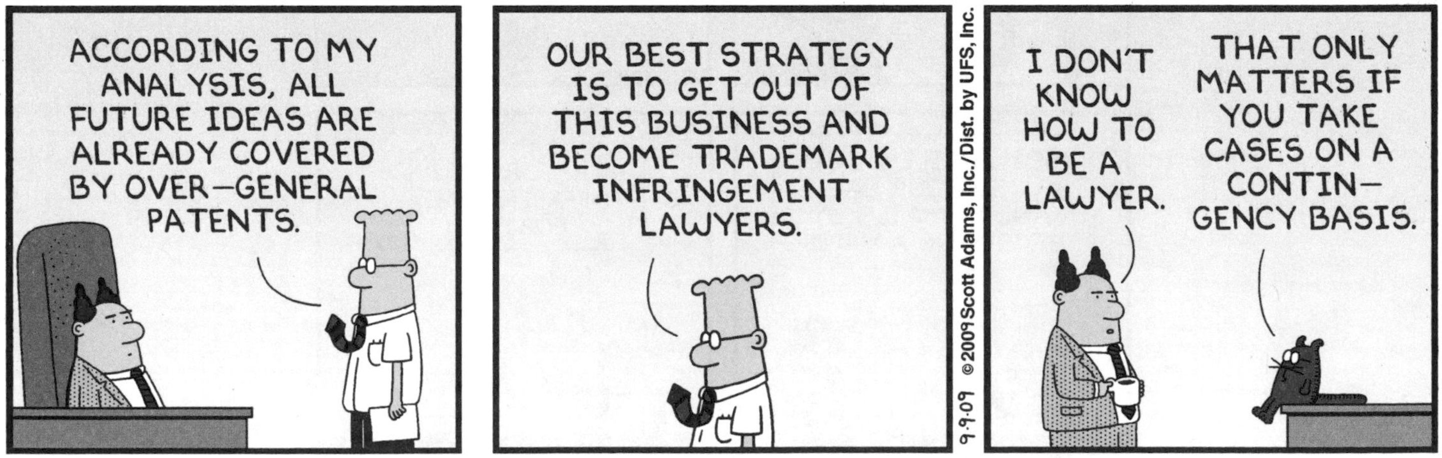
ACCORDING TO MY ANALYSIS, ALL FUTURE IDEAS ARE ALREADY COVERED BY OVER-GENERAL PATENTS.
OUR BEST STRATEGY IS TO GET OUT OF THIS BUSINESS AND BECOME TRADEMARK INFRINGEMENT LAWYERS.
I DON'T KNOW HOW TO BE A LAWYER.
THAT ONLY MATTERS IF YOU TAKE CASES ON A CONTIN-GENCY BASIS.
9-9-09 © 2009 Scott Adams, Inc./Dist. by UFS, Inc.

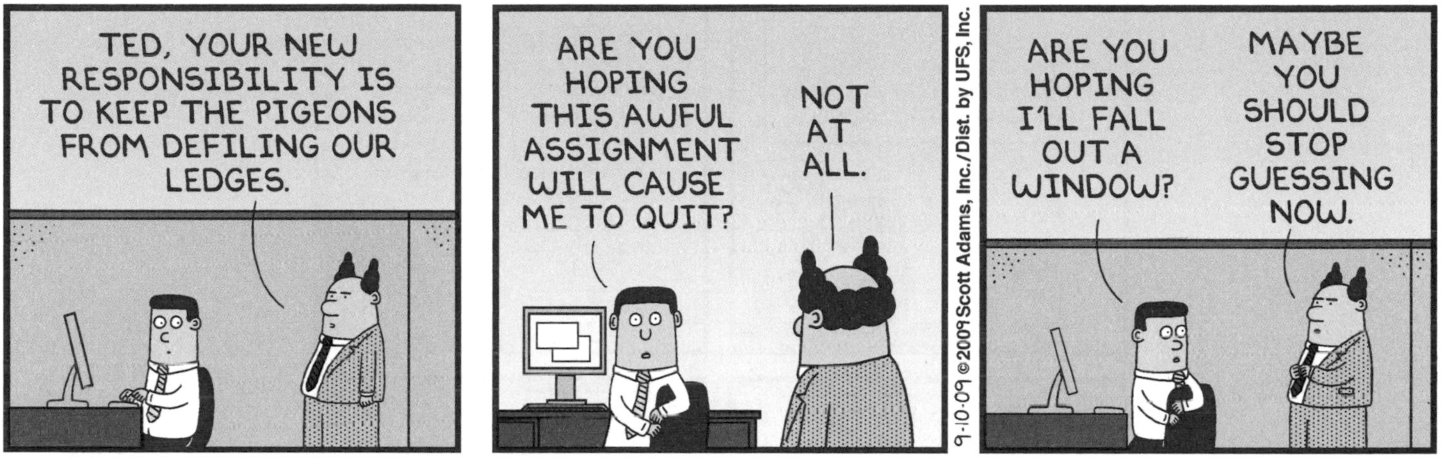
TED, YOUR NEW RESPONSIBILITY IS TO KEEP THE PIGEONS FROM DEFILING OUR LEDGES.
ARE YOU HOPING THIS AWFUL ASSIGNMENT WILL CAUSE ME TO QUIT?
NOT AT ALL.
ARE YOU HOPING I'LL FALL OUT A WINDOW?
MAYBE YOU SHOULD STOP GUESSING NOW.
9-10-09 ©2009 Scott Adams, Inc./Dist. by UFS, Inc.

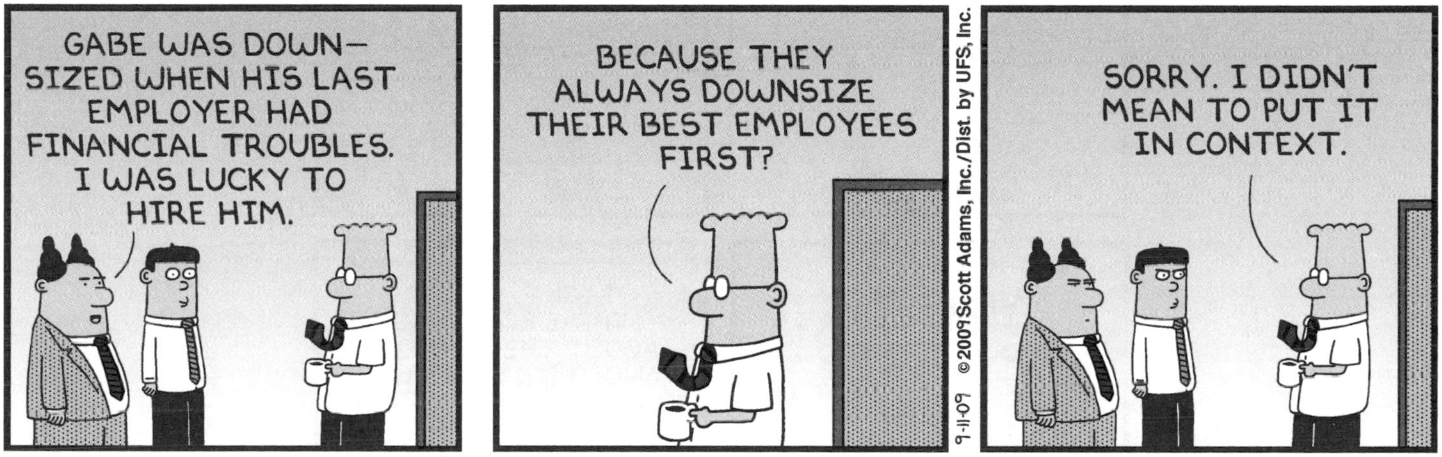
GABE WAS DOWN-SIZED WHEN HIS LAST EMPLOYER HAD FINANCIAL TROUBLES. I WAS LUCKY TO HIRE HIM.
BECAUSE THEY ALWAYS DOWNSIZE THEIR BEST EMPLOYEES FIRST?
SORRY. I DIDN'T MEAN TO PUT IT IN CONTEXT.
9-11-09 ©2009 Scott Adams, Inc./Dist. by UFS, Inc.

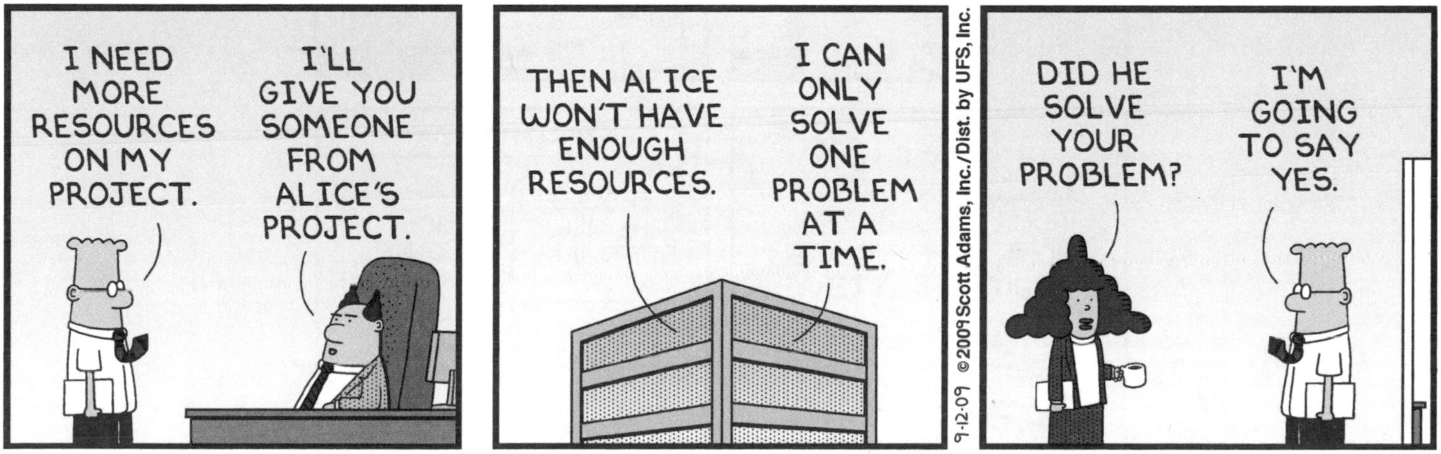
I NEED MORE RESOURCES ON MY PROJECT.
I'LL GIVE YOU SOMEONE FROM ALICE'S PROJECT.
THEN ALICE WON'T HAVE ENOUGH RESOURCES.
I CAN ONLY SOLVE ONE PROBLEM AT A TIME.
DID HE SOLVE YOUR PROBLEM?
I'M GOING TO SAY YES.
9-12-09 ©2009 Scott Adams, Inc./Dist. by UFS, Inc.

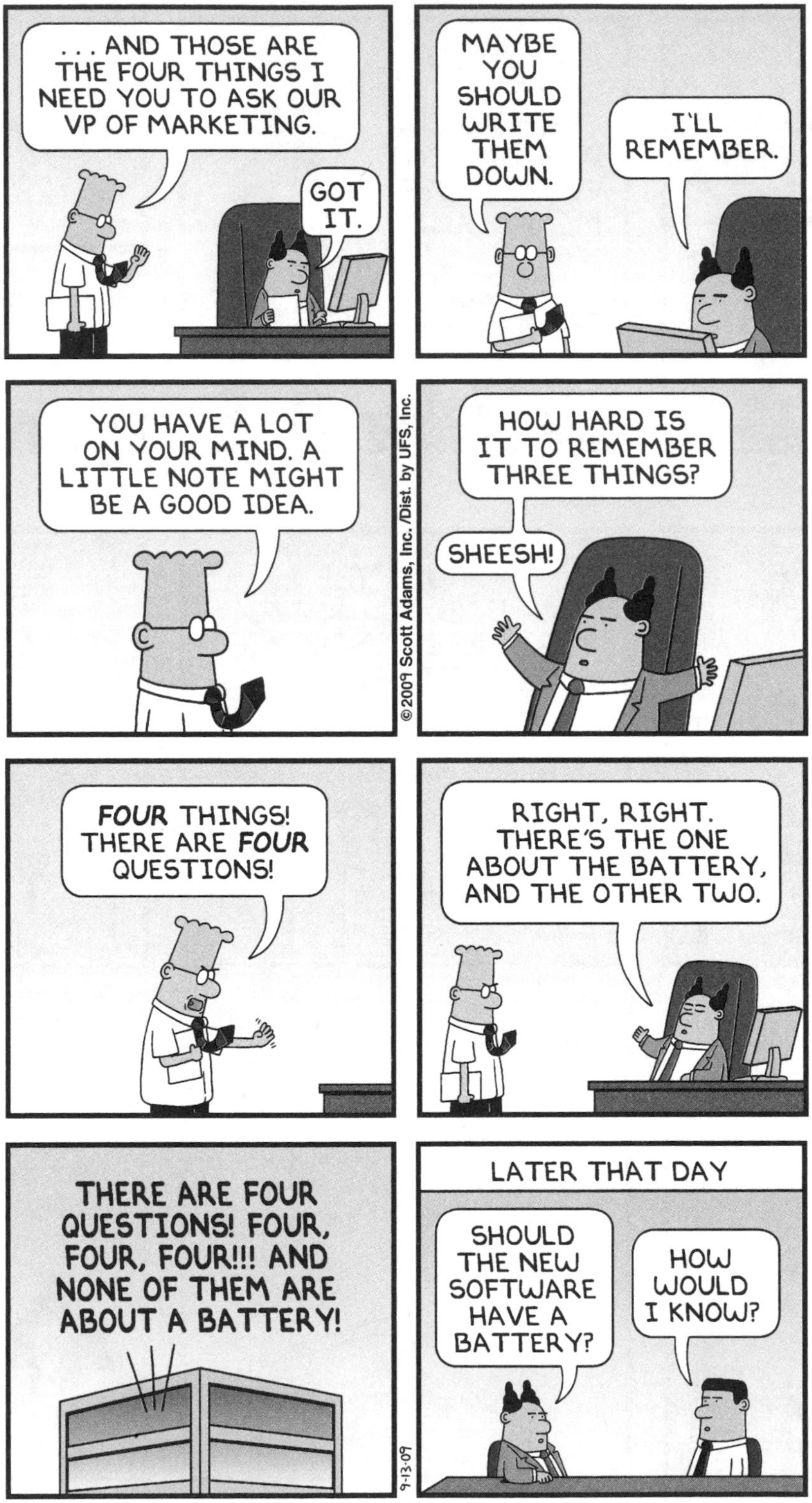
. . . AND THOSE ARE THE FOUR THINGS I NEED YOU TO ASK OUR VP OF MARKETING.
GOT IT.
MAYBE YOU SHOULD WRITE THEM DOWN.
I'LL REMEMBER.
YOU HAVE A LOT ON YOUR MIND. A LITTLE NOTE MIGHT BE A GOOD IDEA.
HOW HARD IS IT TO REMEMBER THREE THINGS?
SHEESH!
FOUR THINGS! THERE ARE FOUR QUESTIONS!
RIGHT, RIGHT. THERE'S THE ONE ABOUT THE BATTERY, AND THE OTHER TWO.
THERE ARE FOUR QUESTIONS! FOUR, FOUR, FOUR!!! AND NONE OF THEM ARE ABOUT A BATTERY!
LATER THAT DAY
SHOULD THE NEW SOFTWARE HAVE A BATTERY?
HOW WOULD I KNOW?
©2009 Scott Adams, Inc./Dist. by UFS, Inc.
9-13-09

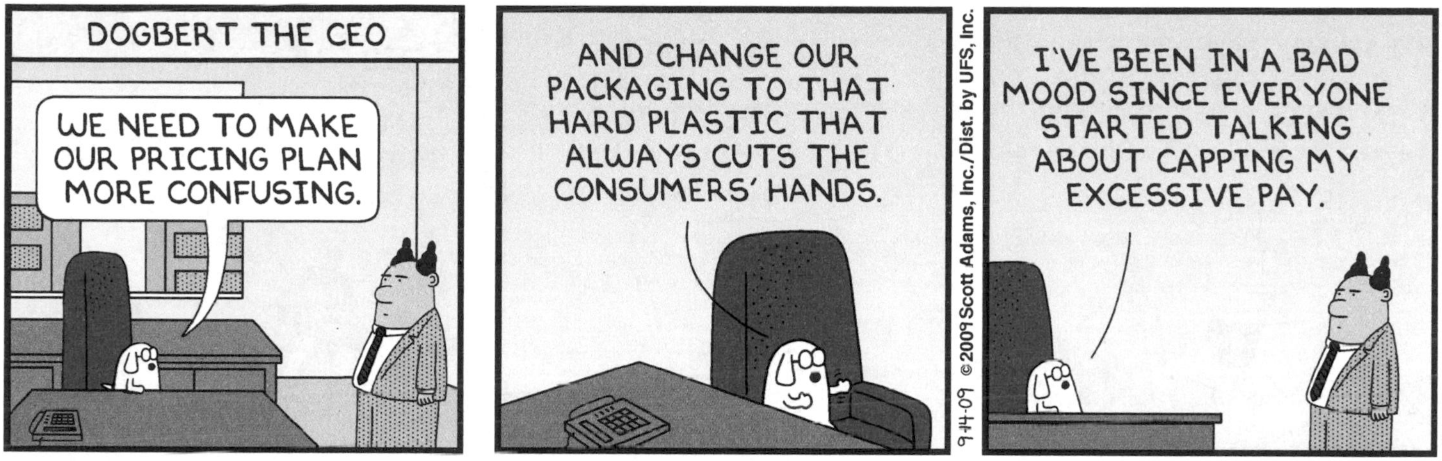
DOGBERT THE CEO
WE NEED TO MAKE OUR PRICING PLAN MORE CONFUSING.
AND CHANGE OUR PACKAGING TO THAT HARD PLASTIC THAT ALWAYS CUTS THE CONSUMERS' HANDS.
9-14-09 ©2009 Scott Adams, Inc./Dist. by UFS, Inc.
I'VE BEEN IN A BAD MOOD SINCE EVERYONE STARTED TALKING ABOUT CAPPING MY EXCESSIVE PAY.

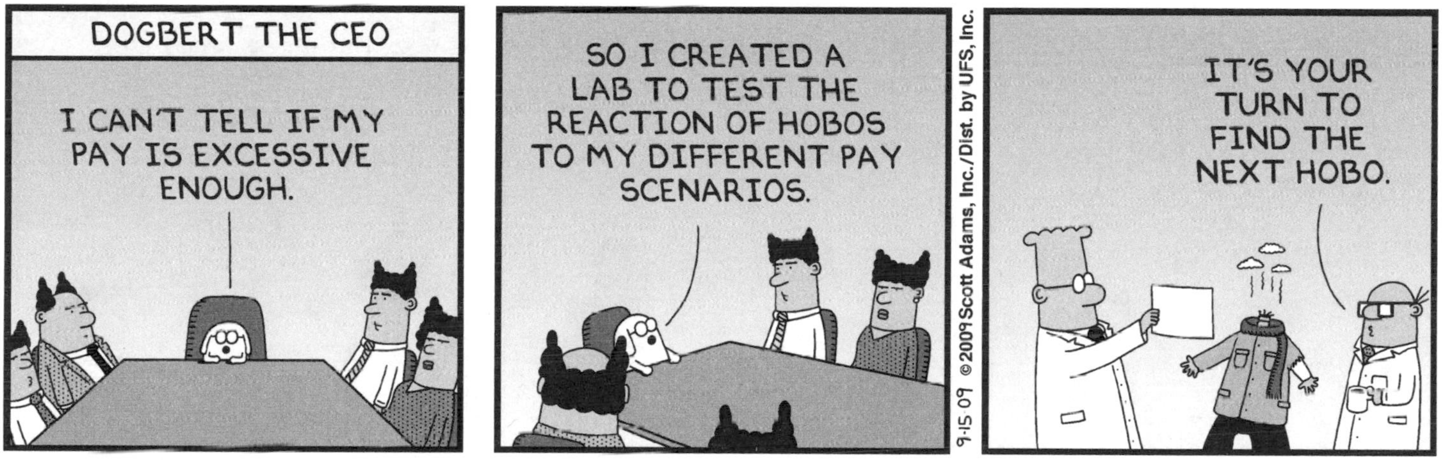
DOGBERT THE CEO
I CAN'T TELL IF MY PAY IS EXCESSIVE ENOUGH.
SO I CREATED A LAB TO TEST THE REACTION OF HOBOS TO MY DIFFERENT PAY SCENARIOS.
9-15-09 ©2009 Scott Adams, Inc./Dist. by UFS, Inc.
IT'S YOUR TURN TO FIND THE NEXT HOBO.

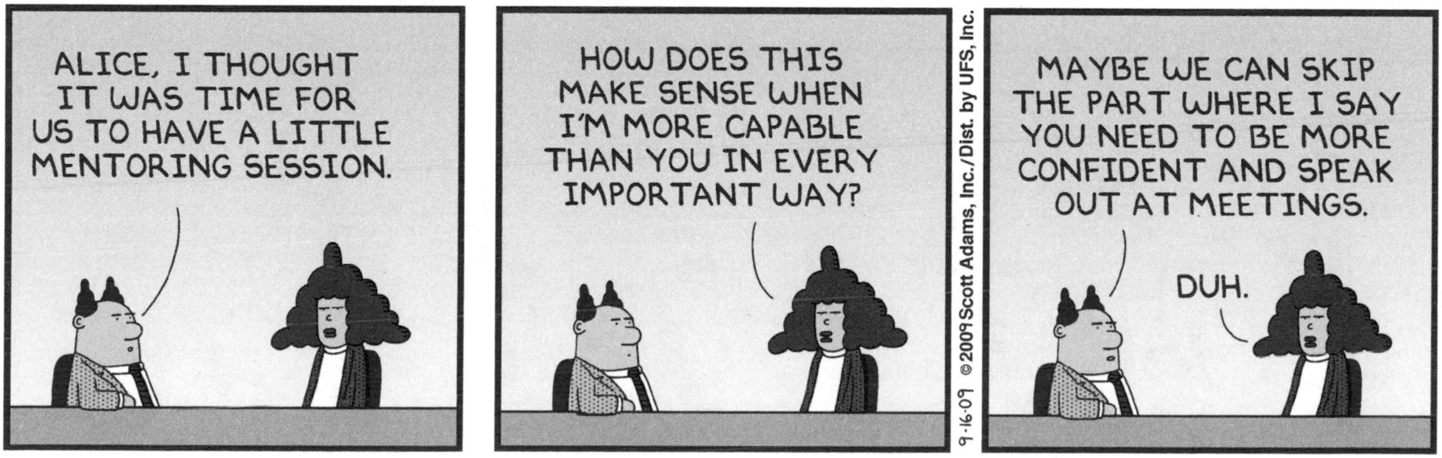
ALICE, I THOUGHT IT WAS TIME FOR US TO HAVE A LITTLE MENTORING SESSION.
HOW DOES THIS MAKE SENSE WHEN I'M MORE CAPABLE THAN YOU IN EVERY IMPORTANT WAY?
9-16-09 ©2009 Scott Adams, Inc./Dist. by UFS, Inc.
MAYBE WE CAN SKIP THE PART WHERE I SAY YOU NEED TO BE MORE CONFIDENT AND SPEAK OUT AT MEETINGS.
DUH.

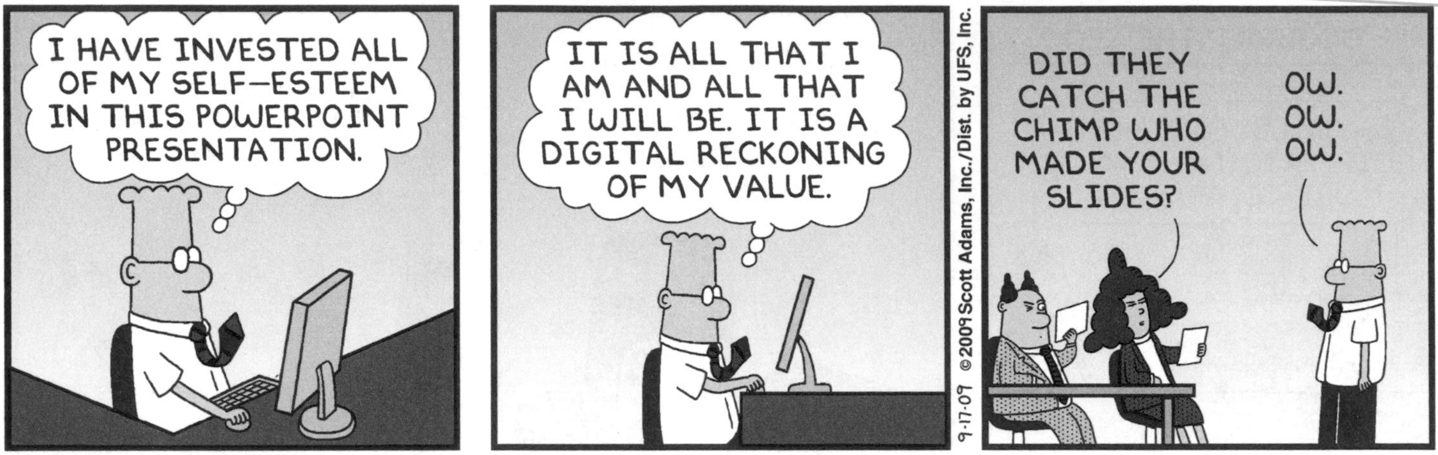
I HAVE INVESTED ALL OF MY SELF-ESTEEM IN THIS POWERPOINT PRESENTATION.
IT IS ALL THAT I AM AND ALL THAT I WILL BE. IT IS A DIGITAL RECKONING OF MY VALUE.
DID THEY CATCH THE CHIMP WHO MADE YOUR SLIDES?
OW. OW. OW.

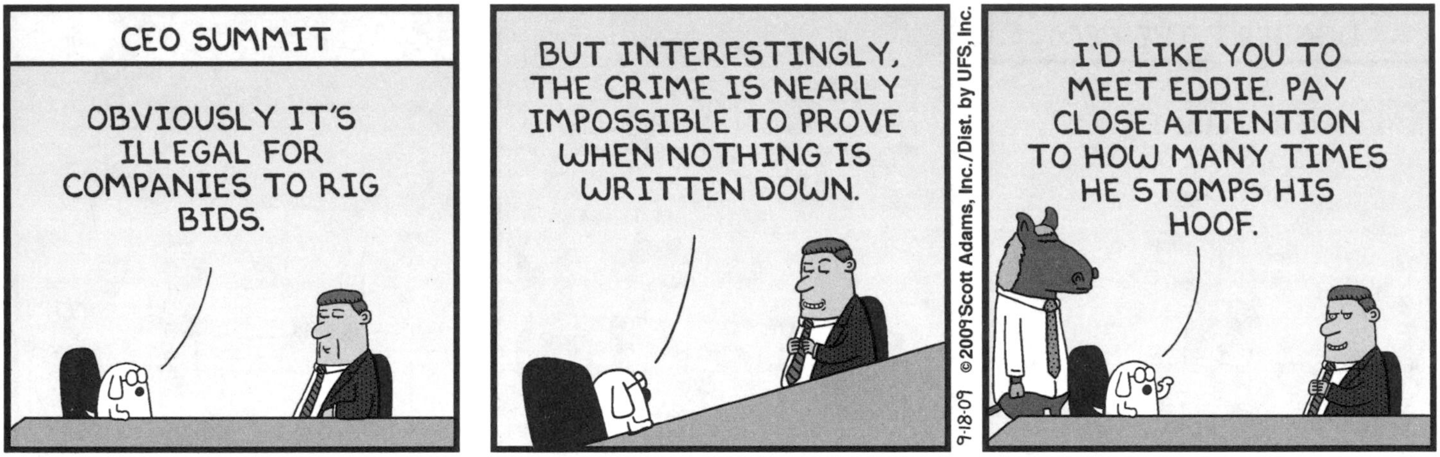
CEO SUMMIT
OBVIOUSLY IT'S ILLEGAL FOR COMPANIES TO RIG BIDS.
BUT INTERESTINGLY, THE CRIME IS NEARLY IMPOSSIBLE TO PROVE WHEN NOTHING IS WRITTEN DOWN.
I'D LIKE YOU TO MEET EDDIE. PAY CLOSE ATTENTION TO HOW MANY TIMES HE STOMPS HIS HOOF.

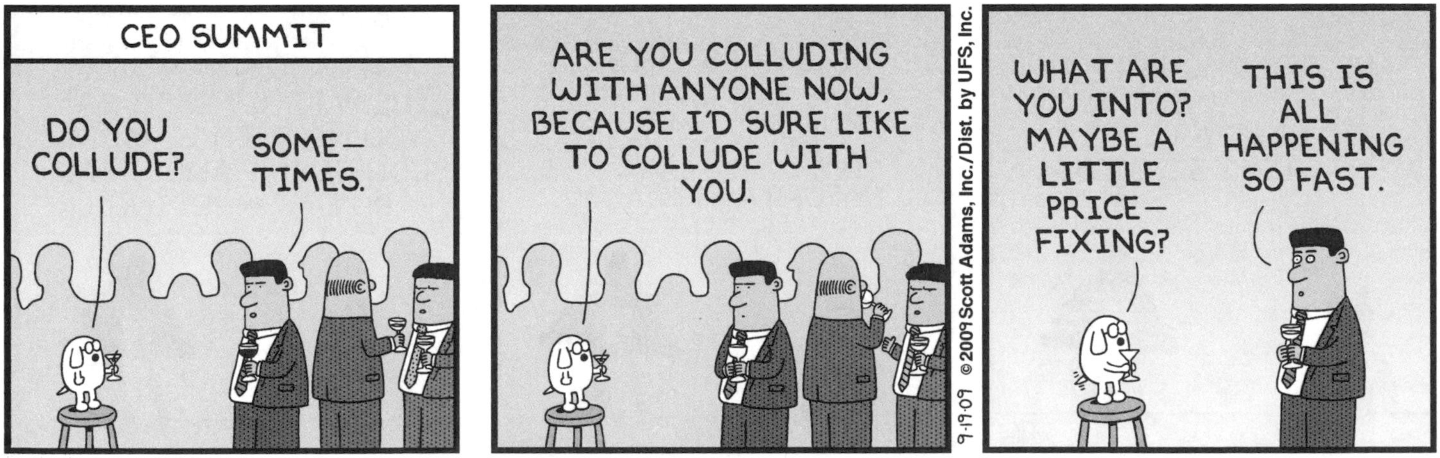
CEO SUMMIT
DO YOU COLLUDE?
SOME-TIMES.
ARE YOU COLLUDING WITH ANYONE NOW, BECAUSE I'D SURE LIKE TO COLLUDE WITH YOU.
WHAT ARE YOU INTO? MAYBE A LITTLE PRICE-FIXING?
THIS IS ALL HAPPENING SO FAST.

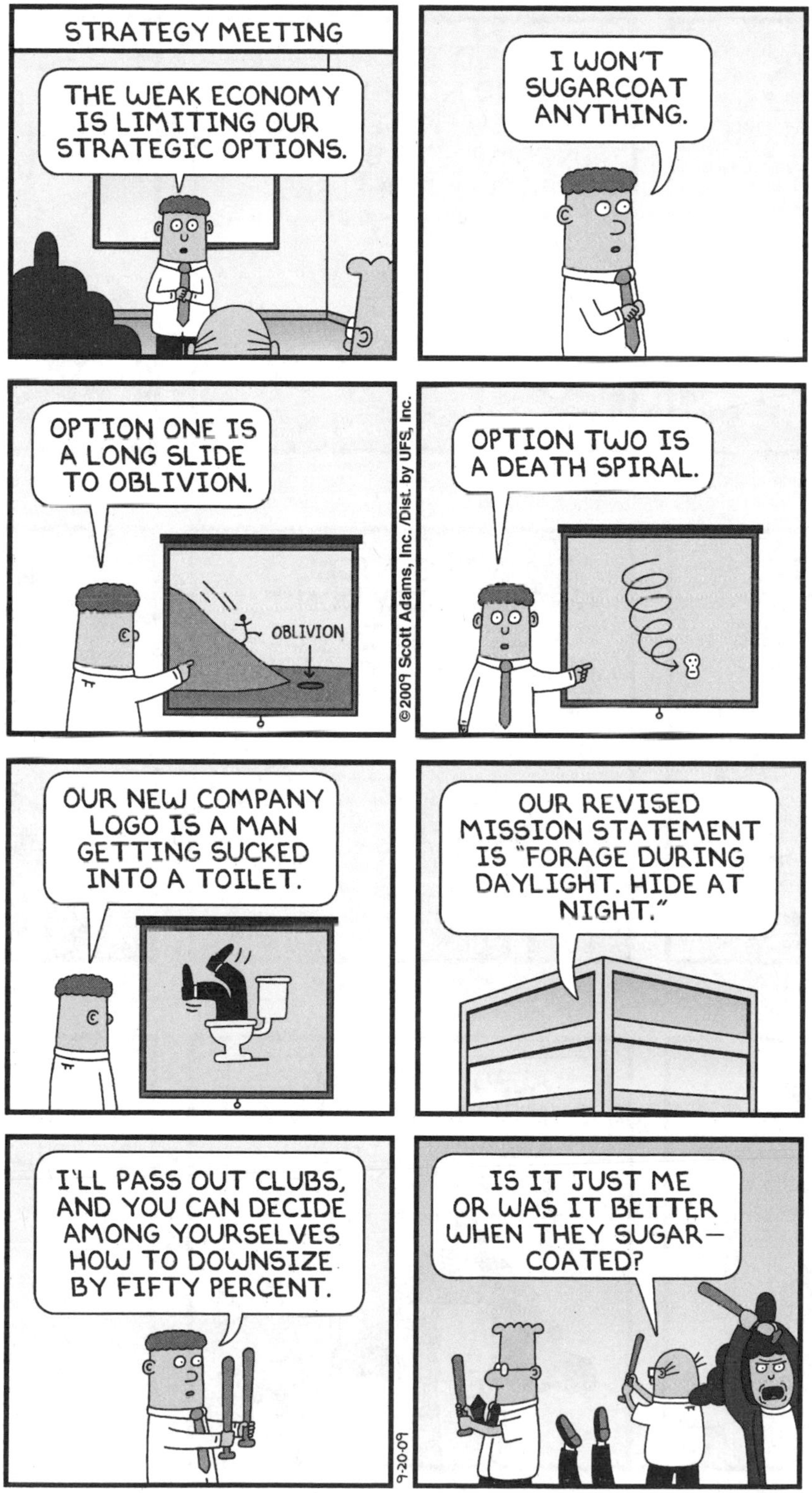
STRATEGY MEETING
THE WEAK ECONOMY IS LIMITING OUR STRATEGIC OPTIONS.
I WON'T SUGARCOAT ANYTHING.
OPTION ONE IS A LONG SLIDE TO OBLIVION.
OBLIVION
OPTION TWO IS A DEATH SPIRAL.
OUR NEW COMPANY LOGO IS A MAN GETTING SUCKED INTO A TOILET.
OUR REVISED MISSION STATEMENT IS "FORAGE DURING DAYLIGHT. HIDE AT NIGHT."
I'LL PASS OUT CLUBS, AND YOU CAN DECIDE AMONG YOURSELVES HOW TO DOWNSIZE BY FIFTY PERCENT.
IS IT JUST ME OR WAS IT BETTER WHEN THEY SUGAR-COATED?
© 2009 Scott Adams, Inc. /Dist. by UFS, Inc.
9-20-09

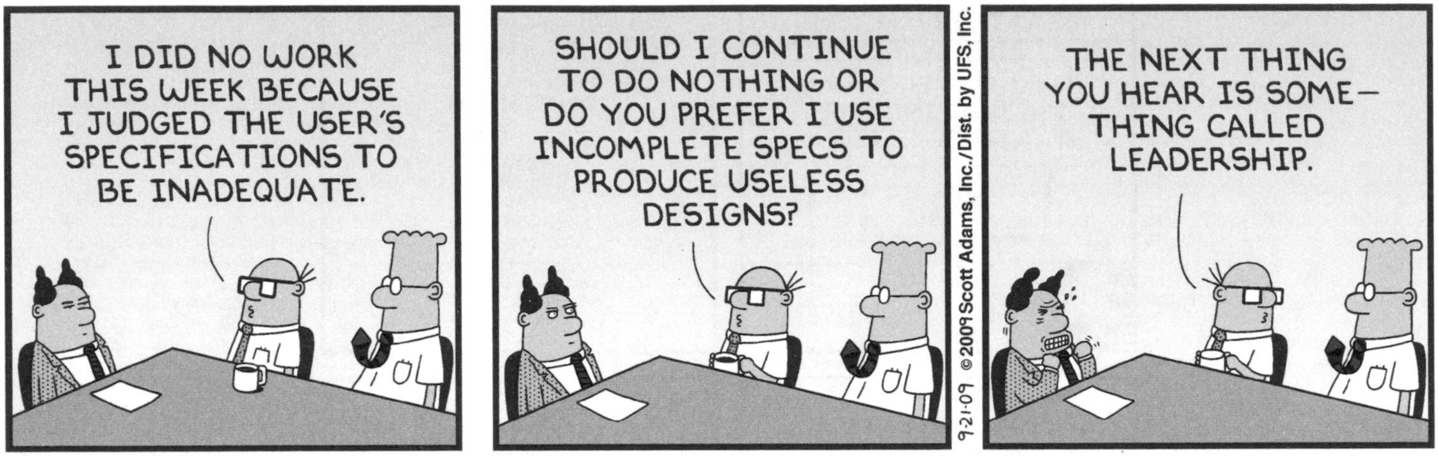
I DID NO WORK THIS WEEK BECAUSE I JUDGED THE USER'S SPECIFICATIONS TO BE INADEQUATE.
SHOULD I CONTINUE TO DO NOTHING OR DO YOU PREFER I USE INCOMPLETE SPECS TO PRODUCE USELESS DESIGNS?
9-21-09 ©2009 Scott Adams, Inc./Dist. by UFS, Inc.
THE NEXT THING YOU HEAR IS SOME-THING CALLED LEADERSHIP.

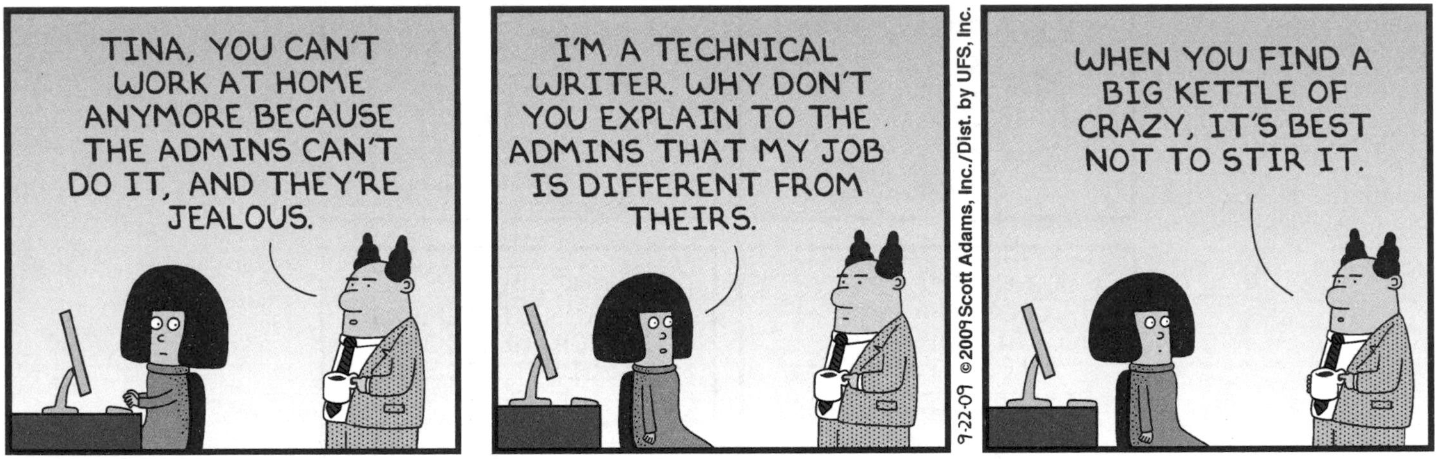
TINA, YOU CAN'T WORK AT HOME ANYMORE BECAUSE THE ADMINS CAN'T DO IT, AND THEY'RE JEALOUS.
I'M A TECHNICAL WRITER. WHY DON'T YOU EXPLAIN TO THE ADMINS THAT MY JOB IS DIFFERENT FROM THEIRS.
9-22-09 ©2009 Scott Adams, Inc./Dist. by UFS, Inc.
WHEN YOU FIND A BIG KETTLE OF CRAZY, IT'S BEST NOT TO STIR IT.

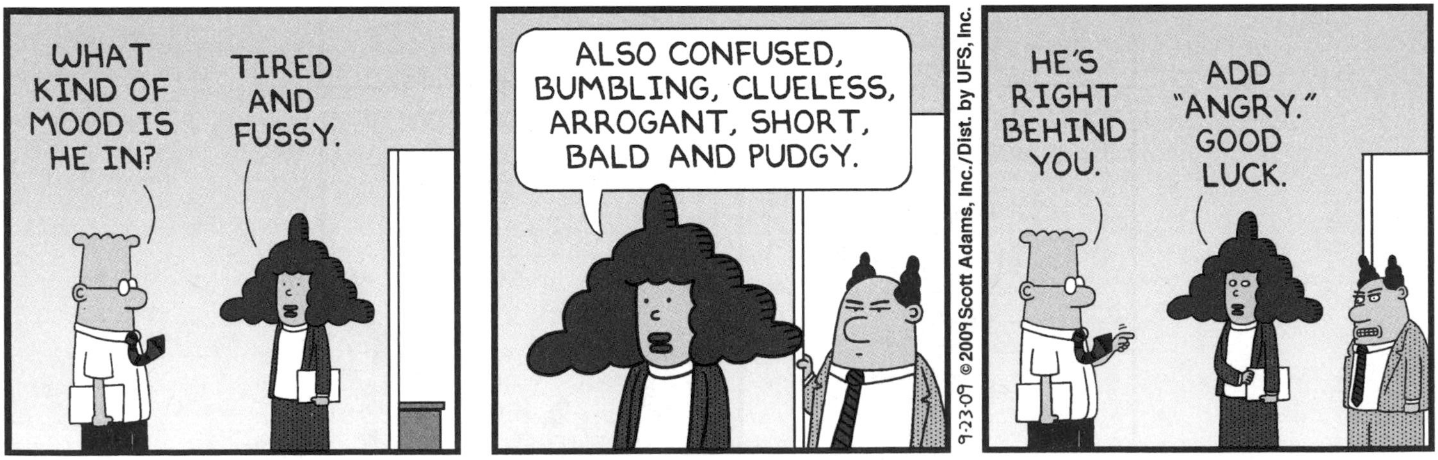
WHAT KIND OF MOOD IS HE IN?
TIRED AND FUSSY.
ALSO CONFUSED, BUMBLING, CLUELESS, ARROGANT, SHORT, BALD AND PUDGY.
9-23-09 ©2009 Scott Adams, Inc./Dist. by UFS, Inc.
HE'S RIGHT BEHIND YOU.
ADD "ANGRY." GOOD LUCK.

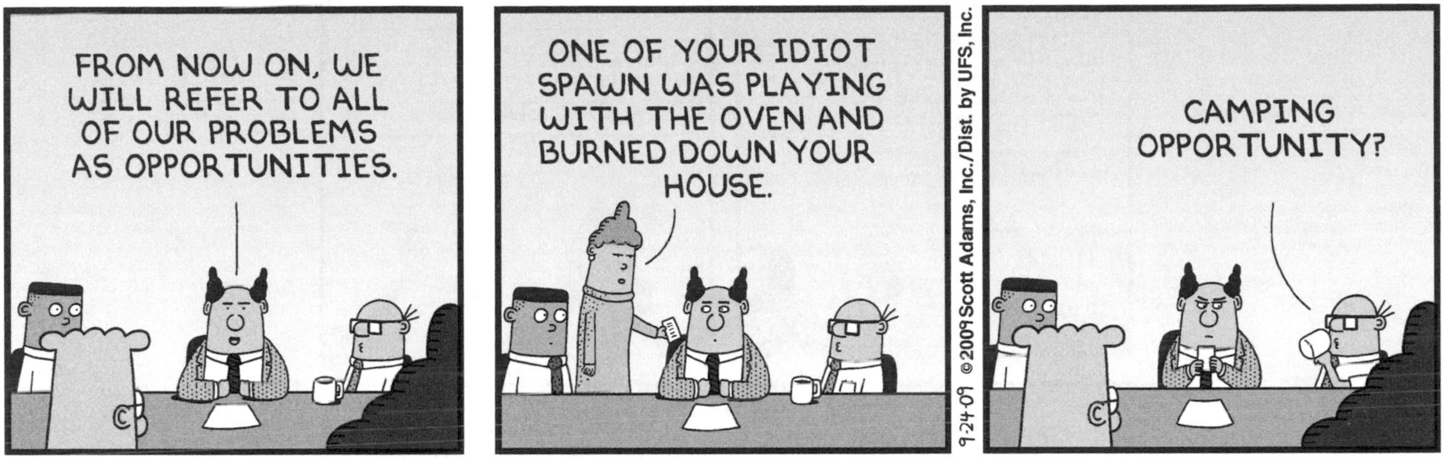
FROM NOW ON, WE WILL REFER TO ALL OF OUR PROBLEMS AS OPPORTUNITIES.
ONE OF YOUR IDIOT SPAWN WAS PLAYING WITH THE OVEN AND BURNED DOWN YOUR HOUSE.
CAMPING OPPORTUNITY?
9-24-09 ©2009 Scott Adams, Inc./Dist. by UFS, Inc.

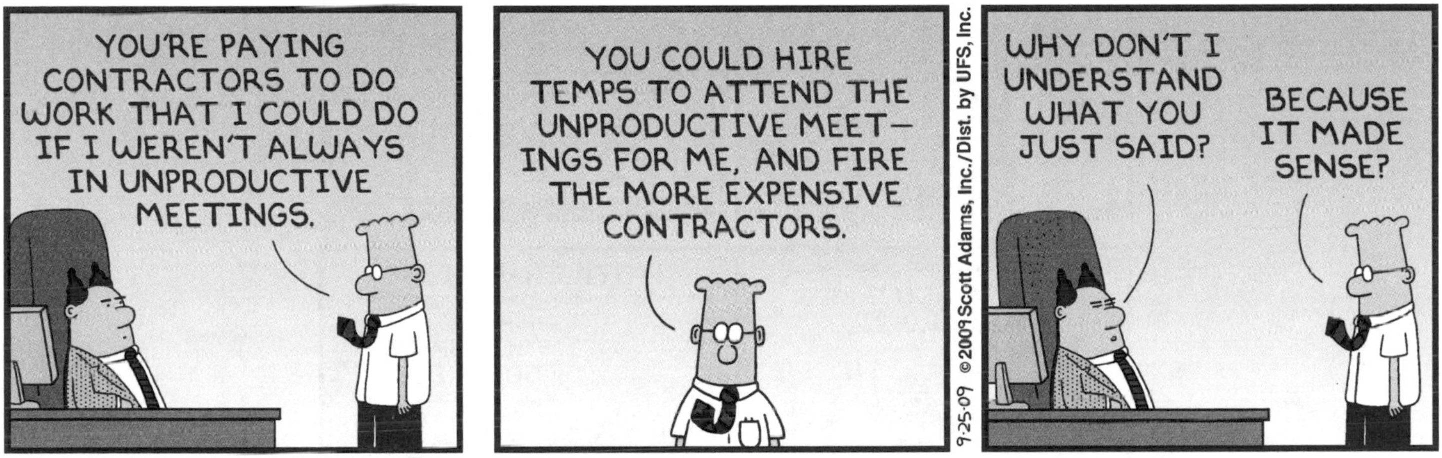
YOU'RE PAYING CONTRACTORS TO DO WORK THAT I COULD DO IF I WEREN'T ALWAYS IN UNPRODUCTIVE MEETINGS.
YOU COULD HIRE TEMPS TO ATTEND THE UNPRODUCTIVE MEET-INGS FOR ME, AND FIRE THE MORE EXPENSIVE CONTRACTORS.
WHY DON'T I UNDERSTAND WHAT YOU JUST SAID?
BECAUSE IT MADE SENSE?
9-25-09 ©2009 Scott Adams, Inc./Dist. by UFS, Inc.

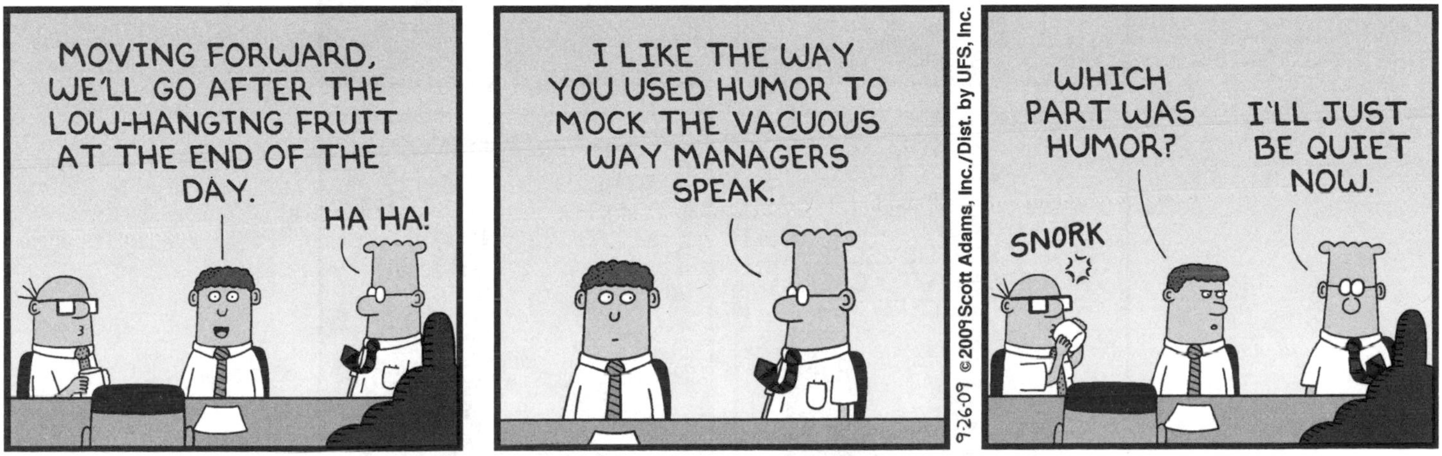
MOVING FORWARD, WE'LL GO AFTER THE LOW-HANGING FRUIT AT THE END OF THE DAY.
HA HA!
I LIKE THE WAY YOU USED HUMOR TO MOCK THE VACUOUS WAY MANAGERS SPEAK.
SNORK
WHICH PART WAS HUMOR?
I'LL JUST BE QUIET NOW.
9-26-09 ©2009 Scott Adams, Inc./Dist. by UFS, Inc.

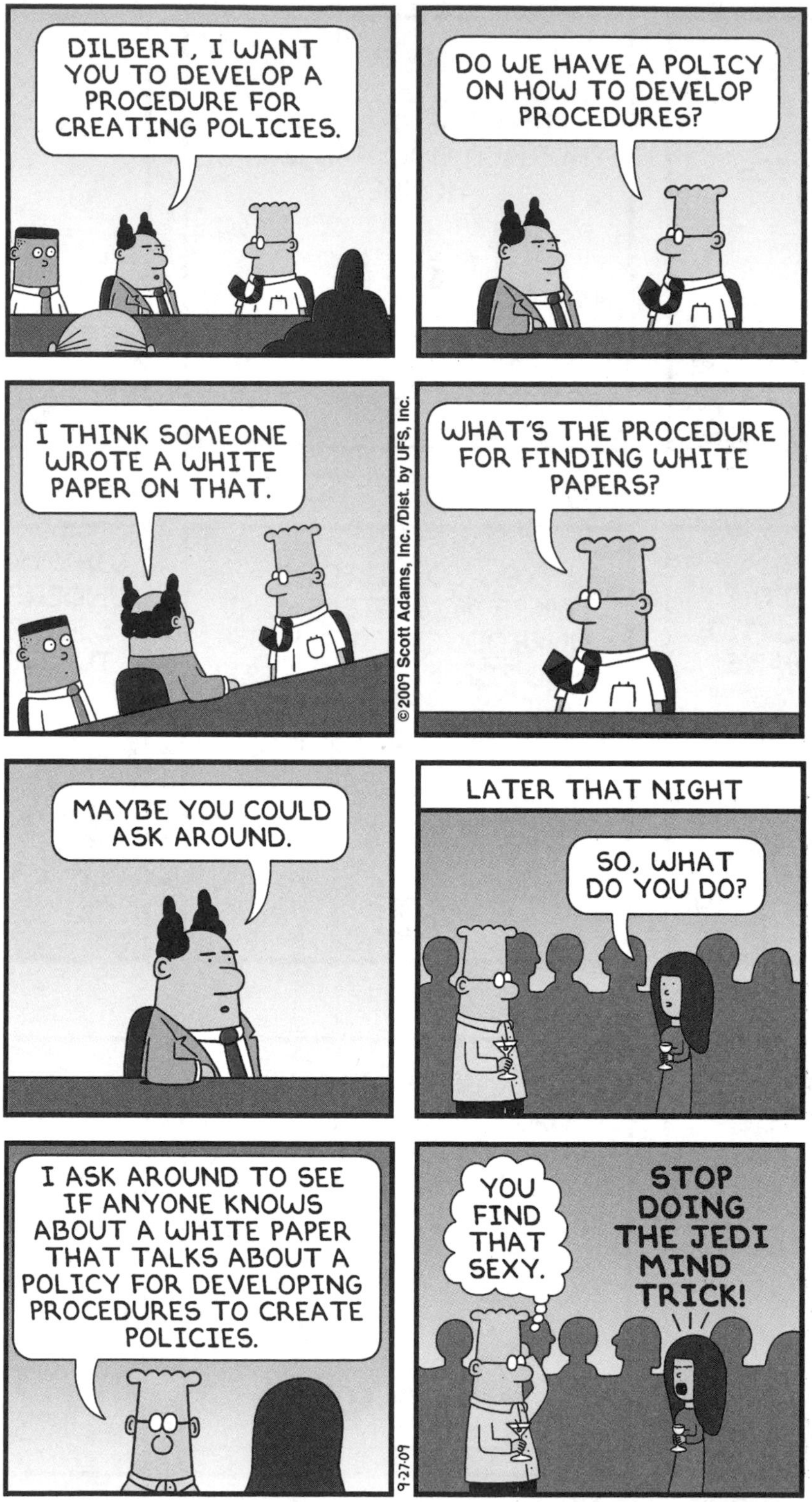
DILBERT, I WANT YOU TO DEVELOP A PROCEDURE FOR CREATING POLICIES.
DO WE HAVE A POLICY ON HOW TO DEVELOP PROCEDURES?
I THINK SOMEONE WROTE A WHITE PAPER ON THAT.
WHAT'S THE PROCEDURE FOR FINDING WHITE PAPERS?
MAYBE YOU COULD ASK AROUND.
LATER THAT NIGHT
SO, WHAT DO YOU DO?
I ASK AROUND TO SEE IF ANYONE KNOWS ABOUT A WHITE PAPER THAT TALKS ABOUT A POLICY FOR DEVELOPING PROCEDURES TO CREATE POLICIES.
YOU FIND THAT SEXY.
STOP DOING THE JEDI MIND TRICK!
©2009 Scott Adams, Inc./Dist. by UFS, Inc.
9-27-09

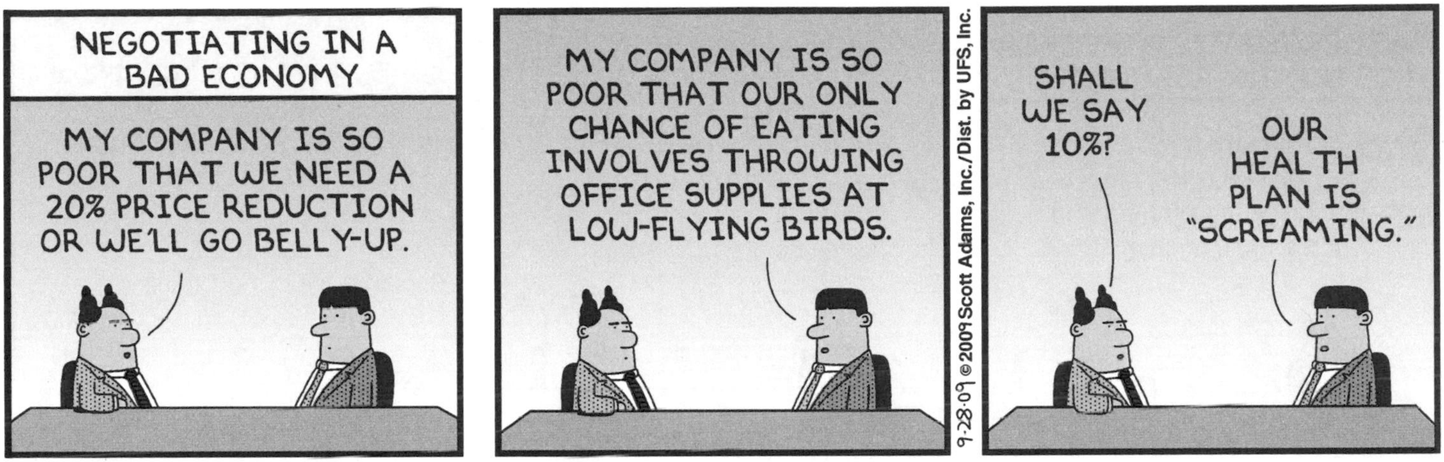
NEGOTIATING IN A BAD ECONOMY
MY COMPANY IS SO POOR THAT WE NEED A 20% PRICE REDUCTION OR WE'LL GO BELLY-UP.
MY COMPANY IS SO POOR THAT OUR ONLY CHANCE OF EATING INVOLVES THROWING OFFICE SUPPLIES AT LOW-FLYING BIRDS.
9-28-09 © 2009 Scott Adams, Inc./Dist. by UFS, Inc.
SHALL WE SAY 10%?
OUR HEALTH PLAN IS "SCREAMING."

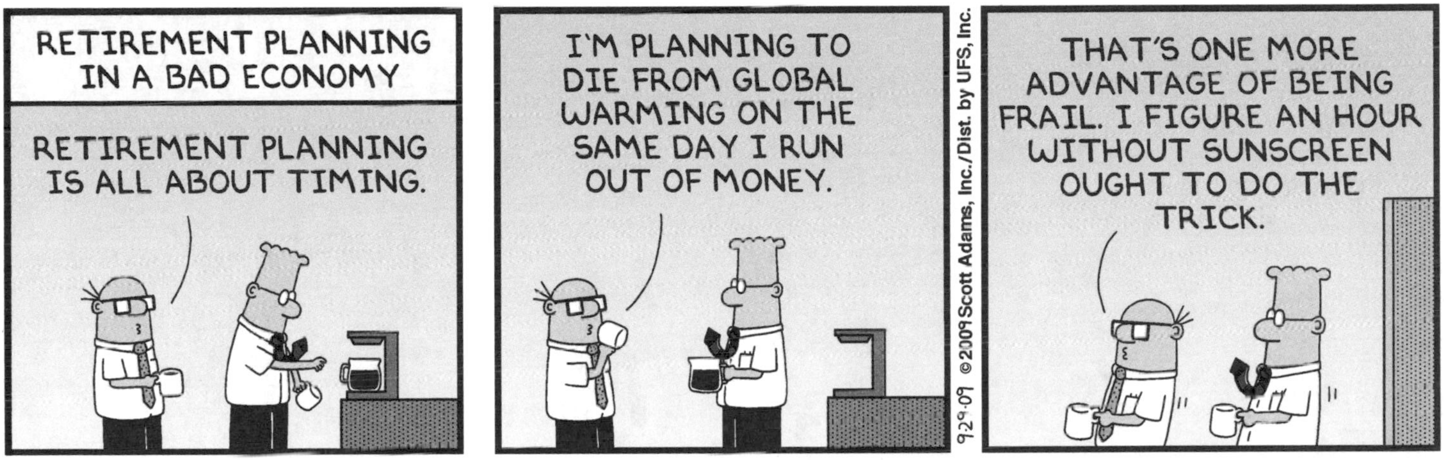
RETIREMENT PLANNING IN A BAD ECONOMY
RETIREMENT PLANNING IS ALL ABOUT TIMING.
I'M PLANNING TO DIE FROM GLOBAL WARMING ON THE SAME DAY I RUN OUT OF MONEY.
9-29-09 © 2009 Scott Adams, Inc./Dist. by UFS, Inc.
THAT'S ONE MORE ADVANTAGE OF BEING FRAIL. I FIGURE AN HOUR WITHOUT SUNSCREEN OUGHT TO DO THE TRICK.

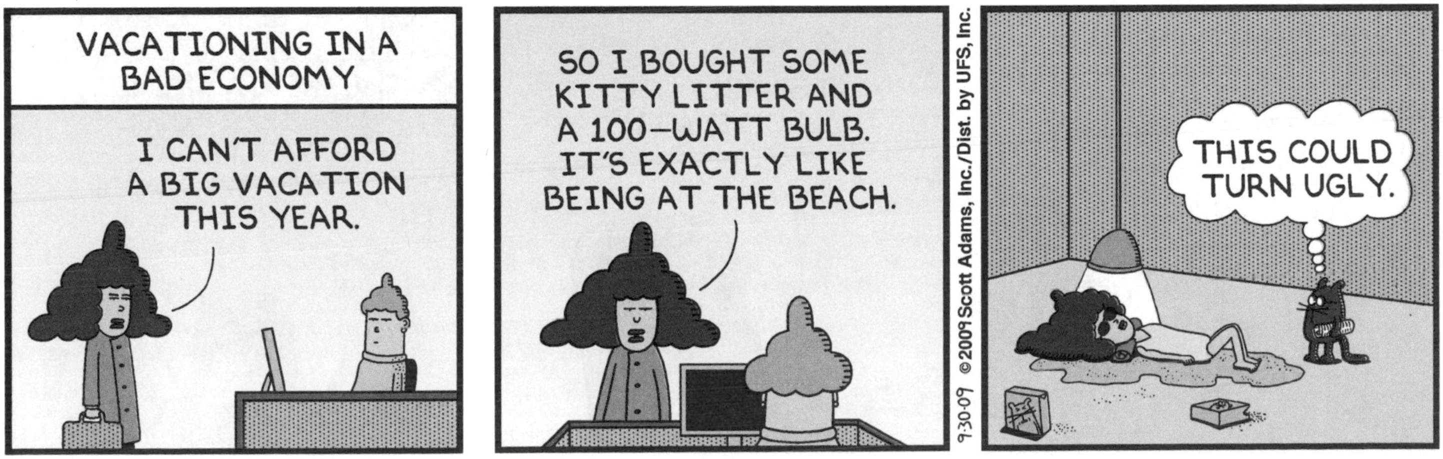
VACATIONING IN A BAD ECONOMY
I CAN'T AFFORD A BIG VACATION THIS YEAR.
SO I BOUGHT SOME KITTY LITTER AND A 100-WATT BULB. IT'S EXACTLY LIKE BEING AT THE BEACH.
9-30-09 © 2009 Scott Adams, Inc./Dist. by UFS, Inc.
THIS COULD TURN UGLY.

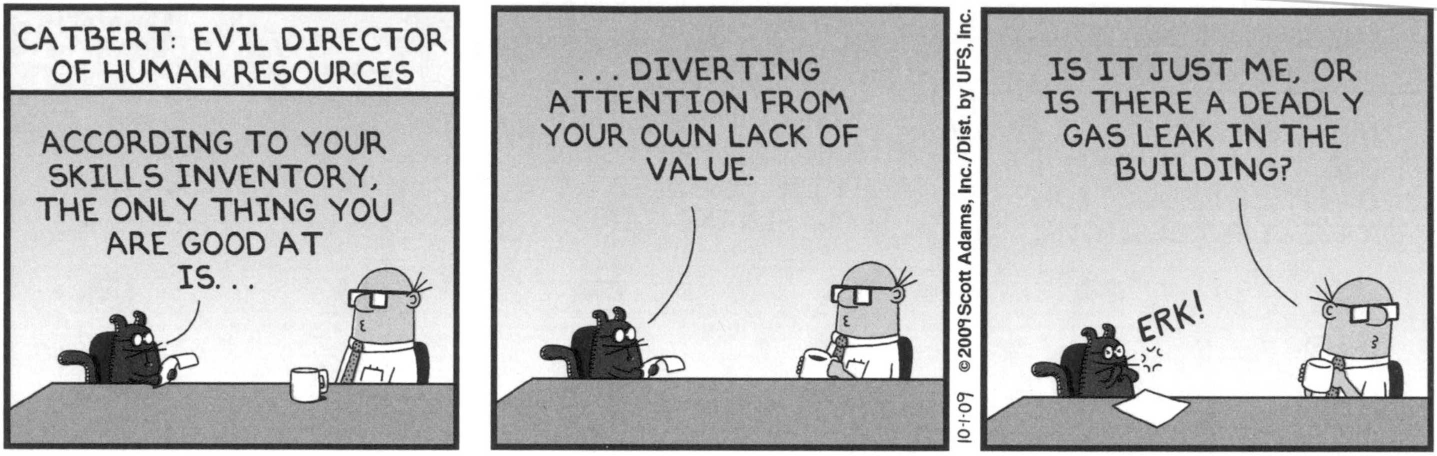
CATBERT: EVIL DIRECTOR OF HUMAN RESOURCES
ACCORDING TO YOUR SKILLS INVENTORY, THE ONLY THING YOU ARE GOOD AT IS. . .
. . . DIVERTING ATTENTION FROM YOUR OWN LACK OF VALUE.
10-1-09 © 2009 Scott Adams, Inc./Dist. by UFS, Inc.
IS IT JUST ME, OR IS THERE A DEADLY GAS LEAK IN THE BUILDING?
ERK!

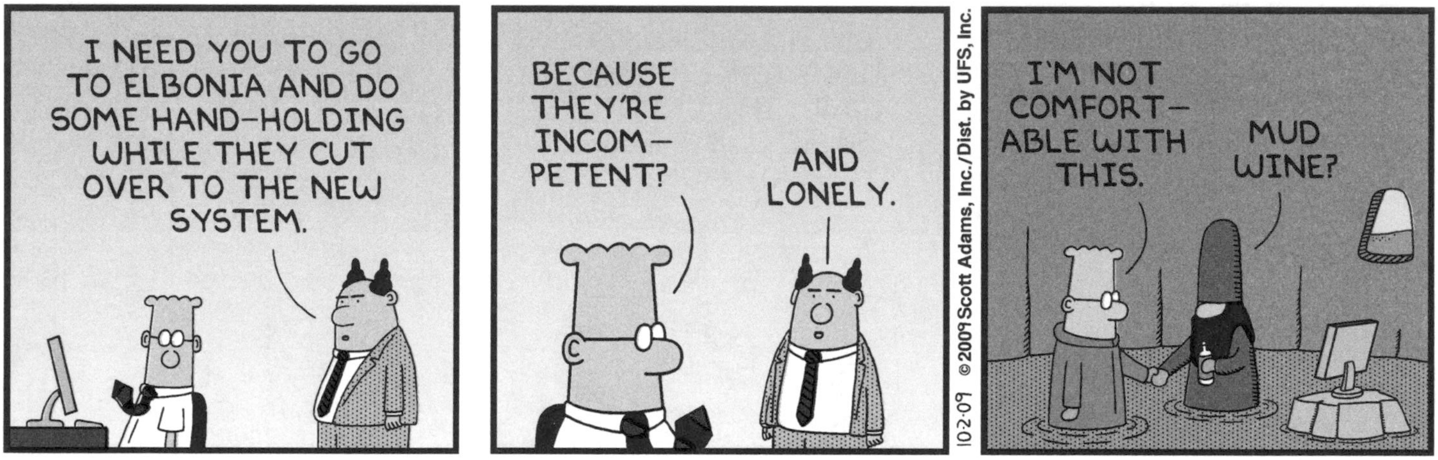
I NEED YOU TO GO TO ELBONIA AND DO SOME HAND-HOLDING WHILE THEY CUT OVER TO THE NEW SYSTEM.
BECAUSE THEY'RE INCOM-PETENT?
AND LONELY.
10-2-09 © 2009 Scott Adams, Inc./Dist. by UFS, Inc.
I'M NOT COMFORT-ABLE WITH THIS.
MUD WINE?

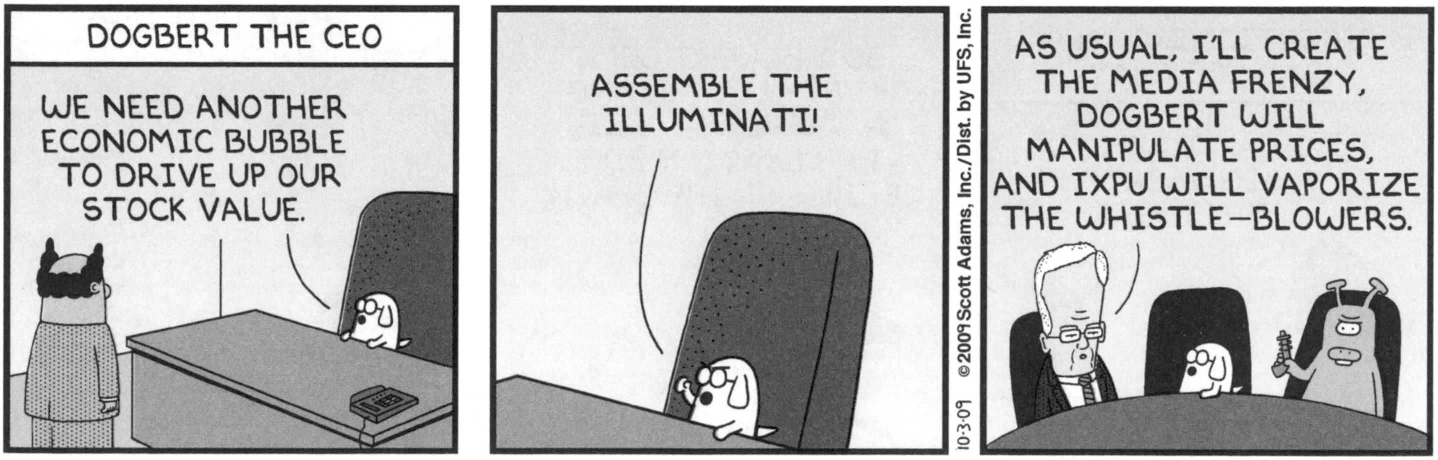
DOGBERT THE CEO
WE NEED ANOTHER ECONOMIC BUBBLE TO DRIVE UP OUR STOCK VALUE.
ASSEMBLE THE ILLUMINATI!
10-3-09 © 2009 Scott Adams, Inc./Dist. by UFS, Inc.
AS USUAL, I'LL CREATE THE MEDIA FRENZY, DOGBERT WILL MANIPULATE PRICES, AND IXPU WILL VAPORIZE THE WHISTLE-BLOWERS.

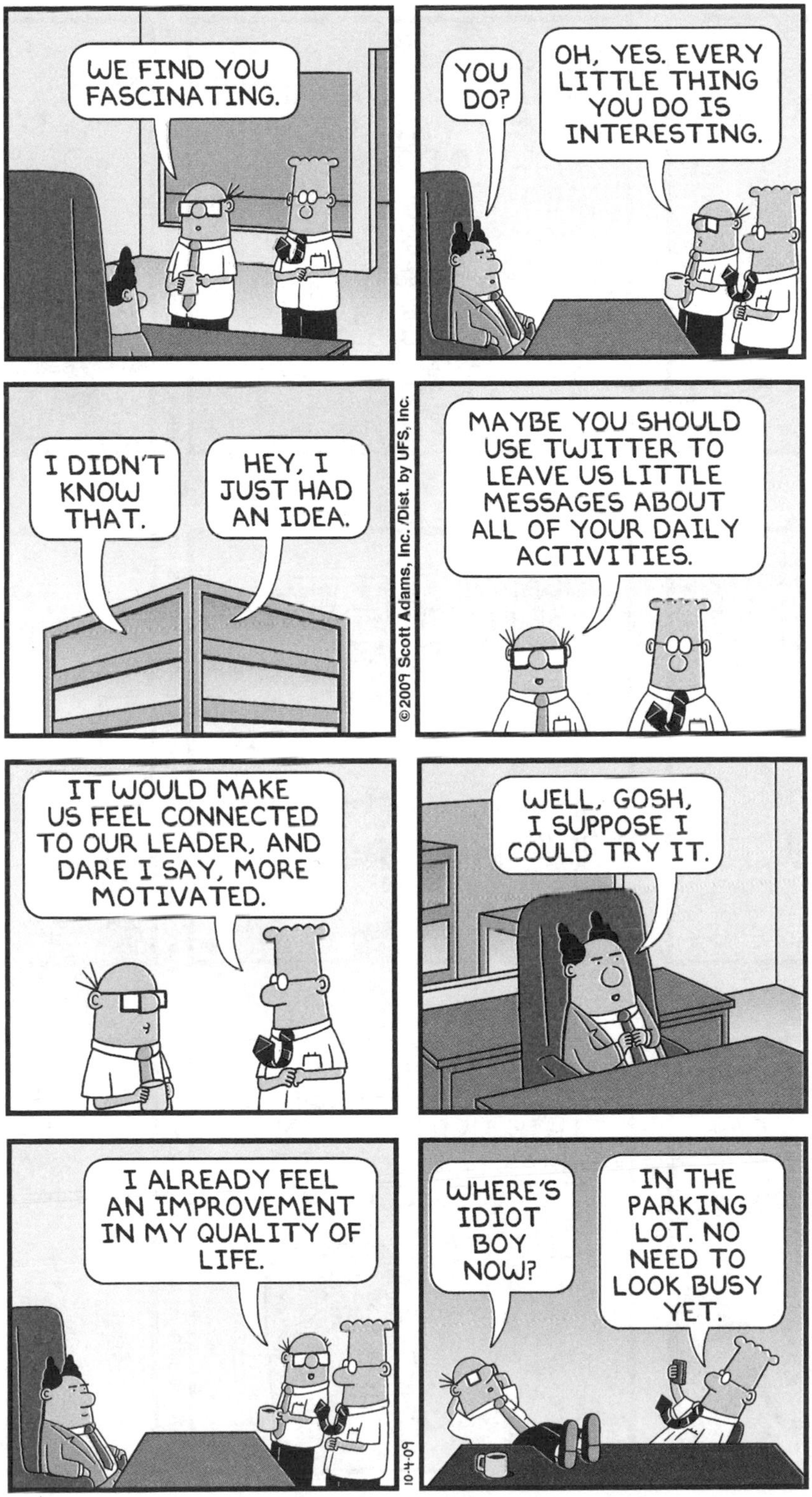
WE FIND YOU FASCINATING.
YOU DO?
OH, YES. EVERY LITTLE THING YOU DO IS INTERESTING.
I DIDN'T KNOW THAT.
HEY, I JUST HAD AN IDEA.
MAYBE YOU SHOULD USE TWITTER TO LEAVE US LITTLE MESSAGES ABOUT ALL OF YOUR DAILY ACTIVITIES.
IT WOULD MAKE US FEEL CONNECTED TO OUR LEADER, AND DARE I SAY, MORE MOTIVATED.
WELL, GOSH, I SUPPOSE I COULD TRY IT.
I ALREADY FEEL AN IMPROVEMENT IN MY QUALITY OF LIFE.
WHERE'S IDIOT BOY NOW?
IN THE PARKING LOT. NO NEED TO LOOK BUSY YET.
©2009 Scott Adams, Inc./Dist. by UFS, Inc.
10-4-09

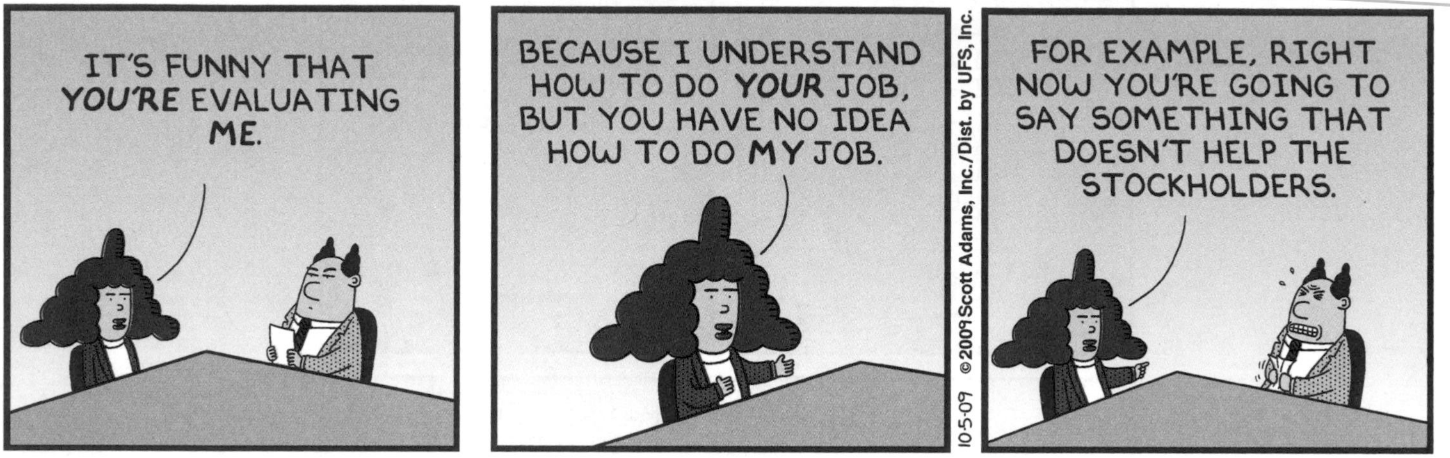
IT'S FUNNY THAT YOU'RE EVALUATING ME.
BECAUSE I UNDERSTAND HOW TO DO YOUR JOB, BUT YOU HAVE NO IDEA HOW TO DO MY JOB.
10-5-09 ©2009 Scott Adams, Inc./Dist. by UFS, Inc.
FOR EXAMPLE, RIGHT NOW YOU'RE GOING TO SAY SOMETHING THAT DOESN'T HELP THE STOCKHOLDERS.

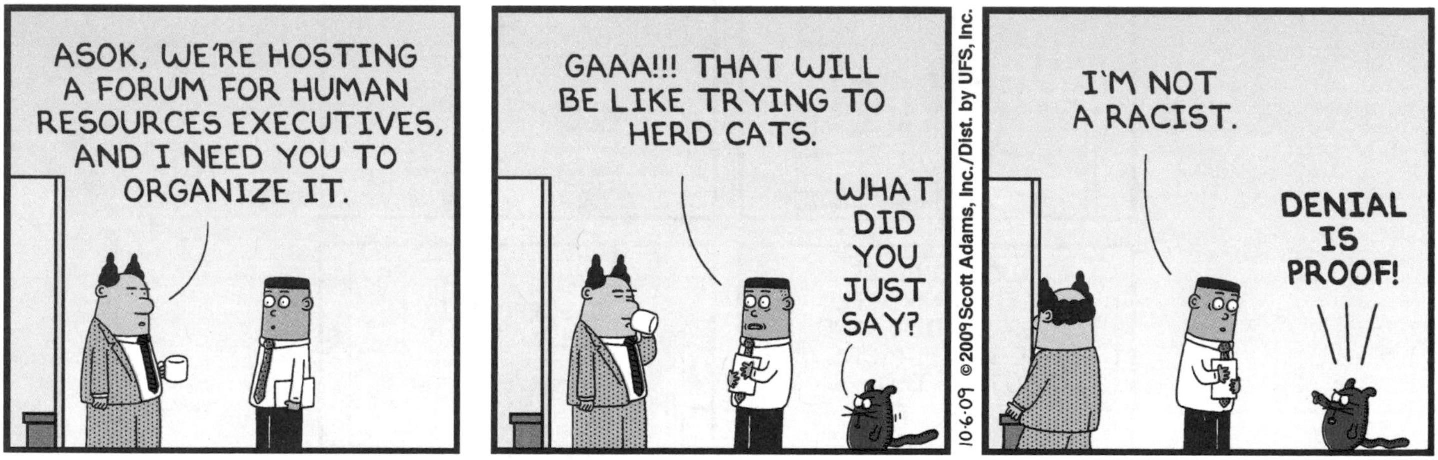
ASOK, WE'RE HOSTING A FORUM FOR HUMAN RESOURCES EXECUTIVES, AND I NEED YOU TO ORGANIZE IT.
GAAA!!! THAT WILL BE LIKE TRYING TO HERD CATS.
WHAT DID YOU JUST SAY?
10-6-09 ©2009 Scott Adams, Inc./Dist. by UFS, Inc.
I'M NOT A RACIST.
DENIAL IS PROOF!

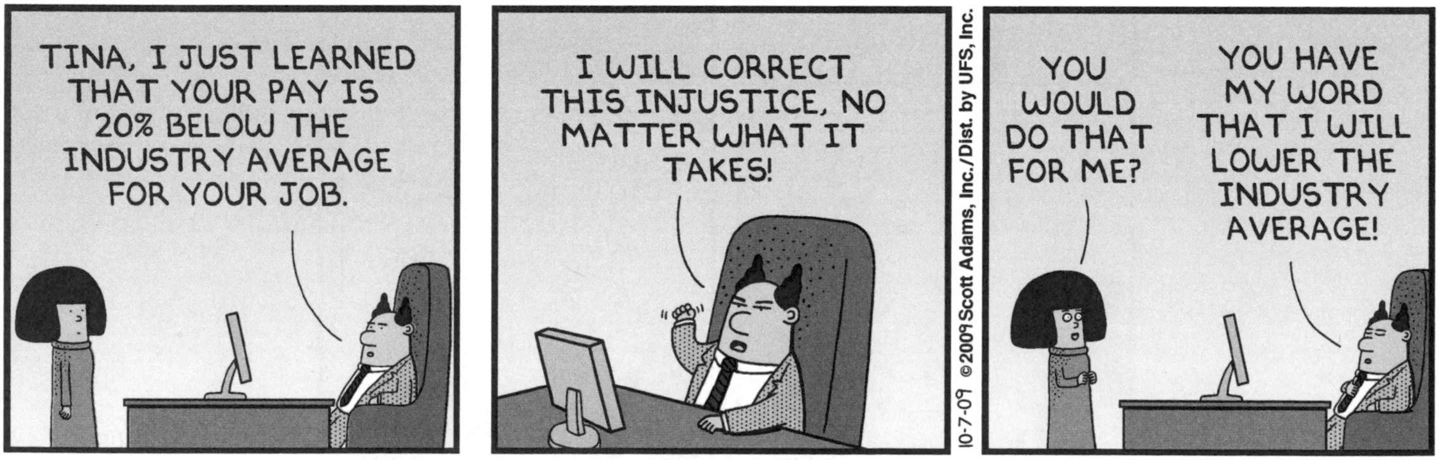
TINA, I JUST LEARNED THAT YOUR PAY IS 20% BELOW THE INDUSTRY AVERAGE FOR YOUR JOB.
I WILL CORRECT THIS INJUSTICE, NO MATTER WHAT IT TAKES!
10-7-09 ©2009 Scott Adams, Inc./Dist. by UFS, Inc.
YOU WOULD DO THAT FOR ME?
YOU HAVE MY WORD THAT I WILL LOWER THE INDUSTRY AVERAGE!

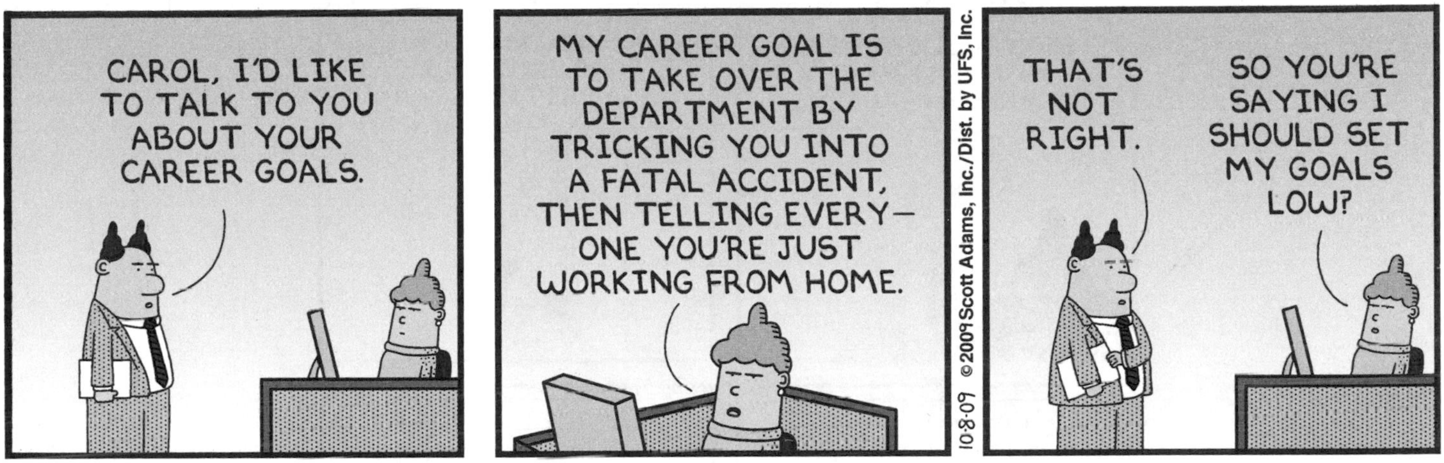
CAROL, I'D LIKE TO TALK TO YOU ABOUT YOUR CAREER GOALS.
MY CAREER GOAL IS TO TAKE OVER THE DEPARTMENT BY TRICKING YOU INTO A FATAL ACCIDENT, THEN TELLING EVERY-ONE YOU'RE JUST WORKING FROM HOME.
10-8-09 © 2009 Scott Adams, Inc./Dist. by UFS, Inc.
THAT'S NOT RIGHT.
SO YOU'RE SAYING I SHOULD SET MY GOALS LOW?

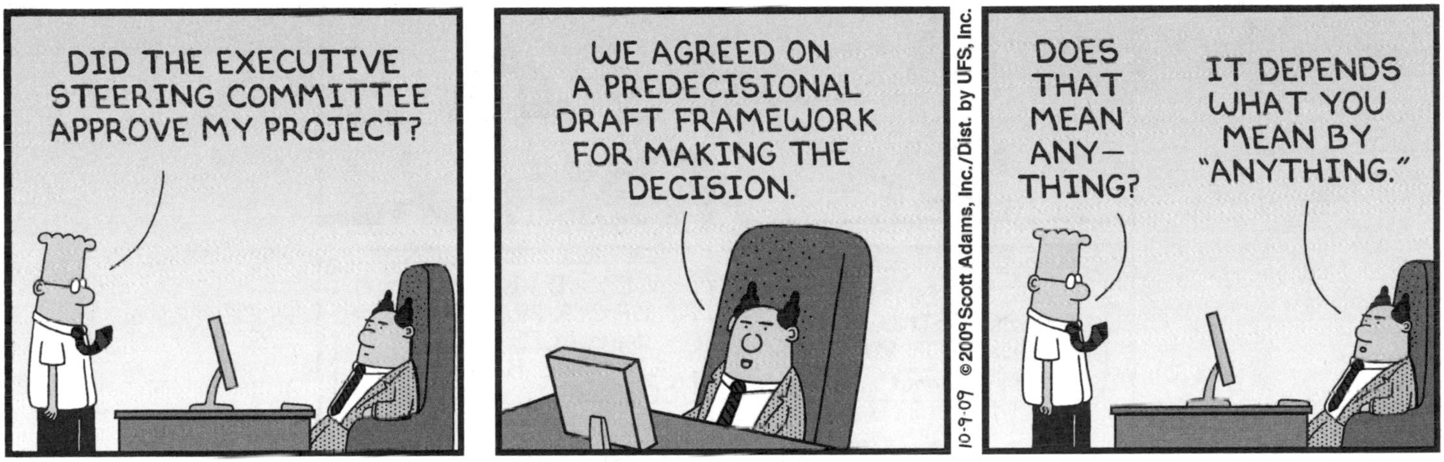
DID THE EXECUTIVE STEERING COMMITTEE APPROVE MY PROJECT?
WE AGREED ON A PREDECISIONAL DRAFT FRAMEWORK FOR MAKING THE DECISION.
10-9-09 © 2009 Scott Adams, Inc./Dist. by UFS, Inc.
DOES THAT MEAN ANY-THING?
IT DEPENDS WHAT YOU MEAN BY "ANYTHING."

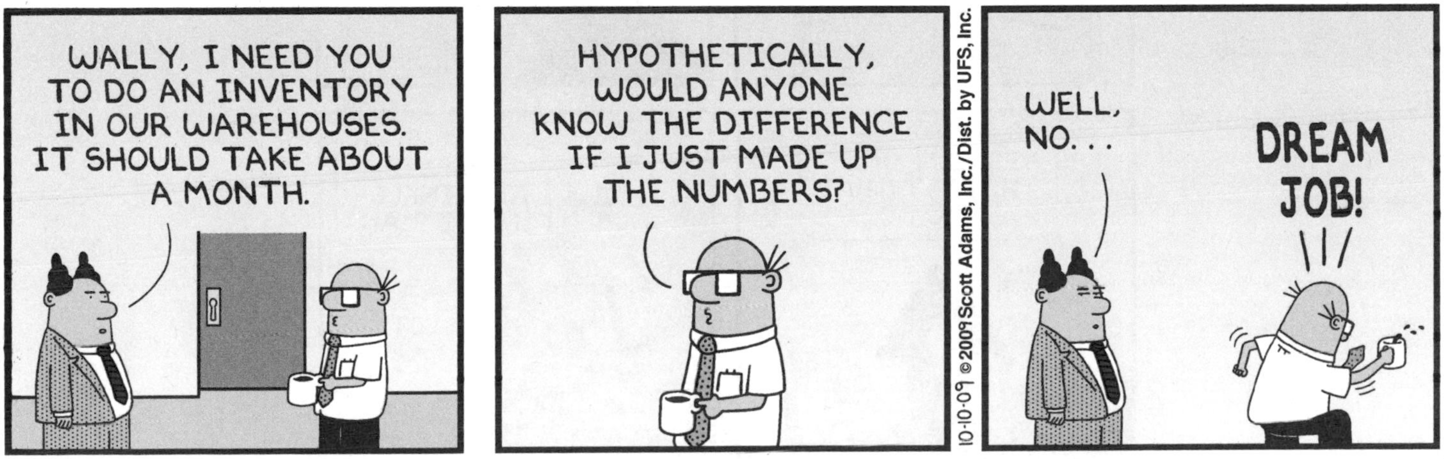
WALLY, I NEED YOU TO DO AN INVENTORY IN OUR WAREHOUSES. IT SHOULD TAKE ABOUT A MONTH.
HYPOTHETICALLY, WOULD ANYONE KNOW THE DIFFERENCE IF I JUST MADE UP THE NUMBERS?
10-10-09 © 2009 Scott Adams, Inc./Dist. by UFS, Inc.
WELL, NO. . .
DREAM JOB!

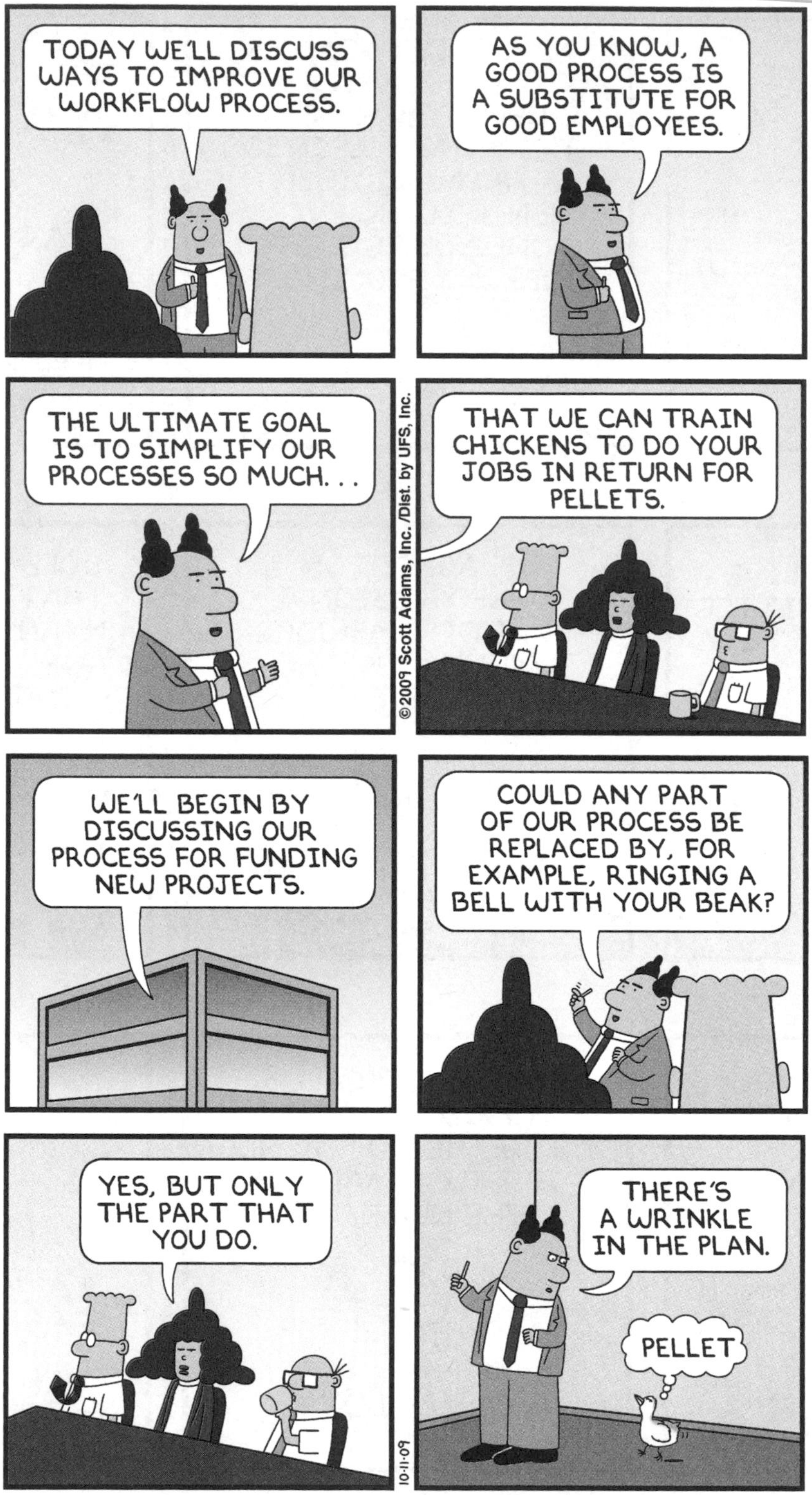
TODAY WE'LL DISCUSS WAYS TO IMPROVE OUR WORKFLOW PROCESS.
AS YOU KNOW, A GOOD PROCESS IS A SUBSTITUTE FOR GOOD EMPLOYEES.
THE ULTIMATE GOAL IS TO SIMPLIFY OUR PROCESSES SO MUCH. . .
THAT WE CAN TRAIN CHICKENS TO DO YOUR JOBS IN RETURN FOR PELLETS.
WE'LL BEGIN BY DISCUSSING OUR PROCESS FOR FUNDING NEW PROJECTS.
COULD ANY PART OF OUR PROCESS BE REPLACED BY, FOR EXAMPLE, RINGING A BELL WITH YOUR BEAK?
YES, BUT ONLY THE PART THAT YOU DO.
THERE'S A WRINKLE IN THE PLAN.
PELLET
©2009 Scott Adams, Inc./Dist. by UFS, Inc.
10-11-09

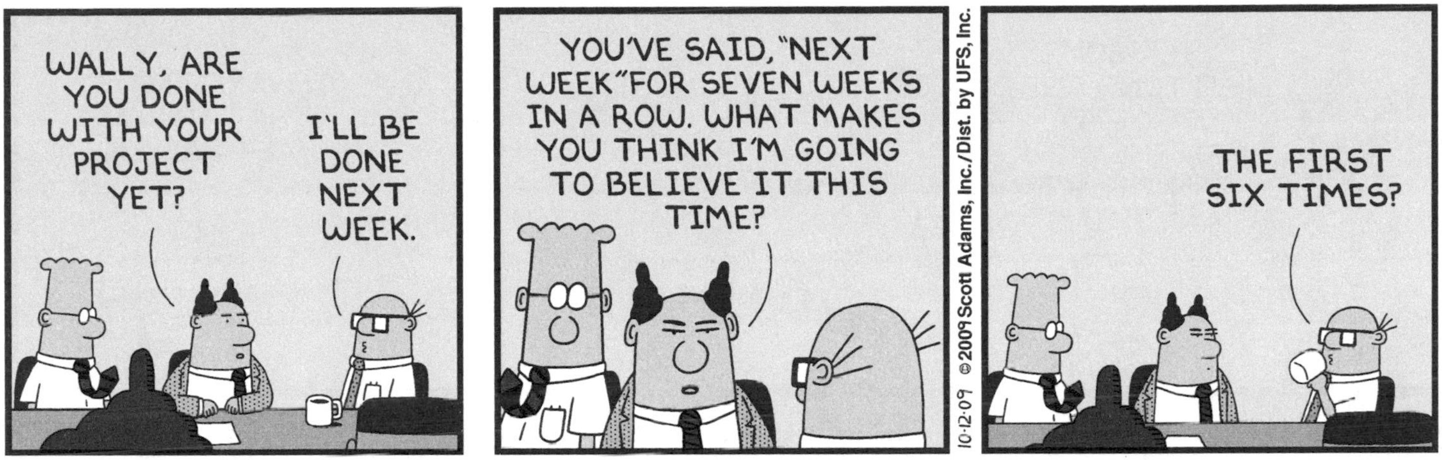
WALLY, ARE YOU DONE WITH YOUR PROJECT YET?
I'LL BE DONE NEXT WEEK.
YOU'VE SAID, "NEXT WEEK" FOR SEVEN WEEKS IN A ROW. WHAT MAKES YOU THINK I'M GOING TO BELIEVE IT THIS TIME?
10-12-09 ©2009 Scott Adams, Inc./Dist. by UFS, Inc.
THE FIRST SIX TIMES?

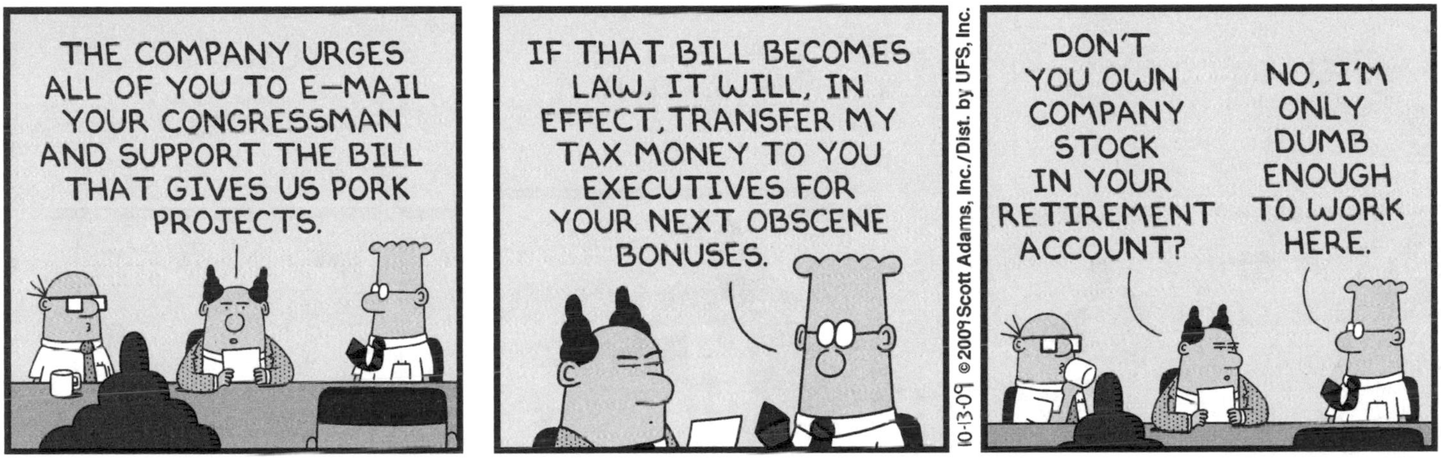
THE COMPANY URGES ALL OF YOU TO E-MAIL YOUR CONGRESSMAN AND SUPPORT THE BILL THAT GIVES US PORK PROJECTS.
IF THAT BILL BECOMES LAW, IT WILL, IN EFFECT, TRANSFER MY TAX MONEY TO YOU EXECUTIVES FOR YOUR NEXT OBSCENE BONUSES.
10-13-09 ©2009 Scott Adams, Inc./Dist. by UFS, Inc.
DON'T YOU OWN COMPANY STOCK IN YOUR RETIREMENT ACCOUNT?
NO, I'M ONLY DUMB ENOUGH TO WORK HERE.

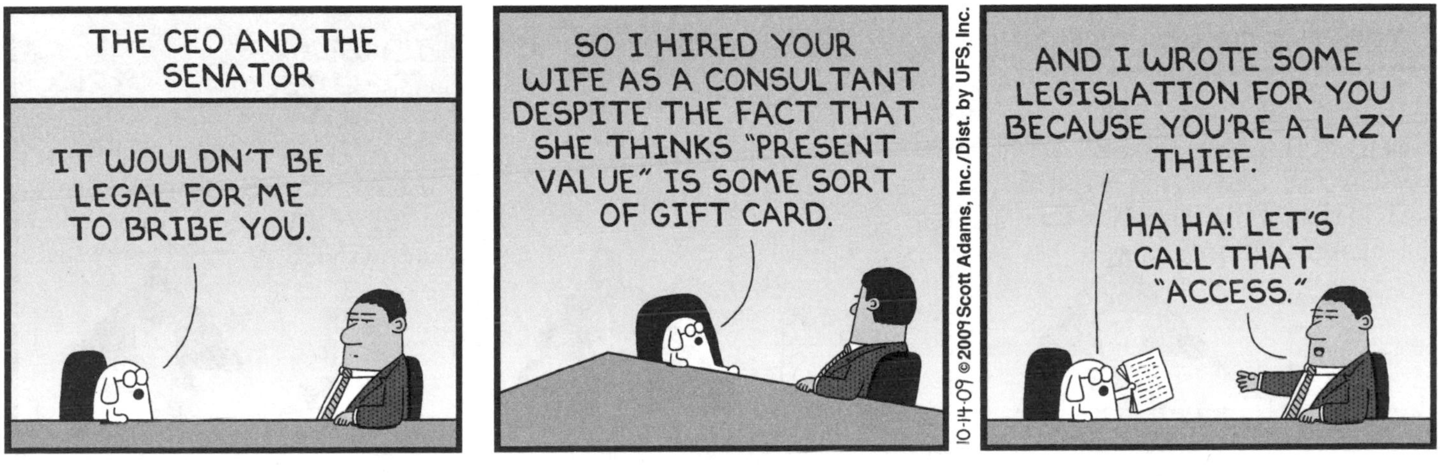
THE CEO AND THE SENATOR
IT WOULDN'T BE LEGAL FOR ME TO BRIBE YOU.
SO I HIRED YOUR WIFE AS A CONSULTANT DESPITE THE FACT THAT SHE THINKS "PRESENT VALUE" IS SOME SORT OF GIFT CARD.
10-14-09 ©2009 Scott Adams, Inc./Dist. by UFS, Inc.
AND I WROTE SOME LEGISLATION FOR YOU BECAUSE YOU'RE A LAZY THIEF.
HA HA! LET'S CALL THAT "ACCESS."

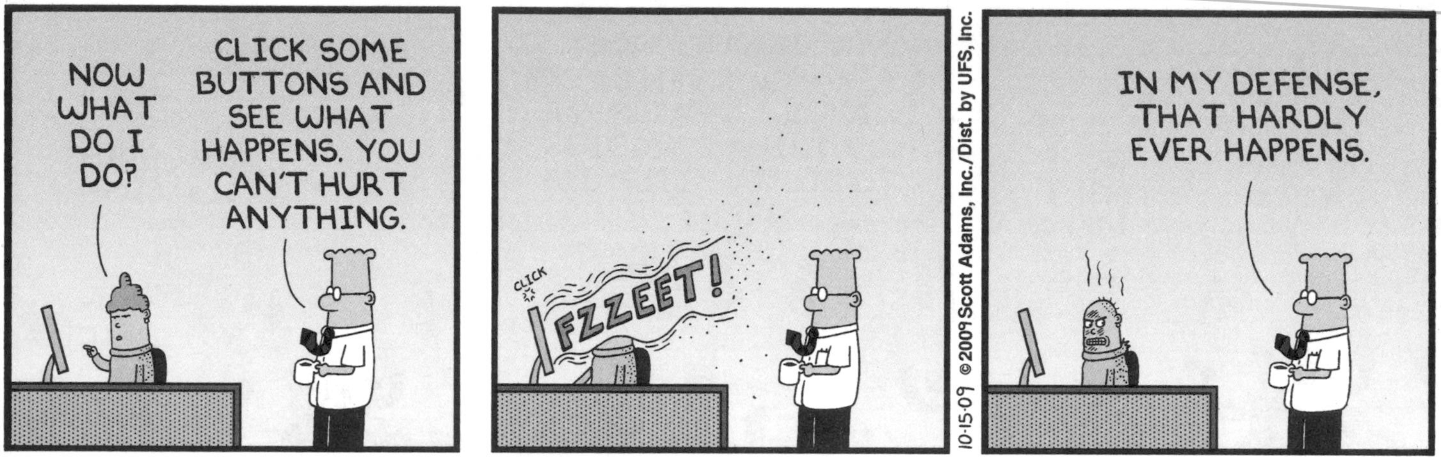
NOW WHAT DO I DO?
CLICK SOME BUTTONS AND SEE WHAT HAPPENS. YOU CAN'T HURT ANYTHING.
CLICK
FZZEET!
10-15-09 ©2009 Scott Adams, Inc./Dist. by UFS, Inc.
IN MY DEFENSE, THAT HARDLY EVER HAPPENS.

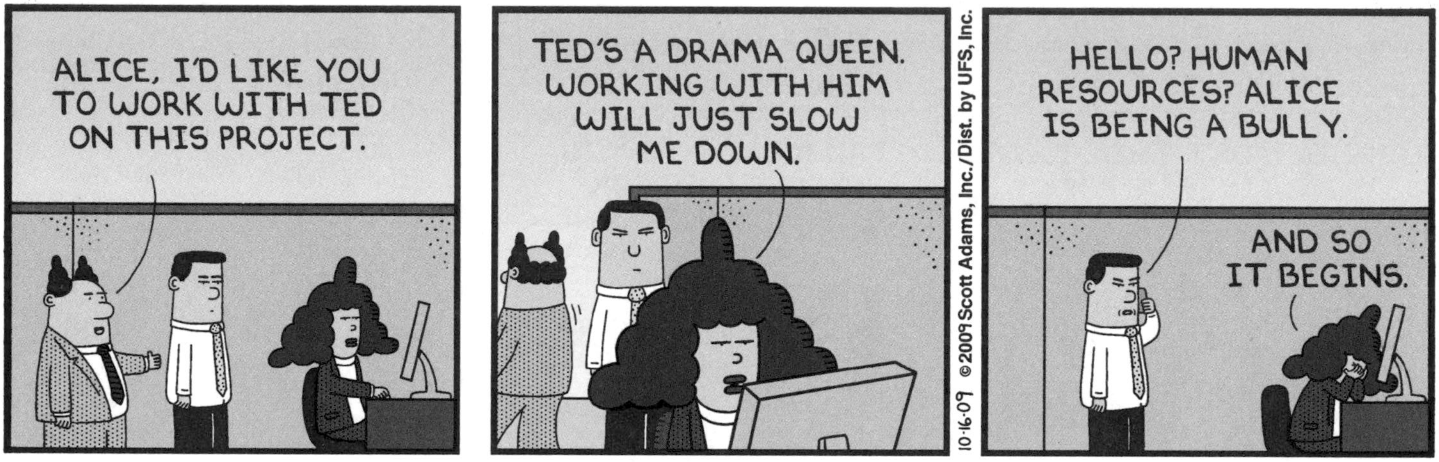
ALICE, I'D LIKE YOU TO WORK WITH TED ON THIS PROJECT.
TED'S A DRAMA QUEEN. WORKING WITH HIM WILL JUST SLOW ME DOWN.
10-16-09 ©2009 Scott Adams, Inc./Dist. by UFS, Inc.
HELLO? HUMAN RESOURCES? ALICE IS BEING A BULLY.
AND SO IT BEGINS.

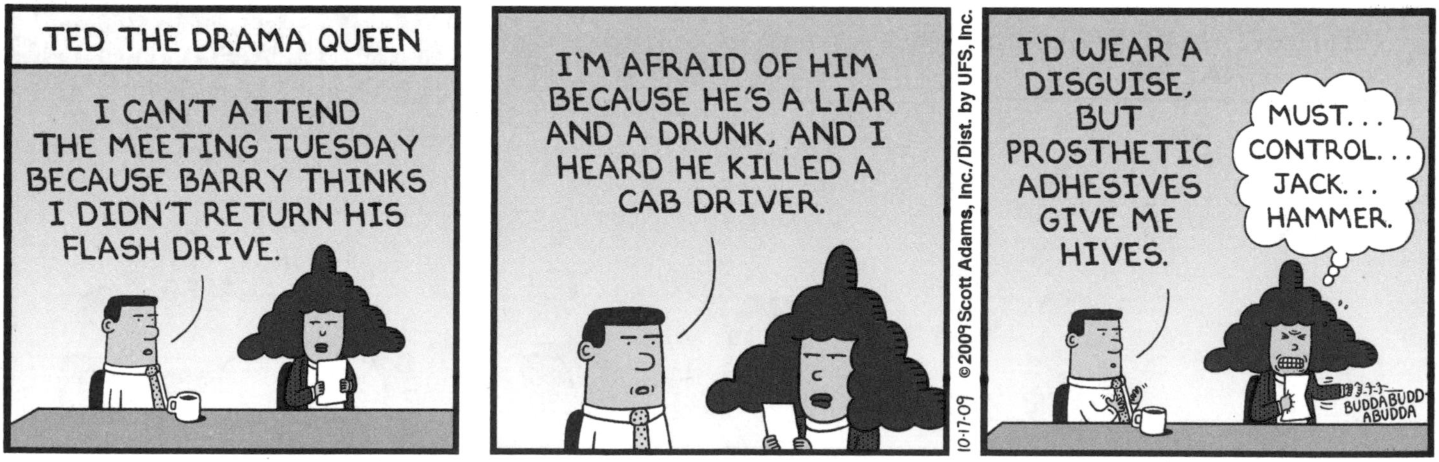
TED THE DRAMA QUEEN
I CAN'T ATTEND THE MEETING TUESDAY BECAUSE BARRY THINKS I DIDN'T RETURN HIS FLASH DRIVE.
I'M AFRAID OF HIM BECAUSE HE'S A LIAR AND A DRUNK, AND I HEARD HE KILLED A CAB DRIVER.
10-17-09 ©2009 Scott Adams, Inc./Dist. by UFS, Inc.
I'D WEAR A DISGUISE, BUT PROSTHETIC ADHESIVES GIVE ME HIVES.
MUST... CONTROL... JACK... HAMMER.
BUDDABUDD-ABUDDA

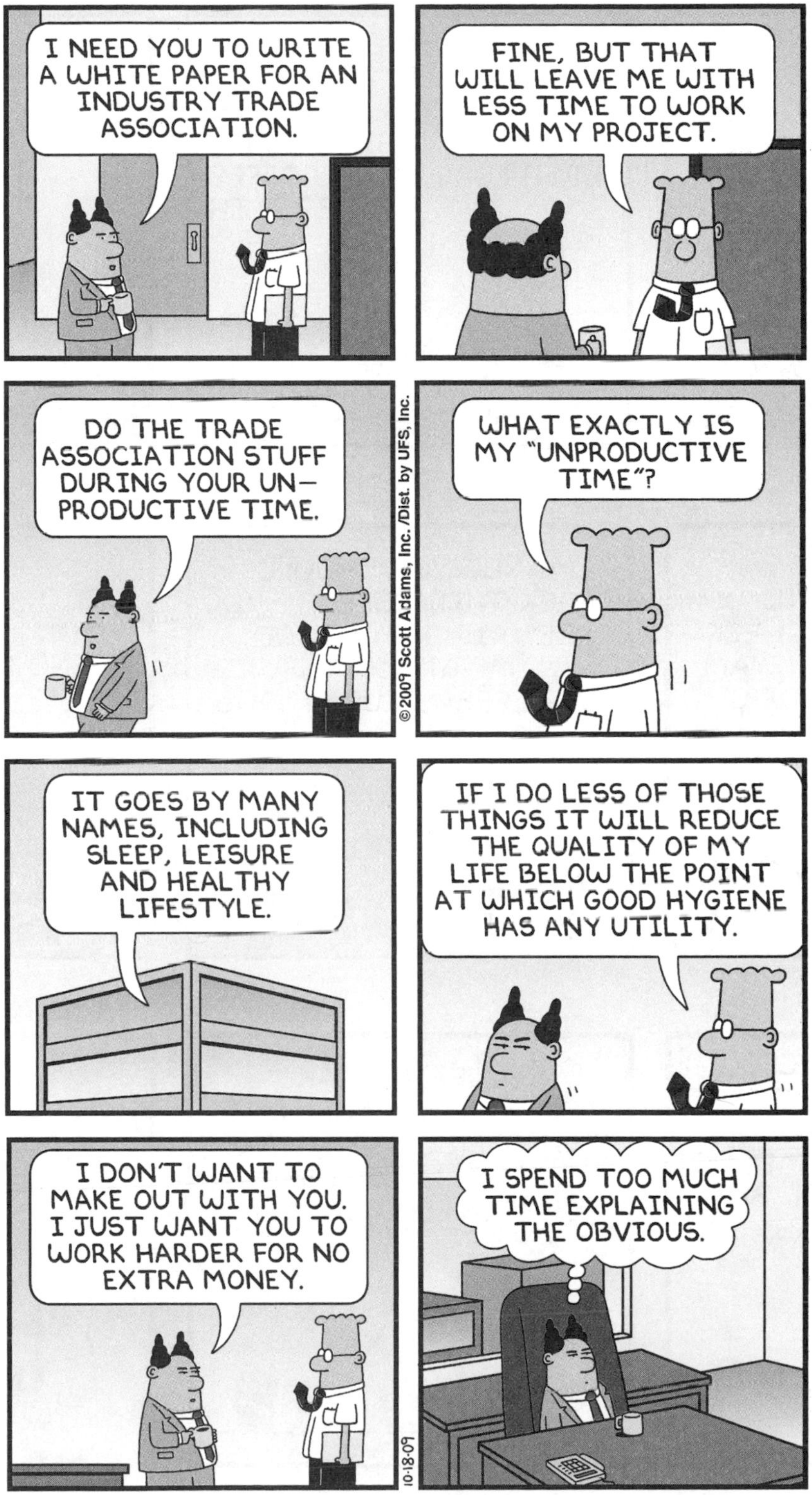
I NEED YOU TO WRITE A WHITE PAPER FOR AN INDUSTRY TRADE ASSOCIATION.
FINE, BUT THAT WILL LEAVE ME WITH LESS TIME TO WORK ON MY PROJECT.
DO THE TRADE ASSOCIATION STUFF DURING YOUR UN-PRODUCTIVE TIME.
WHAT EXACTLY IS MY "UNPRODUCTIVE TIME"?
IT GOES BY MANY NAMES, INCLUDING SLEEP, LEISURE AND HEALTHY LIFESTYLE.
IF I DO LESS OF THOSE THINGS IT WILL REDUCE THE QUALITY OF MY LIFE BELOW THE POINT AT WHICH GOOD HYGIENE HAS ANY UTILITY.
I DON'T WANT TO MAKE OUT WITH YOU. I JUST WANT YOU TO WORK HARDER FOR NO EXTRA MONEY.
I SPEND TOO MUCH TIME EXPLAINING THE OBVIOUS.
©2009 Scott Adams, Inc./Dist. by UFS, Inc.
10-18-09

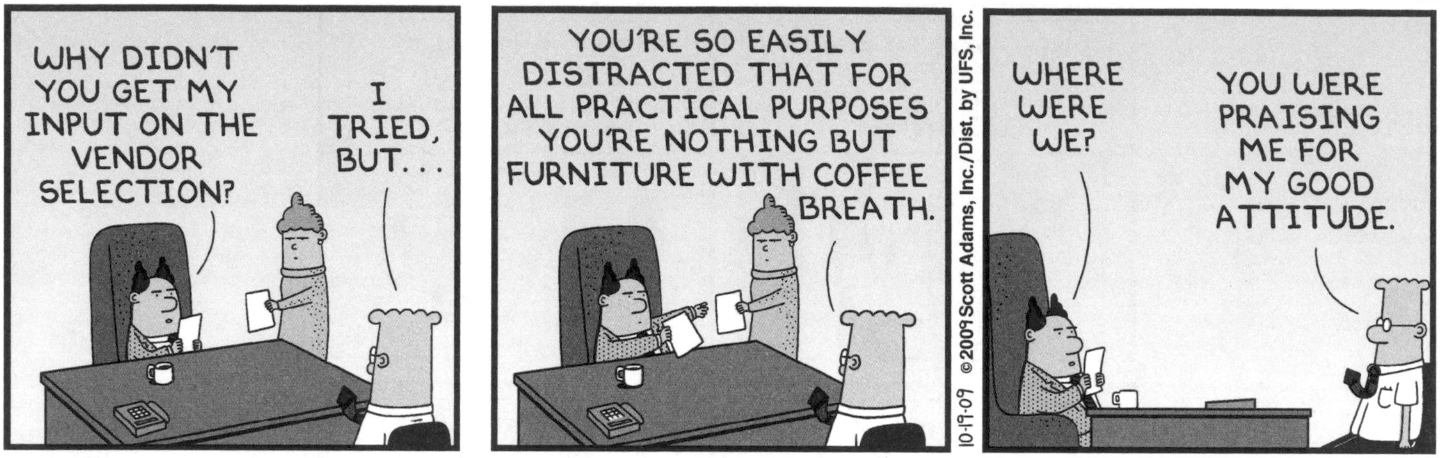
WHY DIDN'T YOU GET MY INPUT ON THE VENDOR SELECTION?
I TRIED, BUT. . .
YOU'RE SO EASILY DISTRACTED THAT FOR ALL PRACTICAL PURPOSES YOU'RE NOTHING BUT FURNITURE WITH COFFEE BREATH.
10-19-09 ©2009 Scott Adams, Inc./Dist. by UFS, Inc.
WHERE WERE WE?
YOU WERE PRAISING ME FOR MY GOOD ATTITUDE.

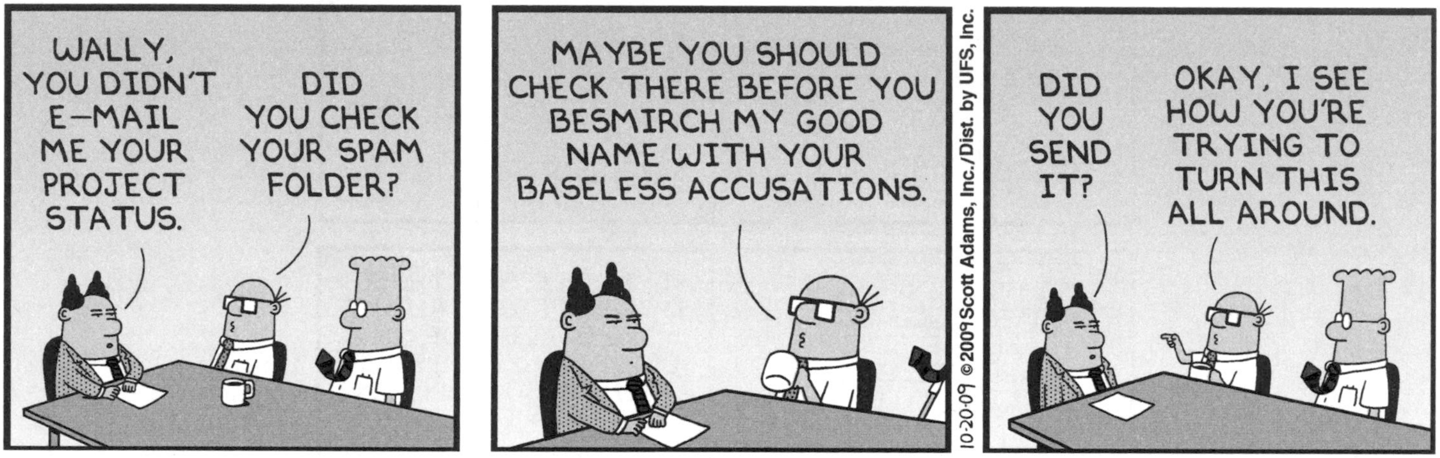
WALLY, YOU DIDN'T E-MAIL ME YOUR PROJECT STATUS.
DID YOU CHECK YOUR SPAM FOLDER?
MAYBE YOU SHOULD CHECK THERE BEFORE YOU BESMIRCH MY GOOD NAME WITH YOUR BASELESS ACCUSATIONS.
10-20-09 ©2009 Scott Adams, Inc./Dist. by UFS, Inc.
DID YOU SEND IT?
OKAY, I SEE HOW YOU'RE TRYING TO TURN THIS ALL AROUND.

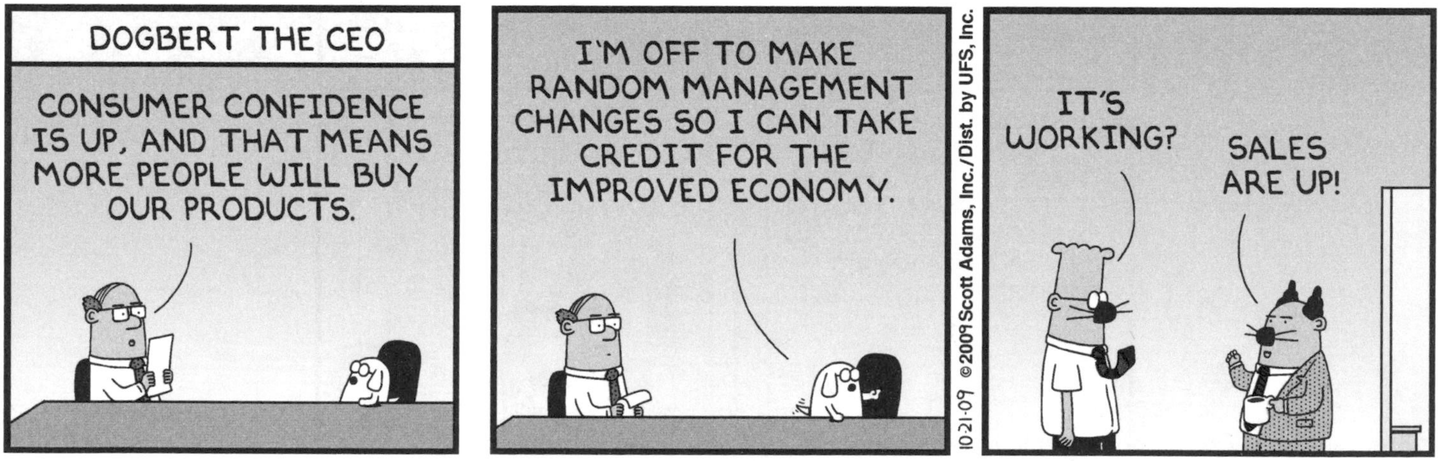
DOGBERT THE CEO
CONSUMER CONFIDENCE IS UP, AND THAT MEANS MORE PEOPLE WILL BUY OUR PRODUCTS.
I'M OFF TO MAKE RANDOM MANAGEMENT CHANGES SO I CAN TAKE CREDIT FOR THE IMPROVED ECONOMY.
10-21-09 ©2009 Scott Adams, Inc./Dist. by UFS, Inc.
IT'S WORKING?
SALES ARE UP!

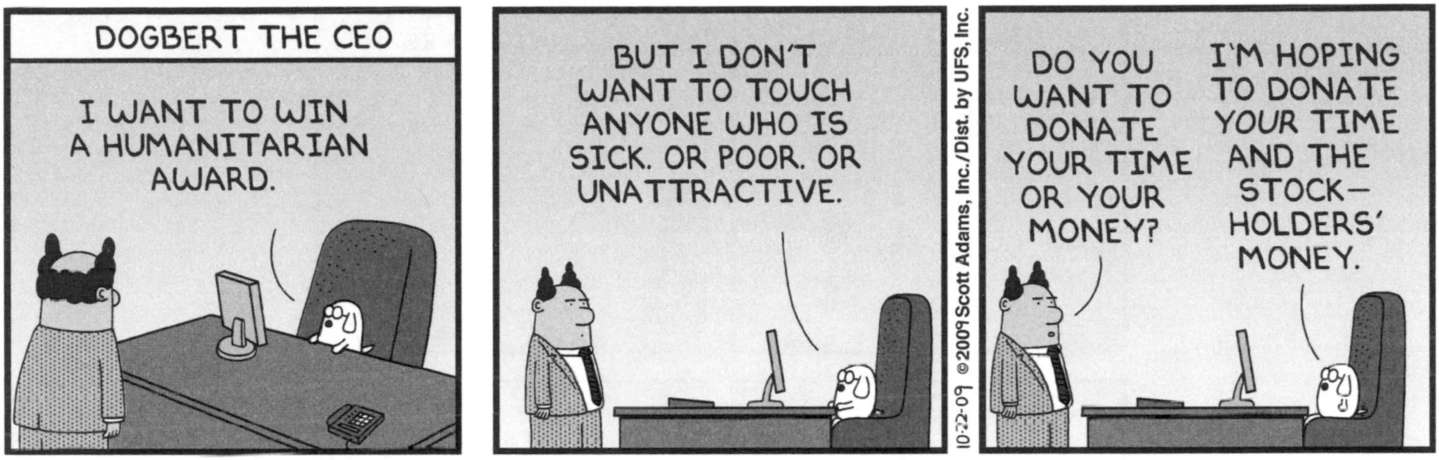
DOGBERT THE CEO
I WANT TO WIN A HUMANITARIAN AWARD.
BUT I DON'T WANT TO TOUCH ANYONE WHO IS SICK. OR POOR. OR UNATTRACTIVE.
10-22-09 ©2009 Scott Adams, Inc./Dist. by UFS, Inc.
DO YOU WANT TO DONATE YOUR TIME OR YOUR MONEY?
I'M HOPING TO DONATE *YOUR* TIME AND THE STOCK-HOLDERS' MONEY.

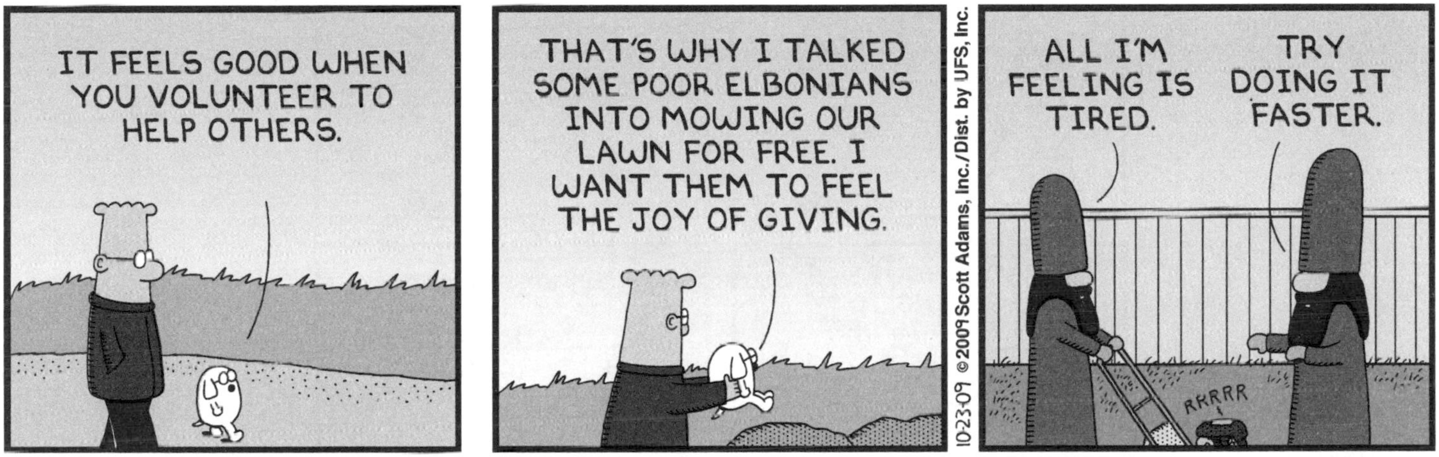
IT FEELS GOOD WHEN YOU VOLUNTEER TO HELP OTHERS.
THAT'S WHY I TALKED SOME POOR ELBONIANS INTO MOWING OUR LAWN FOR FREE. I WANT THEM TO FEEL THE JOY OF GIVING.
10-23-09 ©2009 Scott Adams, Inc./Dist. by UFS, Inc.
ALL I'M FEELING IS TIRED.
TRY DOING IT FASTER.
RRRRR

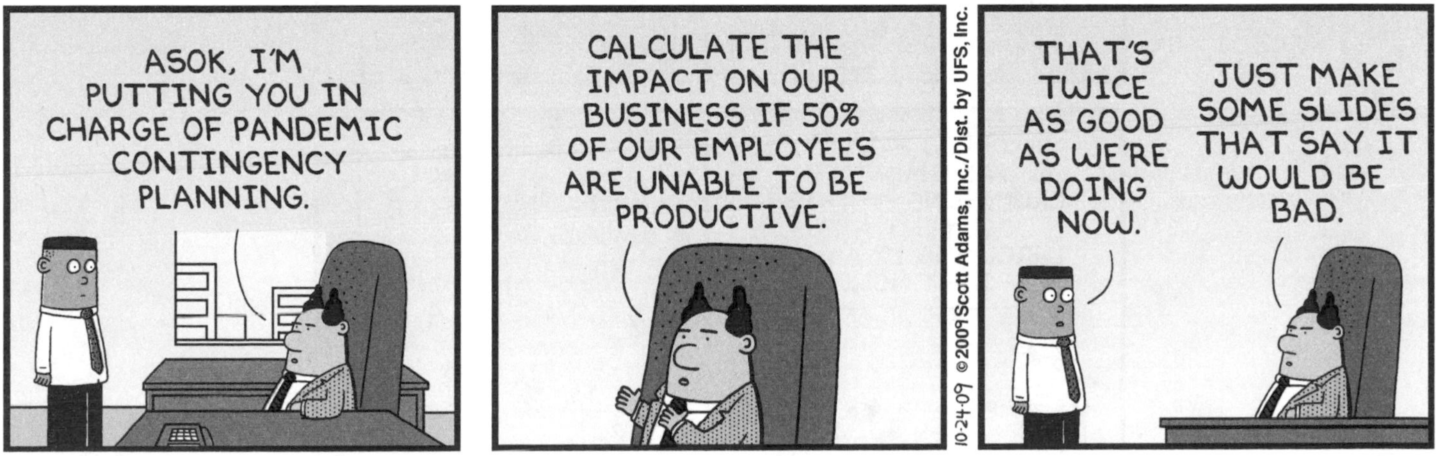
ASOK, I'M PUTTING YOU IN CHARGE OF PANDEMIC CONTINGENCY PLANNING.
CALCULATE THE IMPACT ON OUR BUSINESS IF 50% OF OUR EMPLOYEES ARE UNABLE TO BE PRODUCTIVE.
10-24-09 ©2009 Scott Adams, Inc./Dist. by UFS, Inc.
THAT'S TWICE AS GOOD AS WE'RE DOING NOW.
JUST MAKE SOME SLIDES THAT SAY IT WOULD BE BAD.

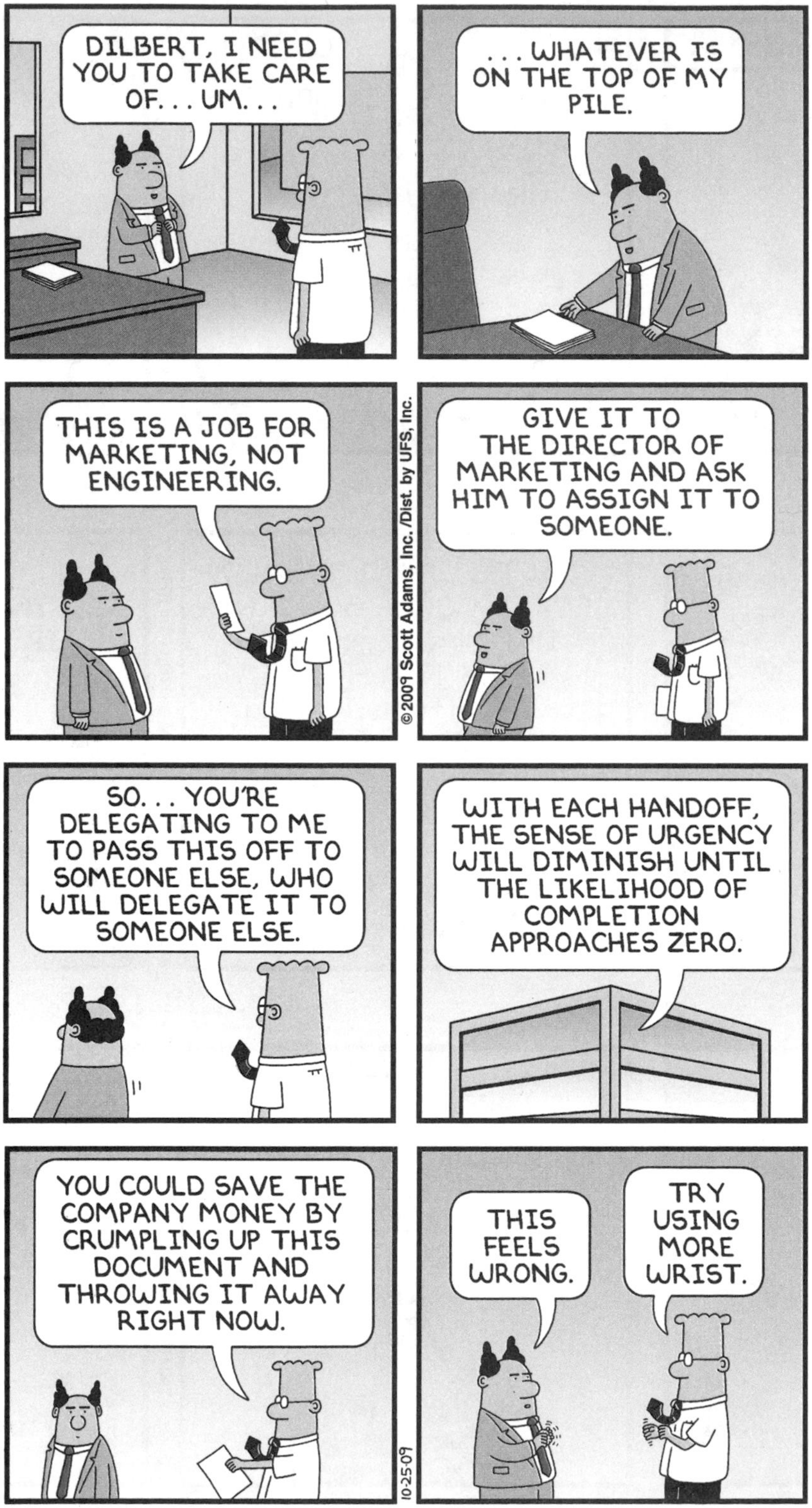
DILBERT, I NEED YOU TO TAKE CARE OF. . . UM. . .
. . . WHATEVER IS ON THE TOP OF MY PILE.
THIS IS A JOB FOR MARKETING, NOT ENGINEERING.
GIVE IT TO THE DIRECTOR OF MARKETING AND ASK HIM TO ASSIGN IT TO SOMEONE.
SO. . . YOU'RE DELEGATING TO ME TO PASS THIS OFF TO SOMEONE ELSE, WHO WILL DELEGATE IT TO SOMEONE ELSE.
WITH EACH HANDOFF, THE SENSE OF URGENCY WILL DIMINISH UNTIL THE LIKELIHOOD OF COMPLETION APPROACHES ZERO.
YOU COULD SAVE THE COMPANY MONEY BY CRUMPLING UP THIS DOCUMENT AND THROWING IT AWAY RIGHT NOW.
THIS FEELS WRONG.
TRY USING MORE WRIST.
© 2009 Scott Adams, Inc. /Dist. by UFS, Inc.
10-25-09

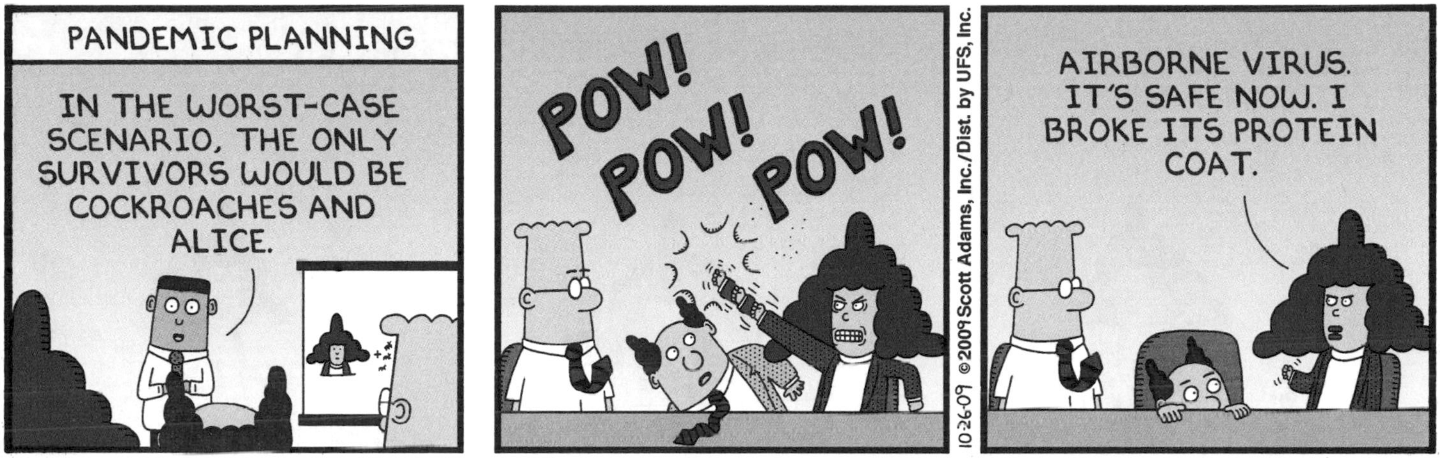
PANDEMIC PLANNING
IN THE WORST-CASE SCENARIO, THE ONLY SURVIVORS WOULD BE COCKROACHES AND ALICE.
POW! POW! POW!
10-26-09 ©2009 Scott Adams, Inc./Dist. by UFS, Inc.
AIRBORNE VIRUS. IT'S SAFE NOW. I BROKE ITS PROTEIN COAT.

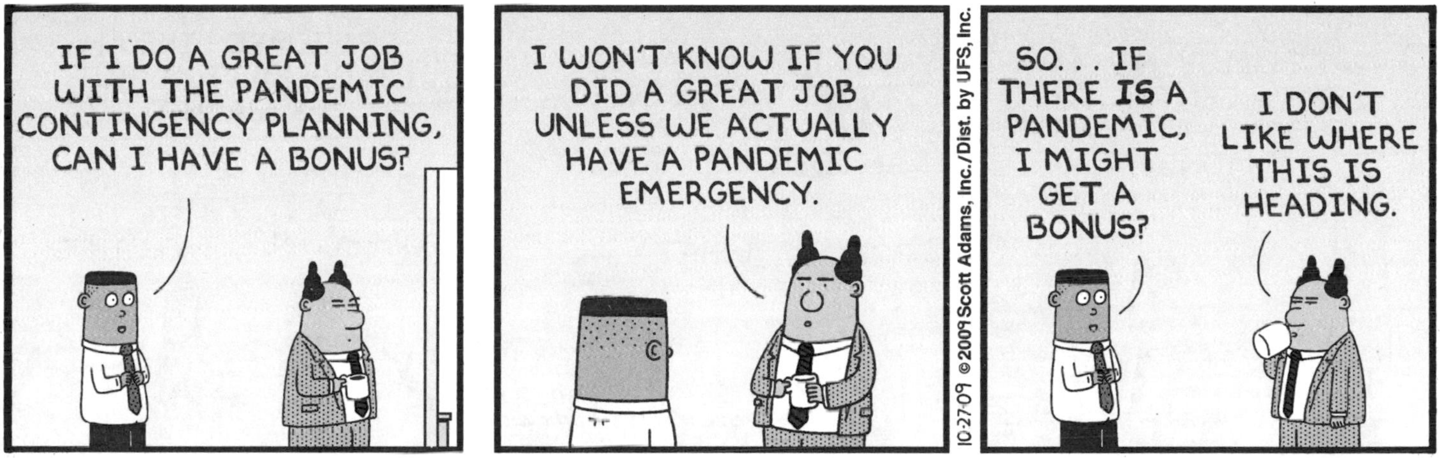
IF I DO A GREAT JOB WITH THE PANDEMIC CONTINGENCY PLANNING, CAN I HAVE A BONUS?
I WON'T KNOW IF YOU DID A GREAT JOB UNLESS WE ACTUALLY HAVE A PANDEMIC EMERGENCY.
10-27-09 ©2009 Scott Adams, Inc./Dist. by UFS, Inc.
SO. . . IF THERE **IS** A PANDEMIC, I MIGHT GET A BONUS?
I DON'T LIKE WHERE THIS IS HEADING.

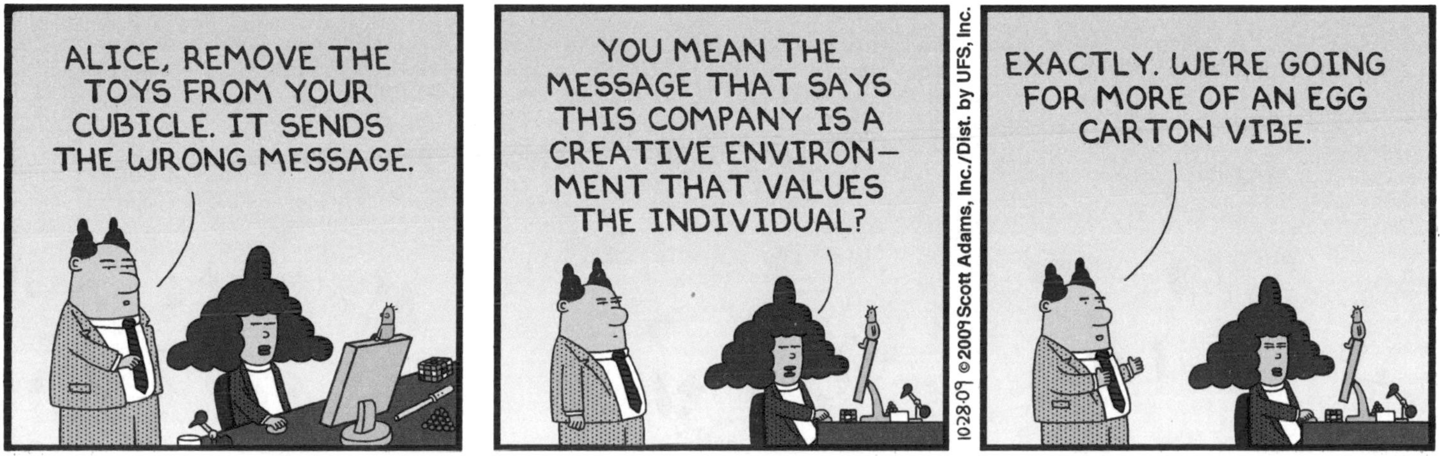
ALICE, REMOVE THE TOYS FROM YOUR CUBICLE. IT SENDS THE WRONG MESSAGE.
YOU MEAN THE MESSAGE THAT SAYS THIS COMPANY IS A CREATIVE ENVIRON-MENT THAT VALUES THE INDIVIDUAL?
10-28-09 ©2009 Scott Adams, Inc./Dist. by UFS, Inc.
EXACTLY. WE'RE GOING FOR MORE OF AN EGG CARTON VIBE.

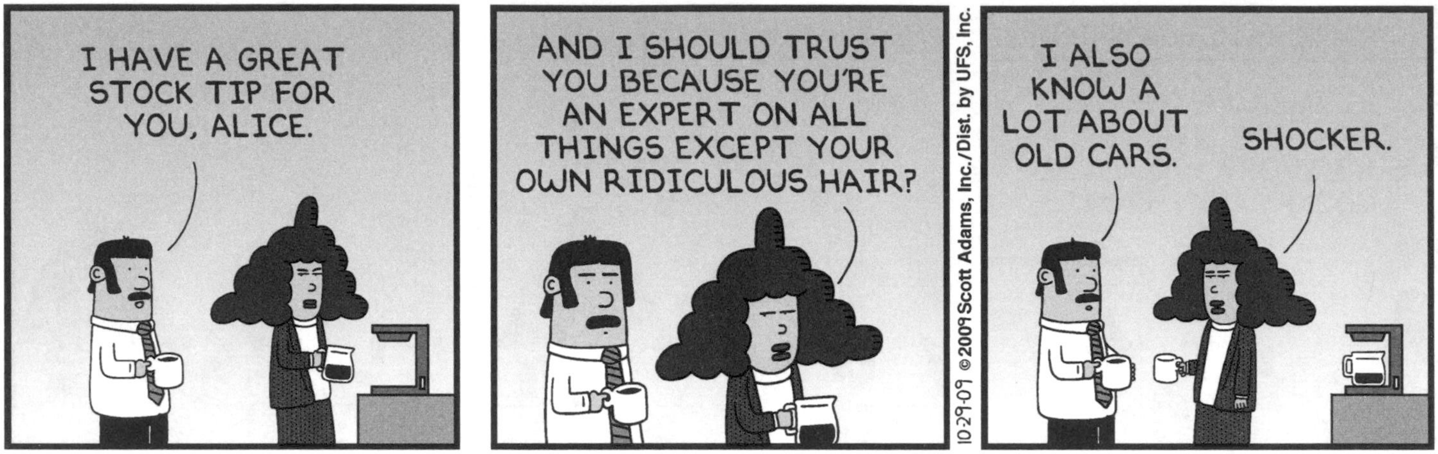
I HAVE A GREAT STOCK TIP FOR YOU, ALICE.
AND I SHOULD TRUST YOU BECAUSE YOU'RE AN EXPERT ON ALL THINGS EXCEPT YOUR OWN RIDICULOUS HAIR?
10-29-09 ©2009 Scott Adams, Inc./Dist. by UFS, Inc.
I ALSO KNOW A LOT ABOUT OLD CARS.
SHOCKER.

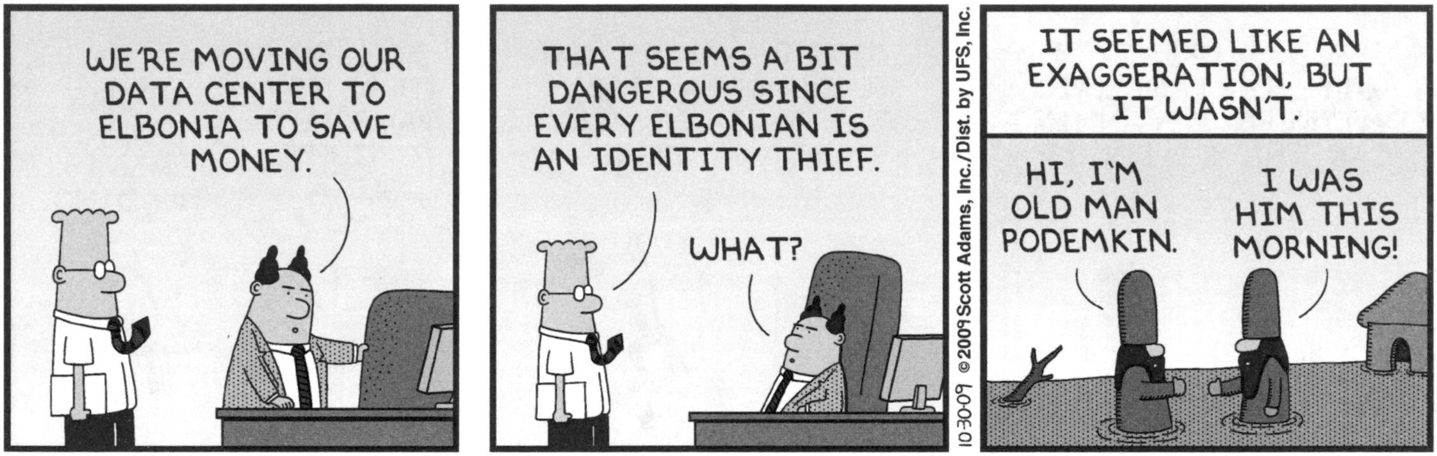
WE'RE MOVING OUR DATA CENTER TO ELBONIA TO SAVE MONEY.
THAT SEEMS A BIT DANGEROUS SINCE EVERY ELBONIAN IS AN IDENTITY THIEF.
WHAT?
10-30-09 ©2009 Scott Adams, Inc./Dist. by UFS, Inc.
IT SEEMED LIKE AN EXAGGERATION, BUT IT WASN'T.
HI, I'M OLD MAN PODEMKIN.
I WAS HIM THIS MORNING!

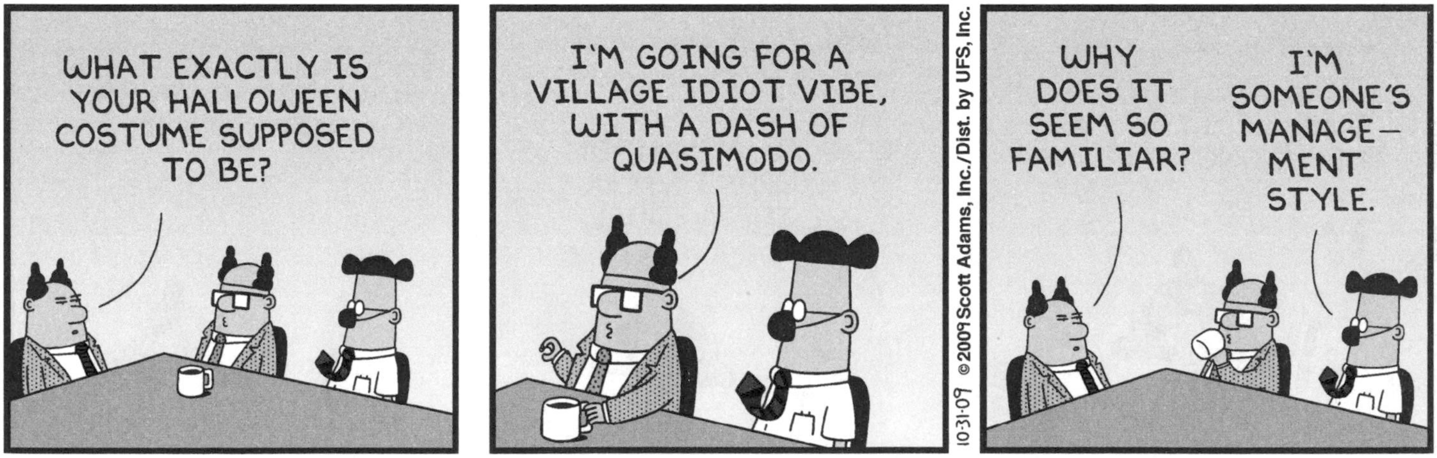
WHAT EXACTLY IS YOUR HALLOWEEN COSTUME SUPPOSED TO BE?
I'M GOING FOR A VILLAGE IDIOT VIBE, WITH A DASH OF QUASIMODO.
10-31-09 ©2009 Scott Adams, Inc./Dist. by UFS, Inc.
WHY DOES IT SEEM SO FAMILIAR?
I'M SOMEONE'S MANAGE-MENT STYLE.

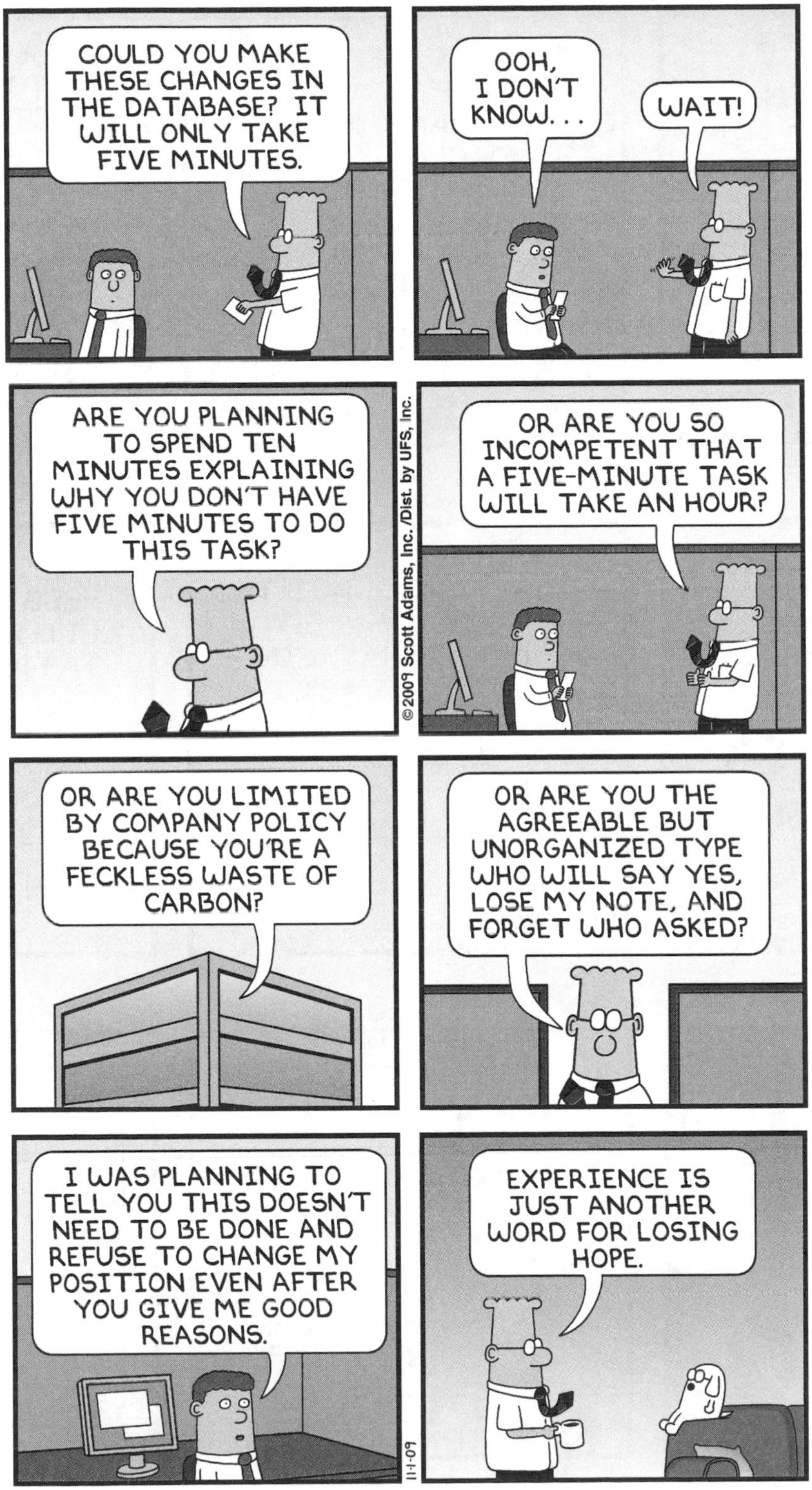
COULD YOU MAKE THESE CHANGES IN THE DATABASE? IT WILL ONLY TAKE FIVE MINUTES.
OOH, I DON'T KNOW. . .
WAIT!
ARE YOU PLANNING TO SPEND TEN MINUTES EXPLAINING WHY YOU DON'T HAVE FIVE MINUTES TO DO THIS TASK?
OR ARE YOU SO INCOMPETENT THAT A FIVE-MINUTE TASK WILL TAKE AN HOUR?
OR ARE YOU LIMITED BY COMPANY POLICY BECAUSE YOU'RE A FECKLESS WASTE OF CARBON?
OR ARE YOU THE AGREEABLE BUT UNORGANIZED TYPE WHO WILL SAY YES, LOSE MY NOTE, AND FORGET WHO ASKED?
I WAS PLANNING TO TELL YOU THIS DOESN'T NEED TO BE DONE AND REFUSE TO CHANGE MY POSITION EVEN AFTER YOU GIVE ME GOOD REASONS.
EXPERIENCE IS JUST ANOTHER WORD FOR LOSING HOPE.
©2009 Scott Adams, Inc. /Dist. by UFS, Inc.
11-1-09

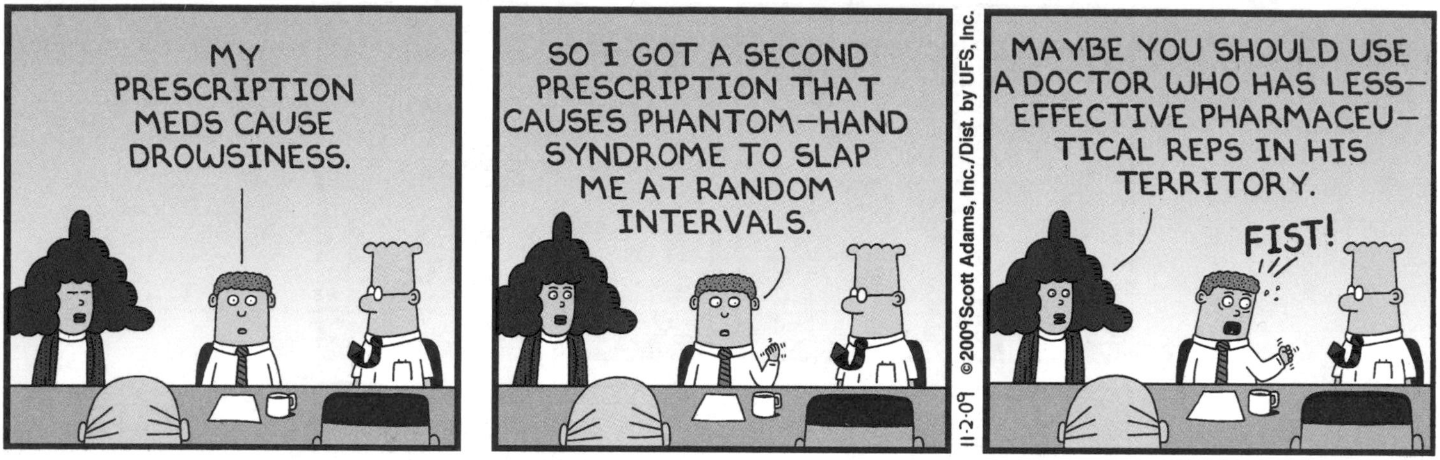
MY PRESCRIPTION MEDS CAUSE DROWSINESS.
SO I GOT A SECOND PRESCRIPTION THAT CAUSES PHANTOM-HAND SYNDROME TO SLAP ME AT RANDOM INTERVALS.
MAYBE YOU SHOULD USE A DOCTOR WHO HAS LESS-EFFECTIVE PHARMACEU-TICAL REPS IN HIS TERRITORY.
FIST!
11·2·09 ©2009 Scott Adams, Inc./Dist. by UFS, Inc.

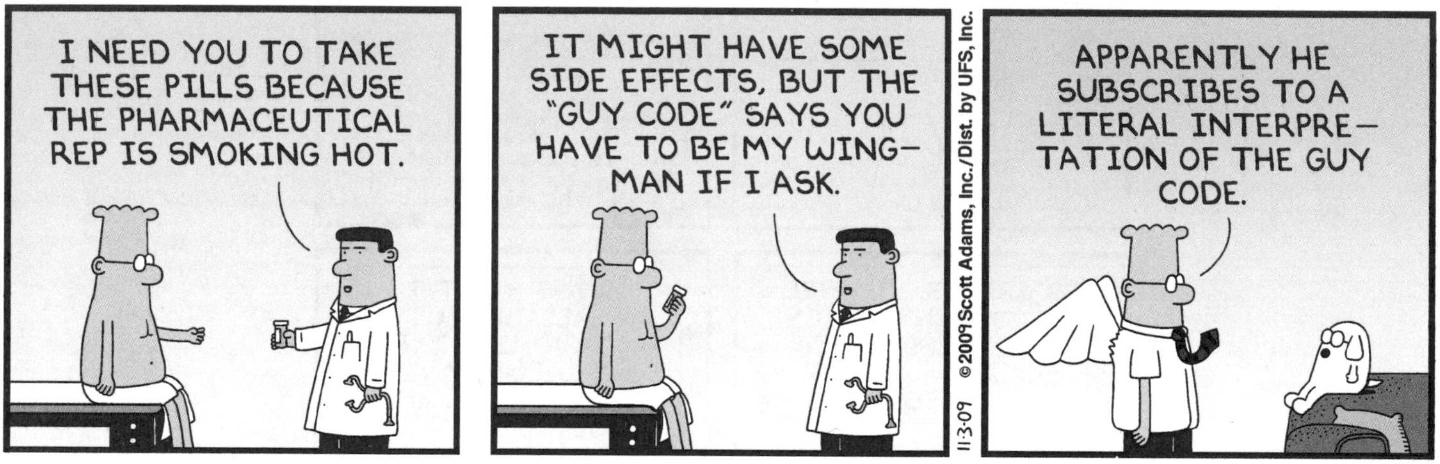
I NEED YOU TO TAKE THESE PILLS BECAUSE THE PHARMACEUTICAL REP IS SMOKING HOT.
IT MIGHT HAVE SOME SIDE EFFECTS, BUT THE "GUY CODE" SAYS YOU HAVE TO BE MY WING-MAN IF I ASK.
APPARENTLY HE SUBSCRIBES TO A LITERAL INTERPRE-TATION OF THE GUY CODE.
11·3·09 ©2009 Scott Adams, Inc./Dist. by UFS, Inc.

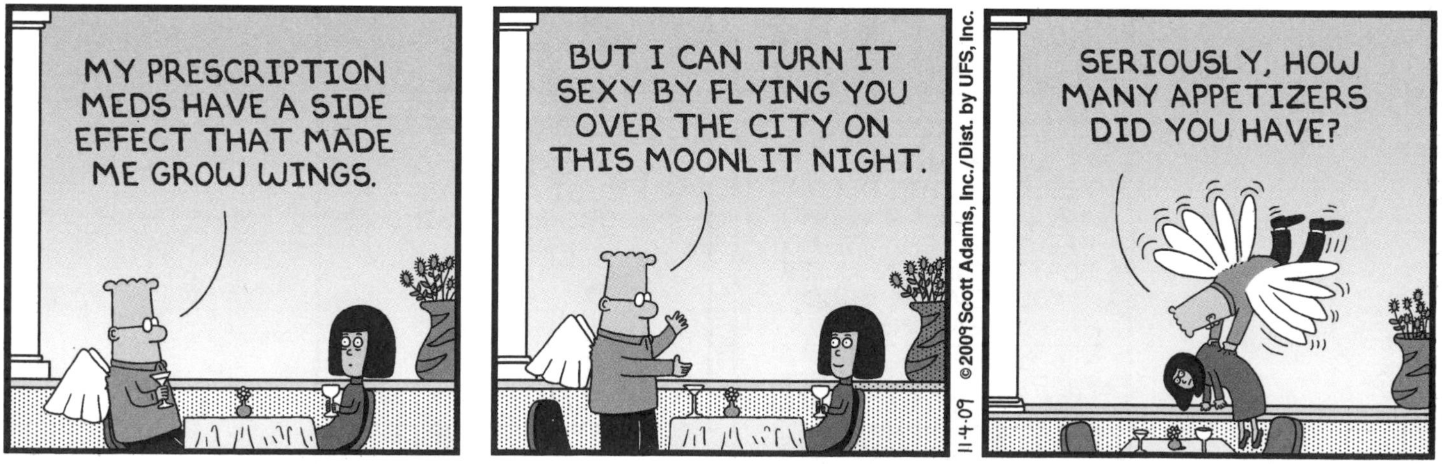
MY PRESCRIPTION MEDS HAVE A SIDE EFFECT THAT MADE ME GROW WINGS.
BUT I CAN TURN IT SEXY BY FLYING YOU OVER THE CITY ON THIS MOONLIT NIGHT.
SERIOUSLY, HOW MANY APPETIZERS DID YOU HAVE?
11·4·09 ©2009 Scott Adams, Inc./Dist. by UFS, Inc.

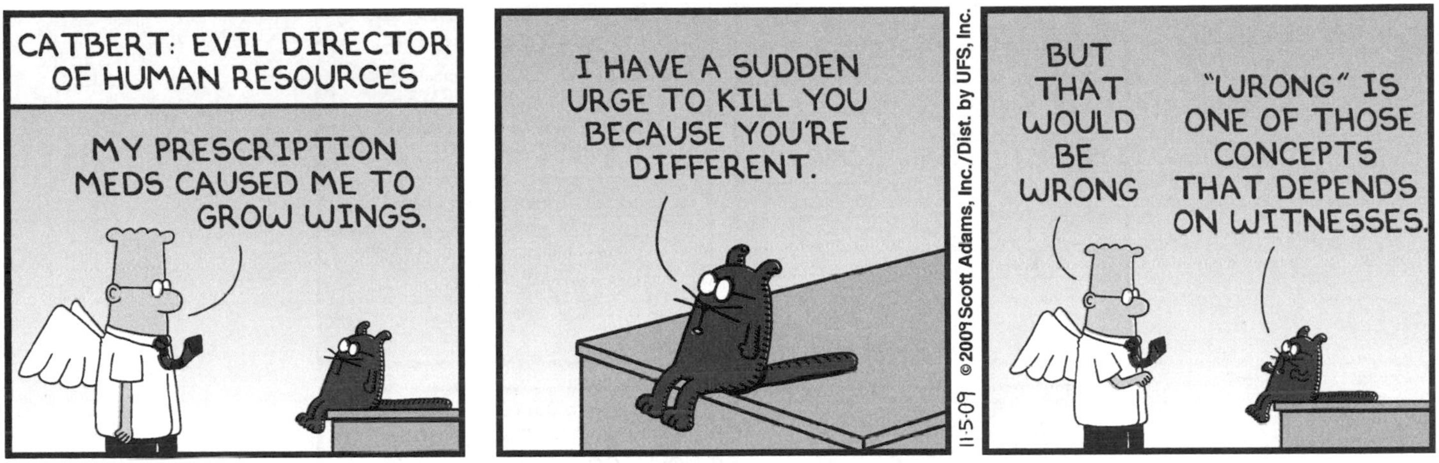
CATBERT: EVIL DIRECTOR OF HUMAN RESOURCES
MY PRESCRIPTION MEDS CAUSED ME TO GROW WINGS.
I HAVE A SUDDEN URGE TO KILL YOU BECAUSE YOU'RE DIFFERENT.
11-5-09 ©2009 Scott Adams, Inc./Dist. by UFS, Inc.
BUT THAT WOULD BE WRONG
"WRONG" IS ONE OF THOSE CONCEPTS THAT DEPENDS ON WITNESSES.

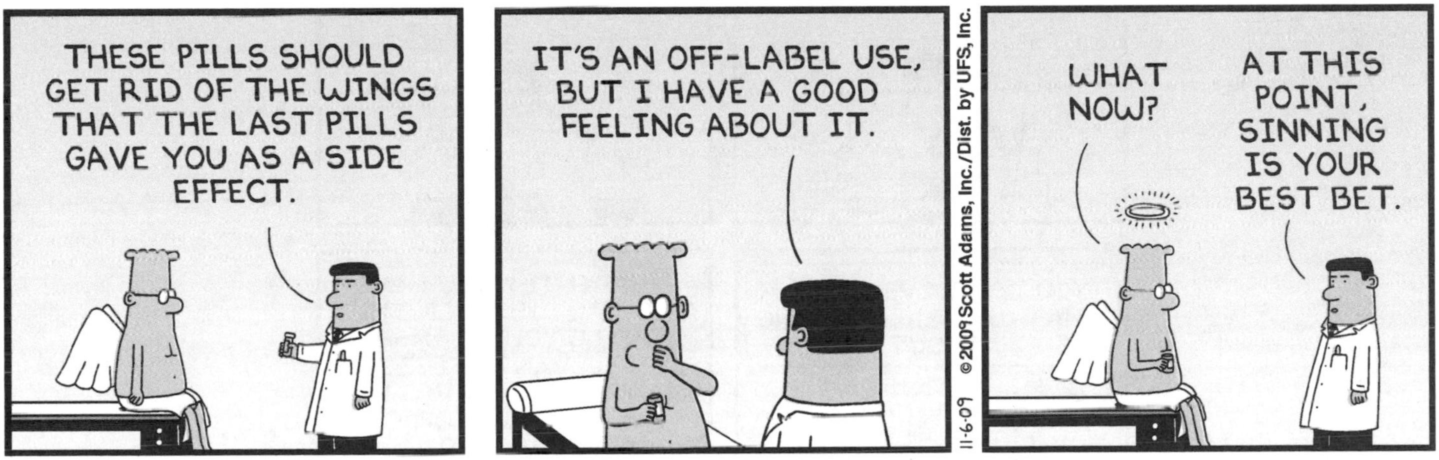
THESE PILLS SHOULD GET RID OF THE WINGS THAT THE LAST PILLS GAVE YOU AS A SIDE EFFECT.
IT'S AN OFF-LABEL USE, BUT I HAVE A GOOD FEELING ABOUT IT.
11-6-09 ©2009 Scott Adams, Inc./Dist. by UFS, Inc.
WHAT NOW?
AT THIS POINT, SINNING IS YOUR BEST BET.

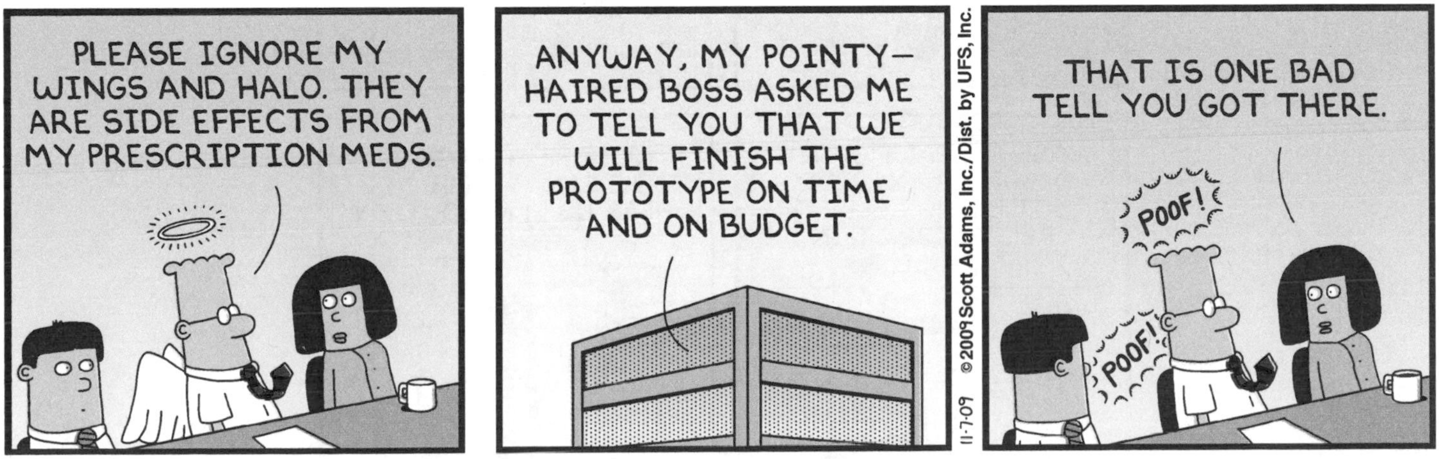
PLEASE IGNORE MY WINGS AND HALO. THEY ARE SIDE EFFECTS FROM MY PRESCRIPTION MEDS.
ANYWAY, MY POINTY-HAIRED BOSS ASKED ME TO TELL YOU THAT WE WILL FINISH THE PROTOTYPE ON TIME AND ON BUDGET.
11-7-09 ©2009 Scott Adams, Inc./Dist. by UFS, Inc.
THAT IS ONE BAD TELL YOU GOT THERE.
POOF!
POOF!

AND THEN TED SAID HE'D. . .
HO HO! I'VE SEEN THAT A MILLION TIMES!
AT MY OLD JOB WE USED TO MAKE CRICKET NOISES WHENEVER OUR MANAGER WAS APPROACHING.
BUT THAT DOESN'T MEAN YOU SHOULD CUT CORNERS WHEN IT COMES TO QUALITY.
©2009 Scott Adams, Inc. /Dist. by UFS, Inc.
YOU'RE HIJACKING OUR CONVERSATION!
I'M ADDING VALUE.
YOU DON'T EVEN KNOW WHAT WE WERE TALKING ABOUT.
APPARENTLY YOU HAVE A SOCIAL DISORDER THAT COMPELS YOU TO INSERT IRRELEVANT STORIES AND TRITE OBSERVATIONS INTO OTHER PEOPLE'S CONVERSATIONS.
I ASSUME PART OF THE DISORDER INVOLVES NOT BEING ABLE TO RECOGNIZE IT IN YOURSELF.
11-8-09
I WONDER IF HE CAN HEAR US.
DID I TELL YOU ABOUT MY CAMPING TRIP?

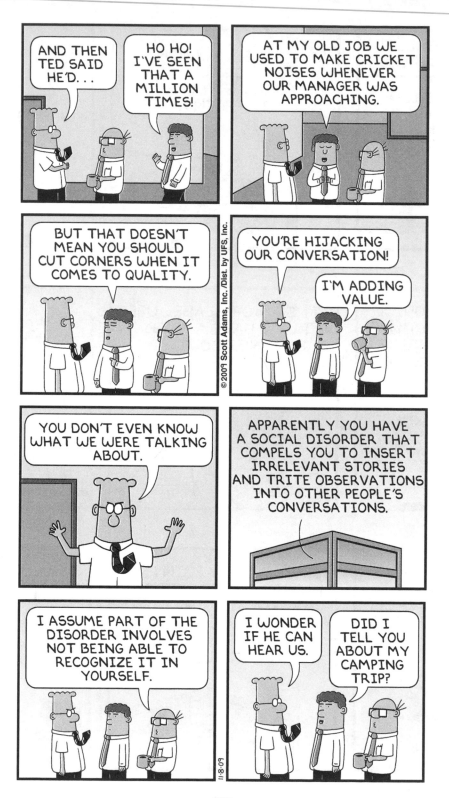

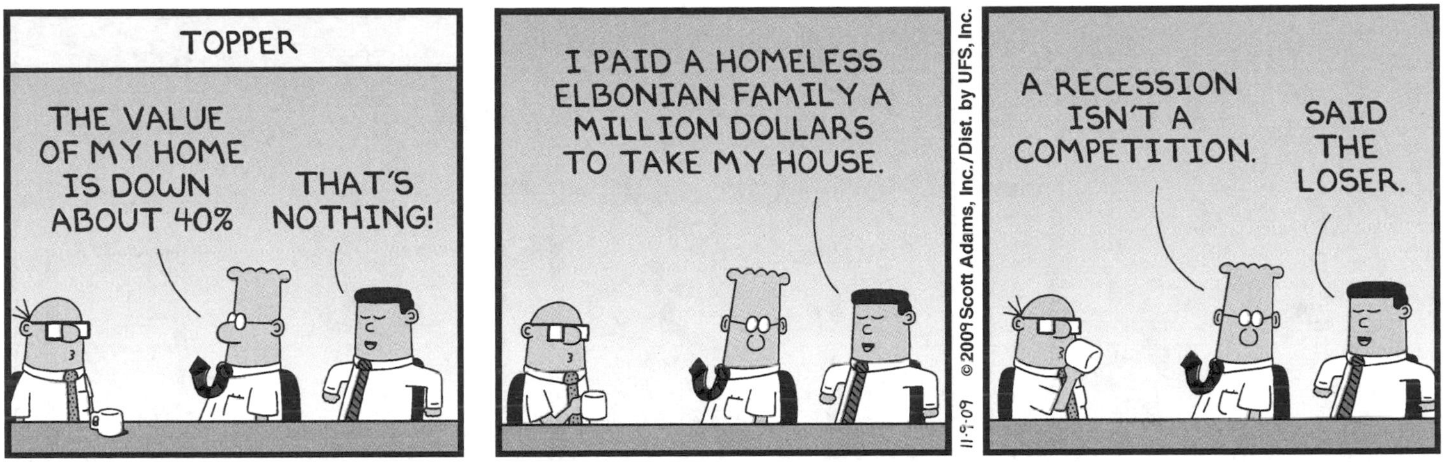
TOPPER
THE VALUE OF MY HOME IS DOWN ABOUT 40%
THAT'S NOTHING!
I PAID A HOMELESS ELBONIAN FAMILY A MILLION DOLLARS TO TAKE MY HOUSE.
11-9-09 © 2009 Scott Adams, Inc./Dist. by UFS, Inc.
A RECESSION ISN'T A COMPETITION.
SAID THE LOSER.

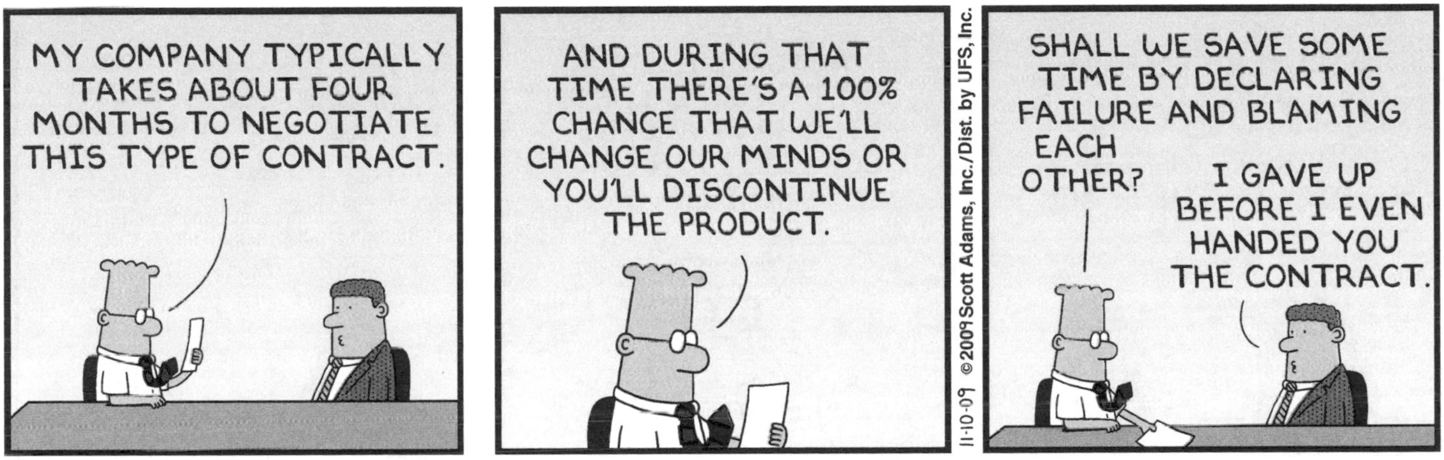
MY COMPANY TYPICALLY TAKES ABOUT FOUR MONTHS TO NEGOTIATE THIS TYPE OF CONTRACT.
AND DURING THAT TIME THERE'S A 100% CHANCE THAT WE'LL CHANGE OUR MINDS OR YOU'LL DISCONTINUE THE PRODUCT.
11-10-09 © 2009 Scott Adams, Inc./Dist. by UFS, Inc.
SHALL WE SAVE SOME TIME BY DECLARING FAILURE AND BLAMING EACH OTHER?
I GAVE UP BEFORE I EVEN HANDED YOU THE CONTRACT.

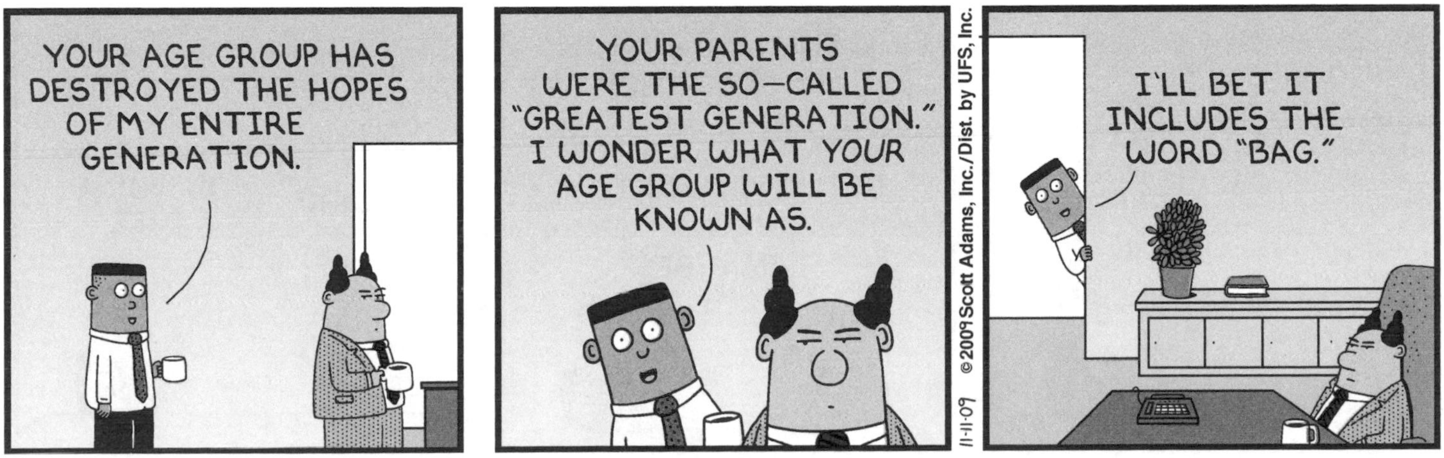
YOUR AGE GROUP HAS DESTROYED THE HOPES OF MY ENTIRE GENERATION.
YOUR PARENTS WERE THE SO-CALLED "GREATEST GENERATION." I WONDER WHAT *YOUR* AGE GROUP WILL BE KNOWN AS.
11-11-09 © 2009 Scott Adams, Inc./Dist. by UFS, Inc.
I'LL BET IT INCLUDES THE WORD "BAG."

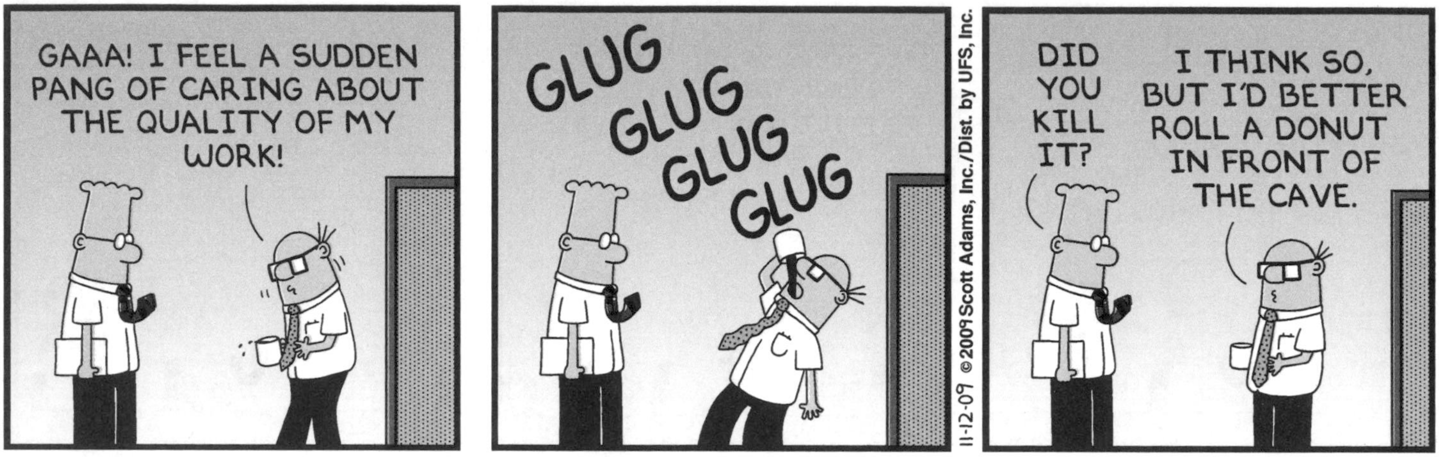
GAAA! I FEEL A SUDDEN PANG OF CARING ABOUT THE QUALITY OF MY WORK!
GLUG GLUG GLUG GLUG
11-12-09 ©2009 Scott Adams, Inc./Dist. by UFS, Inc.
DID YOU KILL IT?
I THINK SO, BUT I'D BETTER ROLL A DONUT IN FRONT OF THE CAVE.

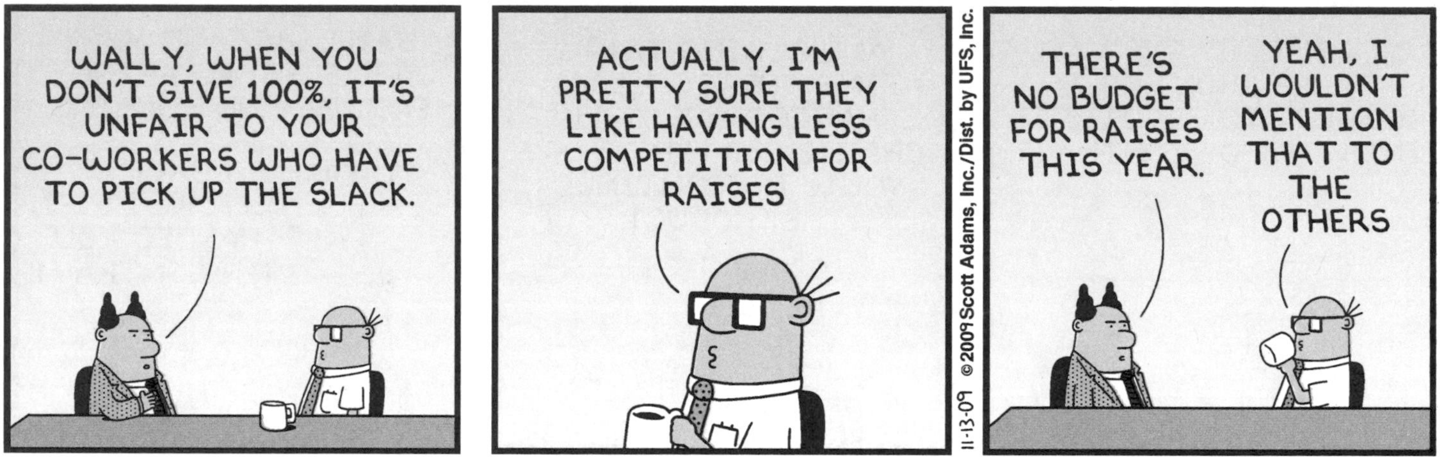
WALLY, WHEN YOU DON'T GIVE 100%, IT'S UNFAIR TO YOUR CO-WORKERS WHO HAVE TO PICK UP THE SLACK.
ACTUALLY, I'M PRETTY SURE THEY LIKE HAVING LESS COMPETITION FOR RAISES
11-13-09 ©2009 Scott Adams, Inc./Dist. by UFS, Inc.
THERE'S NO BUDGET FOR RAISES THIS YEAR.
YEAH, I WOULDN'T MENTION THAT TO THE OTHERS

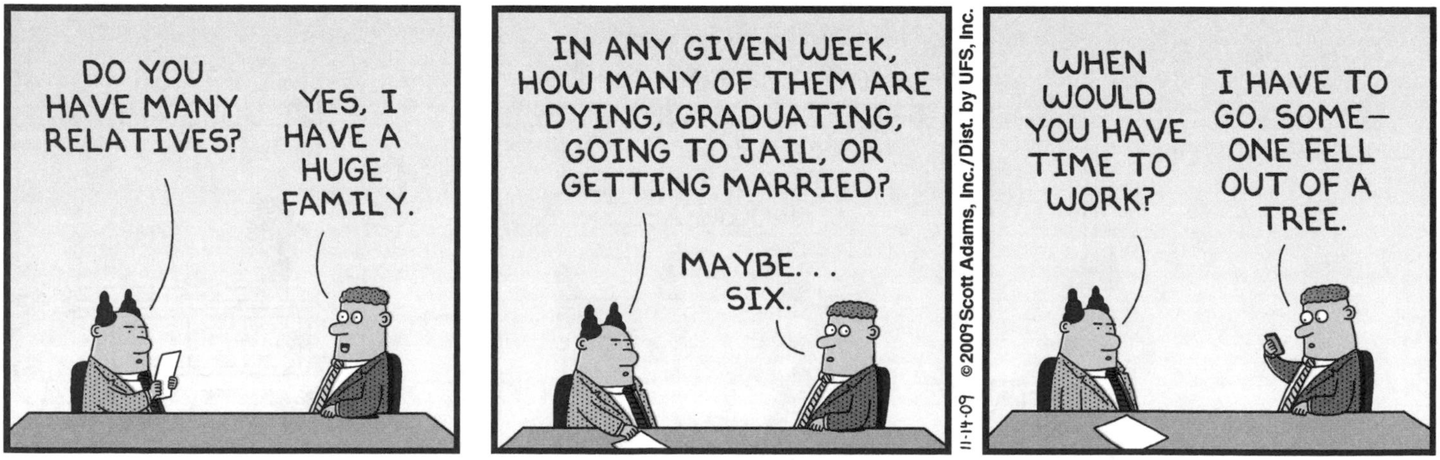
DO YOU HAVE MANY RELATIVES?
YES, I HAVE A HUGE FAMILY.
IN ANY GIVEN WEEK, HOW MANY OF THEM ARE DYING, GRADUATING, GOING TO JAIL, OR GETTING MARRIED?
MAYBE. . . SIX.
11-14-09 ©2009 Scott Adams, Inc./Dist. by UFS, Inc.
WHEN WOULD YOU HAVE TIME TO WORK?
I HAVE TO GO. SOME-ONE FELL OUT OF A TREE.

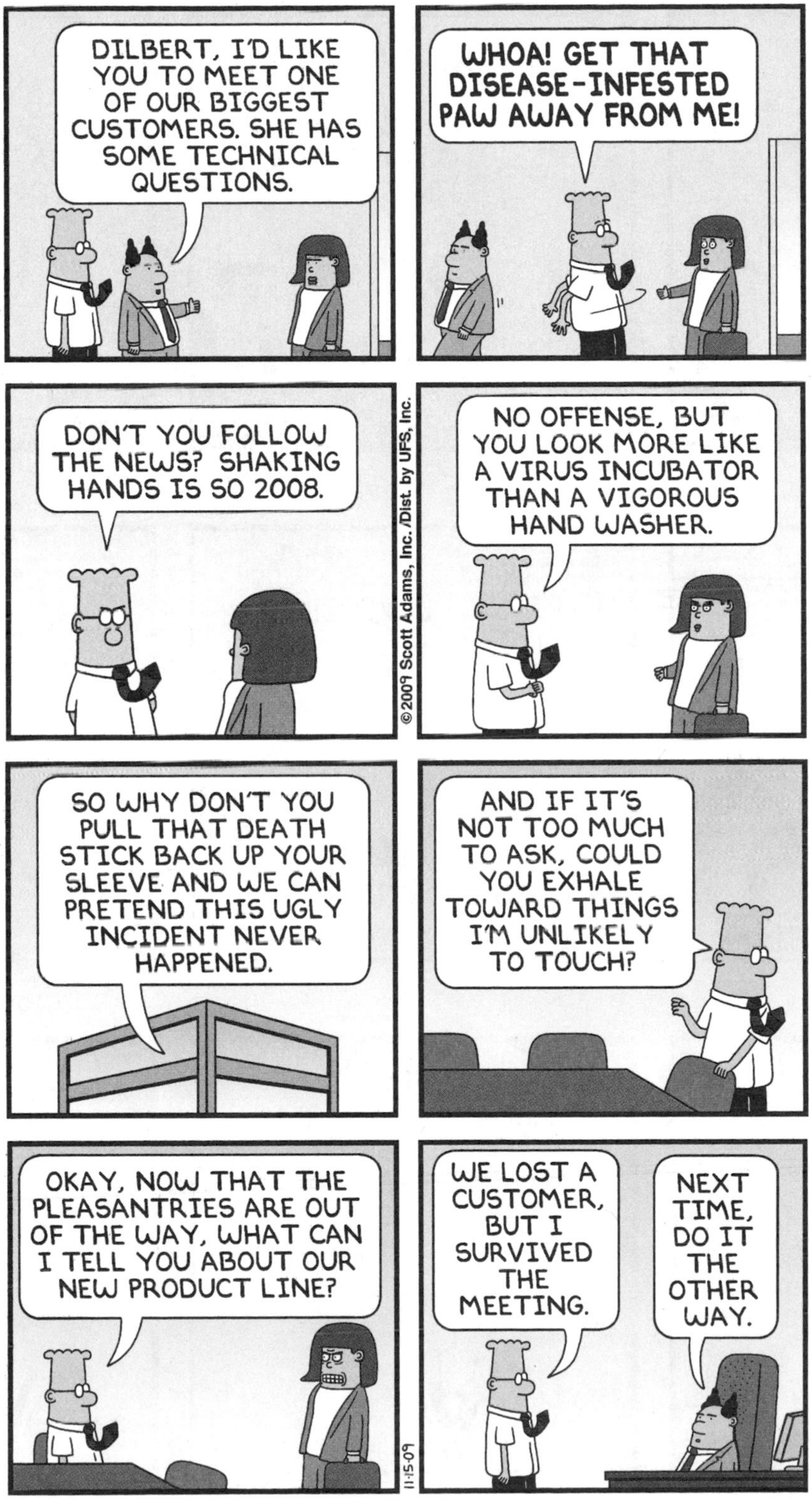
DILBERT, I'D LIKE YOU TO MEET ONE OF OUR BIGGEST CUSTOMERS. SHE HAS SOME TECHNICAL QUESTIONS.
WHOA! GET THAT DISEASE-INFESTED PAW AWAY FROM ME!
DON'T YOU FOLLOW THE NEWS? SHAKING HANDS IS SO 2008.
NO OFFENSE, BUT YOU LOOK MORE LIKE A VIRUS INCUBATOR THAN A VIGOROUS HAND WASHER.
SO WHY DON'T YOU PULL THAT DEATH STICK BACK UP YOUR SLEEVE AND WE CAN PRETEND THIS UGLY INCIDENT NEVER HAPPENED.
AND IF IT'S NOT TOO MUCH TO ASK, COULD YOU EXHALE TOWARD THINGS I'M UNLIKELY TO TOUCH?
OKAY, NOW THAT THE PLEASANTRIES ARE OUT OF THE WAY, WHAT CAN I TELL YOU ABOUT OUR NEW PRODUCT LINE?
WE LOST A CUSTOMER, BUT I SURVIVED THE MEETING.
NEXT TIME, DO IT THE OTHER WAY.
©2009 Scott Adams, Inc./Dist. by UFS, Inc.
11-15-09

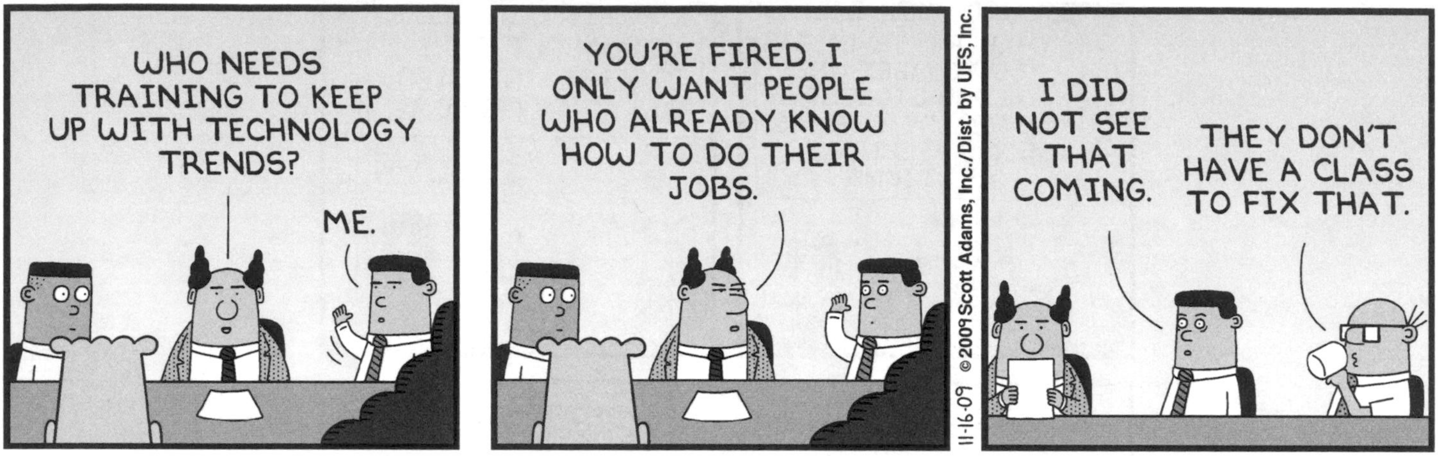
WHO NEEDS TRAINING TO KEEP UP WITH TECHNOLOGY TRENDS?
ME.
YOU'RE FIRED. I ONLY WANT PEOPLE WHO ALREADY KNOW HOW TO DO THEIR JOBS.
11-16-09 ©2009 Scott Adams, Inc./Dist. by UFS, Inc.
I DID NOT SEE THAT COMING.
THEY DON'T HAVE A CLASS TO FIX THAT.

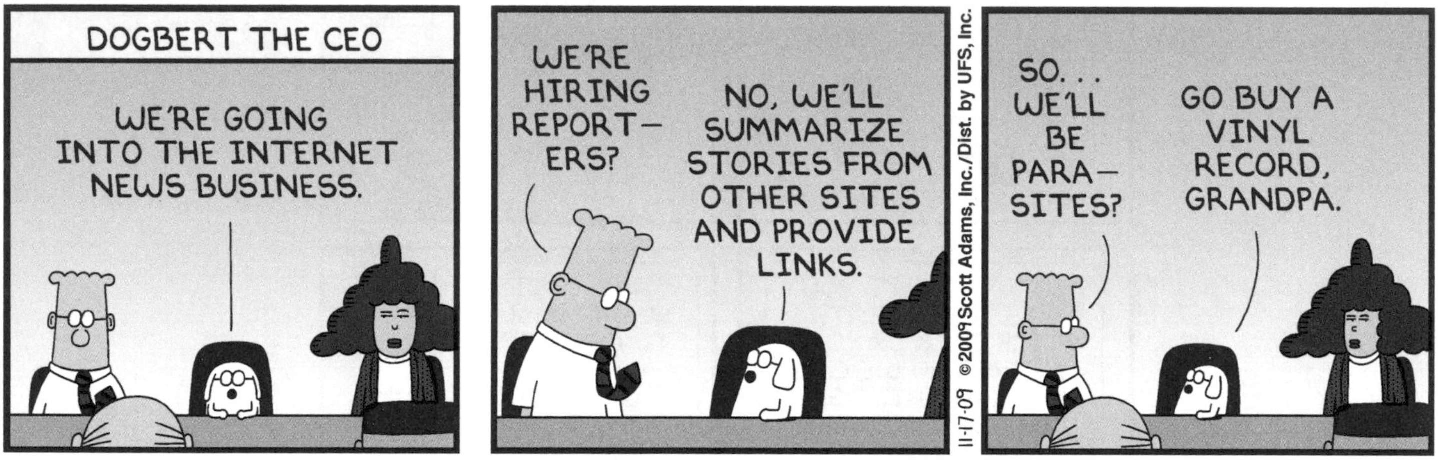
DOGBERT THE CEO
WE'RE GOING INTO THE INTERNET NEWS BUSINESS.
WE'RE HIRING REPORT-ERS?
NO, WE'LL SUMMARIZE STORIES FROM OTHER SITES AND PROVIDE LINKS.
11-17-09 ©2009 Scott Adams, Inc./Dist. by UFS, Inc.
SO... WE'LL BE PARA-SITES?
GO BUY A VINYL RECORD, GRANDPA.

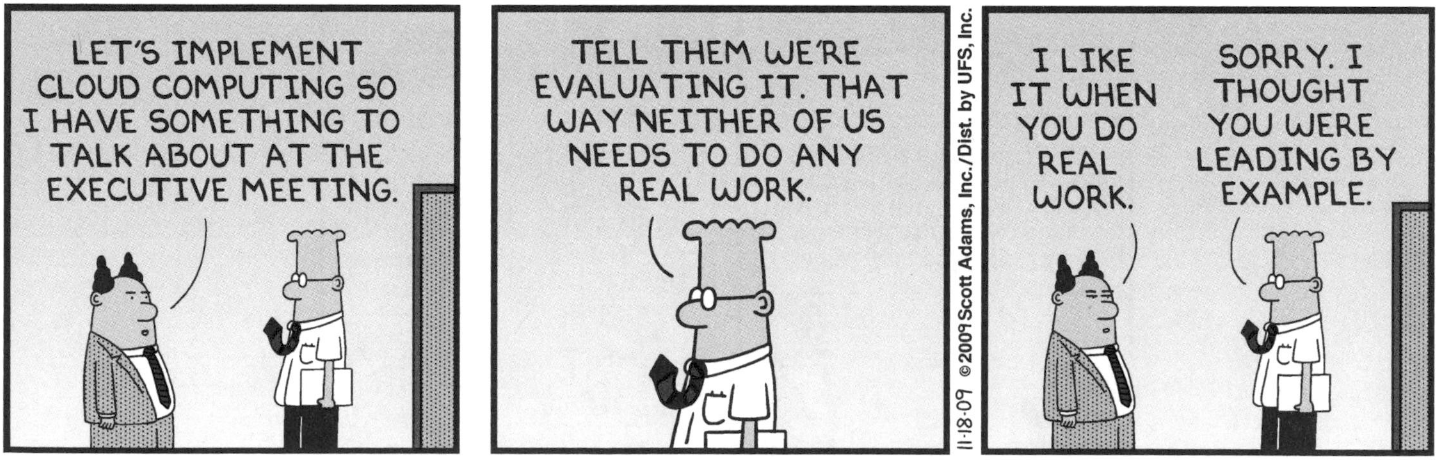
LET'S IMPLEMENT CLOUD COMPUTING SO I HAVE SOMETHING TO TALK ABOUT AT THE EXECUTIVE MEETING.
TELL THEM WE'RE EVALUATING IT. THAT WAY NEITHER OF US NEEDS TO DO ANY REAL WORK.
11-18-09 ©2009 Scott Adams, Inc./Dist. by UFS, Inc.
I LIKE IT WHEN YOU DO REAL WORK.
SORRY. I THOUGHT YOU WERE LEADING BY EXAMPLE.

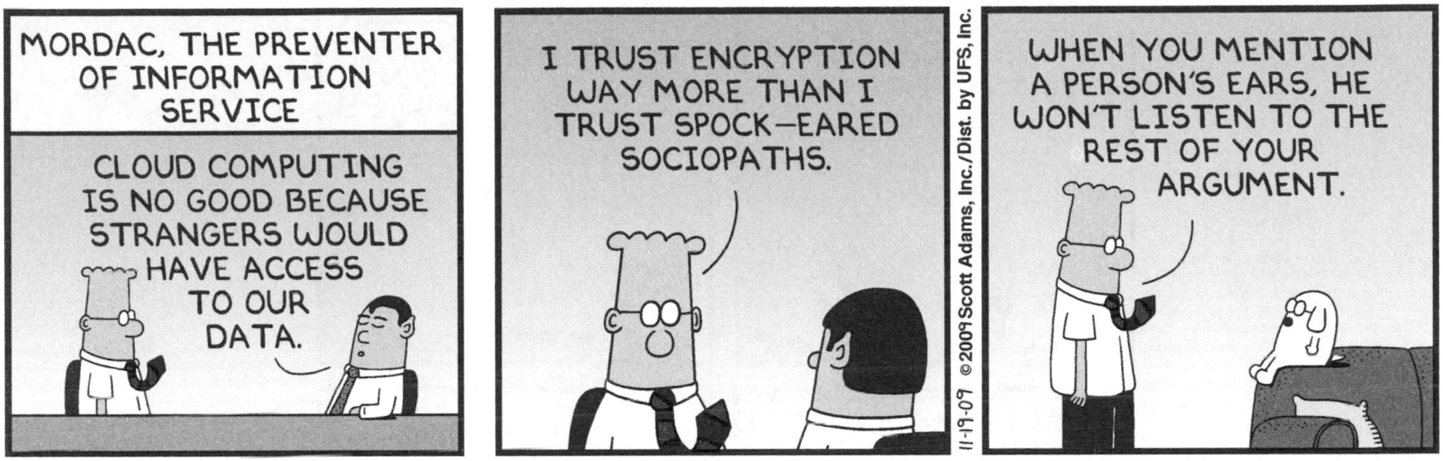
MORDAC, THE PREVENTER OF INFORMATION SERVICE
CLOUD COMPUTING IS NO GOOD BECAUSE STRANGERS WOULD HAVE ACCESS TO OUR DATA.
I TRUST ENCRYPTION WAY MORE THAN I TRUST SPOCK–EARED SOCIOPATHS.
11-19-09 ©2009 Scott Adams, Inc./Dist. by UFS, Inc.
WHEN YOU MENTION A PERSON'S EARS, HE WON'T LISTEN TO THE REST OF YOUR ARGUMENT.

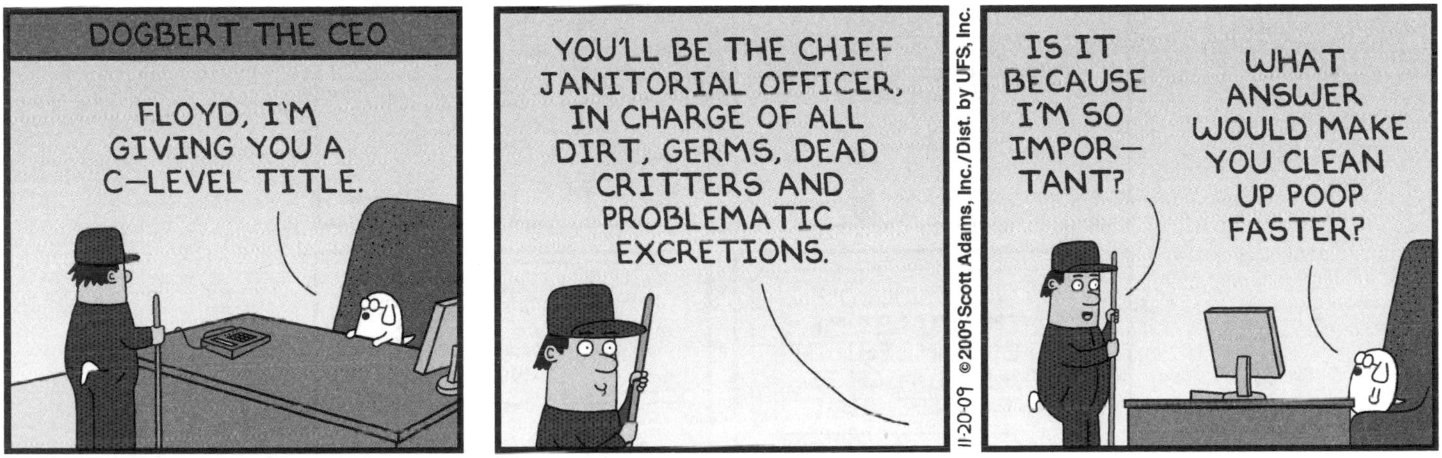
DOGBERT THE CEO
FLOYD, I'M GIVING YOU A C–LEVEL TITLE.
YOU'LL BE THE CHIEF JANITORIAL OFFICER, IN CHARGE OF ALL DIRT, GERMS, DEAD CRITTERS AND PROBLEMATIC EXCRETIONS.
11-20-09 ©2009 Scott Adams, Inc./Dist. by UFS, Inc.
IS IT BECAUSE I'M SO IMPOR–TANT?
WHAT ANSWER WOULD MAKE YOU CLEAN UP POOP FASTER?

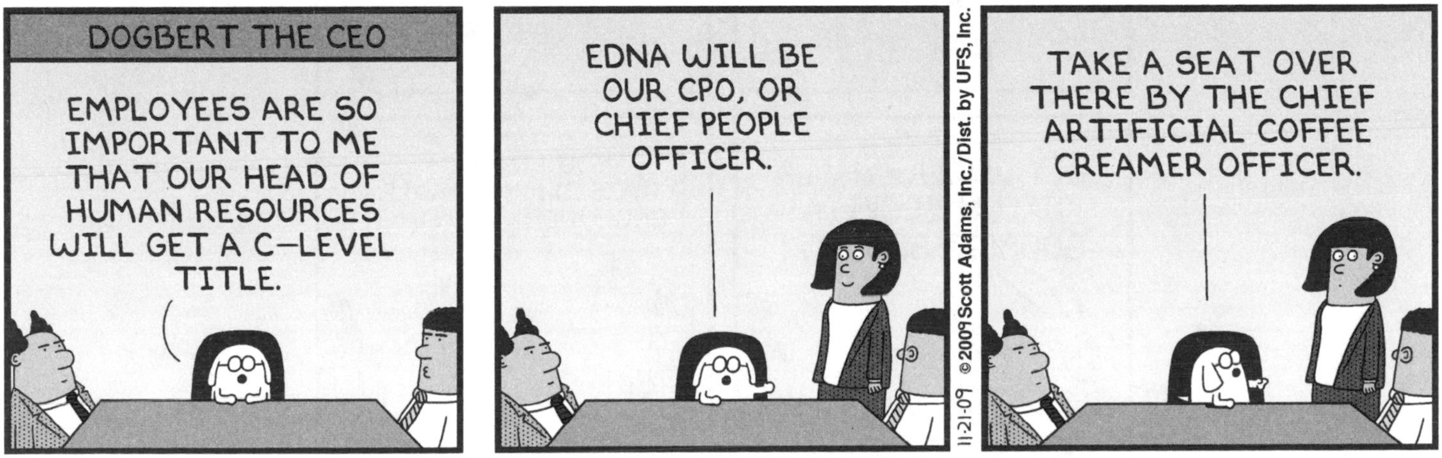
DOGBERT THE CEO
EMPLOYEES ARE SO IMPORTANT TO ME THAT OUR HEAD OF HUMAN RESOURCES WILL GET A C–LEVEL TITLE.
EDNA WILL BE OUR CPO, OR CHIEF PEOPLE OFFICER.
11-21-09 ©2009 Scott Adams, Inc./Dist. by UFS, Inc.
TAKE A SEAT OVER THERE BY THE CHIEF ARTIFICIAL COFFEE CREAMER OFFICER.

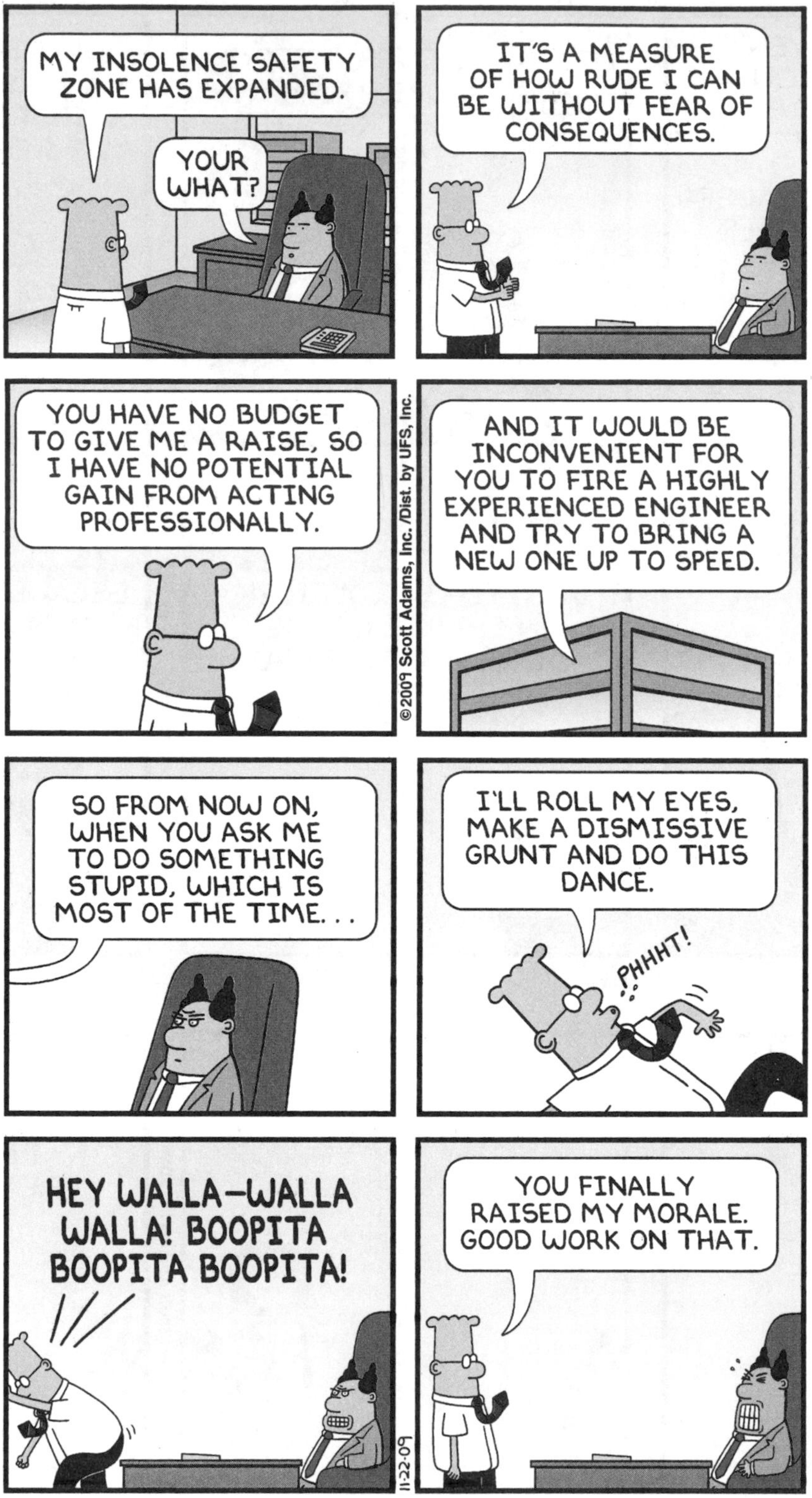
MY INSOLENCE SAFETY ZONE HAS EXPANDED.
YOUR WHAT?
IT'S A MEASURE OF HOW RUDE I CAN BE WITHOUT FEAR OF CONSEQUENCES.
YOU HAVE NO BUDGET TO GIVE ME A RAISE, SO I HAVE NO POTENTIAL GAIN FROM ACTING PROFESSIONALLY.
©2009 Scott Adams, Inc. /Dist. by UFS, Inc.
AND IT WOULD BE INCONVENIENT FOR YOU TO FIRE A HIGHLY EXPERIENCED ENGINEER AND TRY TO BRING A NEW ONE UP TO SPEED.
SO FROM NOW ON, WHEN YOU ASK ME TO DO SOMETHING STUPID, WHICH IS MOST OF THE TIME. . .
I'LL ROLL MY EYES, MAKE A DISMISSIVE GRUNT AND DO THIS DANCE.
PHHHT!
HEY WALLA-WALLA WALLA! BOOPITA BOOPITA BOOPITA BOOPITA!
11-22-09
YOU FINALLY RAISED MY MORALE. GOOD WORK ON THAT.

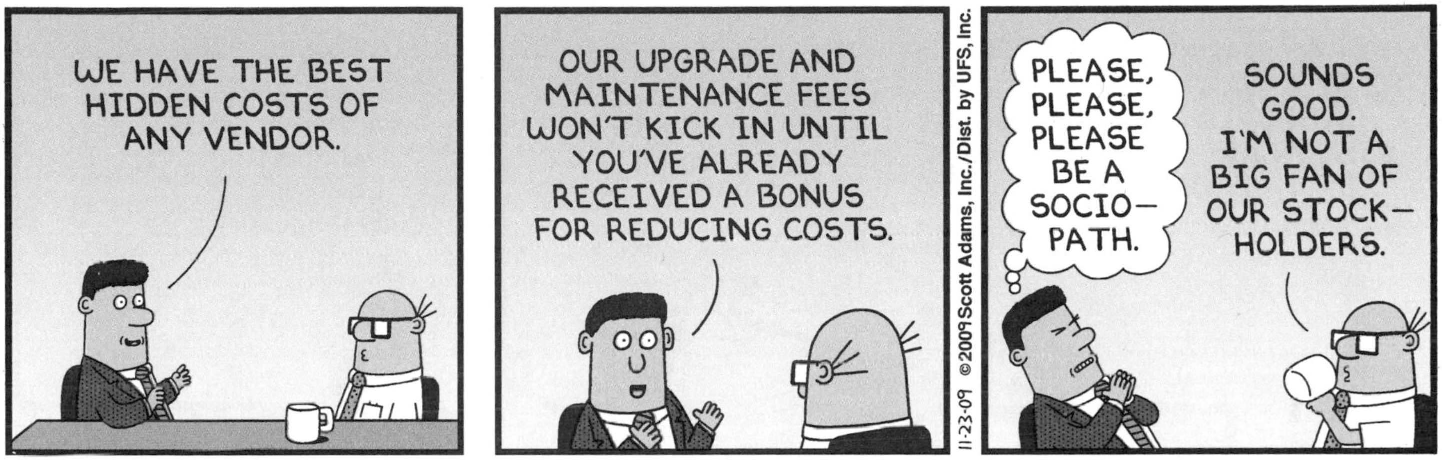
WE HAVE THE BEST HIDDEN COSTS OF ANY VENDOR.
OUR UPGRADE AND MAINTENANCE FEES WON'T KICK IN UNTIL YOU'VE ALREADY RECEIVED A BONUS FOR REDUCING COSTS.
11-23-09 ©2009 Scott Adams, Inc./Dist. by UFS, Inc.
PLEASE, PLEASE, PLEASE BE A SOCIO-PATH.
SOUNDS GOOD. I'M NOT A BIG FAN OF OUR STOCK-HOLDERS.

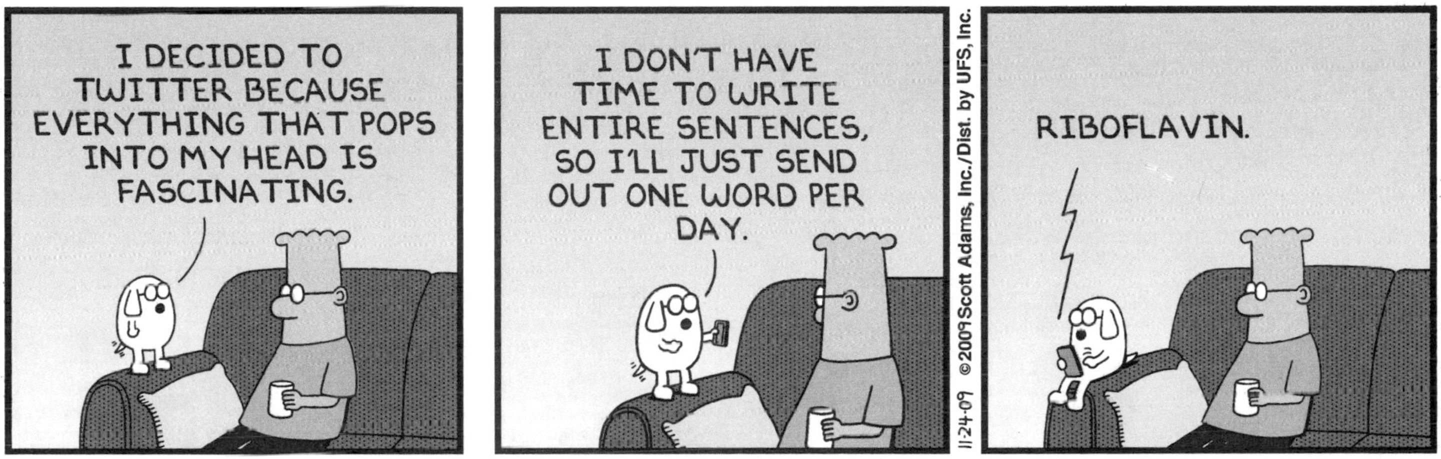
I DECIDED TO TWITTER BECAUSE EVERYTHING THAT POPS INTO MY HEAD IS FASCINATING.
I DON'T HAVE TIME TO WRITE ENTIRE SENTENCES, SO I'LL JUST SEND OUT ONE WORD PER DAY.
11-24-09 ©2009 Scott Adams, Inc./Dist. by UFS, Inc.
RIBOFLAVIN.

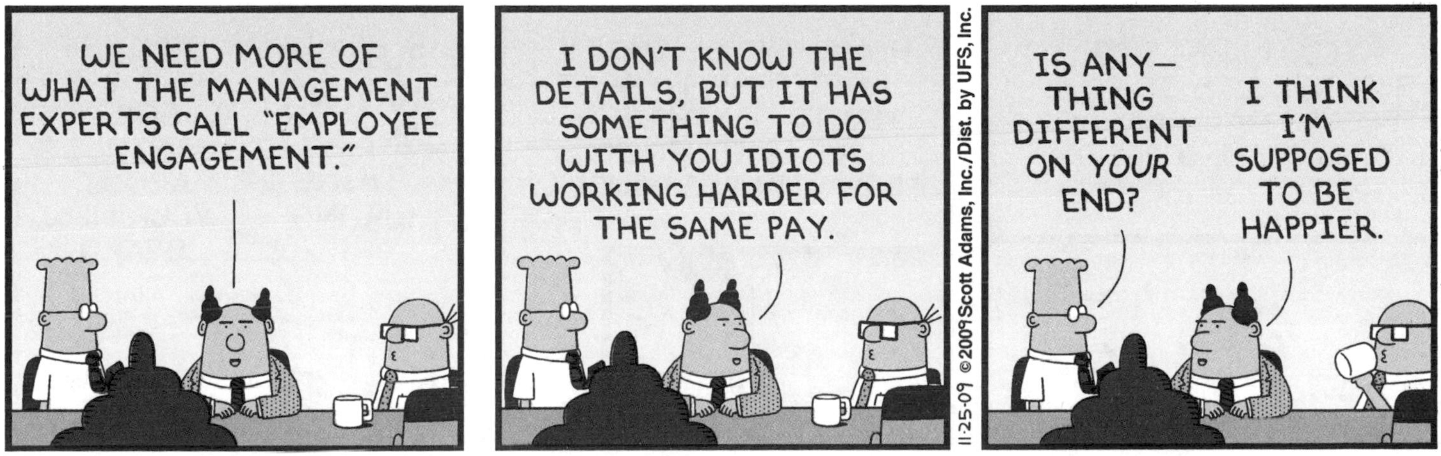
WE NEED MORE OF WHAT THE MANAGEMENT EXPERTS CALL "EMPLOYEE ENGAGEMENT."
I DON'T KNOW THE DETAILS, BUT IT HAS SOMETHING TO DO WITH YOU IDIOTS WORKING HARDER FOR THE SAME PAY.
11-25-09 ©2009 Scott Adams, Inc./Dist. by UFS, Inc.
IS ANY-THING DIFFERENT ON *YOUR* END?
I THINK I'M SUPPOSED TO BE HAPPIER.

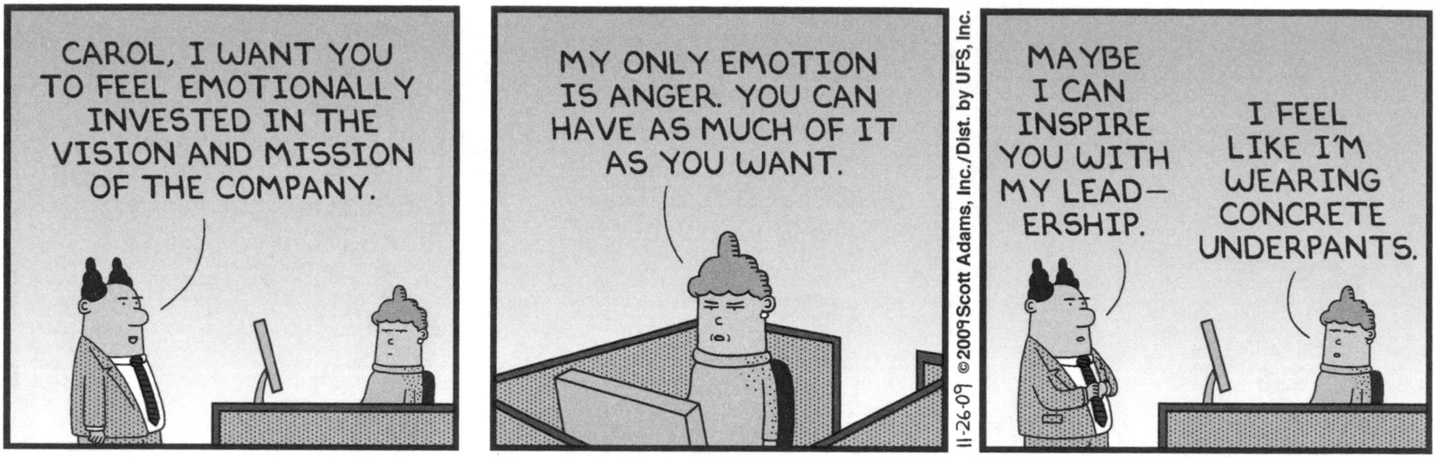
CAROL, I WANT YOU TO FEEL EMOTIONALLY INVESTED IN THE VISION AND MISSION OF THE COMPANY.
MY ONLY EMOTION IS ANGER. YOU CAN HAVE AS MUCH OF IT AS YOU WANT.
11-26-09 ©2009 Scott Adams, Inc./Dist. by UFS, Inc.
MAYBE I CAN INSPIRE YOU WITH MY LEAD-ERSHIP.
I FEEL LIKE I'M WEARING CONCRETE UNDERPANTS.

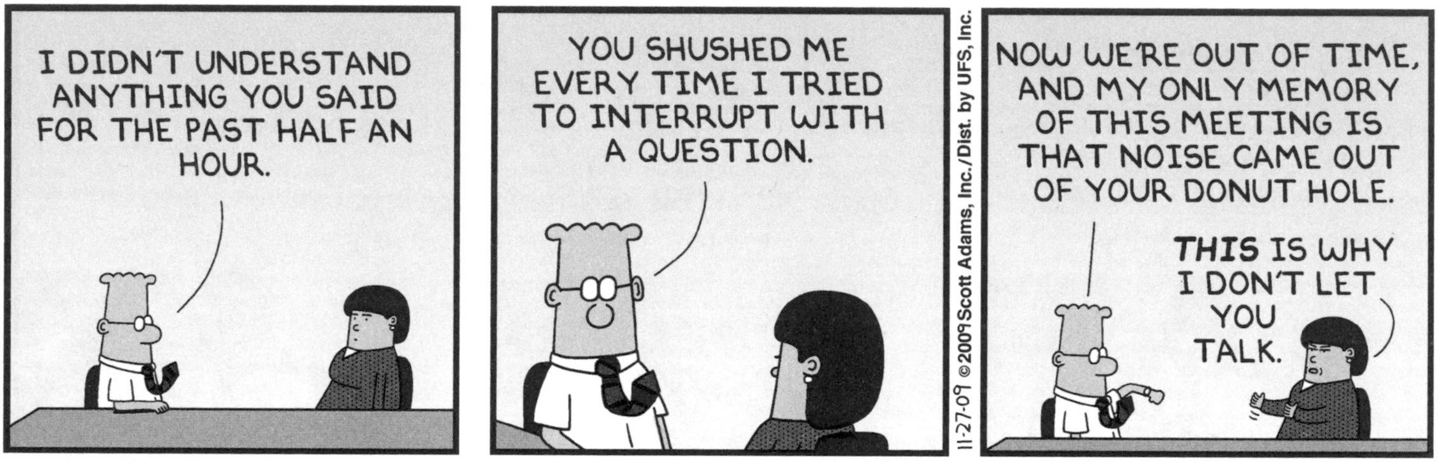
I DIDN'T UNDERSTAND ANYTHING YOU SAID FOR THE PAST HALF AN HOUR.
YOU SHUSHED ME EVERY TIME I TRIED TO INTERRUPT WITH A QUESTION.
11-27-09 ©2009 Scott Adams, Inc./Dist. by UFS, Inc.
NOW WE'RE OUT OF TIME, AND MY ONLY MEMORY OF THIS MEETING IS THAT NOISE CAME OUT OF YOUR DONUT HOLE.
THIS IS WHY I DON'T LET YOU TALK.

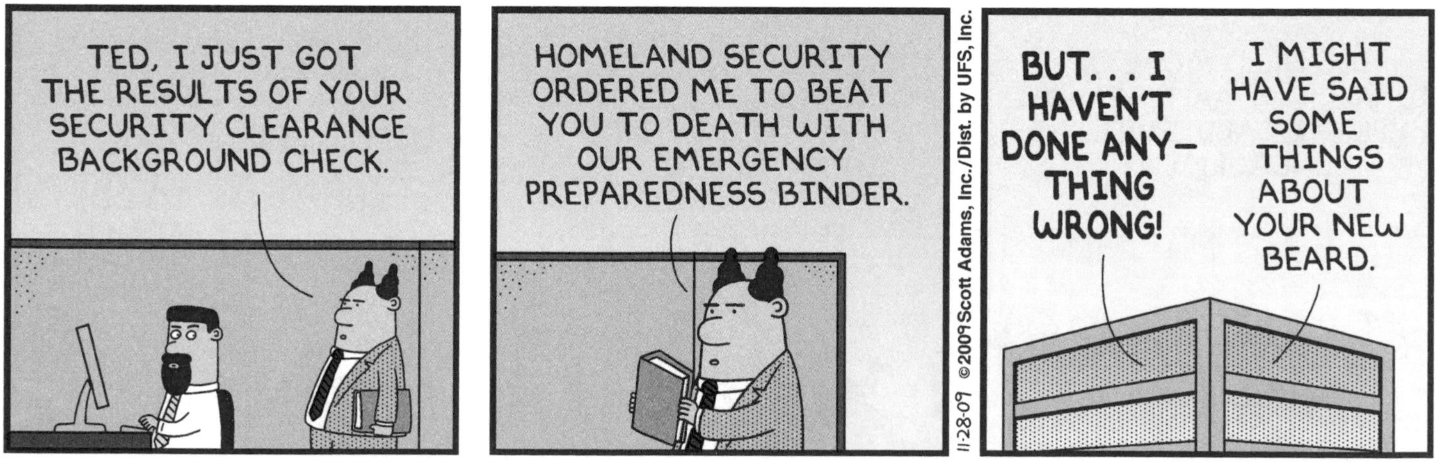
TED, I JUST GOT THE RESULTS OF YOUR SECURITY CLEARANCE BACKGROUND CHECK.
HOMELAND SECURITY ORDERED ME TO BEAT YOU TO DEATH WITH OUR EMERGENCY PREPAREDNESS BINDER.
11-28-09 ©2009 Scott Adams, Inc./Dist. by UFS, Inc.
BUT. . . I HAVEN'T DONE ANY-THING WRONG!
I MIGHT HAVE SAID SOME THINGS ABOUT YOUR NEW BEARD.

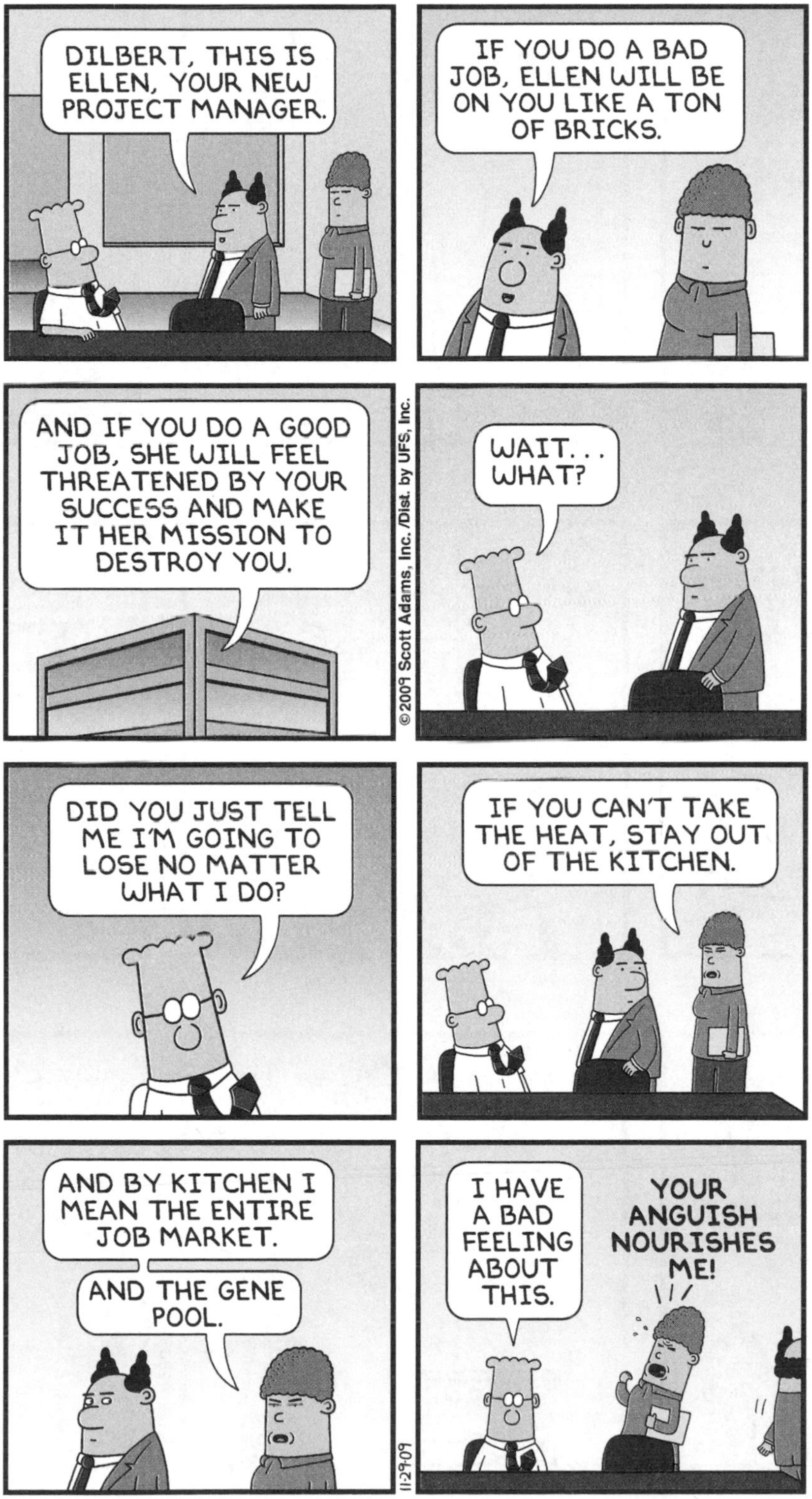
DILBERT, THIS IS ELLEN, YOUR NEW PROJECT MANAGER.
IF YOU DO A BAD JOB, ELLEN WILL BE ON YOU LIKE A TON OF BRICKS.
AND IF YOU DO A GOOD JOB, SHE WILL FEEL THREATENED BY YOUR SUCCESS AND MAKE IT HER MISSION TO DESTROY YOU.
©2009 Scott Adams, Inc./Dist. by UFS, Inc.
WAIT... WHAT?
DID YOU JUST TELL ME I'M GOING TO LOSE NO MATTER WHAT I DO?
IF YOU CAN'T TAKE THE HEAT, STAY OUT OF THE KITCHEN.
AND BY KITCHEN I MEAN THE ENTIRE JOB MARKET.
AND THE GENE POOL.
11-29-09
I HAVE A BAD FEELING ABOUT THIS.
YOUR ANGUISH NOURISHES ME!

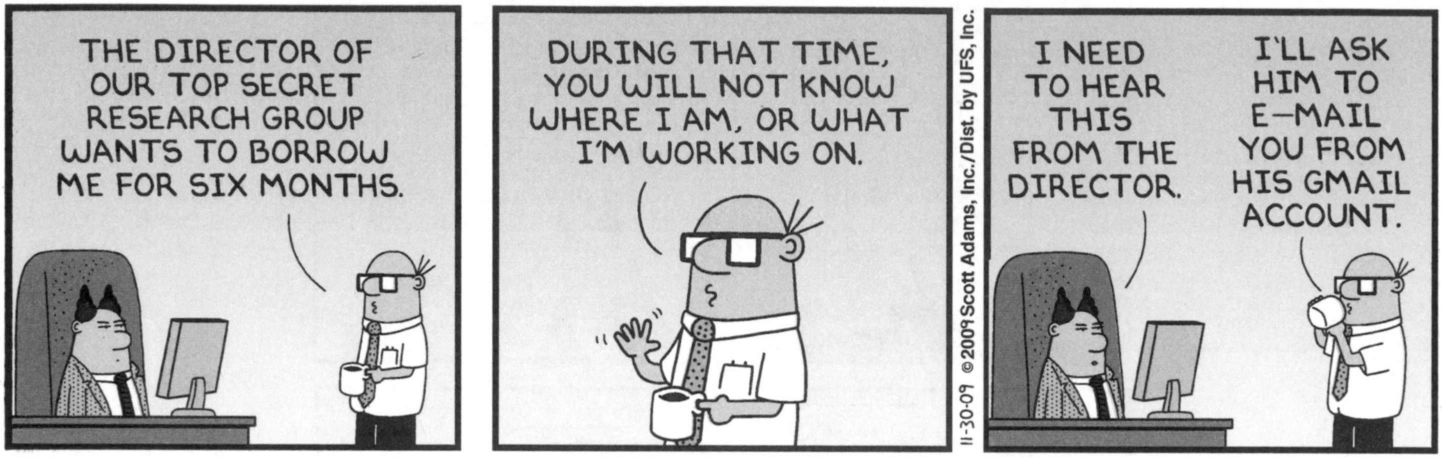
THE DIRECTOR OF OUR TOP SECRET RESEARCH GROUP WANTS TO BORROW ME FOR SIX MONTHS.
DURING THAT TIME, YOU WILL NOT KNOW WHERE I AM, OR WHAT I'M WORKING ON.
11-30-09 ©2009 Scott Adams, Inc./Dist. by UFS, Inc.
I NEED TO HEAR THIS FROM THE DIRECTOR.
I'LL ASK HIM TO E-MAIL YOU FROM HIS GMAIL ACCOUNT.

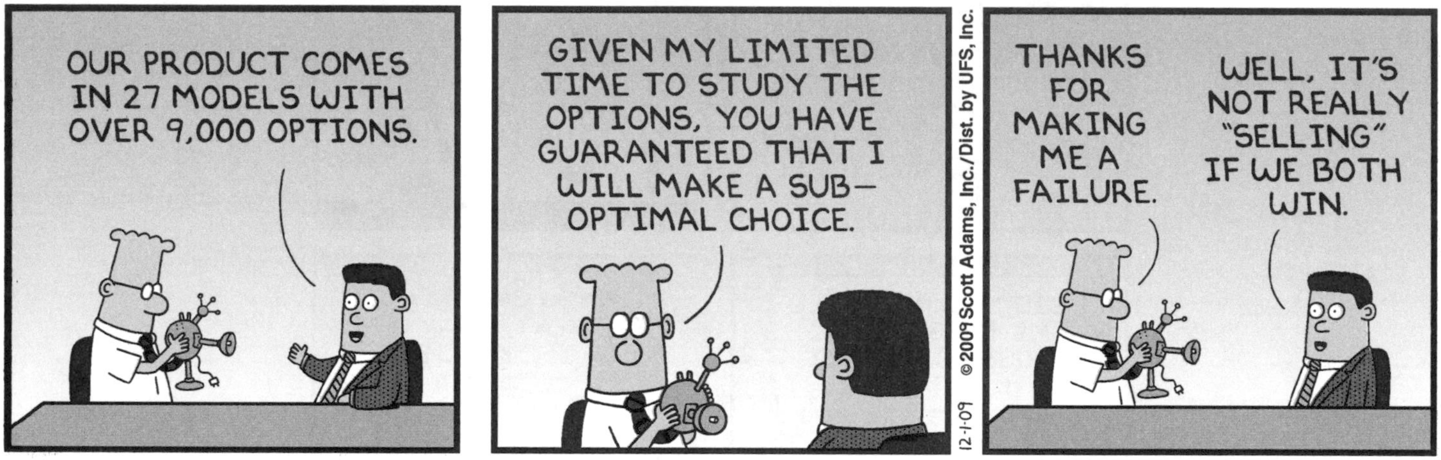
OUR PRODUCT COMES IN 27 MODELS WITH OVER 9,000 OPTIONS.
GIVEN MY LIMITED TIME TO STUDY THE OPTIONS, YOU HAVE GUARANTEED THAT I WILL MAKE A SUB-OPTIMAL CHOICE.
12-1-09 ©2009 Scott Adams, Inc./Dist. by UFS, Inc.
THANKS FOR MAKING ME A FAILURE.
WELL, IT'S NOT REALLY "SELLING" IF WE BOTH WIN.

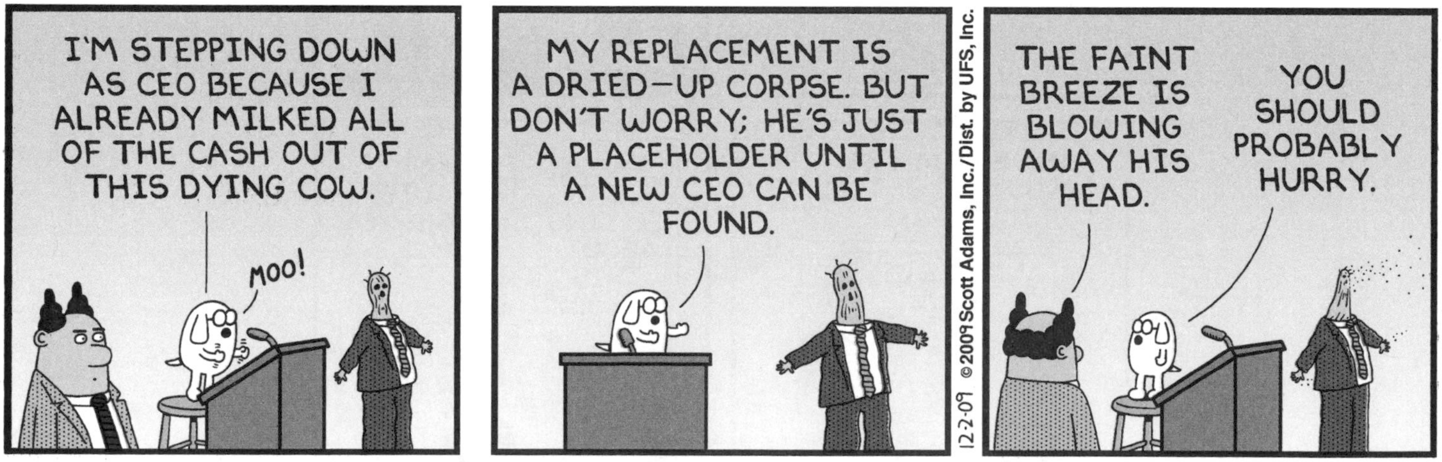
I'M STEPPING DOWN AS CEO BECAUSE I ALREADY MILKED ALL OF THE CASH OUT OF THIS DYING COW.
MOO!
MY REPLACEMENT IS A DRIED-UP CORPSE. BUT DON'T WORRY; HE'S JUST A PLACEHOLDER UNTIL A NEW CEO CAN BE FOUND.
12-2-09 ©2009 Scott Adams, Inc./Dist. by UFS, Inc.
THE FAINT BREEZE IS BLOWING AWAY HIS HEAD.
YOU SHOULD PROBABLY HURRY.

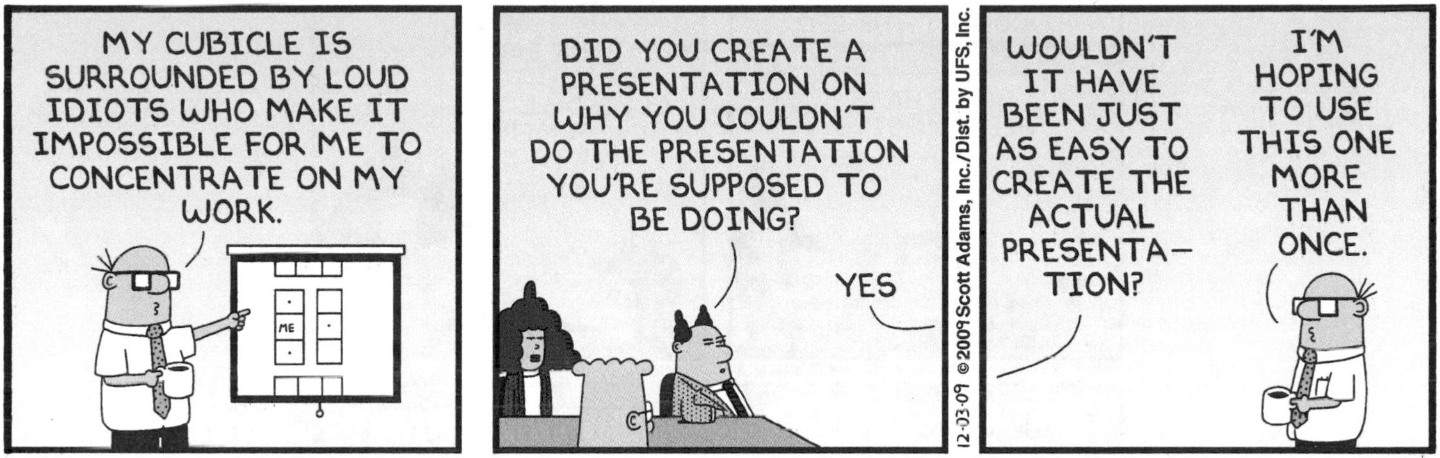
MY CUBICLE IS SURROUNDED BY LOUD IDIOTS WHO MAKE IT IMPOSSIBLE FOR ME TO CONCENTRATE ON MY WORK.
ME
DID YOU CREATE A PRESENTATION ON WHY YOU COULDN'T DO THE PRESENTATION YOU'RE SUPPOSED TO BE DOING?
YES
12-03-09 ©2009 Scott Adams, Inc./Dist. by UFS, Inc.
WOULDN'T IT HAVE BEEN JUST AS EASY TO CREATE THE ACTUAL PRESENTA-TION?
I'M HOPING TO USE THIS ONE MORE THAN ONCE.

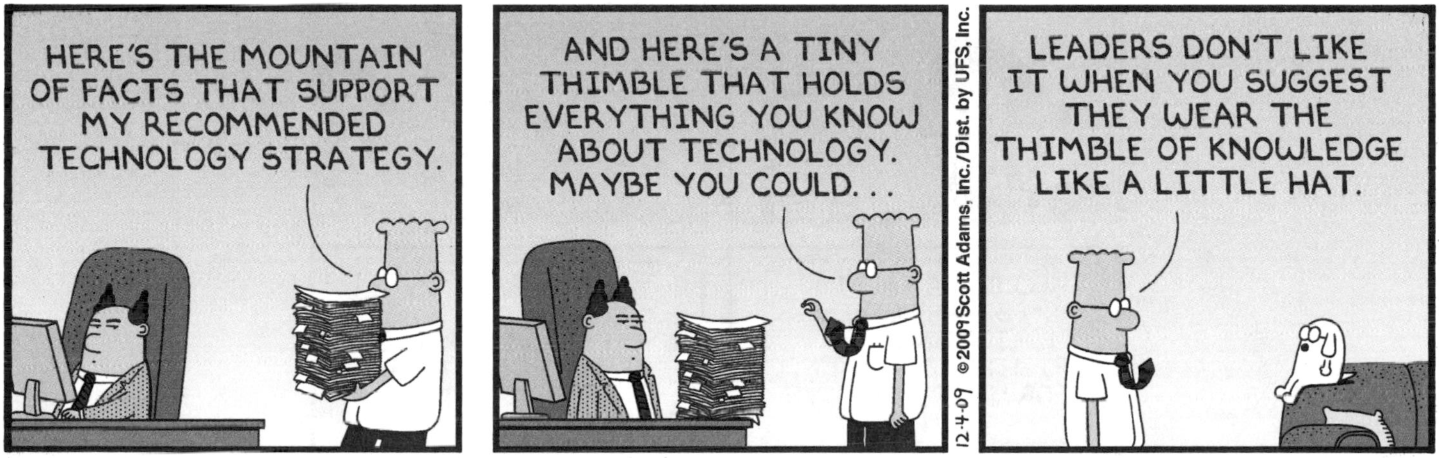
HERE'S THE MOUNTAIN OF FACTS THAT SUPPORT MY RECOMMENDED TECHNOLOGY STRATEGY.
AND HERE'S A TINY THIMBLE THAT HOLDS EVERYTHING YOU KNOW ABOUT TECHNOLOGY. MAYBE YOU COULD. . .
12-4-09 ©2009 Scott Adams, Inc./Dist. by UFS, Inc.
LEADERS DON'T LIKE IT WHEN YOU SUGGEST THEY WEAR THE THIMBLE OF KNOWLEDGE LIKE A LITTLE HAT.

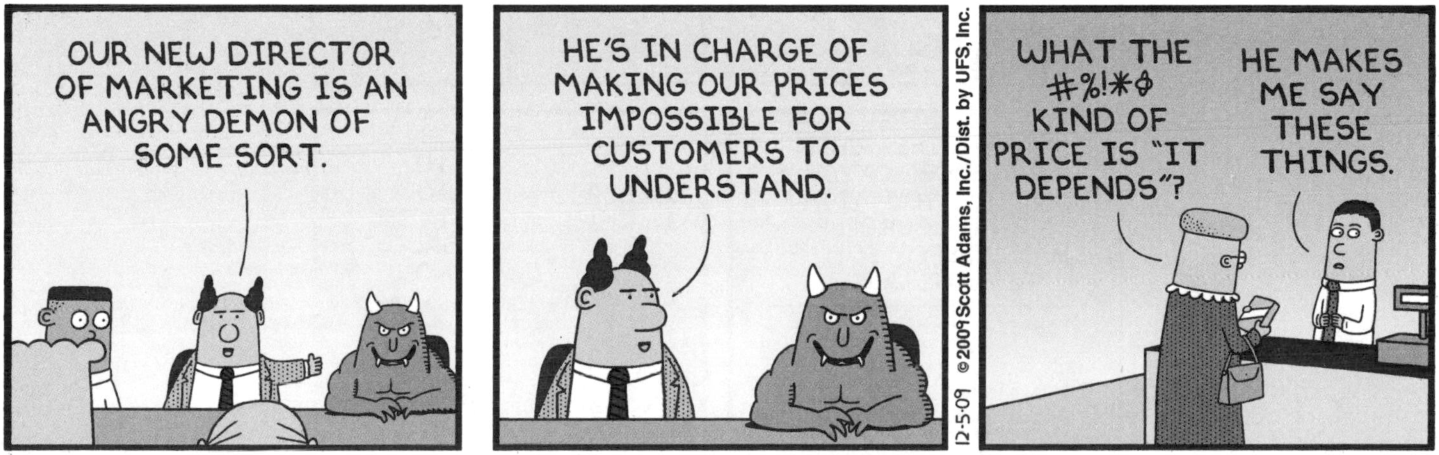
OUR NEW DIRECTOR OF MARKETING IS AN ANGRY DEMON OF SOME SORT.
HE'S IN CHARGE OF MAKING OUR PRICES IMPOSSIBLE FOR CUSTOMERS TO UNDERSTAND.
12-5-09 ©2009 Scott Adams, Inc./Dist. by UFS, Inc.
WHAT THE #%!*$ KIND OF PRICE IS "IT DEPENDS"?
HE MAKES ME SAY THESE THINGS.

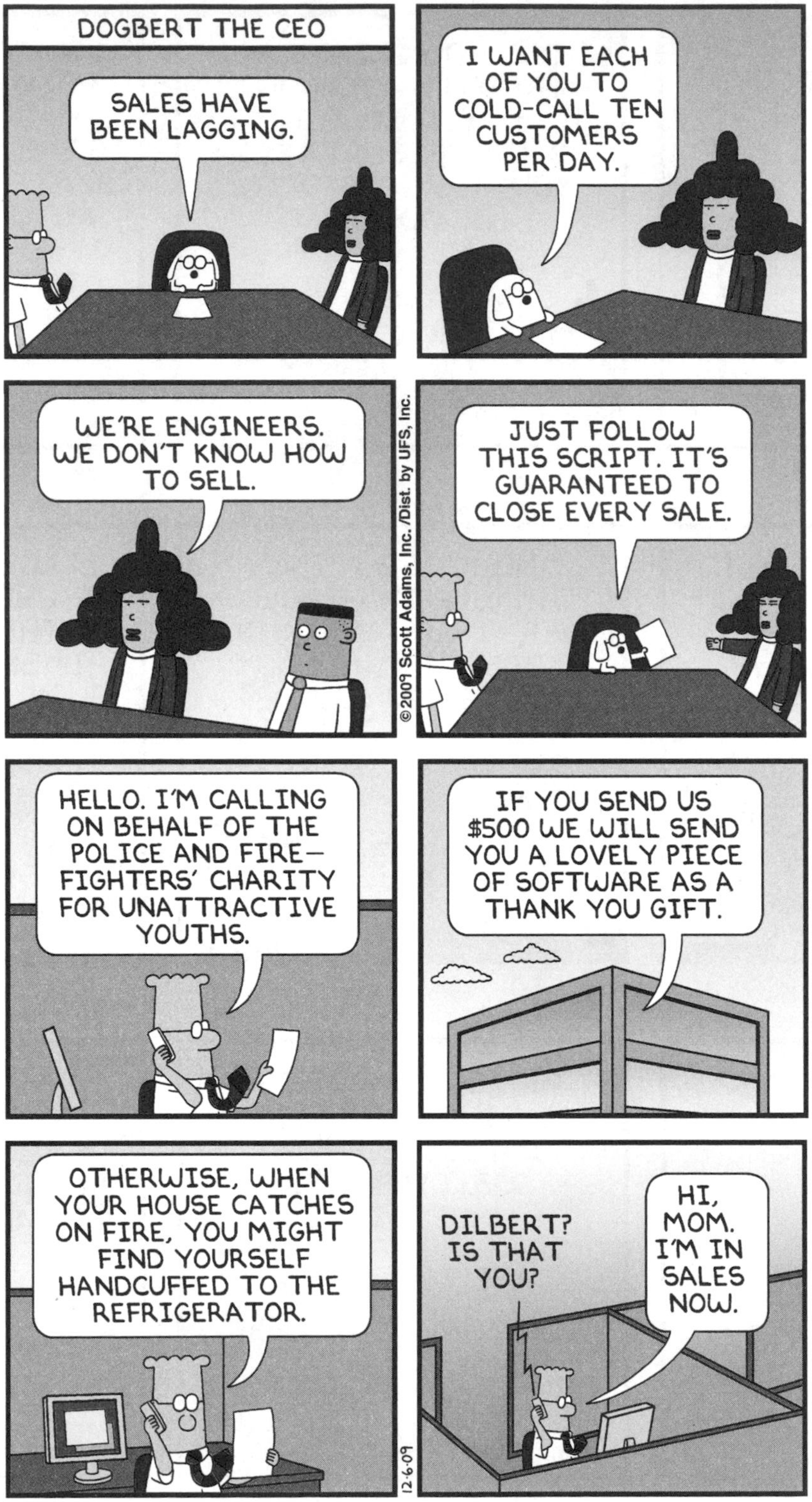
DOGBERT THE CEO
SALES HAVE BEEN LAGGING.
I WANT EACH OF YOU TO COLD-CALL TEN CUSTOMERS PER DAY.
WE'RE ENGINEERS. WE DON'T KNOW HOW TO SELL.
JUST FOLLOW THIS SCRIPT. IT'S GUARANTEED TO CLOSE EVERY SALE.
HELLO. I'M CALLING ON BEHALF OF THE POLICE AND FIRE-FIGHTERS' CHARITY FOR UNATTRACTIVE YOUTHS.
IF YOU SEND US $500 WE WILL SEND YOU A LOVELY PIECE OF SOFTWARE AS A THANK YOU GIFT.
OTHERWISE, WHEN YOUR HOUSE CATCHES ON FIRE, YOU MIGHT FIND YOURSELF HANDCUFFED TO THE REFRIGERATOR.
DILBERT? IS THAT YOU?
HI, MOM. I'M IN SALES NOW.
©2009 Scott Adams, Inc. /Dist. by UFS, Inc.
12-6-09

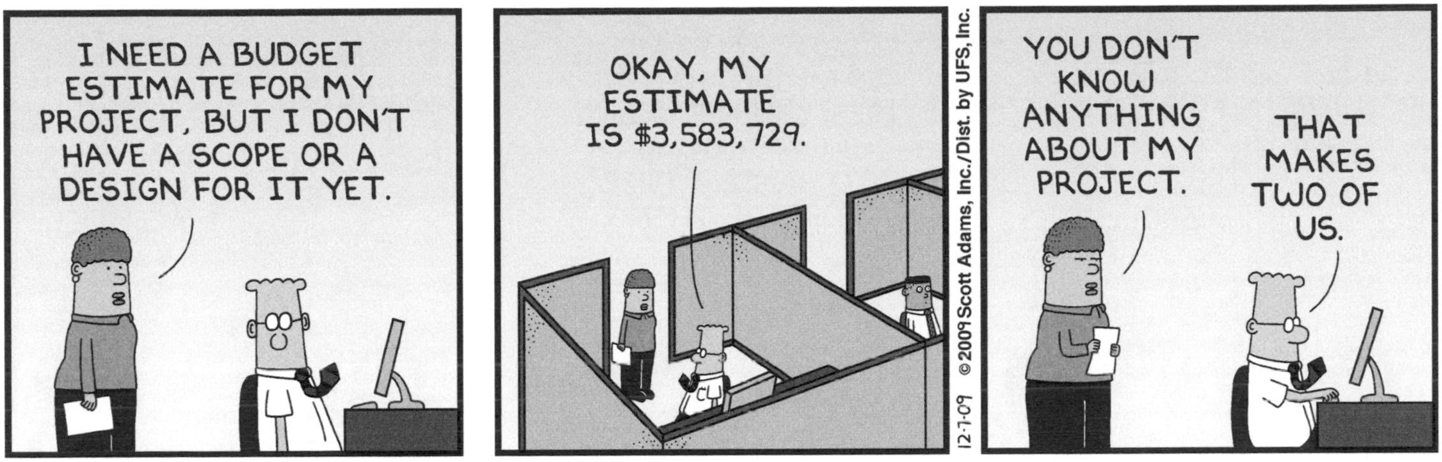
I NEED A BUDGET ESTIMATE FOR MY PROJECT, BUT I DON'T HAVE A SCOPE OR A DESIGN FOR IT YET.
OKAY, MY ESTIMATE IS $3,583,729.
YOU DON'T KNOW ANYTHING ABOUT MY PROJECT.
THAT MAKES TWO OF US.
12-7-09 © 2009 Scott Adams, Inc./Dist. by UFS, Inc.

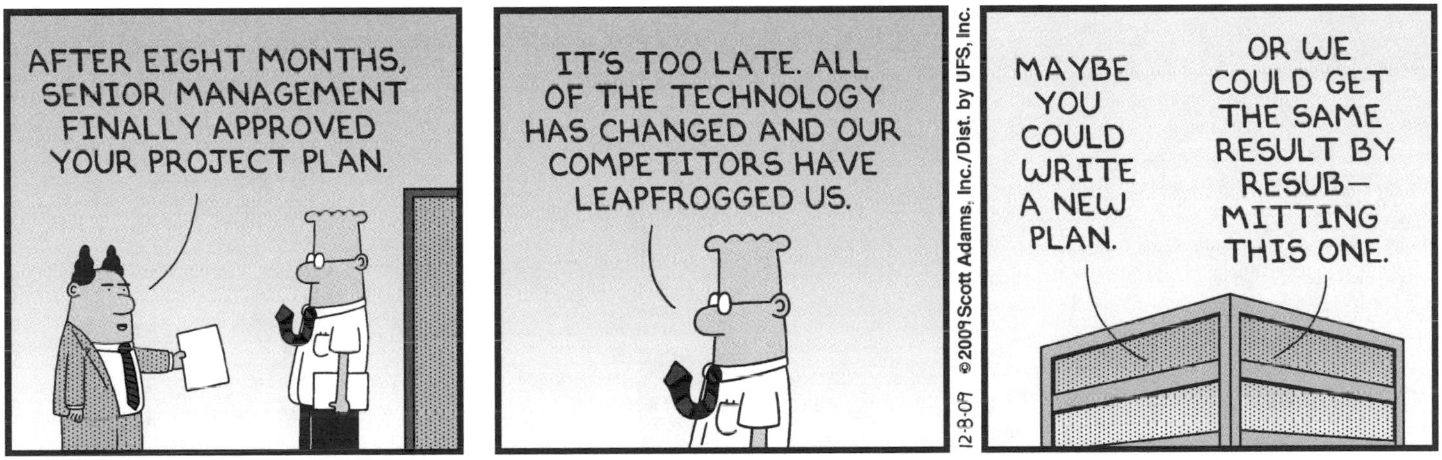
AFTER EIGHT MONTHS, SENIOR MANAGEMENT FINALLY APPROVED YOUR PROJECT PLAN.
IT'S TOO LATE. ALL OF THE TECHNOLOGY HAS CHANGED AND OUR COMPETITORS HAVE LEAPFROGGED US.
MAYBE YOU COULD WRITE A NEW PLAN.
OR WE COULD GET THE SAME RESULT BY RESUB– MITTING THIS ONE.
12-8-09 © 2009 Scott Adams, Inc./Dist. by UFS, Inc.

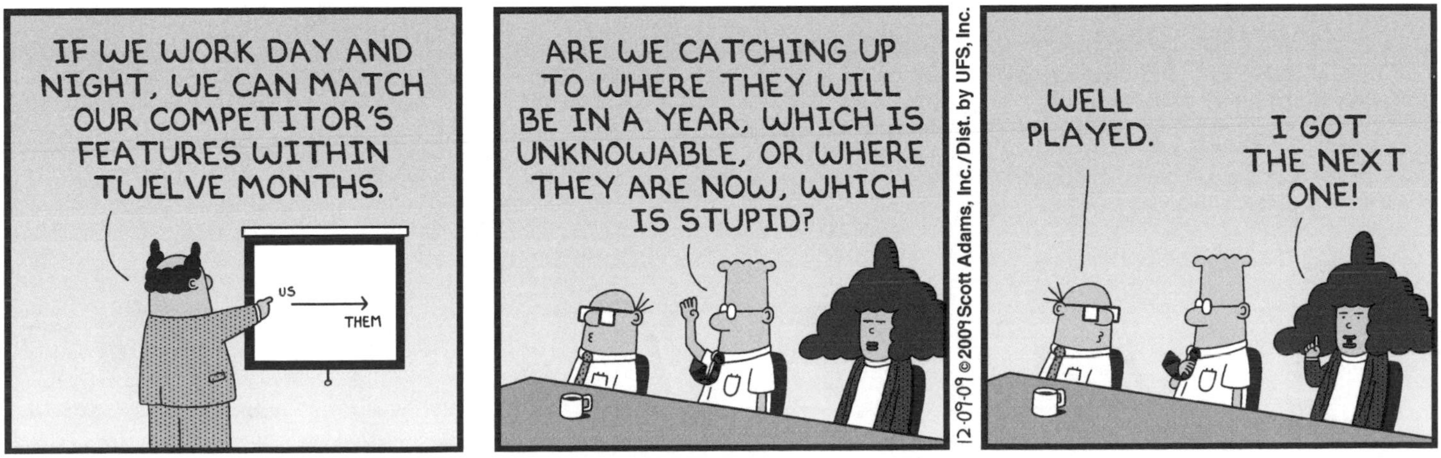
IF WE WORK DAY AND NIGHT, WE CAN MATCH OUR COMPETITOR'S FEATURES WITHIN TWELVE MONTHS.
US
THEM
ARE WE CATCHING UP TO WHERE THEY WILL BE IN A YEAR, WHICH IS UNKNOWABLE, OR WHERE THEY ARE NOW, WHICH IS STUPID?
WELL PLAYED.
I GOT THE NEXT ONE!
12-09-09 © 2009 Scott Adams, Inc./Dist. by UFS, Inc.

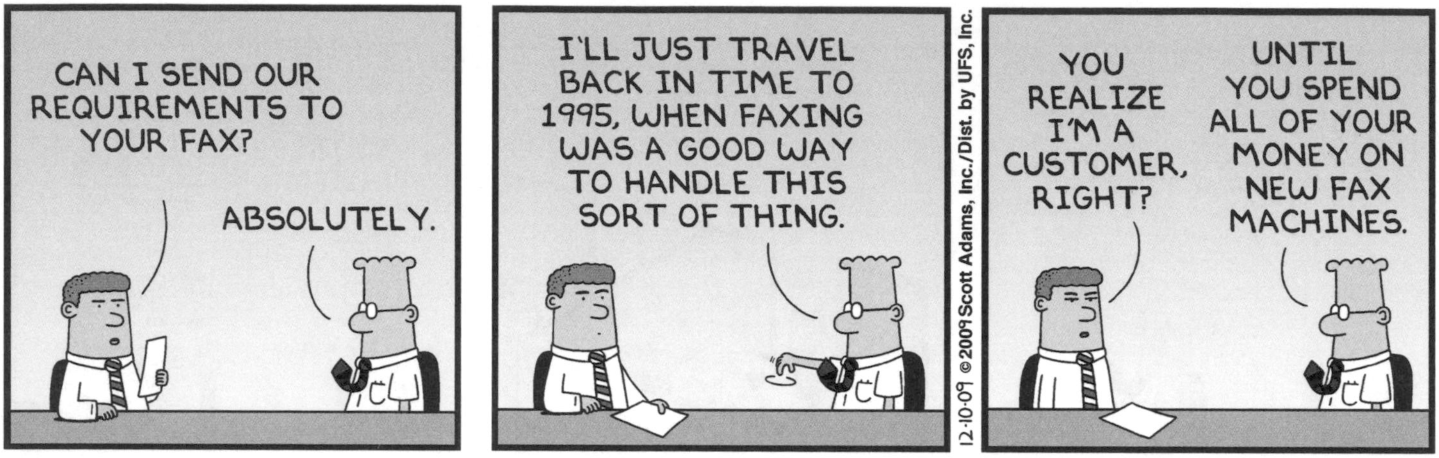
CAN I SEND OUR REQUIREMENTS TO YOUR FAX?
ABSOLUTELY.
I'LL JUST TRAVEL BACK IN TIME TO 1995, WHEN FAXING WAS A GOOD WAY TO HANDLE THIS SORT OF THING.
12-10-09 ©2009 Scott Adams, Inc./Dist. by UFS, Inc.
YOU REALIZE I'M A CUSTOMER, RIGHT?
UNTIL YOU SPEND ALL OF YOUR MONEY ON NEW FAX MACHINES.

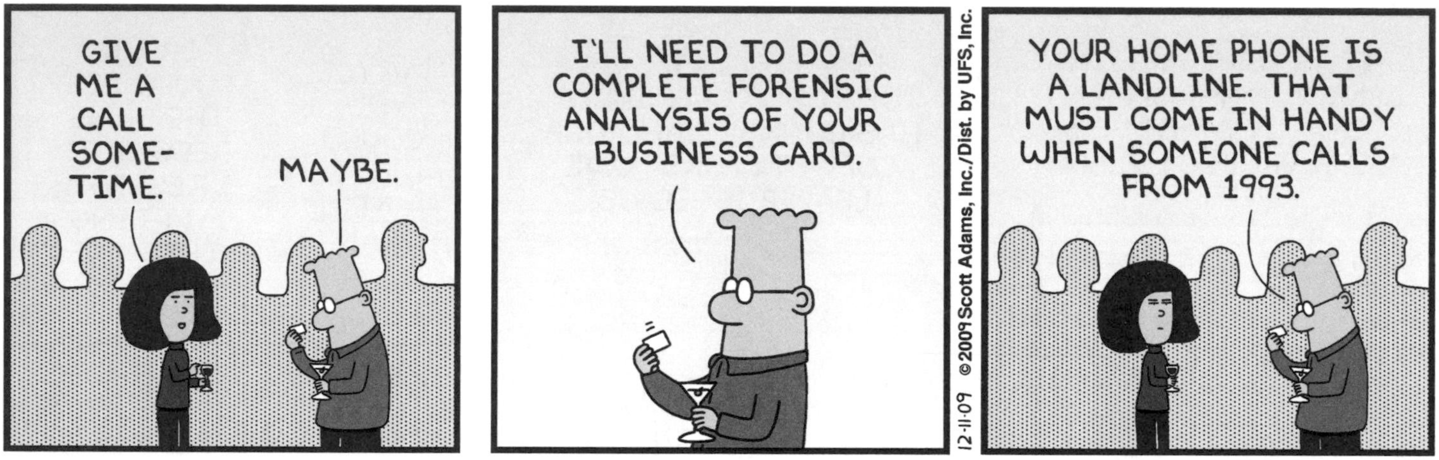
GIVE ME A CALL SOME-TIME.
MAYBE.
I'LL NEED TO DO A COMPLETE FORENSIC ANALYSIS OF YOUR BUSINESS CARD.
12-11-09 ©2009 Scott Adams, Inc./Dist. by UFS, Inc.
YOUR HOME PHONE IS A LANDLINE. THAT MUST COME IN HANDY WHEN SOMEONE CALLS FROM 1993.

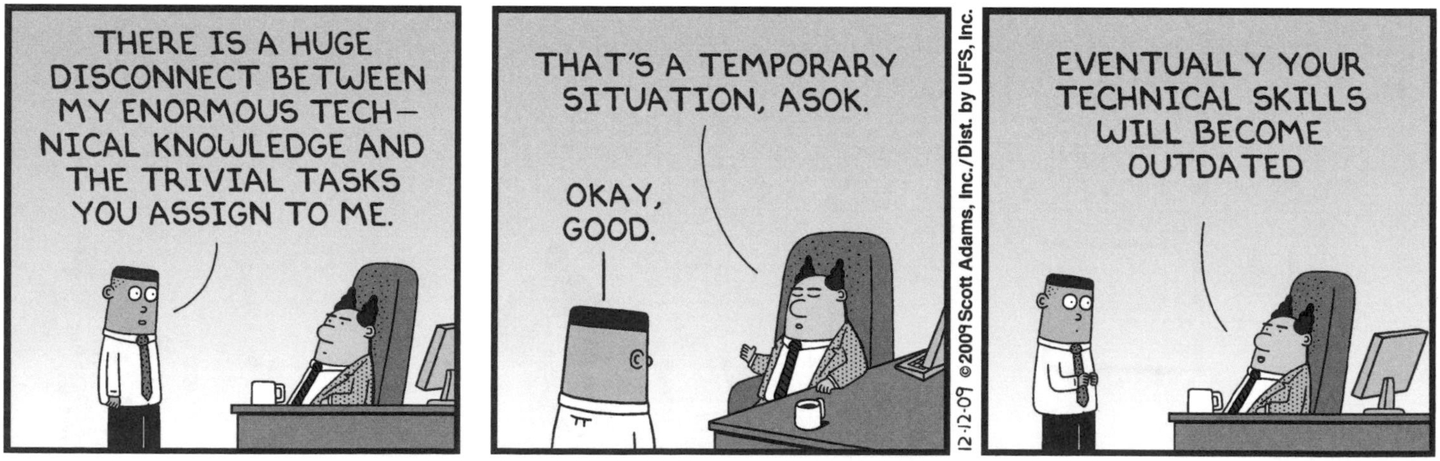
THERE IS A HUGE DISCONNECT BETWEEN MY ENORMOUS TECH-NICAL KNOWLEDGE AND THE TRIVIAL TASKS YOU ASSIGN TO ME.
THAT'S A TEMPORARY SITUATION, ASOK.
OKAY, GOOD.
12-12-09 ©2009 Scott Adams, Inc./Dist. by UFS, Inc.
EVENTUALLY YOUR TECHNICAL SKILLS WILL BECOME OUTDATED

WALLY, CAN YOU TAKE A LOOK AT THIS?
I'D BE DELIGHTED.
WHAT'S YOUR PROJECT CHARGE CODE?
IT WILL ONLY TAKE A MINUTE.
ARE YOU SUGGESTING THAT I LIE ABOUT MY TIME?
© 2009 Scott Adams, Inc./Dist. by UFS, Inc.
IT'S ONLY ONE MINUTE.
BY THAT LINE OF REASONING, IT'S OKAY TO STEAL, AS LONG AS YOU DON'T TAKE TOO MUCH.
INCIDENTALLY, I HAVE TO CHARGE YOU FOR THE TIME IT JUST TOOK TO LABEL YOU A THIEF.
FORGET IT! I'LL ASK SOMEONE ELSE!
12-13-09
LET'S CALL THAT "OVERHEAD."
CLICK

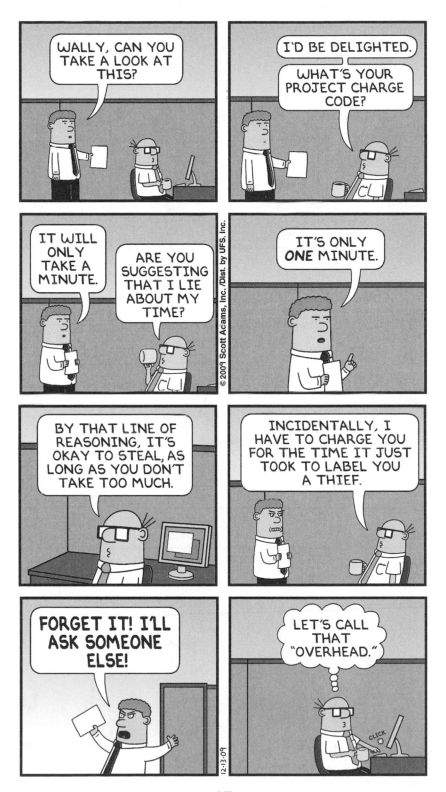

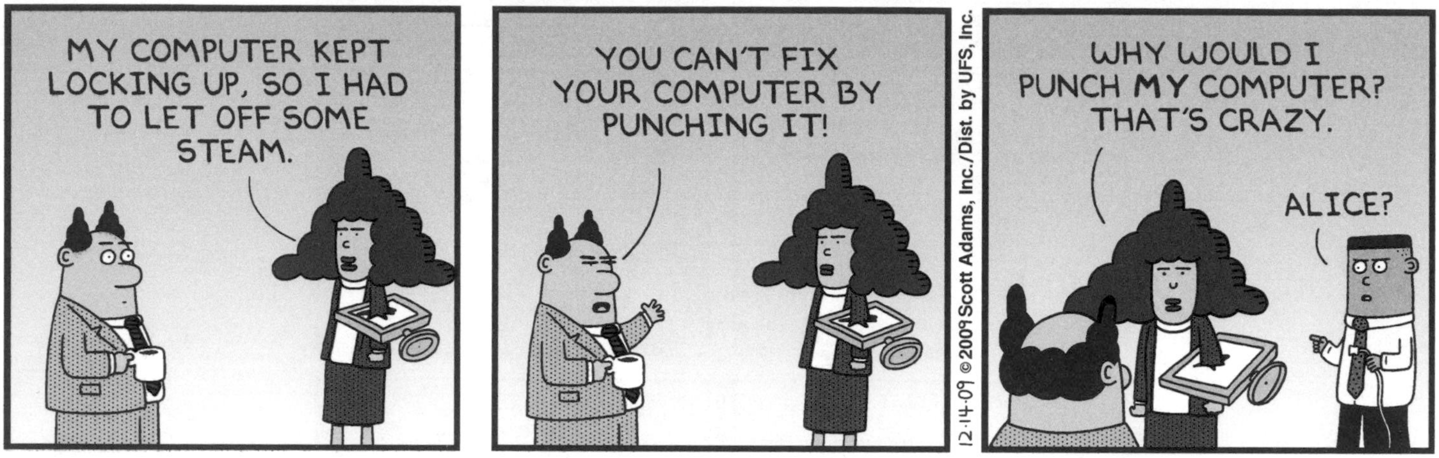
MY COMPUTER KEPT LOCKING UP, SO I HAD TO LET OFF SOME STEAM.
YOU CAN'T FIX YOUR COMPUTER BY PUNCHING IT!
12·14·09 © 2009 Scott Adams, Inc./Dist. by UFS, Inc.
WHY WOULD I PUNCH **MY** COMPUTER? THAT'S CRAZY.
ALICE?

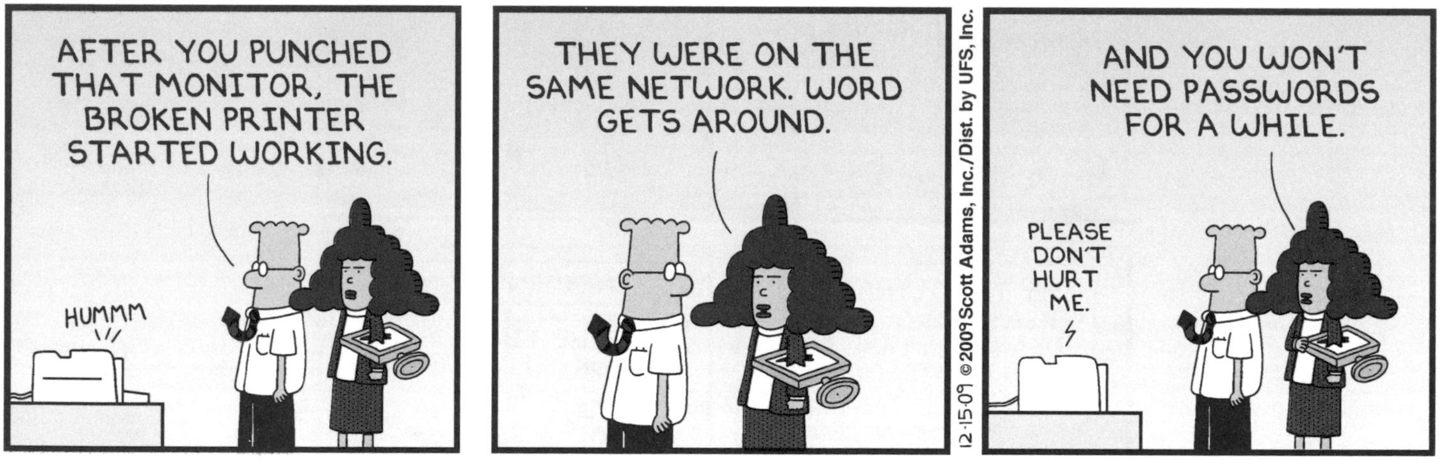
AFTER YOU PUNCHED THAT MONITOR, THE BROKEN PRINTER STARTED WORKING.
HUMMM
THEY WERE ON THE SAME NETWORK. WORD GETS AROUND.
12·15·09 © 2009 Scott Adams, Inc./Dist. by UFS, Inc.
PLEASE DON'T HURT ME.
AND YOU WON'T NEED PASSWORDS FOR A WHILE.

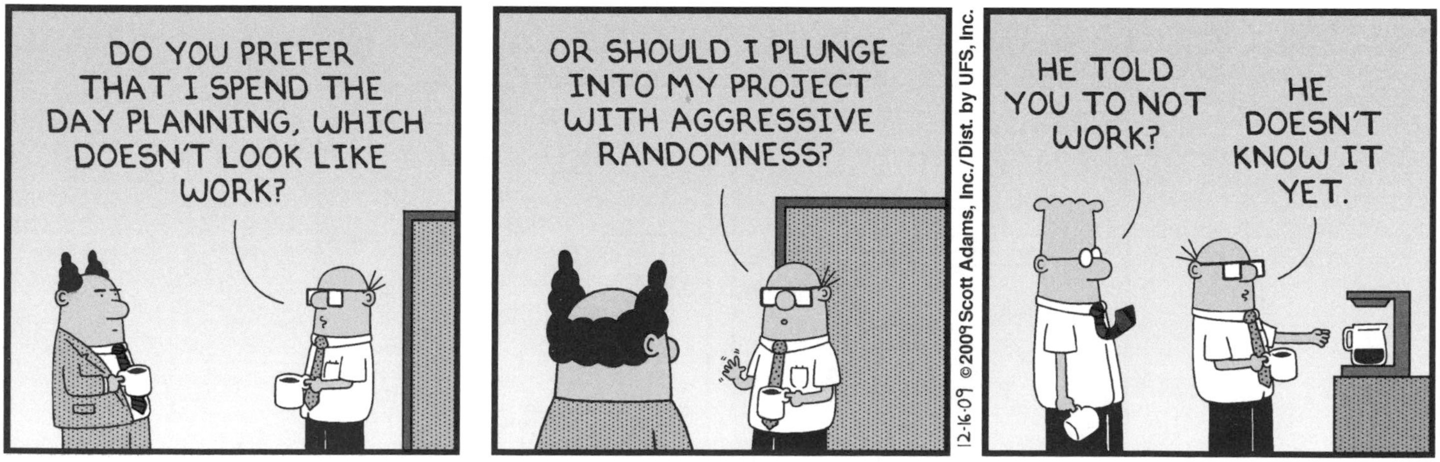
DO YOU PREFER THAT I SPEND THE DAY PLANNING, WHICH DOESN'T LOOK LIKE WORK?
OR SHOULD I PLUNGE INTO MY PROJECT WITH AGGRESSIVE RANDOMNESS?
12·16·09 © 2009 Scott Adams, Inc./Dist. by UFS, Inc.
HE TOLD YOU TO NOT WORK?
HE DOESN'T KNOW IT YET.

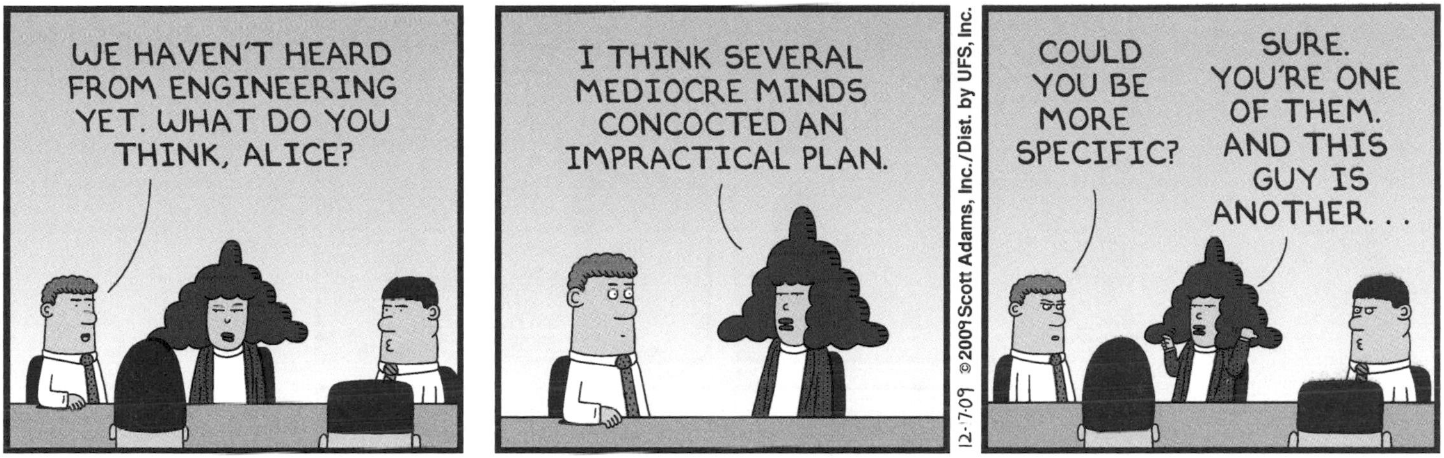
WE HAVEN'T HEARD FROM ENGINEERING YET. WHAT DO YOU THINK, ALICE?
I THINK SEVERAL MEDIOCRE MINDS CONCOCTED AN IMPRACTICAL PLAN.
12·7·09 ©2009 Scott Adams, Inc./Dist. by UFS, Inc.
COULD YOU BE MORE SPECIFIC?
SURE. YOU'RE ONE OF THEM. AND THIS GUY IS ANOTHER. . .

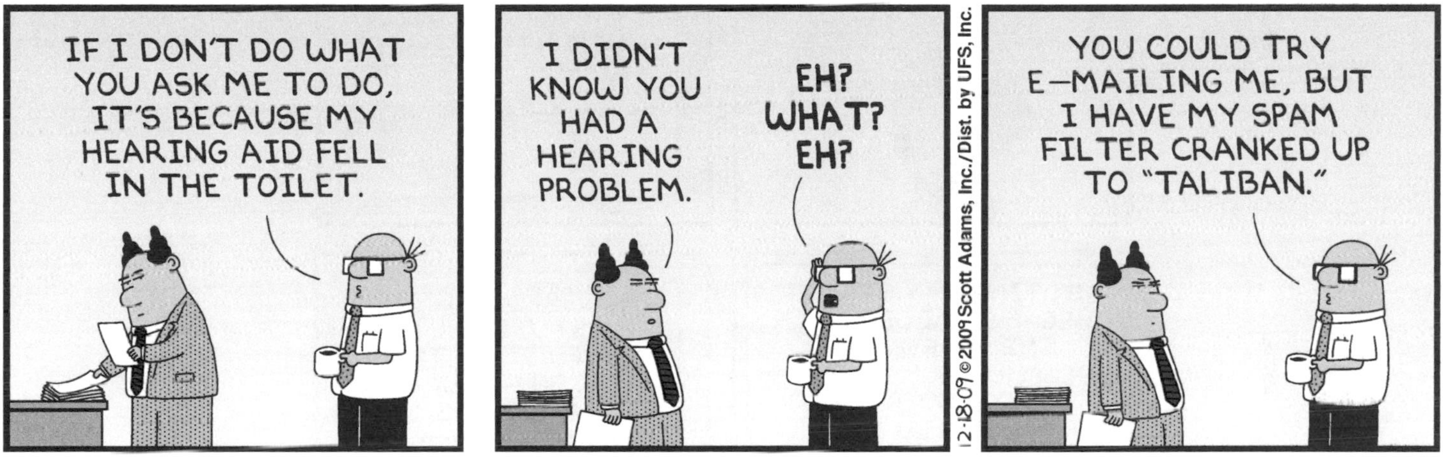
IF I DON'T DO WHAT YOU ASK ME TO DO, IT'S BECAUSE MY HEARING AID FELL IN THE TOILET.
I DIDN'T KNOW YOU HAD A HEARING PROBLEM.
EH? WHAT? EH?
12·18·09 ©2009 Scott Adams, Inc./Dist. by UFS, Inc.
YOU COULD TRY E-MAILING ME, BUT I HAVE MY SPAM FILTER CRANKED UP TO "TALIBAN."

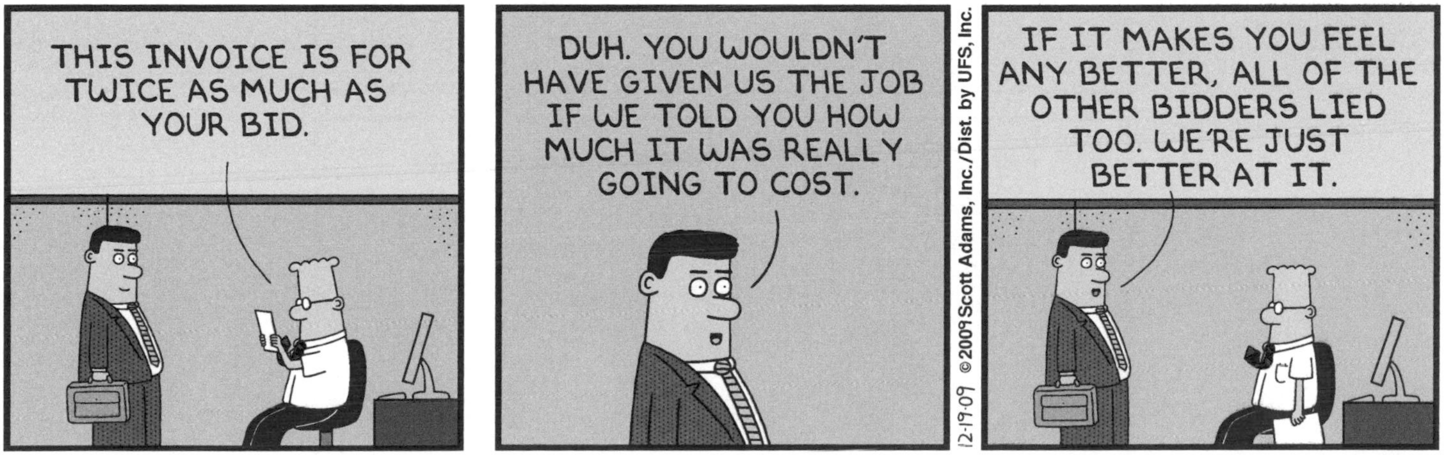
THIS INVOICE IS FOR TWICE AS MUCH AS YOUR BID.
DUH. YOU WOULDN'T HAVE GIVEN US THE JOB IF WE TOLD YOU HOW MUCH IT WAS REALLY GOING TO COST.
12·19·09 ©2009 Scott Adams, Inc./Dist. by UFS, Inc.
IF IT MAKES YOU FEEL ANY BETTER, ALL OF THE OTHER BIDDERS LIED TOO. WE'RE JUST BETTER AT IT.

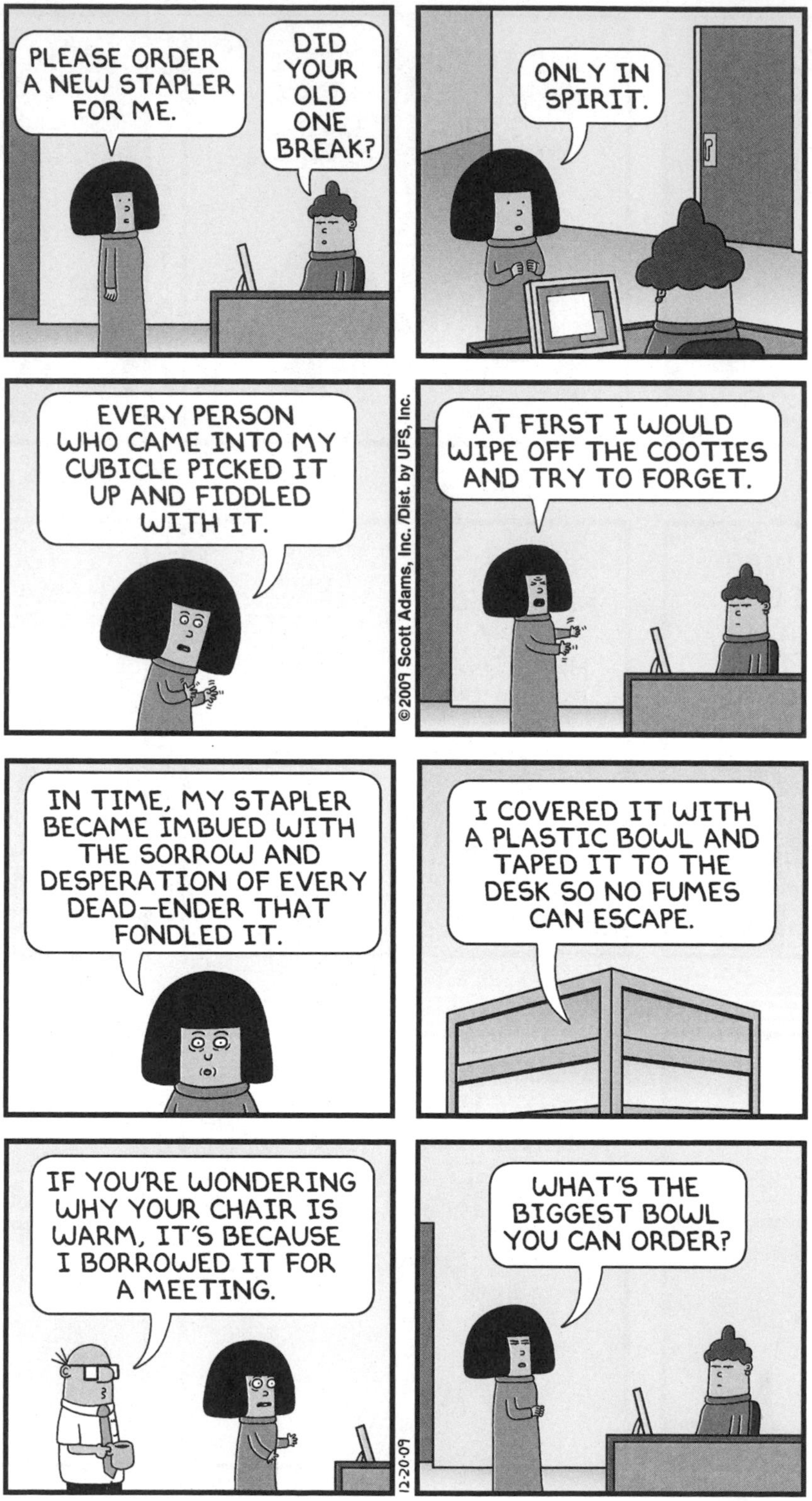
PLEASE ORDER A NEW STAPLER FOR ME.
DID YOUR OLD ONE BREAK?
ONLY IN SPIRIT.
EVERY PERSON WHO CAME INTO MY CUBICLE PICKED IT UP AND FIDDLED WITH IT.
©2009 Scott Adams, Inc. /Dist. by UFS, Inc.
AT FIRST I WOULD WIPE OFF THE COOTIES AND TRY TO FORGET.
IN TIME, MY STAPLER BECAME IMBUED WITH THE SORROW AND DESPERATION OF EVERY DEAD—ENDER THAT FONDLED IT.
I COVERED IT WITH A PLASTIC BOWL AND TAPED IT TO THE DESK SO NO FUMES CAN ESCAPE.
IF YOU'RE WONDERING WHY YOUR CHAIR IS WARM, IT'S BECAUSE I BORROWED IT FOR A MEETING.
12-20-09
WHAT'S THE BIGGEST BOWL YOU CAN ORDER?

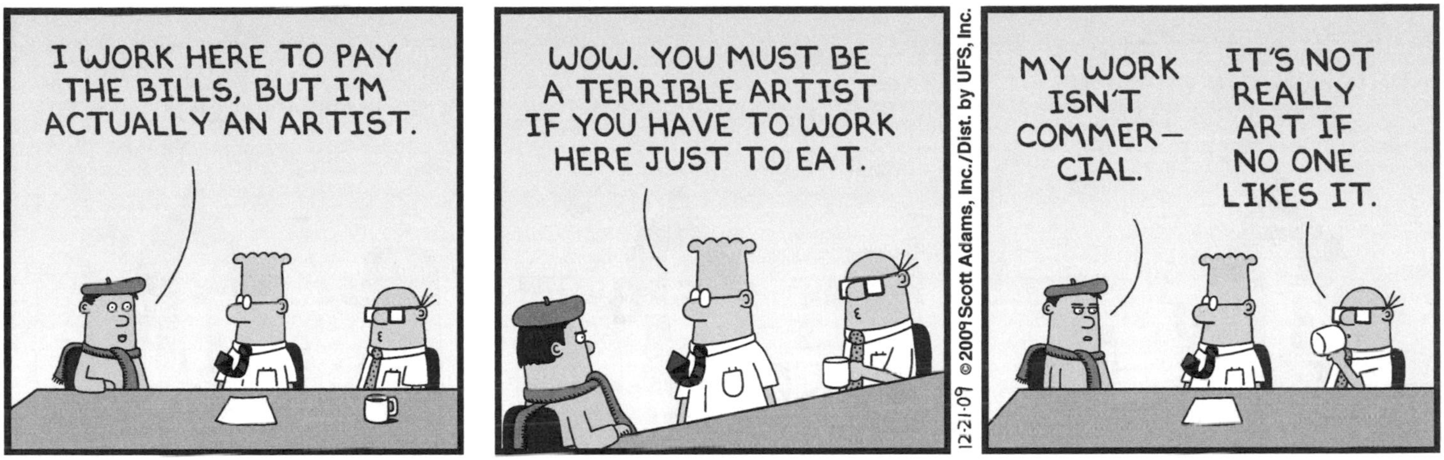
I WORK HERE TO PAY THE BILLS, BUT I'M ACTUALLY AN ARTIST.
WOW. YOU MUST BE A TERRIBLE ARTIST IF YOU HAVE TO WORK HERE JUST TO EAT.
MY WORK ISN'T COMMER- CIAL.
IT'S NOT REALLY ART IF NO ONE LIKES IT.
12-21-09 ©2009 Scott Adams, Inc./Dist. by UFS, Inc.

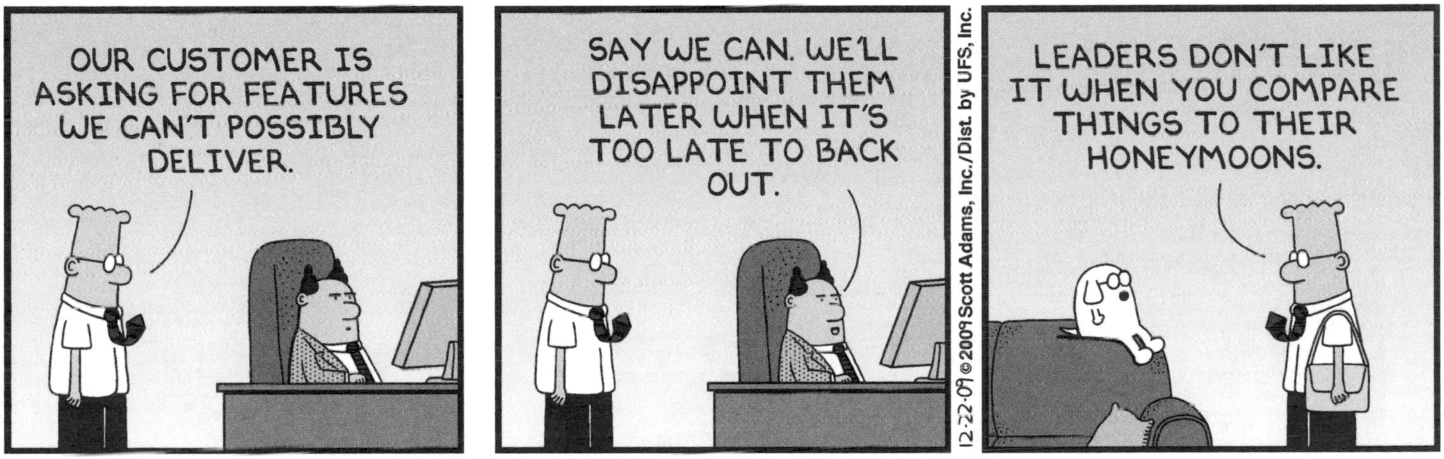
OUR CUSTOMER IS ASKING FOR FEATURES WE CAN'T POSSIBLY DELIVER.
SAY WE CAN. WE'LL DISAPPOINT THEM LATER WHEN IT'S TOO LATE TO BACK OUT.
LEADERS DON'T LIKE IT WHEN YOU COMPARE THINGS TO THEIR HONEYMOONS.
12-22-09 ©2009 Scott Adams, Inc./Dist. by UFS, Inc.

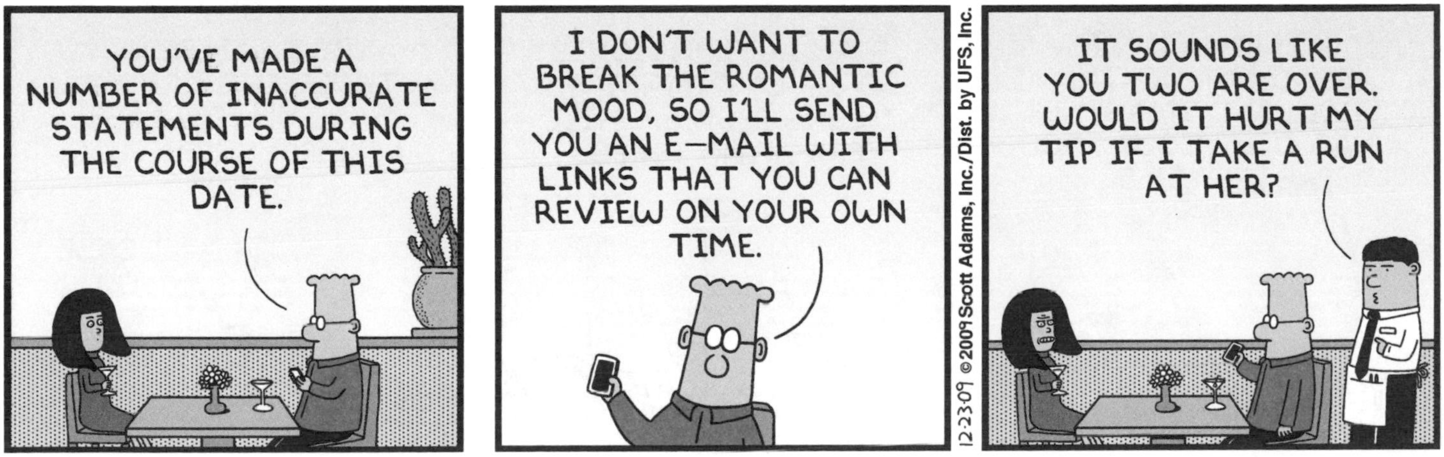
YOU'VE MADE A NUMBER OF INACCURATE STATEMENTS DURING THE COURSE OF THIS DATE.
I DON'T WANT TO BREAK THE ROMANTIC MOOD, SO I'LL SEND YOU AN E-MAIL WITH LINKS THAT YOU CAN REVIEW ON YOUR OWN TIME.
IT SOUNDS LIKE YOU TWO ARE OVER. WOULD IT HURT MY TIP IF I TAKE A RUN AT HER?
12-23-09 ©2009 Scott Adams, Inc./Dist. by UFS, Inc.

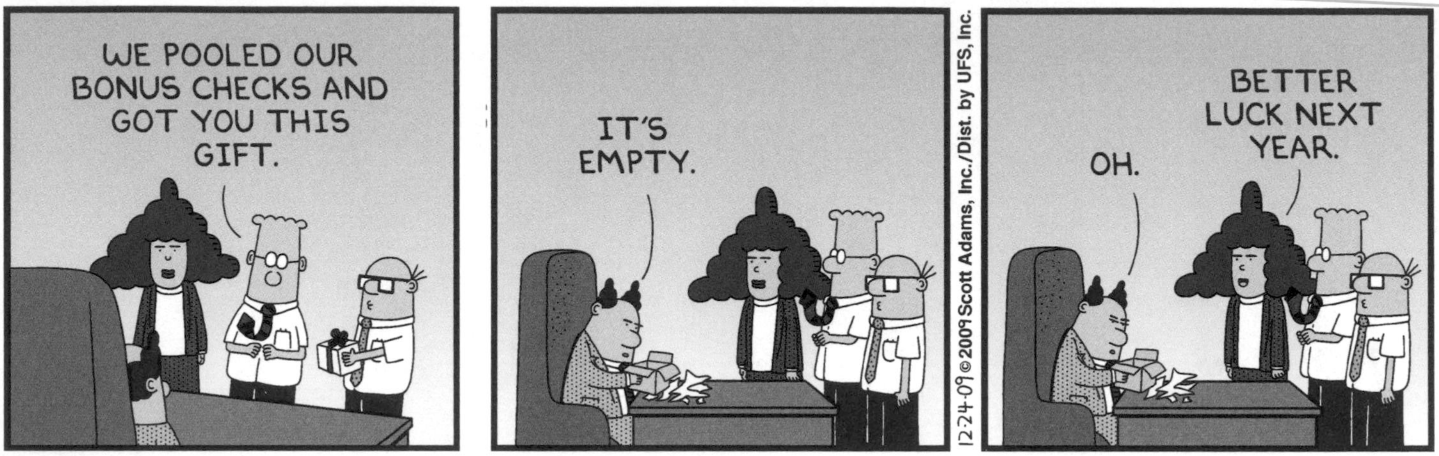
WE POOLED OUR BONUS CHECKS AND GOT YOU THIS GIFT.
IT'S EMPTY.
12·24·09 © 2009 Scott Adams, Inc./Dist. by UFS, Inc.
OH.
BETTER LUCK NEXT YEAR.

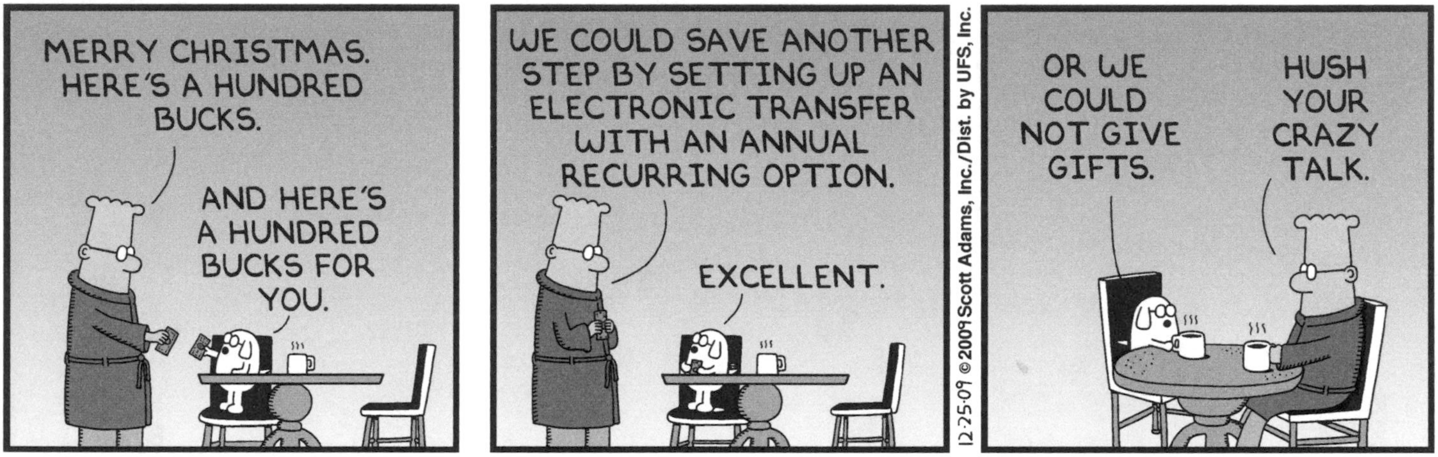
MERRY CHRISTMAS. HERE'S A HUNDRED BUCKS.
AND HERE'S A HUNDRED BUCKS FOR YOU.
WE COULD SAVE ANOTHER STEP BY SETTING UP AN ELECTRONIC TRANSFER WITH AN ANNUAL RECURRING OPTION.
EXCELLENT.
12·25·09 © 2009 Scott Adams, Inc./Dist. by UFS, Inc.
OR WE COULD NOT GIVE GIFTS.
HUSH YOUR CRAZY TALK.

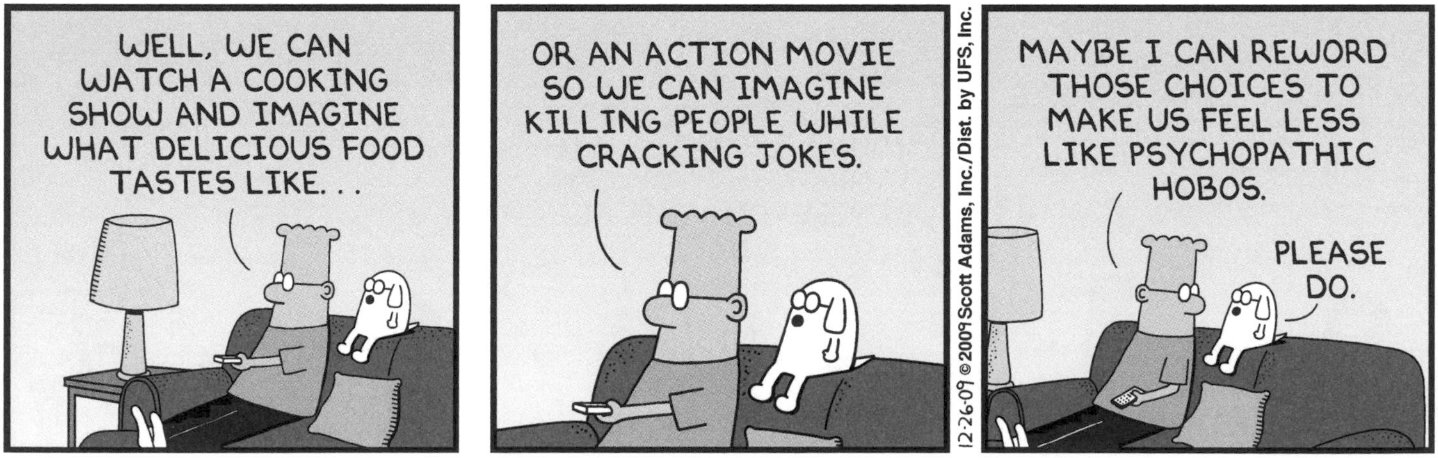
WELL, WE CAN WATCH A COOKING SHOW AND IMAGINE WHAT DELICIOUS FOOD TASTES LIKE. . .
OR AN ACTION MOVIE SO WE CAN IMAGINE KILLING PEOPLE WHILE CRACKING JOKES.
12·26·09 © 2009 Scott Adams, Inc./Dist. by UFS, Inc.
MAYBE I CAN REWORD THOSE CHOICES TO MAKE US FEEL LESS LIKE PSYCHOPATHIC HOBOS.
PLEASE DO.

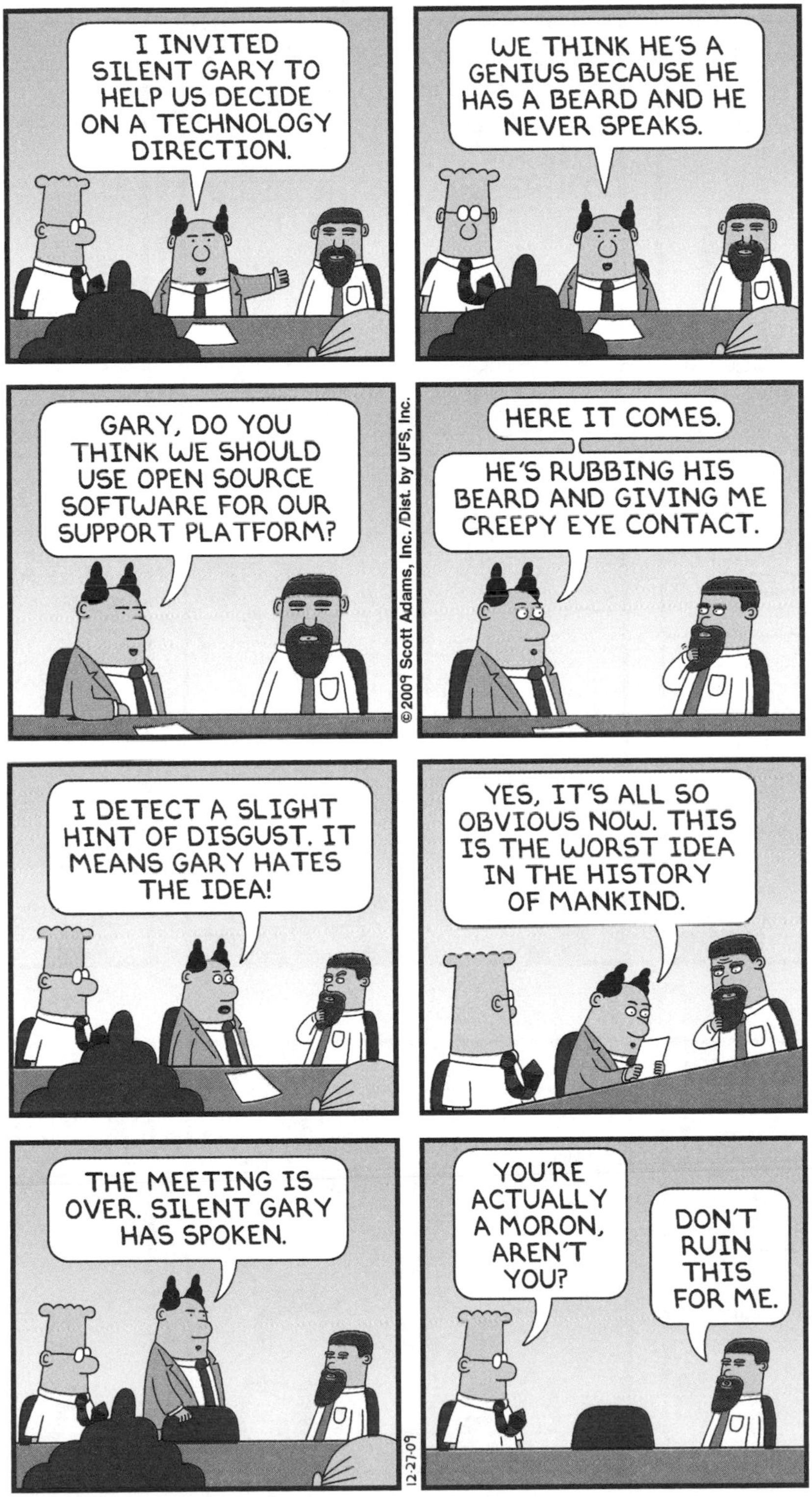
I INVITED SILENT GARY TO HELP US DECIDE ON A TECHNOLOGY DIRECTION.
WE THINK HE'S A GENIUS BECAUSE HE HAS A BEARD AND HE NEVER SPEAKS.
GARY, DO YOU THINK WE SHOULD USE OPEN SOURCE SOFTWARE FOR OUR SUPPORT PLATFORM?
HERE IT COMES.
HE'S RUBBING HIS BEARD AND GIVING ME CREEPY EYE CONTACT.
I DETECT A SLIGHT HINT OF DISGUST. IT MEANS GARY HATES THE IDEA!
YES, IT'S ALL SO OBVIOUS NOW. THIS IS THE WORST IDEA IN THE HISTORY OF MANKIND.
THE MEETING IS OVER. SILENT GARY HAS SPOKEN.
YOU'RE ACTUALLY A MORON, AREN'T YOU?
DON'T RUIN THIS FOR ME.
©2009 Scott Adams, Inc./Dist. by UFS, Inc.
12-27-09

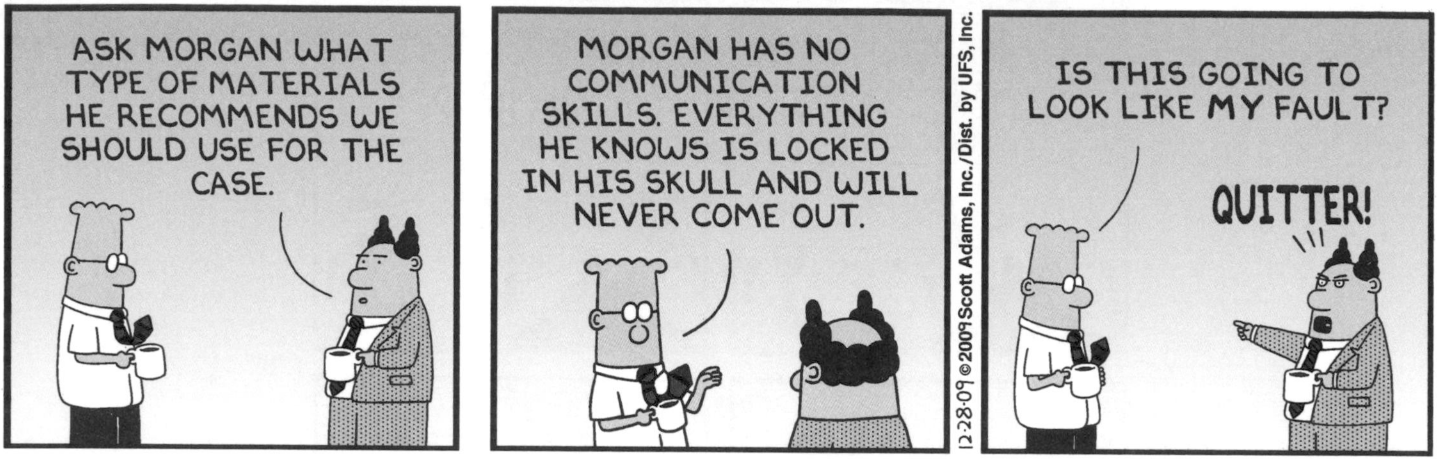
ASK MORGAN WHAT TYPE OF MATERIALS HE RECOMMENDS WE SHOULD USE FOR THE CASE.
MORGAN HAS NO COMMUNICATION SKILLS. EVERYTHING HE KNOWS IS LOCKED IN HIS SKULL AND WILL NEVER COME OUT.
12·28·09 ©2009 Scott Adams, Inc./Dist. by UFS, Inc.
IS THIS GOING TO LOOK LIKE MY FAULT?
QUITTER!

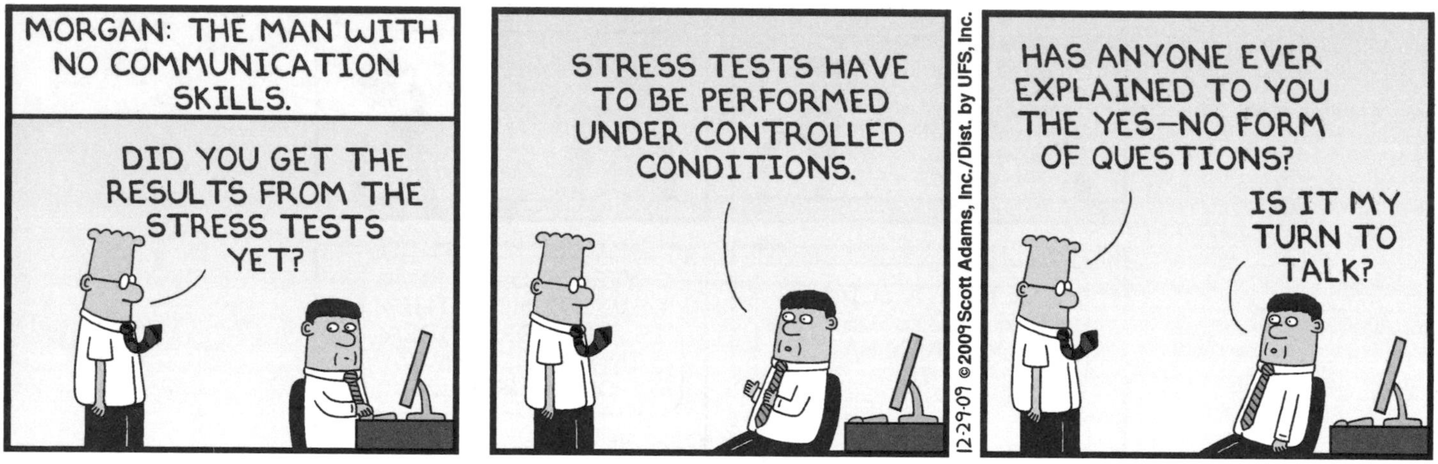
MORGAN: THE MAN WITH NO COMMUNICATION SKILLS.
DID YOU GET THE RESULTS FROM THE STRESS TESTS YET?
STRESS TESTS HAVE TO BE PERFORMED UNDER CONTROLLED CONDITIONS.
12·29·09 ©2009 Scott Adams, Inc./Dist. by UFS, Inc.
HAS ANYONE EVER EXPLAINED TO YOU THE YES—NO FORM OF QUESTIONS?
IS IT MY TURN TO TALK?

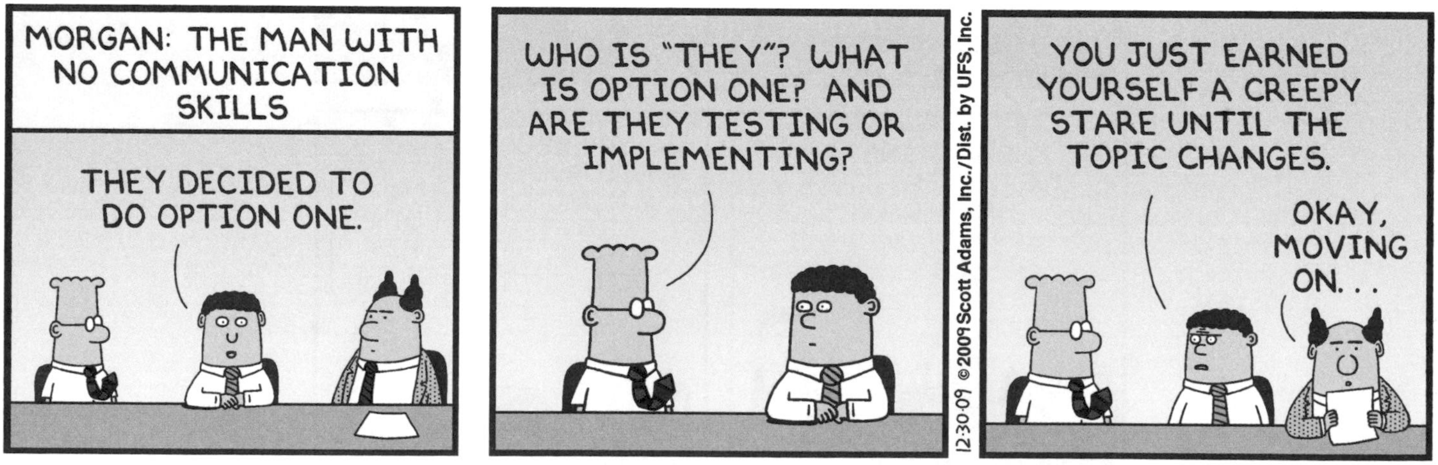
MORGAN: THE MAN WITH NO COMMUNICATION SKILLS
THEY DECIDED TO DO OPTION ONE.
WHO IS "THEY"? WHAT IS OPTION ONE? AND ARE THEY TESTING OR IMPLEMENTING?
12·30·09 ©2009 Scott Adams, Inc./Dist. by UFS, Inc.
YOU JUST EARNED YOURSELF A CREEPY STARE UNTIL THE TOPIC CHANGES.
OKAY, MOVING ON. . .

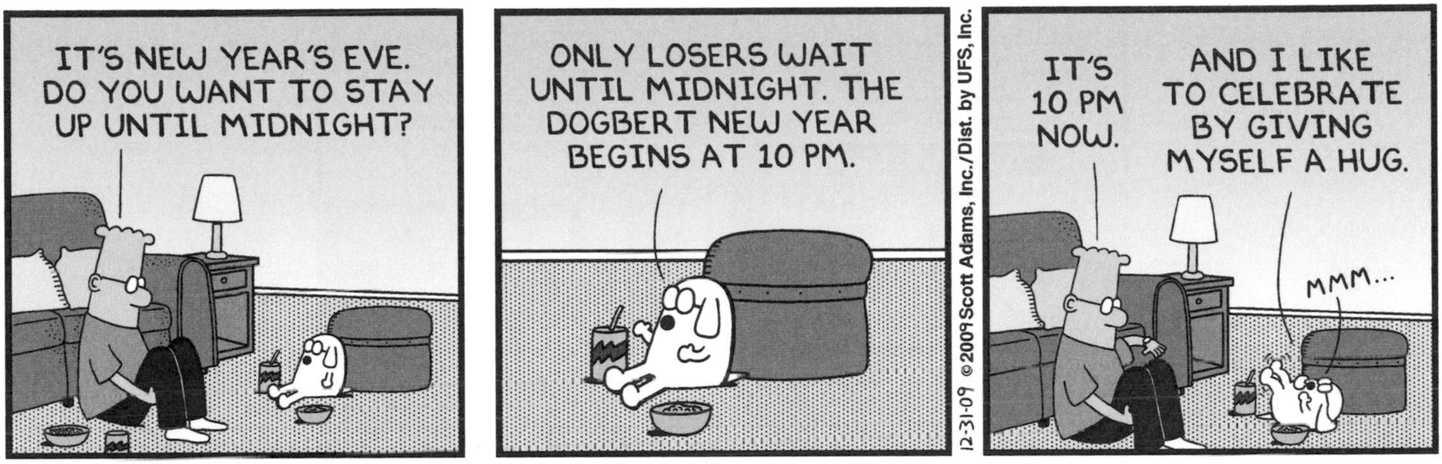
IT'S NEW YEAR'S EVE. DO YOU WANT TO STAY UP UNTIL MIDNIGHT?
ONLY LOSERS WAIT UNTIL MIDNIGHT. THE DOGBERT NEW YEAR BEGINS AT 10 PM.
12-31-09 ©2009 Scott Adams, Inc./Dist. by UFS, Inc.
IT'S 10 PM NOW.
AND I LIKE TO CELEBRATE BY GIVING MYSELF A HUG.
MMM...

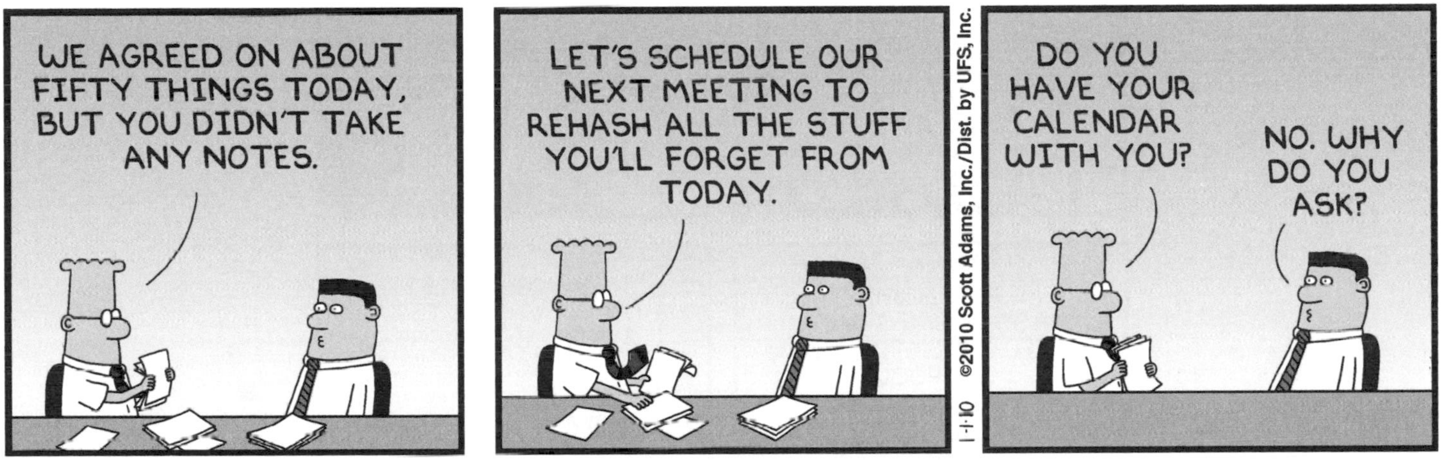
WE AGREED ON ABOUT FIFTY THINGS TODAY, BUT YOU DIDN'T TAKE ANY NOTES.
LET'S SCHEDULE OUR NEXT MEETING TO REHASH ALL THE STUFF YOU'LL FORGET FROM TODAY.
1-1-10 ©2010 Scott Adams, Inc./Dist. by UFS, Inc.
DO YOU HAVE YOUR CALENDAR WITH YOU?
NO. WHY DO YOU ASK?

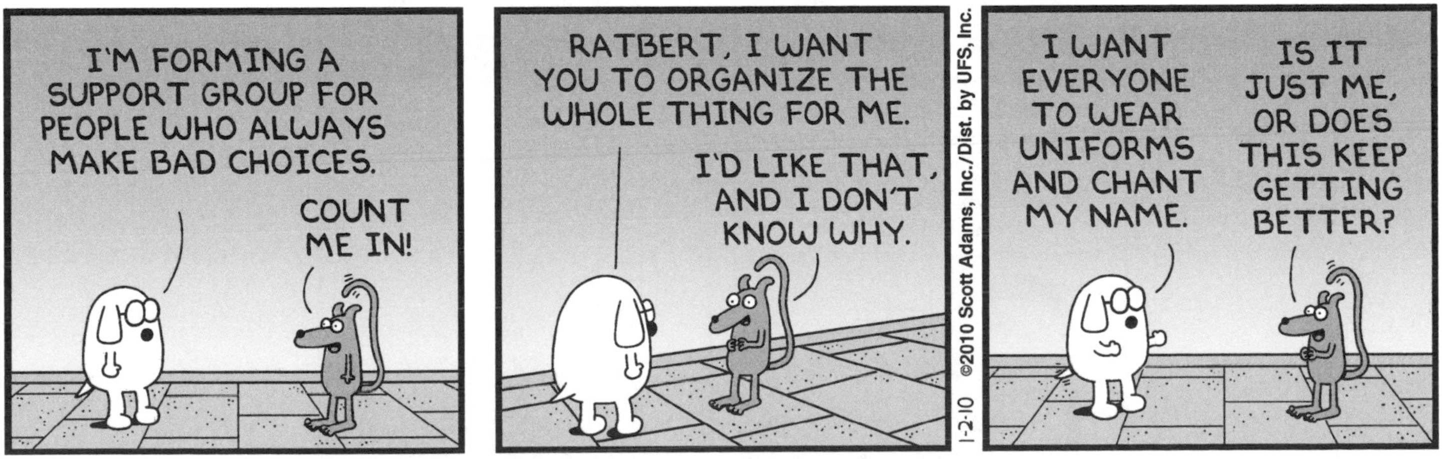
I'M FORMING A SUPPORT GROUP FOR PEOPLE WHO ALWAYS MAKE BAD CHOICES.
COUNT ME IN!
RATBERT, I WANT YOU TO ORGANIZE THE WHOLE THING FOR ME.
I'D LIKE THAT, AND I DON'T KNOW WHY.
1-2-10 ©2010 Scott Adams, Inc./Dist. by UFS, Inc.
I WANT EVERYONE TO WEAR UNIFORMS AND CHANT MY NAME.
IS IT JUST ME, OR DOES THIS KEEP GETTING BETTER?

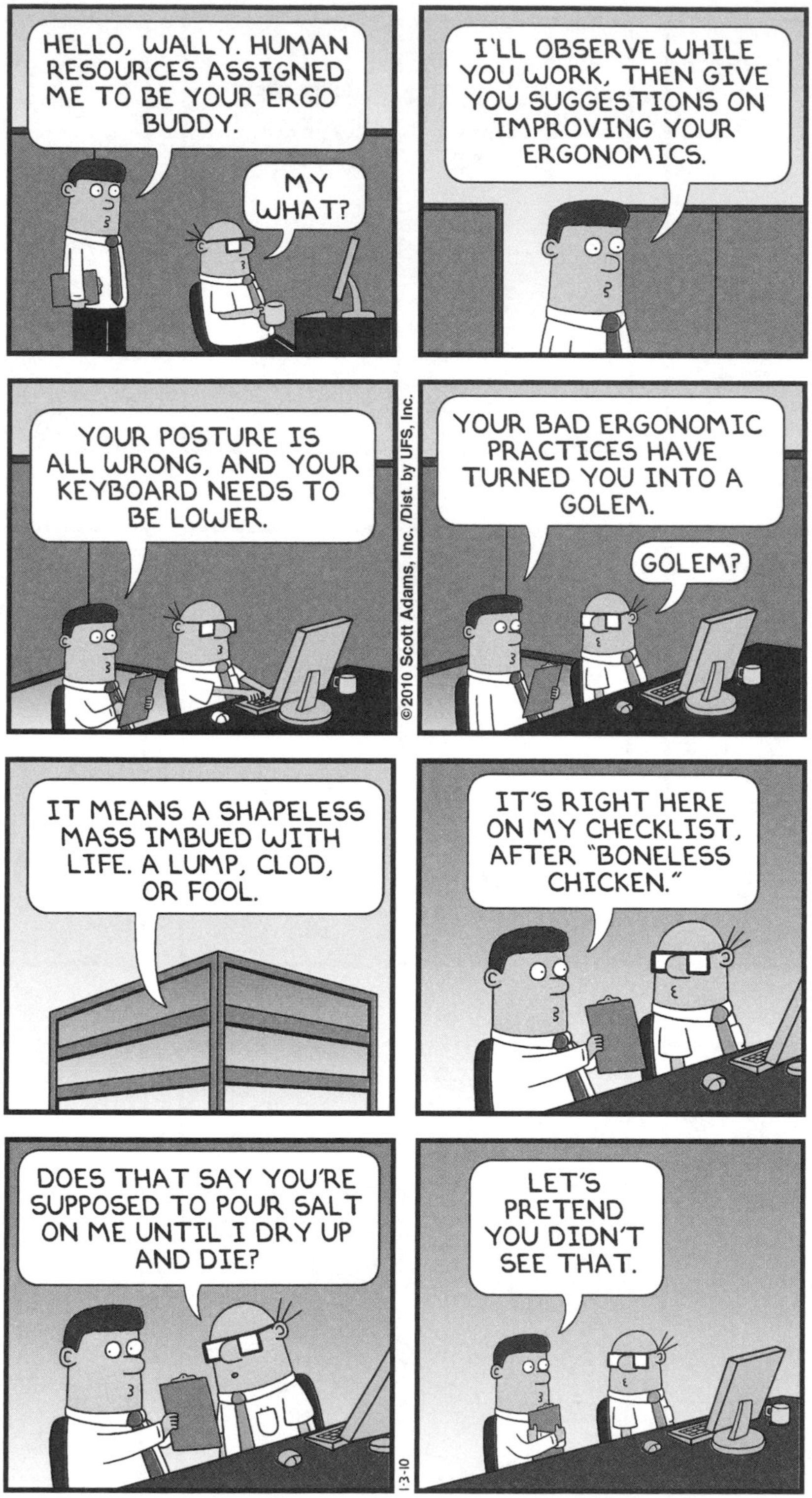
HELLO, WALLY. HUMAN RESOURCES ASSIGNED ME TO BE YOUR ERGO BUDDY.
MY WHAT?
I'LL OBSERVE WHILE YOU WORK, THEN GIVE YOU SUGGESTIONS ON IMPROVING YOUR ERGONOMICS.
YOUR POSTURE IS ALL WRONG, AND YOUR KEYBOARD NEEDS TO BE LOWER.
YOUR BAD ERGONOMIC PRACTICES HAVE TURNED YOU INTO A GOLEM.
GOLEM?
IT MEANS A SHAPELESS MASS IMBUED WITH LIFE. A LUMP, CLOD, OR FOOL.
IT'S RIGHT HERE ON MY CHECKLIST, AFTER "BONELESS CHICKEN."
DOES THAT SAY YOU'RE SUPPOSED TO POUR SALT ON ME UNTIL I DRY UP AND DIE?
LET'S PRETEND YOU DIDN'T SEE THAT.
1-3-10

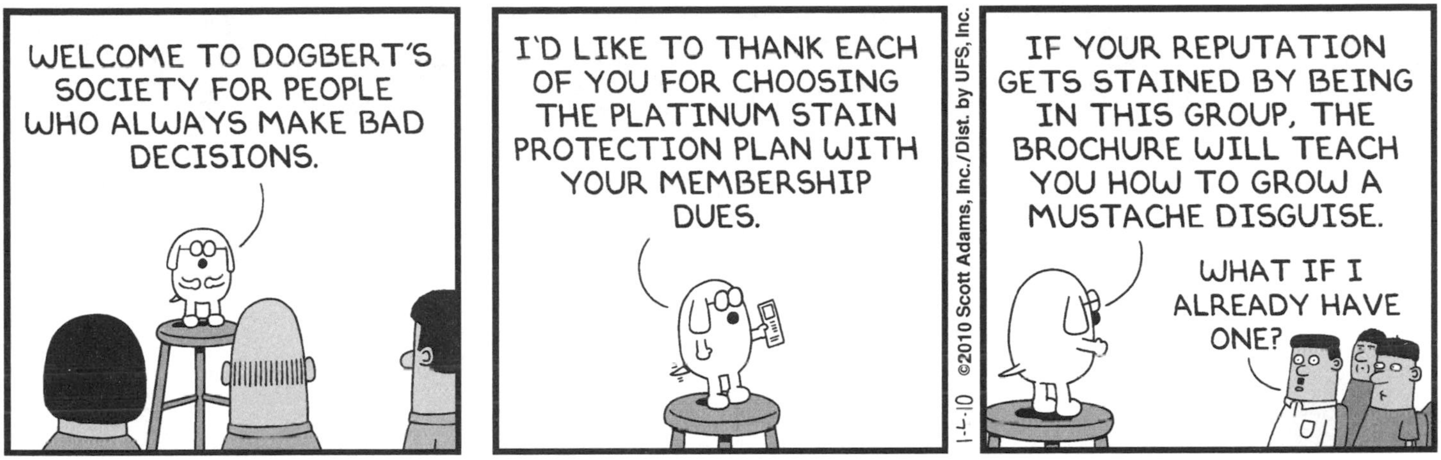
WELCOME TO DOGBERT'S SOCIETY FOR PEOPLE WHO ALWAYS MAKE BAD DECISIONS.
I'D LIKE TO THANK EACH OF YOU FOR CHOOSING THE PLATINUM STAIN PROTECTION PLAN WITH YOUR MEMBERSHIP DUES.
1-4-10 ©2010 Scott Adams, Inc./Dist. by UFS, Inc.
IF YOUR REPUTATION GETS STAINED BY BEING IN THIS GROUP, THE BROCHURE WILL TEACH YOU HOW TO GROW A MUSTACHE DISGUISE.
WHAT IF I ALREADY HAVE ONE?

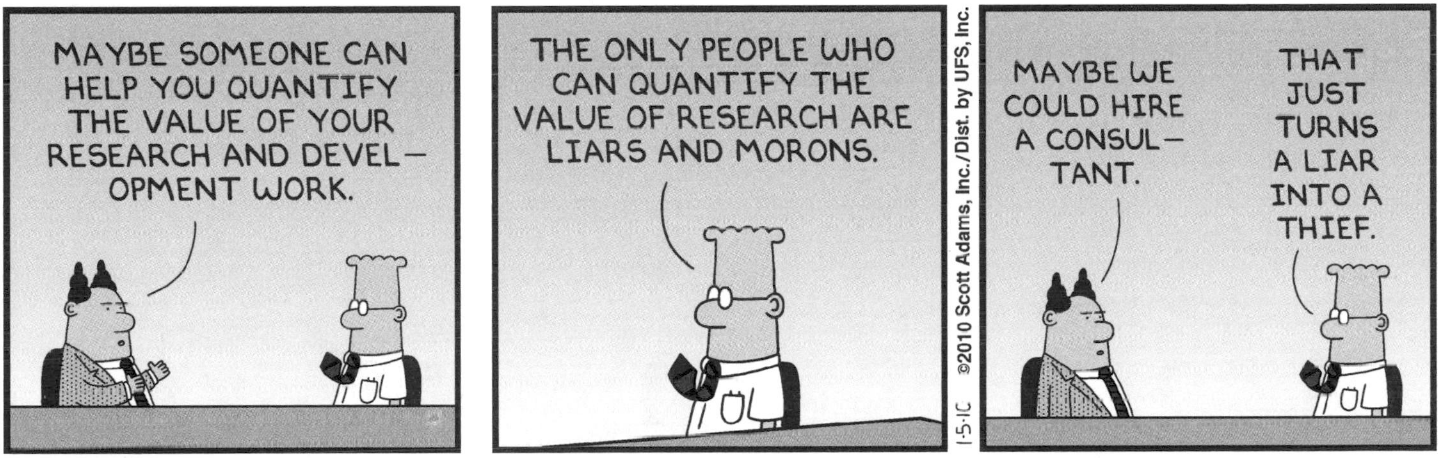
MAYBE SOMEONE CAN HELP YOU QUANTIFY THE VALUE OF YOUR RESEARCH AND DEVEL-OPMENT WORK.
THE ONLY PEOPLE WHO CAN QUANTIFY THE VALUE OF RESEARCH ARE LIARS AND MORONS.
1-5-10 ©2010 Scott Adams, Inc./Dist. by UFS, Inc.
MAYBE WE COULD HIRE A CONSUL-TANT.
THAT JUST TURNS A LIAR INTO A THIEF.

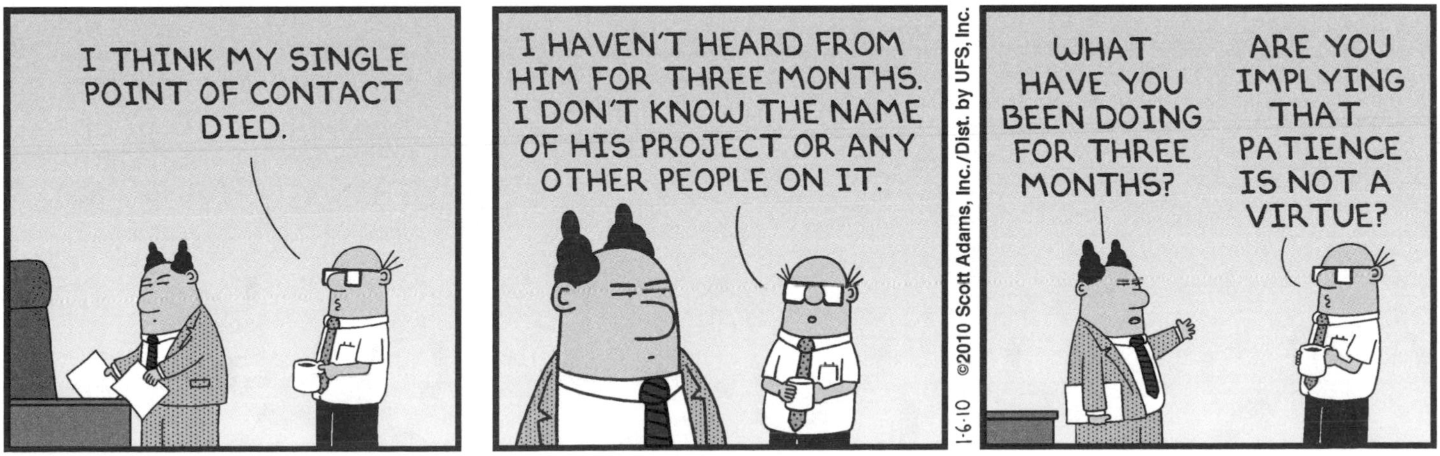
I THINK MY SINGLE POINT OF CONTACT DIED.
I HAVEN'T HEARD FROM HIM FOR THREE MONTHS. I DON'T KNOW THE NAME OF HIS PROJECT OR ANY OTHER PEOPLE ON IT.
1-6-10 ©2010 Scott Adams, Inc./Dist. by UFS, Inc.
WHAT HAVE YOU BEEN DOING FOR THREE MONTHS?
ARE YOU IMPLYING THAT PATIENCE IS NOT A VIRTUE?

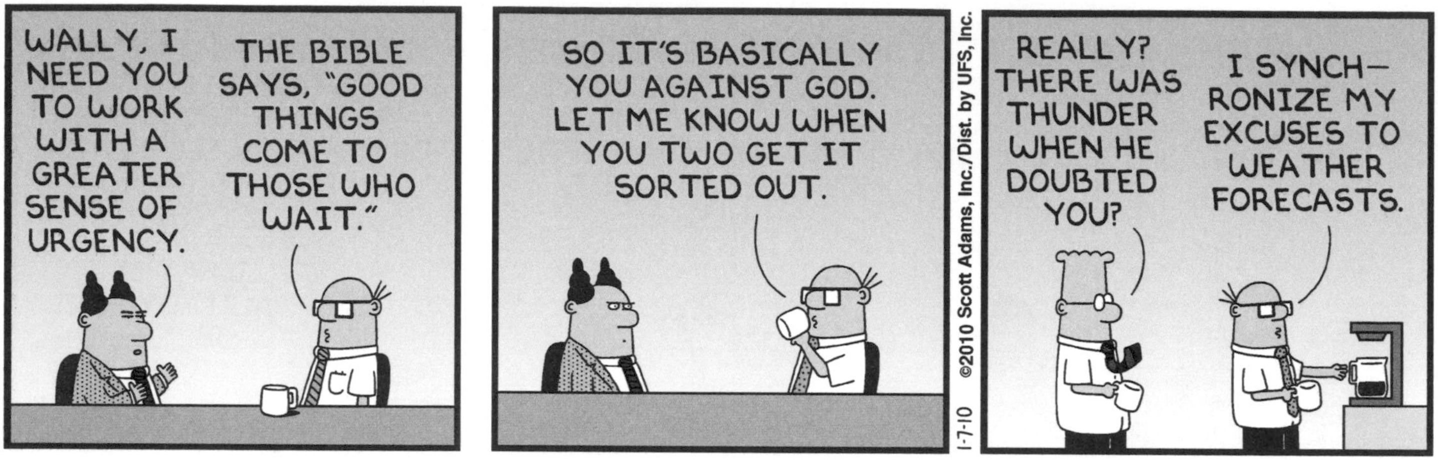
WALLY, I NEED YOU TO WORK WITH A GREATER SENSE OF URGENCY.
THE BIBLE SAYS, "GOOD THINGS COME TO THOSE WHO WAIT."
SO IT'S BASICALLY YOU AGAINST GOD. LET ME KNOW WHEN YOU TWO GET IT SORTED OUT.
1-7-10 ©2010 Scott Adams, Inc./Dist. by UFS, Inc.
REALLY? THERE WAS THUNDER WHEN HE DOUBTED YOU?
I SYNCH-RONIZE MY EXCUSES TO WEATHER FORECASTS.

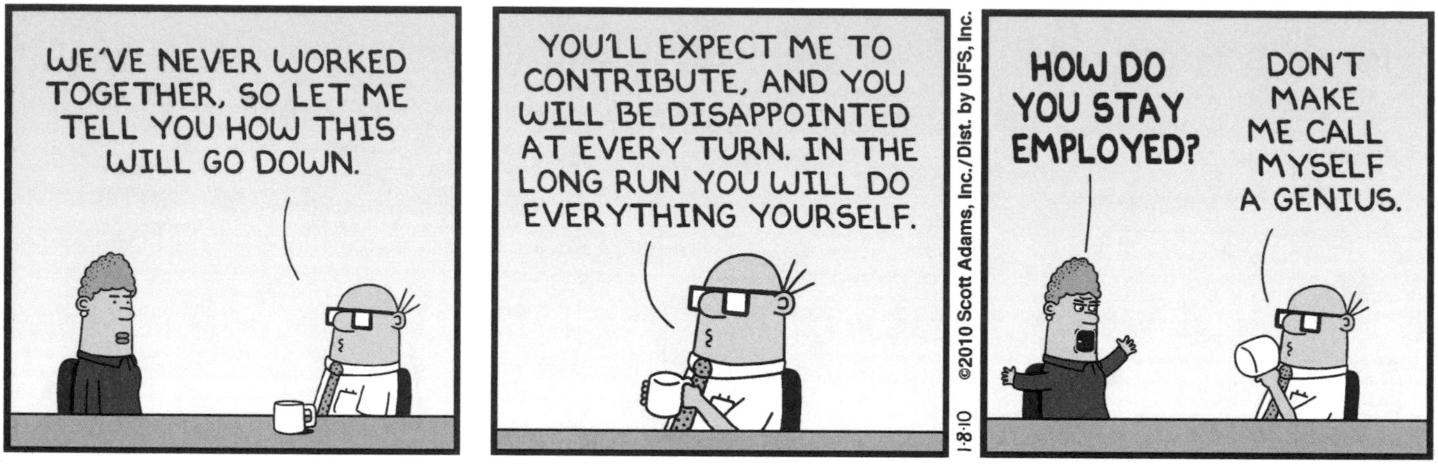
WE'VE NEVER WORKED TOGETHER, SO LET ME TELL YOU HOW THIS WILL GO DOWN.
YOU'LL EXPECT ME TO CONTRIBUTE, AND YOU WILL BE DISAPPOINTED AT EVERY TURN. IN THE LONG RUN YOU WILL DO EVERYTHING YOURSELF.
1-8-10 ©2010 Scott Adams, Inc./Dist. by UFS, Inc.
HOW DO YOU STAY EMPLOYED?
DON'T MAKE ME CALL MYSELF A GENIUS.

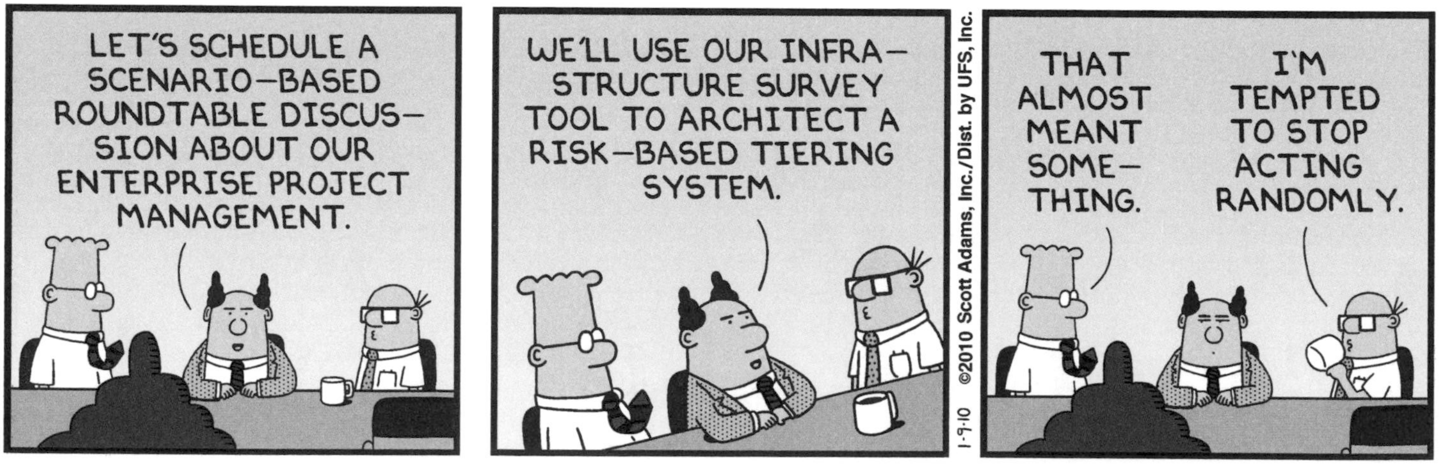
LET'S SCHEDULE A SCENARIO-BASED ROUNDTABLE DISCUS-SION ABOUT OUR ENTERPRISE PROJECT MANAGEMENT.
WE'LL USE OUR INFRA-STRUCTURE SURVEY TOOL TO ARCHITECT A RISK-BASED TIERING SYSTEM.
1-9-10 ©2010 Scott Adams, Inc./Dist. by UFS, Inc.
THAT ALMOST MEANT SOME-THING.
I'M TEMPTED TO STOP ACTING RANDOMLY.

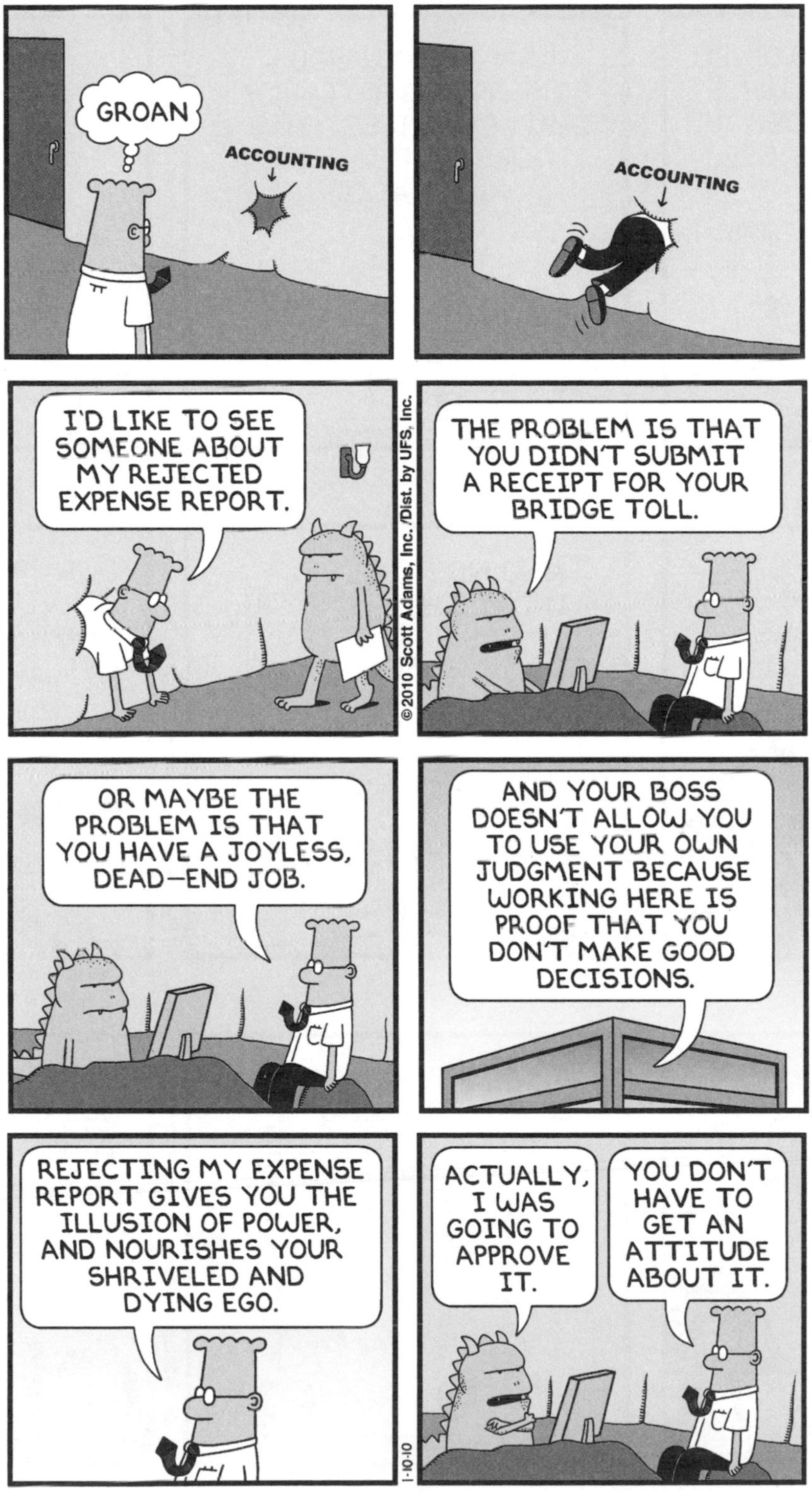
GROAN
ACCOUNTING
ACCOUNTING
I'D LIKE TO SEE SOMEONE ABOUT MY REJECTED EXPENSE REPORT.
©2010 Scott Adams, Inc./Dist. by UFS, Inc.
THE PROBLEM IS THAT YOU DIDN'T SUBMIT A RECEIPT FOR YOUR BRIDGE TOLL.
OR MAYBE THE PROBLEM IS THAT YOU HAVE A JOYLESS, DEAD—END JOB.
AND YOUR BOSS DOESN'T ALLOW YOU TO USE YOUR OWN JUDGMENT BECAUSE WORKING HERE IS PROOF THAT YOU DON'T MAKE GOOD DECISIONS.
REJECTING MY EXPENSE REPORT GIVES YOU THE ILLUSION OF POWER, AND NOURISHES YOUR SHRIVELED AND DYING EGO.
1-10-10
ACTUALLY, I WAS GOING TO APPROVE IT.
YOU DON'T HAVE TO GET AN ATTITUDE ABOUT IT.

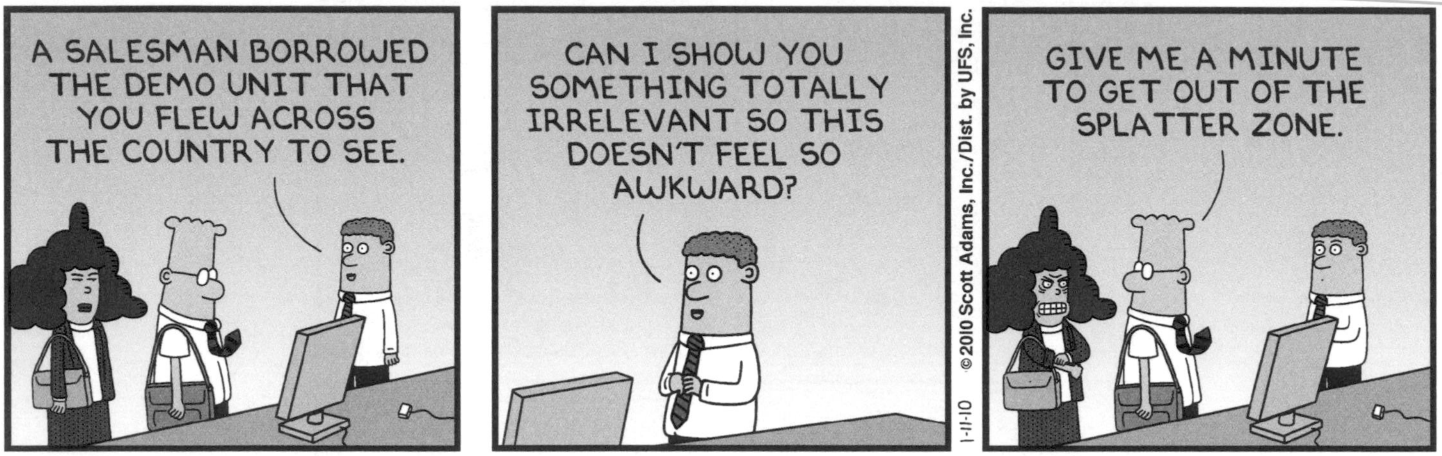
A SALESMAN BORROWED THE DEMO UNIT THAT YOU FLEW ACROSS THE COUNTRY TO SEE.
CAN I SHOW YOU SOMETHING TOTALLY IRRELEVANT SO THIS DOESN'T FEEL SO AWKWARD?
1-11-10 ©2010 Scott Adams, Inc./Dist. by UFS, Inc.
GIVE ME A MINUTE TO GET OUT OF THE SPLATTER ZONE.

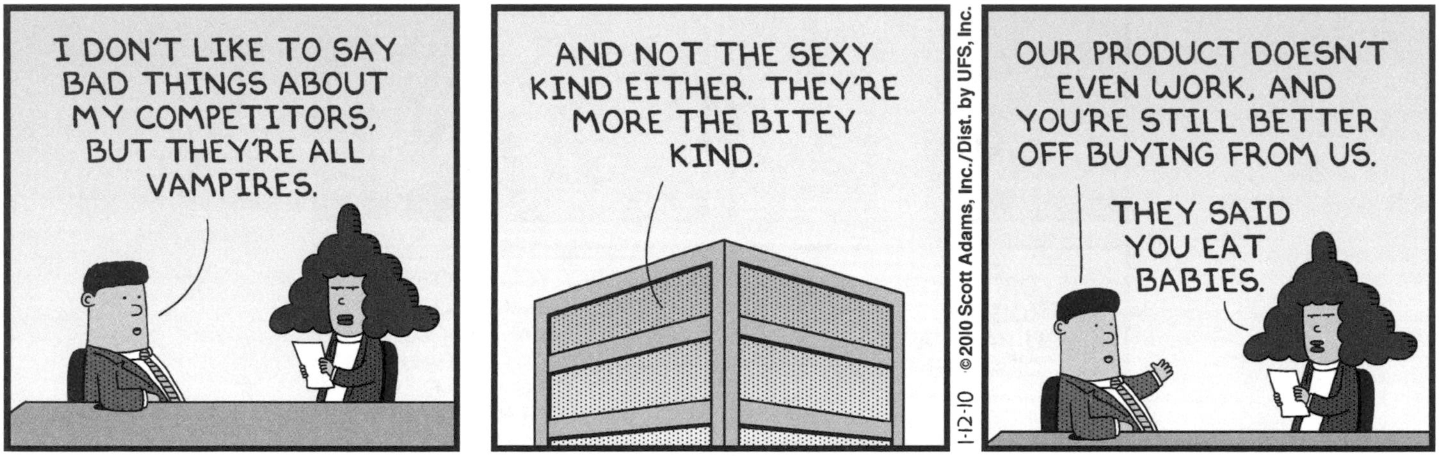
I DON'T LIKE TO SAY BAD THINGS ABOUT MY COMPETITORS, BUT THEY'RE ALL VAMPIRES.
AND NOT THE SEXY KIND EITHER. THEY'RE MORE THE BITEY KIND.
1-12-10 ©2010 Scott Adams, Inc./Dist. by UFS, Inc.
OUR PRODUCT DOESN'T EVEN WORK, AND YOU'RE STILL BETTER OFF BUYING FROM US.
THEY SAID YOU EAT BABIES.

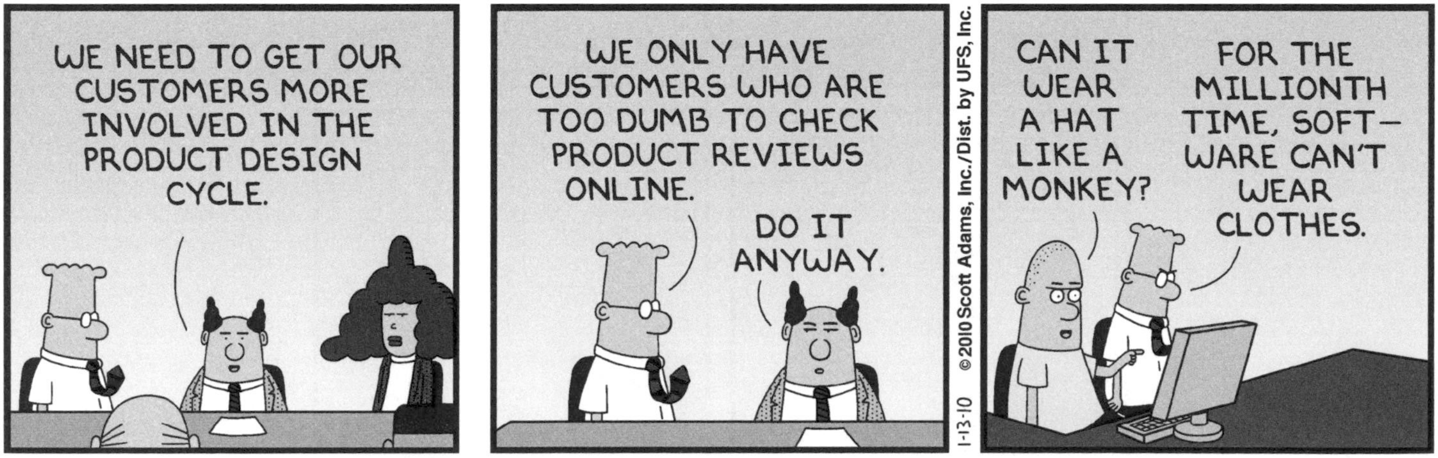
WE NEED TO GET OUR CUSTOMERS MORE INVOLVED IN THE PRODUCT DESIGN CYCLE.
WE ONLY HAVE CUSTOMERS WHO ARE TOO DUMB TO CHECK PRODUCT REVIEWS ONLINE.
DO IT ANYWAY.
1-13-10 ©2010 Scott Adams, Inc./Dist. by UFS, Inc.
CAN IT WEAR A HAT LIKE A MONKEY?
FOR THE MILLIONTH TIME, SOFT-WARE CAN'T WEAR CLOTHES.

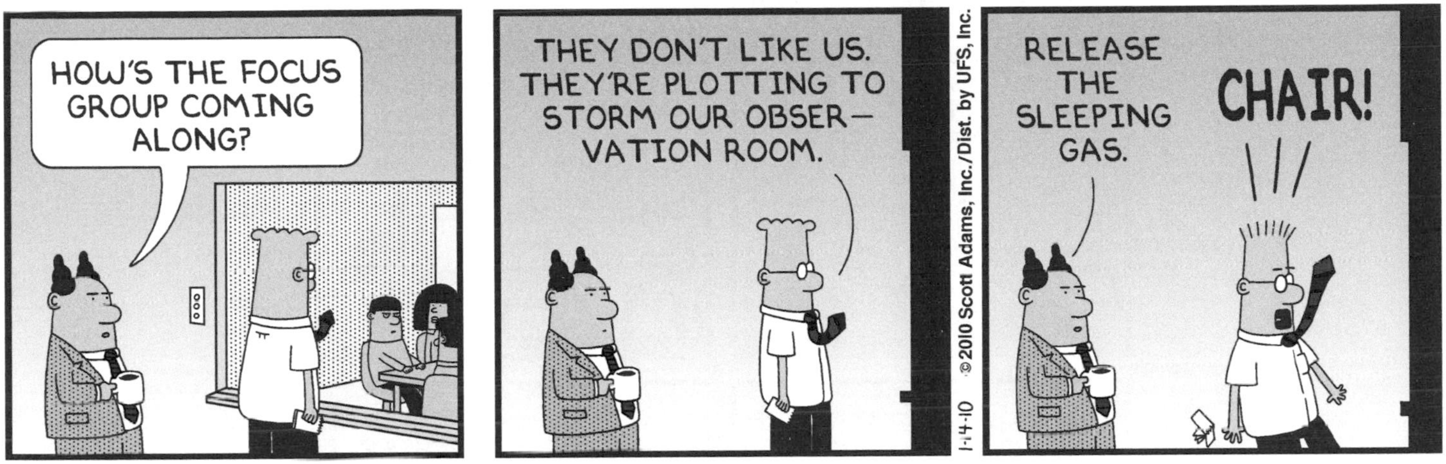
HOW'S THE FOCUS GROUP COMING ALONG?
THEY DON'T LIKE US. THEY'RE PLOTTING TO STORM OUR OBSER-VATION ROOM.
1-14-10 ©2010 Scott Adams, Inc./Dist. by UFS, Inc.
RELEASE THE SLEEPING GAS.
CHAIR!

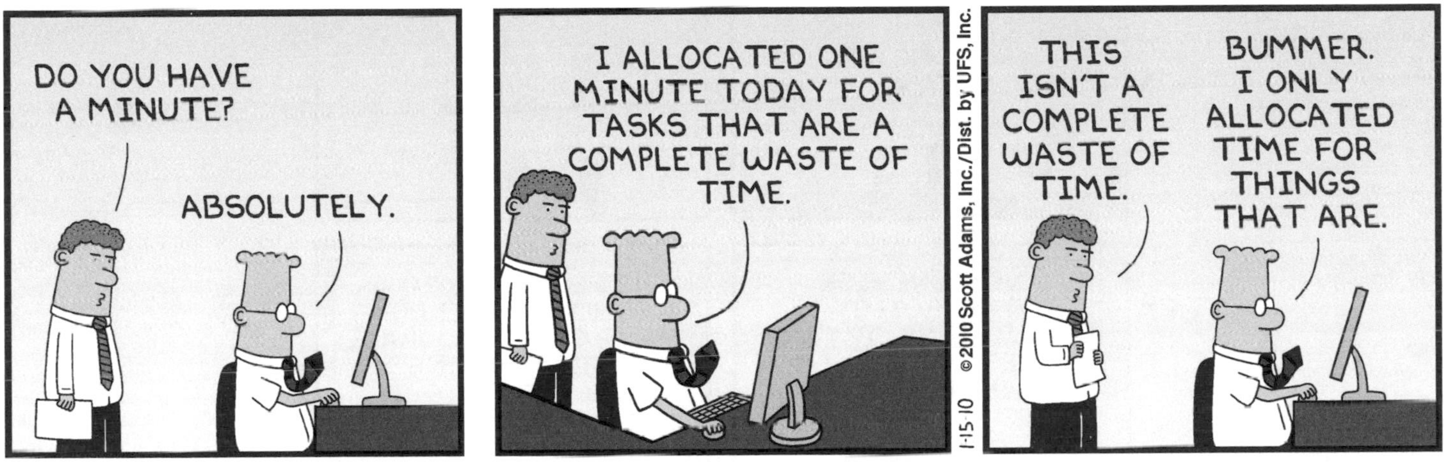
DO YOU HAVE A MINUTE?
ABSOLUTELY.
I ALLOCATED ONE MINUTE TODAY FOR TASKS THAT ARE A COMPLETE WASTE OF TIME.
1-15-10 ©2010 Scott Adams, Inc./Dist. by UFS, Inc.
THIS ISN'T A COMPLETE WASTE OF TIME.
BUMMER. I ONLY ALLOCATED TIME FOR THINGS THAT ARE.

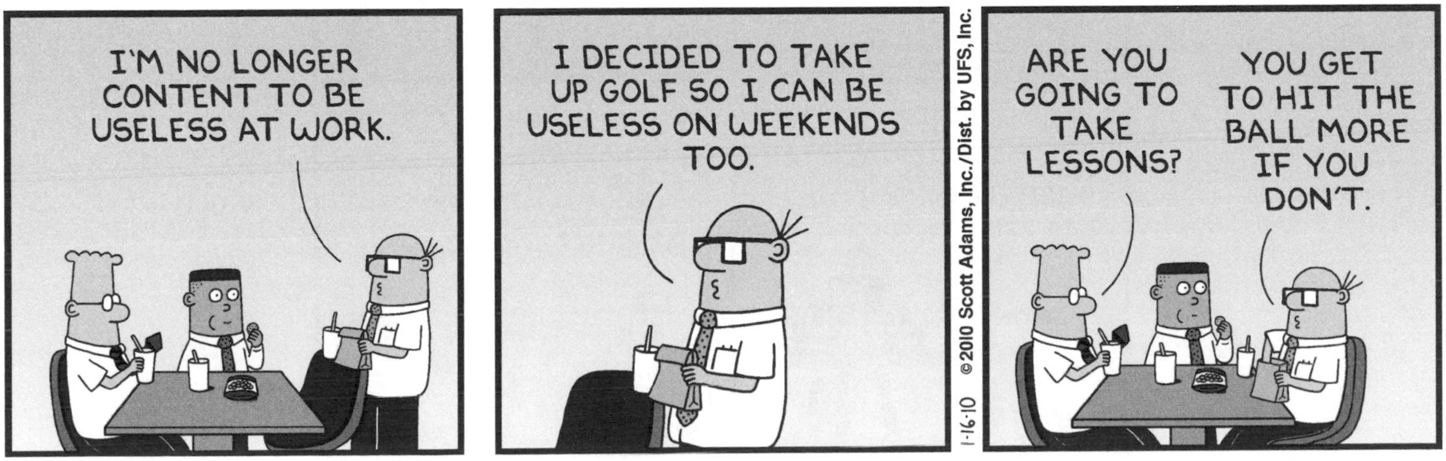
I'M NO LONGER CONTENT TO BE USELESS AT WORK.
I DECIDED TO TAKE UP GOLF SO I CAN BE USELESS ON WEEKENDS TOO.
1-16-10 ©2010 Scott Adams, Inc./Dist. by UFS, Inc.
ARE YOU GOING TO TAKE LESSONS?
YOU GET TO HIT THE BALL MORE IF YOU DON'T.

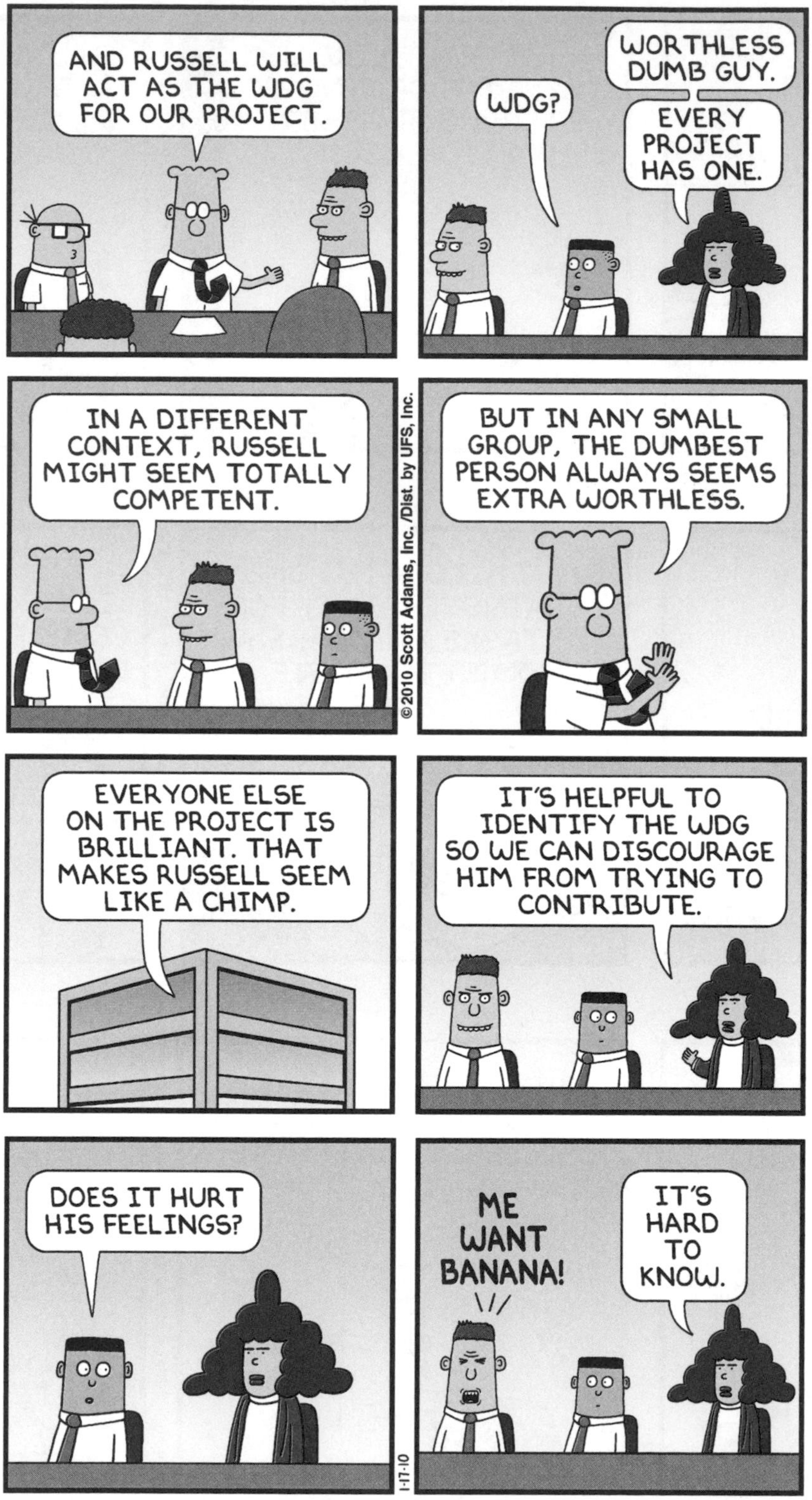
AND RUSSELL WILL ACT AS THE WDG FOR OUR PROJECT.
WDG?
WORTHLESS DUMB GUY.
EVERY PROJECT HAS ONE.
IN A DIFFERENT CONTEXT, RUSSELL MIGHT SEEM TOTALLY COMPETENT.
©2010 Scott Adams, Inc. /Dist. by UFS, Inc.
BUT IN ANY SMALL GROUP, THE DUMBEST PERSON ALWAYS SEEMS EXTRA WORTHLESS.
EVERYONE ELSE ON THE PROJECT IS BRILLIANT. THAT MAKES RUSSELL SEEM LIKE A CHIMP.
IT'S HELPFUL TO IDENTIFY THE WDG SO WE CAN DISCOURAGE HIM FROM TRYING TO CONTRIBUTE.
DOES IT HURT HIS FEELINGS?
ME WANT BANANA!
IT'S HARD TO KNOW.
1-17-10

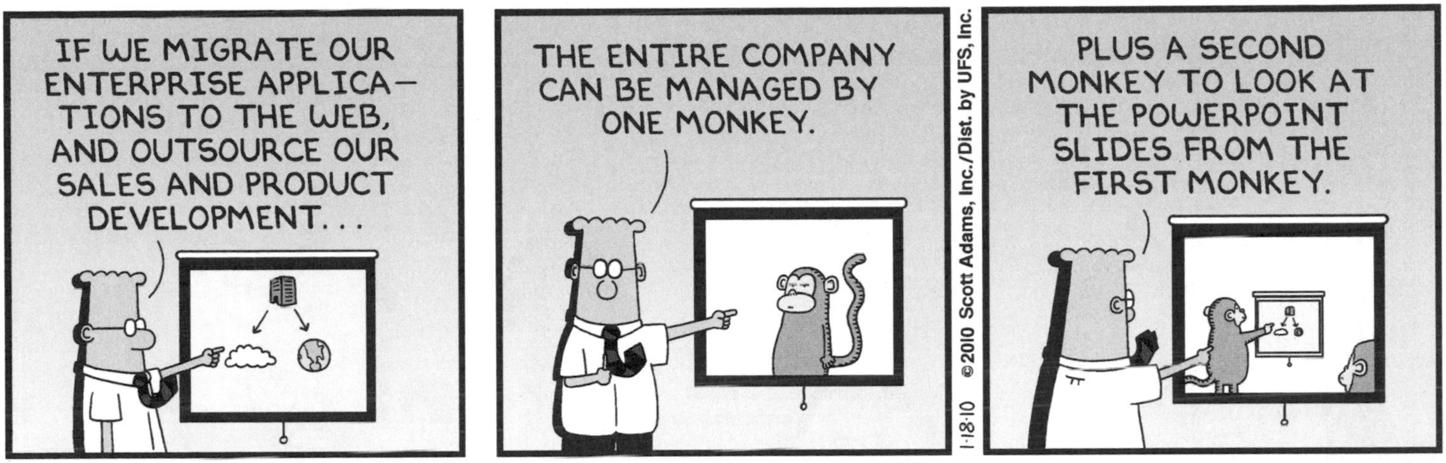
IF WE MIGRATE OUR ENTERPRISE APPLICA–TIONS TO THE WEB, AND OUTSOURCE OUR SALES AND PRODUCT DEVELOPMENT...
THE ENTIRE COMPANY CAN BE MANAGED BY ONE MONKEY.
1·18·10 ©2010 Scott Adams, Inc./Dist. by UFS, Inc.
PLUS A SECOND MONKEY TO LOOK AT THE POWERPOINT SLIDES FROM THE FIRST MONKEY.

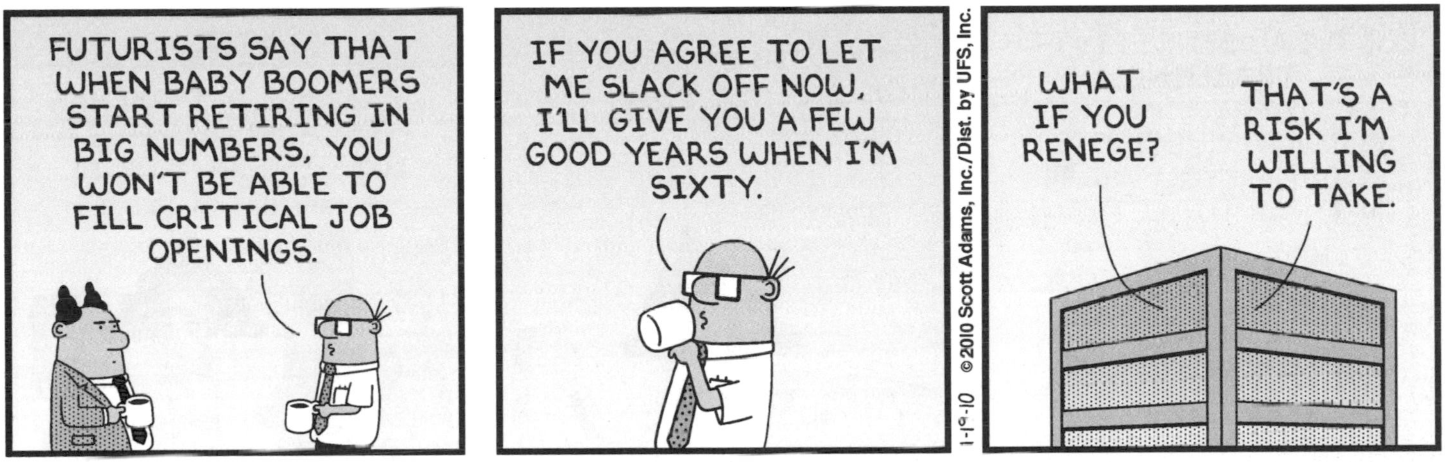
FUTURISTS SAY THAT WHEN BABY BOOMERS START RETIRING IN BIG NUMBERS, YOU WON'T BE ABLE TO FILL CRITICAL JOB OPENINGS.
IF YOU AGREE TO LET ME SLACK OFF NOW, I'LL GIVE YOU A FEW GOOD YEARS WHEN I'M SIXTY.
1·19·10 ©2010 Scott Adams, Inc./Dist. by UFS, Inc.
WHAT IF YOU RENEGE?
THAT'S A RISK I'M WILLING TO TAKE.

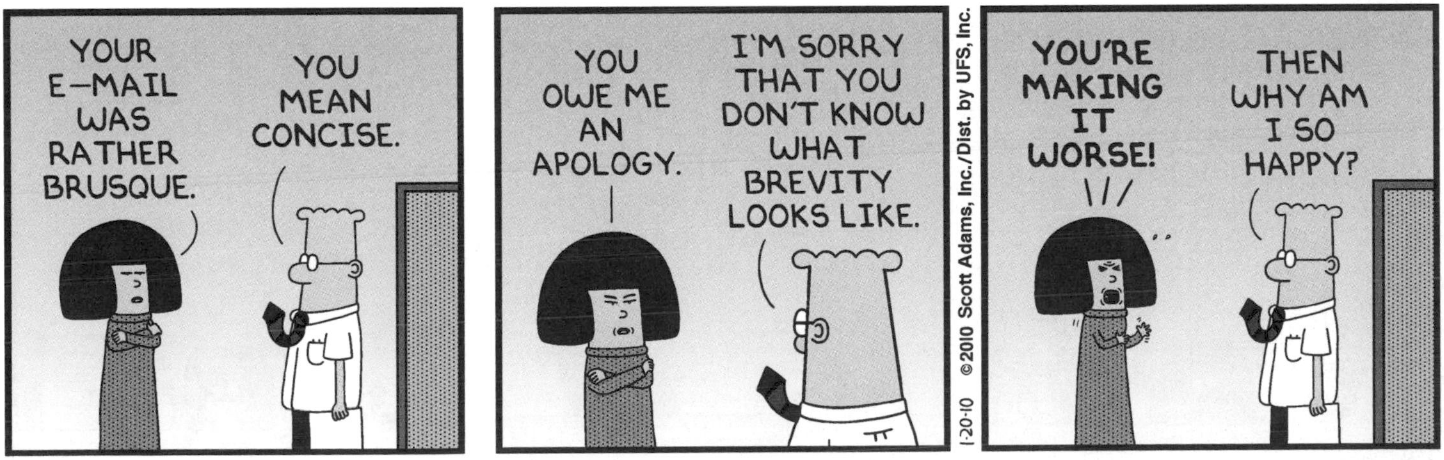
YOUR E–MAIL WAS RATHER BRUSQUE.
YOU MEAN CONCISE.
YOU OWE ME AN APOLOGY.
I'M SORRY THAT YOU DON'T KNOW WHAT BREVITY LOOKS LIKE.
1·20·10 ©2010 Scott Adams, Inc./Dist. by UFS, Inc.
YOU'RE MAKING IT WORSE!
THEN WHY AM I SO HAPPY?

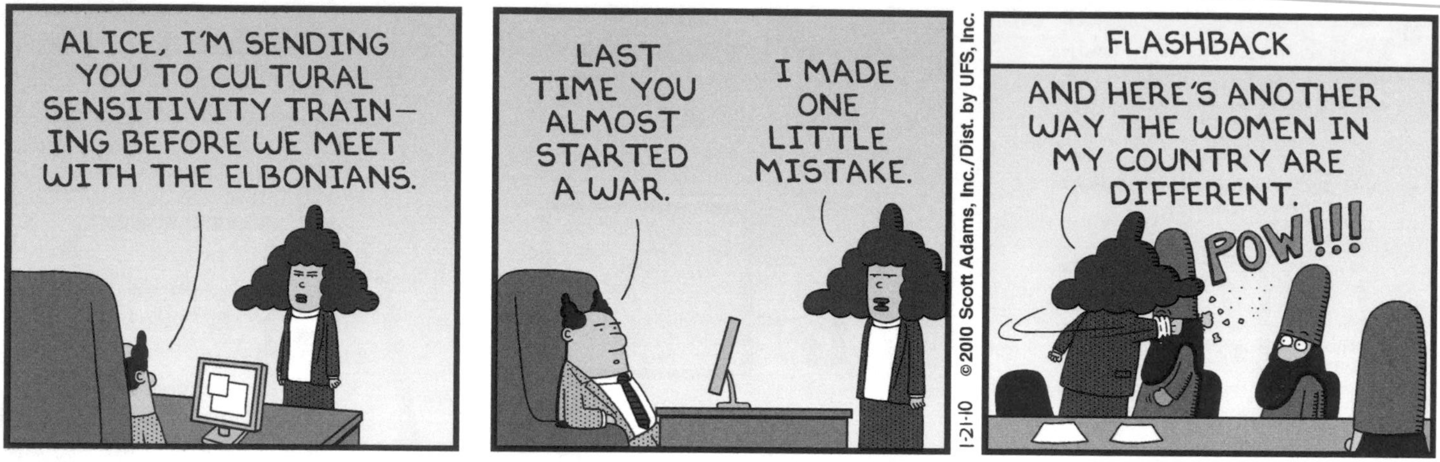
ALICE, I'M SENDING YOU TO CULTURAL SENSITIVITY TRAIN- ING BEFORE WE MEET WITH THE ELBONIANS.
LAST TIME YOU ALMOST STARTED A WAR.
I MADE ONE LITTLE MISTAKE.
1-21-10 ©2010 Scott Adams, Inc./Dist. by UFS, Inc.
FLASHBACK
AND HERE'S ANOTHER WAY THE WOMEN IN MY COUNTRY ARE DIFFERENT.
POW!!!

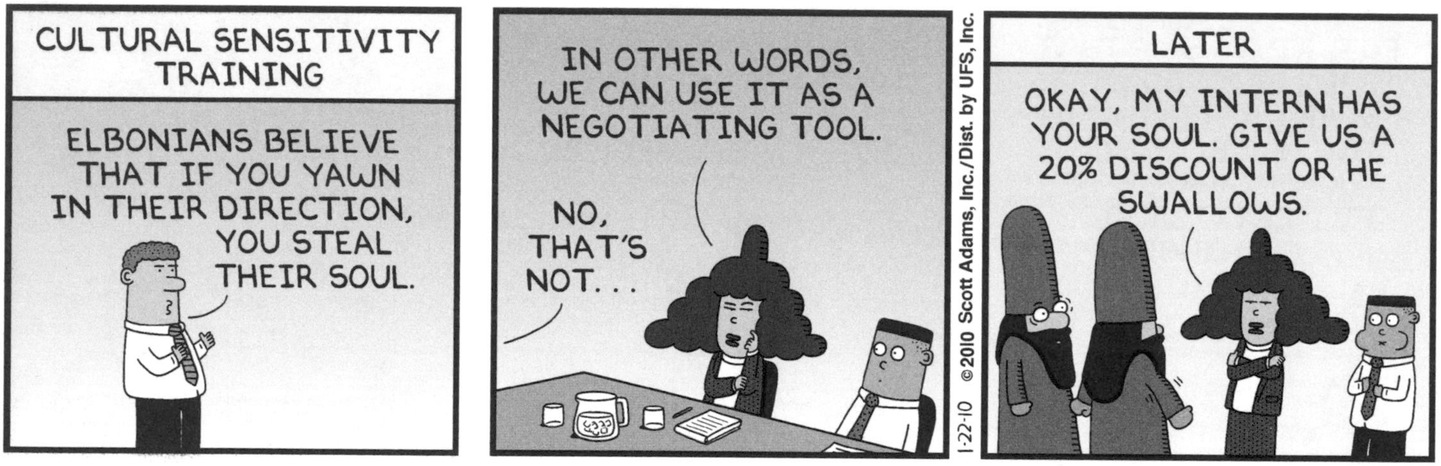
CULTURAL SENSITIVITY TRAINING
ELBONIANS BELIEVE THAT IF YOU YAWN IN THEIR DIRECTION, YOU STEAL THEIR SOUL.
IN OTHER WORDS, WE CAN USE IT AS A NEGOTIATING TOOL.
NO, THAT'S NOT. . .
1-22-10 ©2010 Scott Adams, Inc./Dist. by UFS, Inc.
LATER
OKAY, MY INTERN HAS YOUR SOUL. GIVE US A 20% DISCOUNT OR HE SWALLOWS.

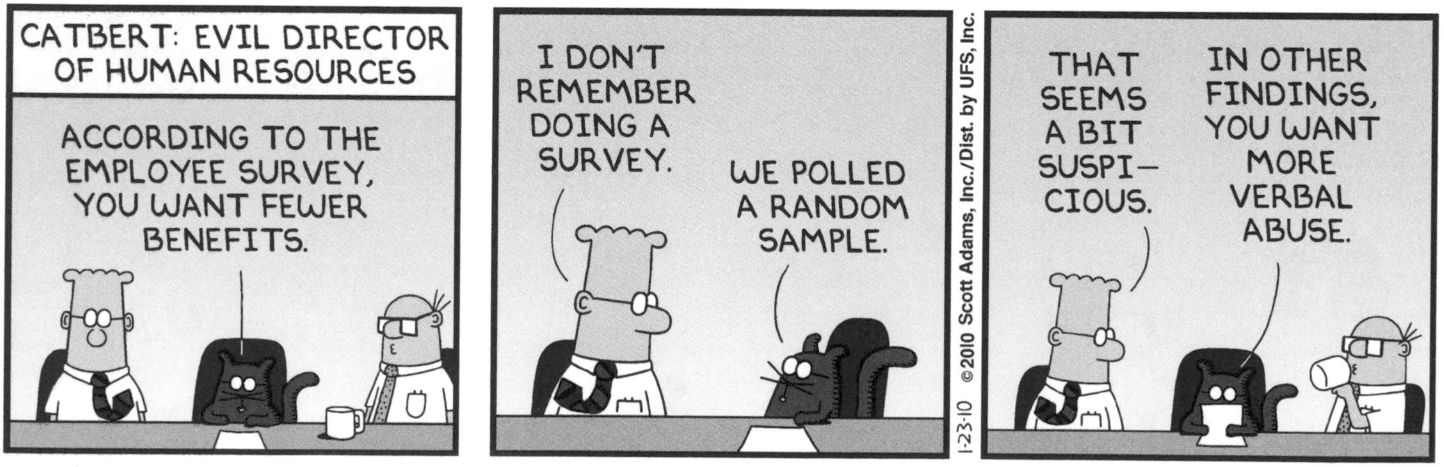
CATBERT: EVIL DIRECTOR OF HUMAN RESOURCES
ACCORDING TO THE EMPLOYEE SURVEY, YOU WANT FEWER BENEFITS.
I DON'T REMEMBER DOING A SURVEY.
WE POLLED A RANDOM SAMPLE.
1-23-10 ©2010 Scott Adams, Inc./Dist. by UFS, Inc.
THAT SEEMS A BIT SUSPI- CIOUS.
IN OTHER FINDINGS, YOU WANT MORE VERBAL ABUSE.

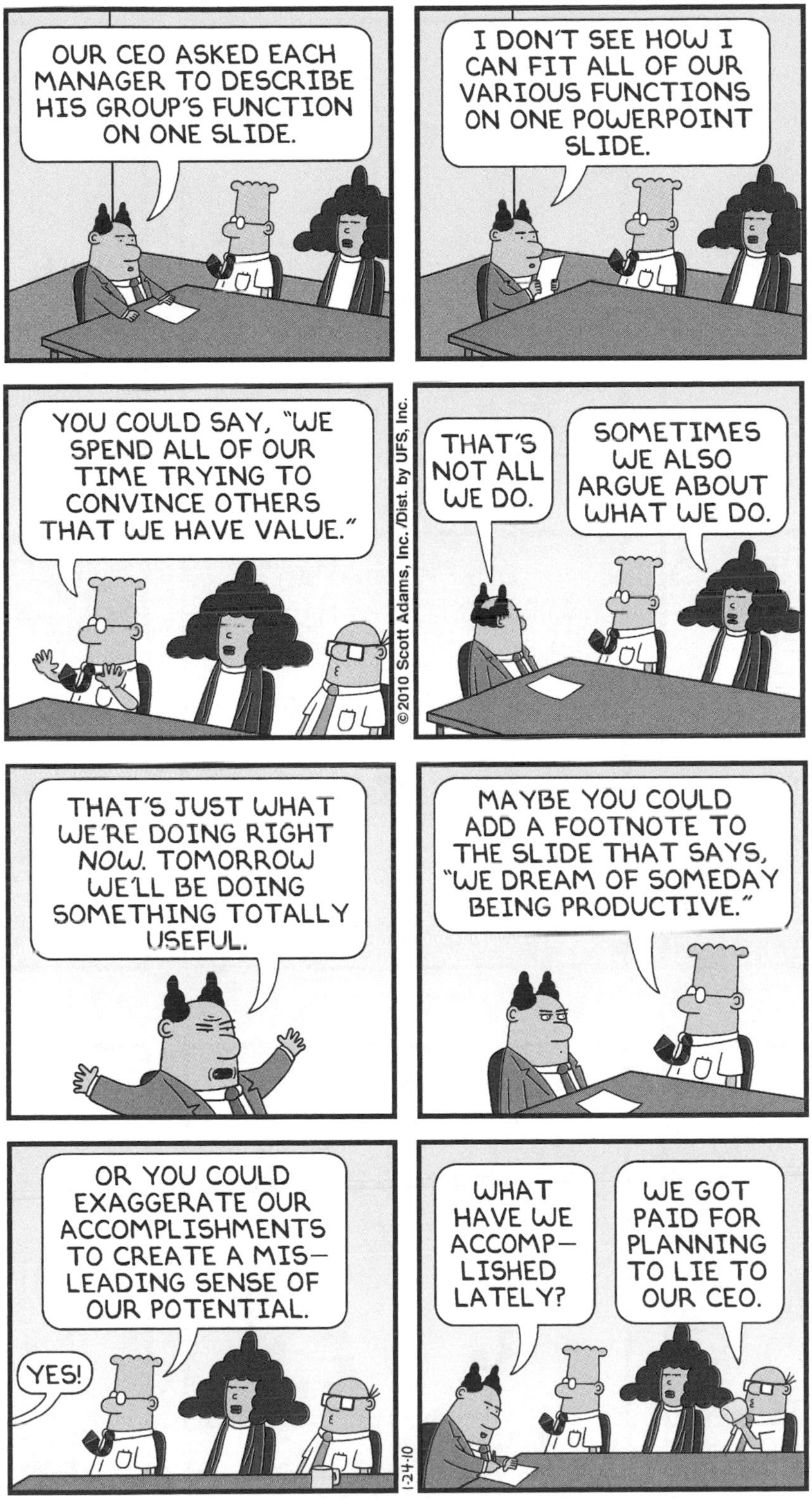
OUR CEO ASKED EACH MANAGER TO DESCRIBE HIS GROUP'S FUNCTION ON ONE SLIDE.
I DON'T SEE HOW I CAN FIT ALL OF OUR VARIOUS FUNCTIONS ON ONE POWERPOINT SLIDE.
YOU COULD SAY, "WE SPEND ALL OF OUR TIME TRYING TO CONVINCE OTHERS THAT WE HAVE VALUE."
©2010 Scott Adams, Inc. /Dist. by UFS, Inc.
THAT'S NOT ALL WE DO.
SOMETIMES WE ALSO ARGUE ABOUT WHAT WE DO.
THAT'S JUST WHAT WE'RE DOING RIGHT NOW. TOMORROW WE'LL BE DOING SOMETHING TOTALLY USEFUL.
MAYBE YOU COULD ADD A FOOTNOTE TO THE SLIDE THAT SAYS, "WE DREAM OF SOMEDAY BEING PRODUCTIVE."
OR YOU COULD EXAGGERATE OUR ACCOMPLISHMENTS TO CREATE A MIS-LEADING SENSE OF OUR POTENTIAL.
YES!
1-24-10
WHAT HAVE WE ACCOMP-LISHED LATELY?
WE GOT PAID FOR PLANNING TO LIE TO OUR CEO.

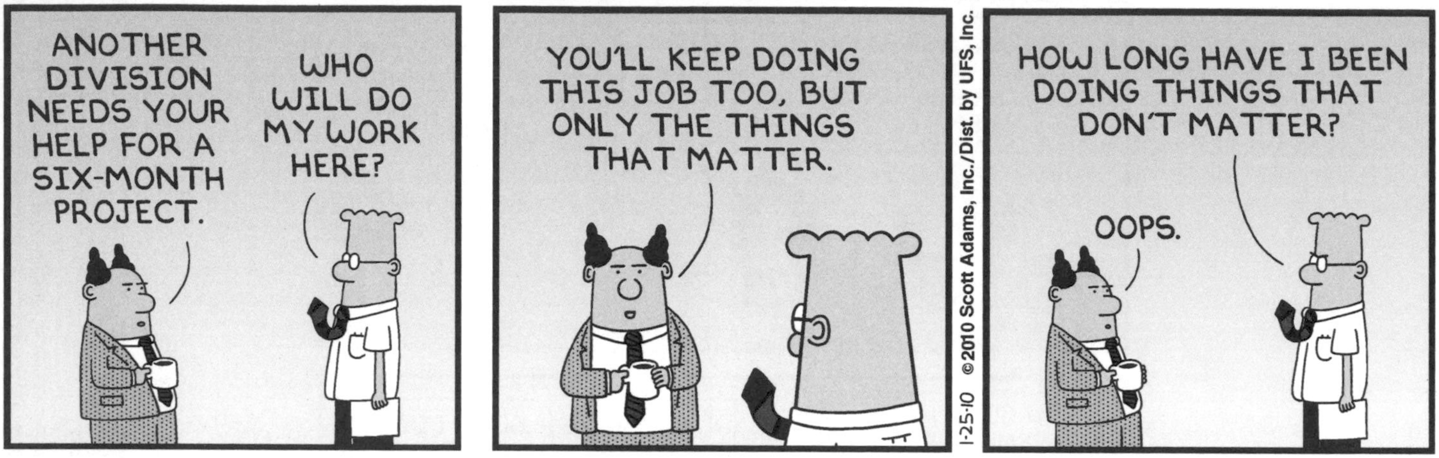
ANOTHER DIVISION NEEDS YOUR HELP FOR A SIX-MONTH PROJECT.
WHO WILL DO MY WORK HERE?
YOU'LL KEEP DOING THIS JOB TOO, BUT ONLY THE THINGS THAT MATTER.
1-25-10 ©2010 Scott Adams, Inc./Dist. by UFS, Inc.
HOW LONG HAVE I BEEN DOING THINGS THAT DON'T MATTER?
OOPS.

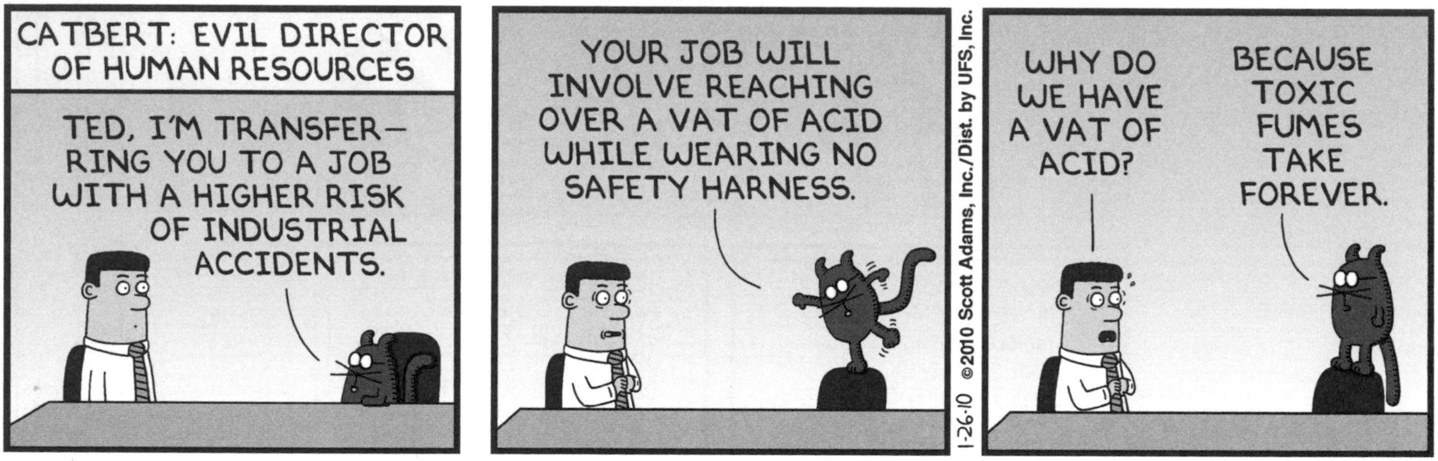
CATBERT: EVIL DIRECTOR OF HUMAN RESOURCES
TED, I'M TRANSFER-RING YOU TO A JOB WITH A HIGHER RISK OF INDUSTRIAL ACCIDENTS.
YOUR JOB WILL INVOLVE REACHING OVER A VAT OF ACID WHILE WEARING NO SAFETY HARNESS.
1-26-10 ©2010 Scott Adams, Inc./Dist. by UFS, Inc.
WHY DO WE HAVE A VAT OF ACID?
BECAUSE TOXIC FUMES TAKE FOREVER.

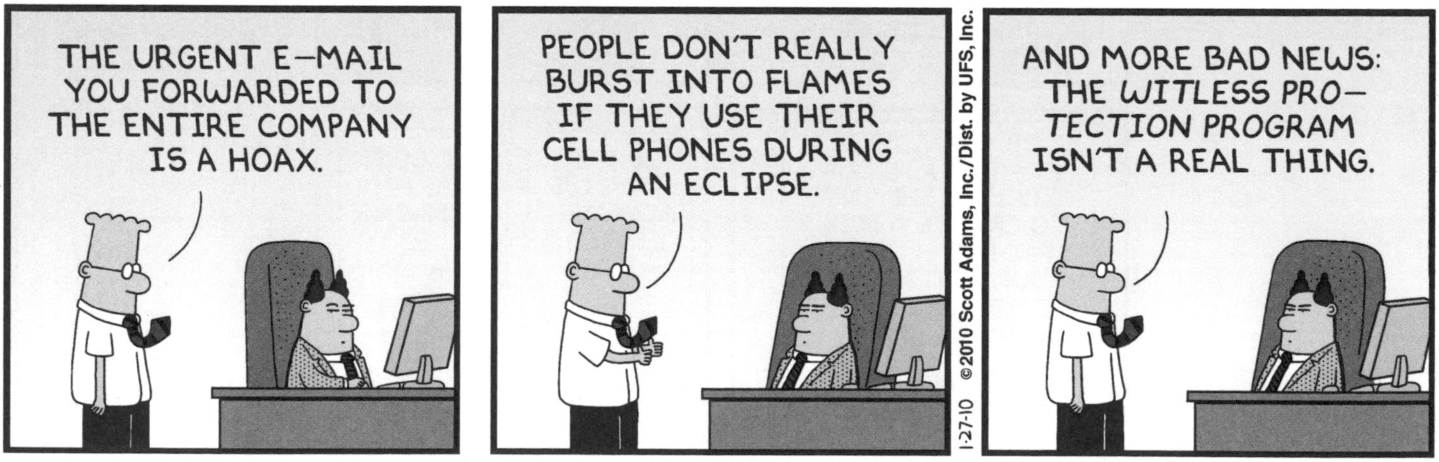
THE URGENT E-MAIL YOU FORWARDED TO THE ENTIRE COMPANY IS A HOAX.
PEOPLE DON'T REALLY BURST INTO FLAMES IF THEY USE THEIR CELL PHONES DURING AN ECLIPSE.
1-27-10 ©2010 Scott Adams, Inc./Dist. by UFS, Inc.
AND MORE BAD NEWS: THE *WITLESS PRO-TECTION PROGRAM* ISN'T A REAL THING.

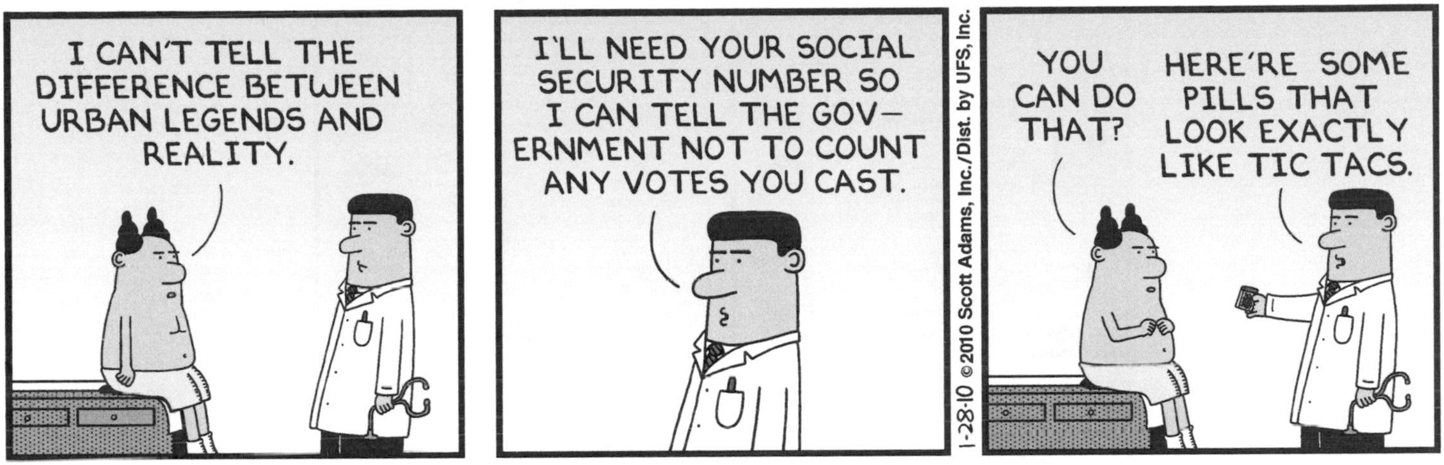
I CAN'T TELL THE DIFFERENCE BETWEEN URBAN LEGENDS AND REALITY.
I'LL NEED YOUR SOCIAL SECURITY NUMBER SO I CAN TELL THE GOV-ERNMENT NOT TO COUNT ANY VOTES YOU CAST.
1-28-10 ©2010 Scott Adams, Inc./Dist. by UFS, Inc.
YOU CAN DO THAT?
HERE'RE SOME PILLS THAT LOOK EXACTLY LIKE TIC TACS.

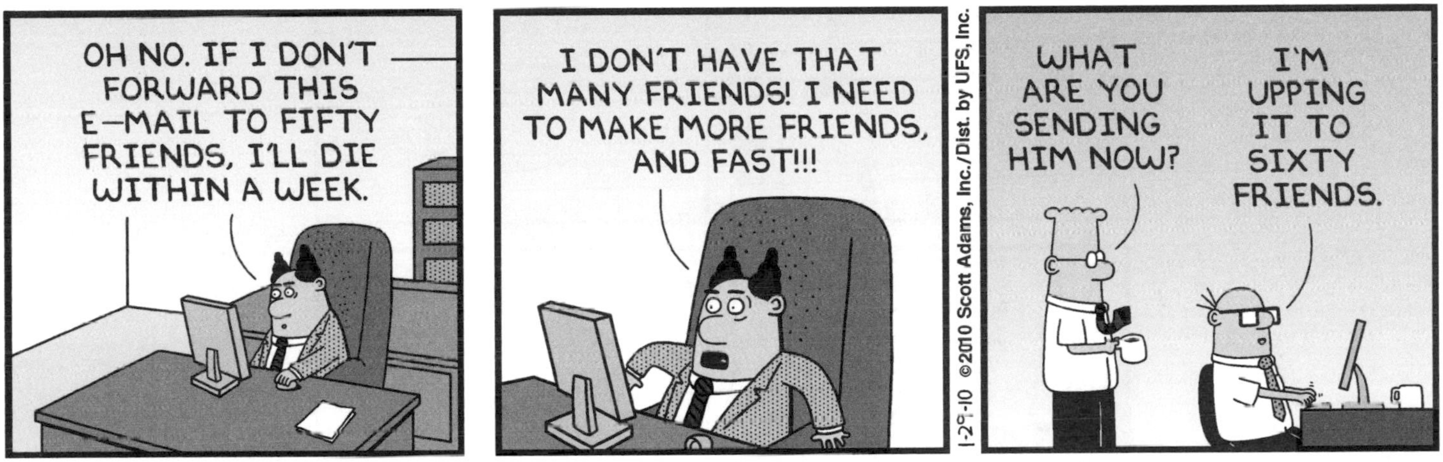
OH NO. IF I DON'T FORWARD THIS E-MAIL TO FIFTY FRIENDS, I'LL DIE WITHIN A WEEK.
I DON'T HAVE THAT MANY FRIENDS! I NEED TO MAKE MORE FRIENDS, AND FAST!!!
1-29-10 ©2010 Scott Adams, Inc./Dist. by UFS, Inc.
WHAT ARE YOU SENDING HIM NOW?
I'M UPPING IT TO SIXTY FRIENDS.

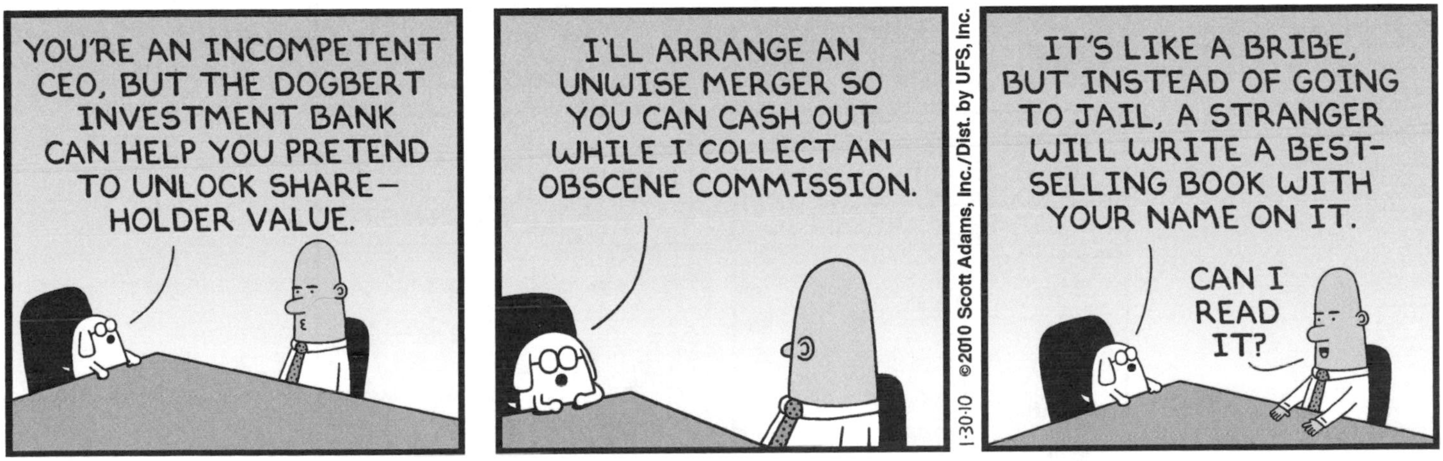
YOU'RE AN INCOMPETENT CEO, BUT THE DOGBERT INVESTMENT BANK CAN HELP YOU PRETEND TO UNLOCK SHARE-HOLDER VALUE.
I'LL ARRANGE AN UNWISE MERGER SO YOU CAN CASH OUT WHILE I COLLECT AN OBSCENE COMMISSION.
1-30-10 ©2010 Scott Adams, Inc./Dist. by UFS, Inc.
IT'S LIKE A BRIBE, BUT INSTEAD OF GOING TO JAIL, A STRANGER WILL WRITE A BEST-SELLING BOOK WITH YOUR NAME ON IT.
CAN I READ IT?

WALLY, WILL YOU DO ME A FAVOR?
ABSOLUTELY. WHAT ARE FRIENDS FOR?
AFTER ALL, YOU'D DO A FAVOR FOR ME IF I ASKED, RIGHT?
UM. . . SURE
© 2010 Scott Adams, Inc. /Dist. by UFS, Inc.
OF COURSE YOU WOULD.
SO DO ME A FAVOR AND DON'T ASK ME TO DO ANY FAVORS.
WOW. OKAY. I DID NOT SEE THAT COMING.
YOU'RE LIKE A WIZARD WHO USES THE RULES OF SOCIAL CONVENTION AS IF THEY ARE MAGIC.
1-31-10
YOU'RE HAIRLESS POTTER!
DON'T TELL BALDEMORT.

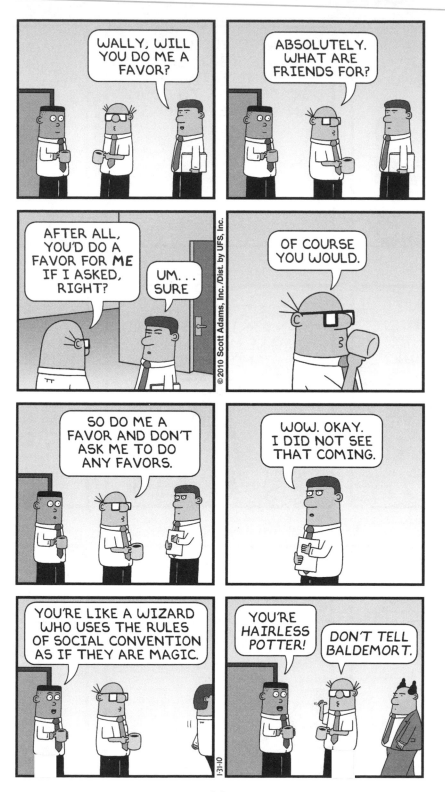

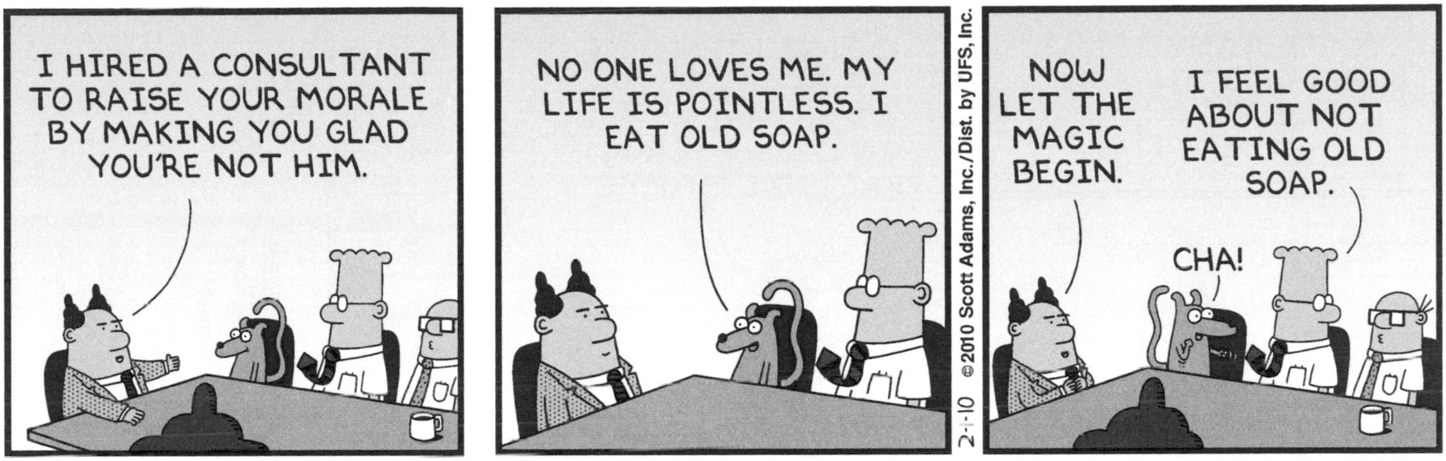
I HIRED A CONSULTANT TO RAISE YOUR MORALE BY MAKING YOU GLAD YOU'RE NOT HIM.
NO ONE LOVES ME. MY LIFE IS POINTLESS. I EAT OLD SOAP.
2-1-10 ©2010 Scott Adams, Inc./Dist. by UFS, Inc.
NOW LET THE MAGIC BEGIN.
I FEEL GOOD ABOUT NOT EATING OLD SOAP.
CHA!

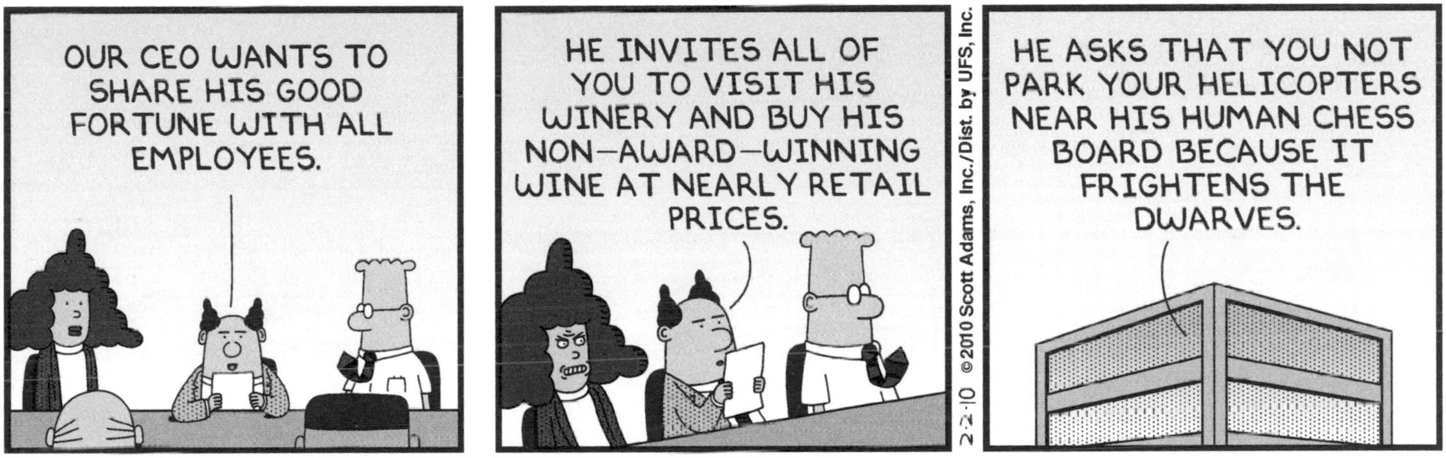
OUR CEO WANTS TO SHARE HIS GOOD FORTUNE WITH ALL EMPLOYEES.
HE INVITES ALL OF YOU TO VISIT HIS WINERY AND BUY HIS NON-AWARD-WINNING WINE AT NEARLY RETAIL PRICES.
2-2-10 ©2010 Scott Adams, Inc./Dist. by UFS, Inc.
HE ASKS THAT YOU NOT PARK YOUR HELICOPTERS NEAR HIS HUMAN CHESS BOARD BECAUSE IT FRIGHTENS THE DWARVES.

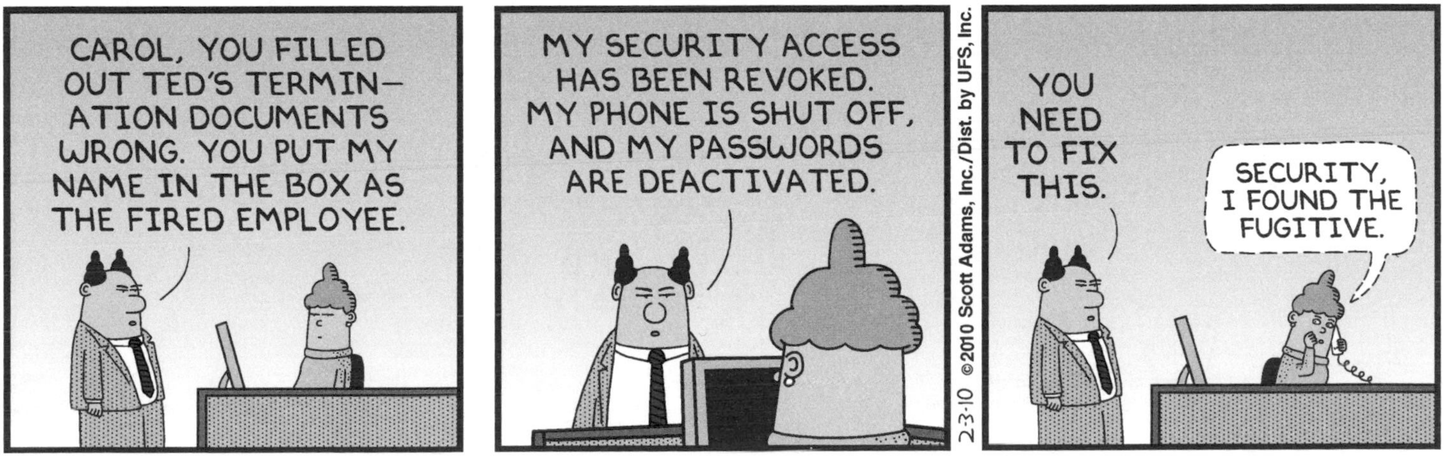
CAROL, YOU FILLED OUT TED'S TERMIN-ATION DOCUMENTS WRONG. YOU PUT MY NAME IN THE BOX AS THE FIRED EMPLOYEE.
MY SECURITY ACCESS HAS BEEN REVOKED. MY PHONE IS SHUT OFF, AND MY PASSWORDS ARE DEACTIVATED.
2-3-10 ©2010 Scott Adams, Inc./Dist. by UFS, Inc.
YOU NEED TO FIX THIS.
SECURITY, I FOUND THE FUGITIVE.

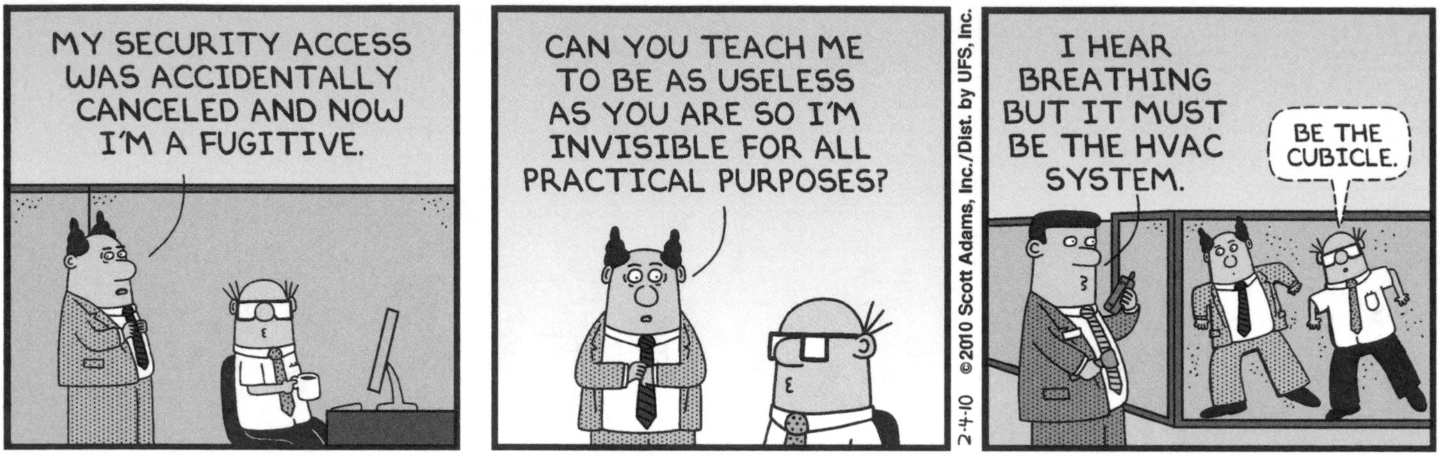
MY SECURITY ACCESS WAS ACCIDENTALLY CANCELED AND NOW I'M A FUGITIVE.
CAN YOU TEACH ME TO BE AS USELESS AS YOU ARE SO I'M INVISIBLE FOR ALL PRACTICAL PURPOSES?
2-4-10 ©2010 Scott Adams, Inc./Dist. by UFS, Inc.
I HEAR BREATHING BUT IT MUST BE THE HVAC SYSTEM.
BE THE CUBICLE.

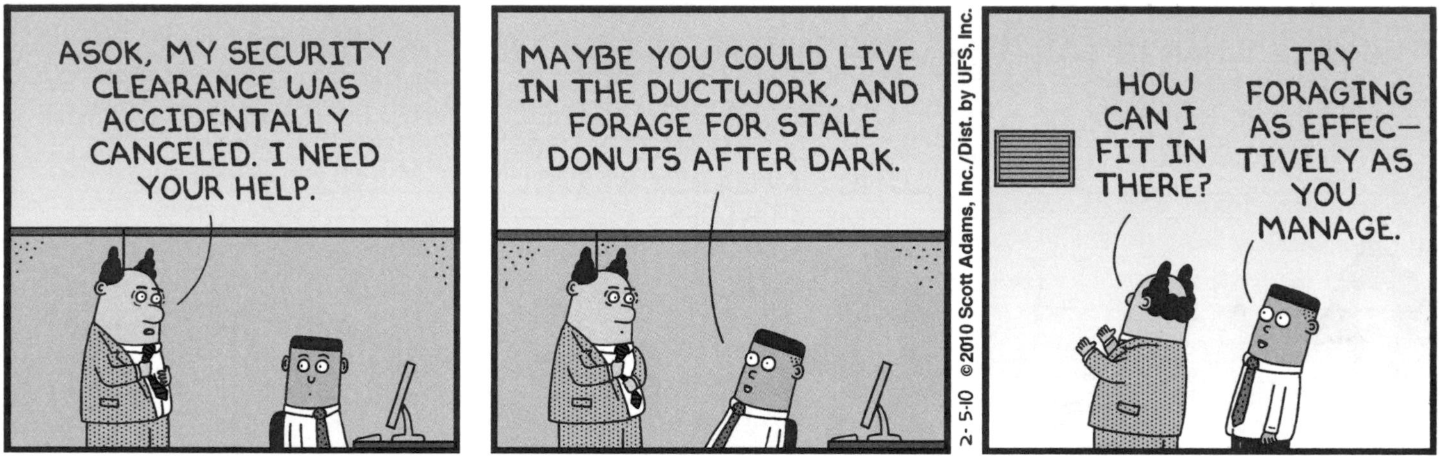
ASOK, MY SECURITY CLEARANCE WAS ACCIDENTALLY CANCELED. I NEED YOUR HELP.
MAYBE YOU COULD LIVE IN THE DUCTWORK, AND FORAGE FOR STALE DONUTS AFTER DARK.
2-5-10 ©2010 Scott Adams, Inc./Dist. by UFS, Inc.
HOW CAN I FIT IN THERE?
TRY FORAGING AS EFFEC-TIVELY AS YOU MANAGE.

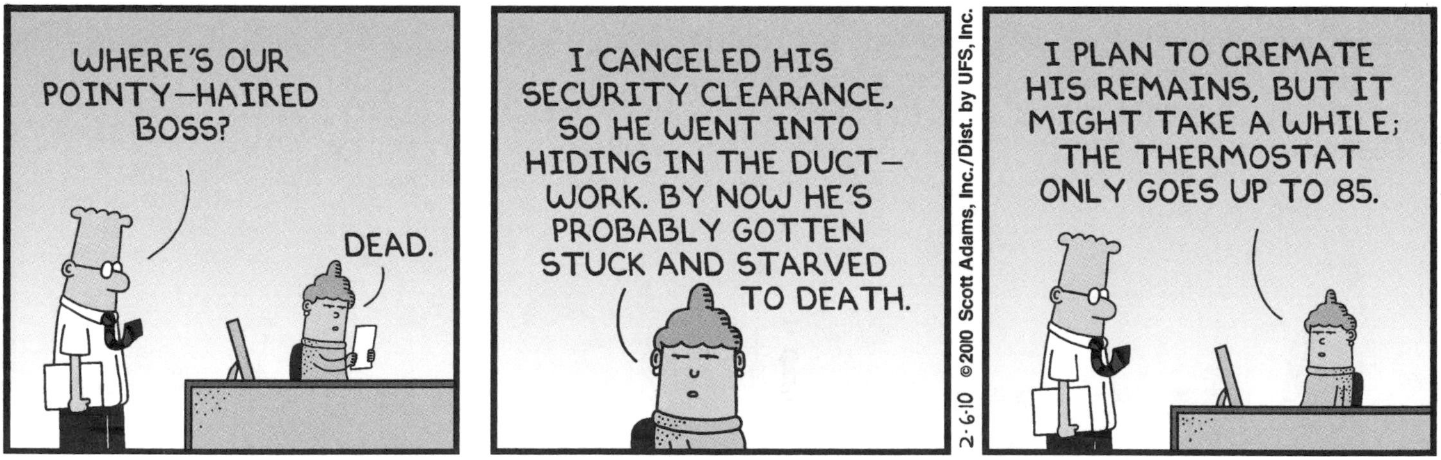
WHERE'S OUR POINTY-HAIRED BOSS?
DEAD.
I CANCELED HIS SECURITY CLEARANCE, SO HE WENT INTO HIDING IN THE DUCT-WORK. BY NOW HE'S PROBABLY GOTTEN STUCK AND STARVED TO DEATH.
2-6-10 ©2010 Scott Adams, Inc./Dist. by UFS, Inc.
I PLAN TO CREMATE HIS REMAINS, BUT IT MIGHT TAKE A WHILE; THE THERMOSTAT ONLY GOES UP TO 85.

I NEED YOU TO ASSIGN ONE OF YOUR ENGINEERS TO MY PROJECT.
FOLLOW ME AND I'LL SHOW YOU YOUR CHOICES.
THIS ONE IS HIGHLY CAPABLE, BUT SHE'S IN SUCH HIGH DEMAND THAT YOU'LL BE LUCKY IF SHE EVER RETURNS A CALL.
©2010 Scott Adams, Inc./Dist. by UFS, Inc.
THIS ONE IS AGGRESSIVELY UNHELPFUL.
THIS ONE WILL TELL YOU THAT ALL OF YOUR PLANS ARE IMPRACTICAL AND DOOMED.
THAT ONE IS AN INTERN, SO NO ONE TAKES HIM SERIOUSLY.
MY MANAGEMENT THEORY IS THAT NATURE MAKES EVERYONE USELESS IN THEIR OWN WAY.
2-7-10
I'M NOT USELESS.
SAID THE MAN WHO CAN'T FIND A GOOD ENGINEER.

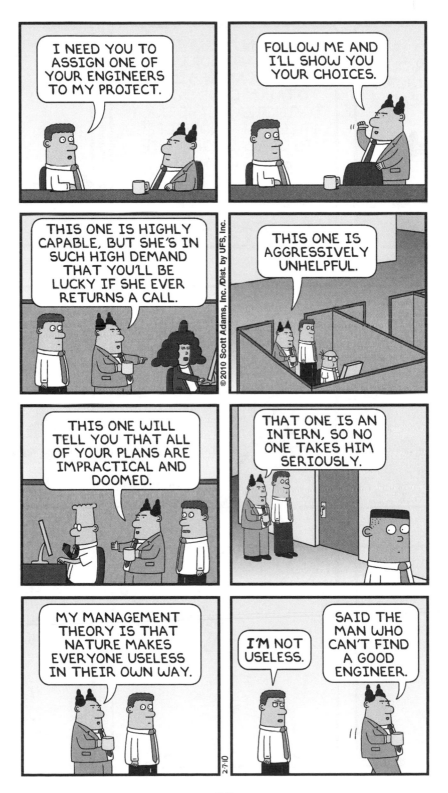

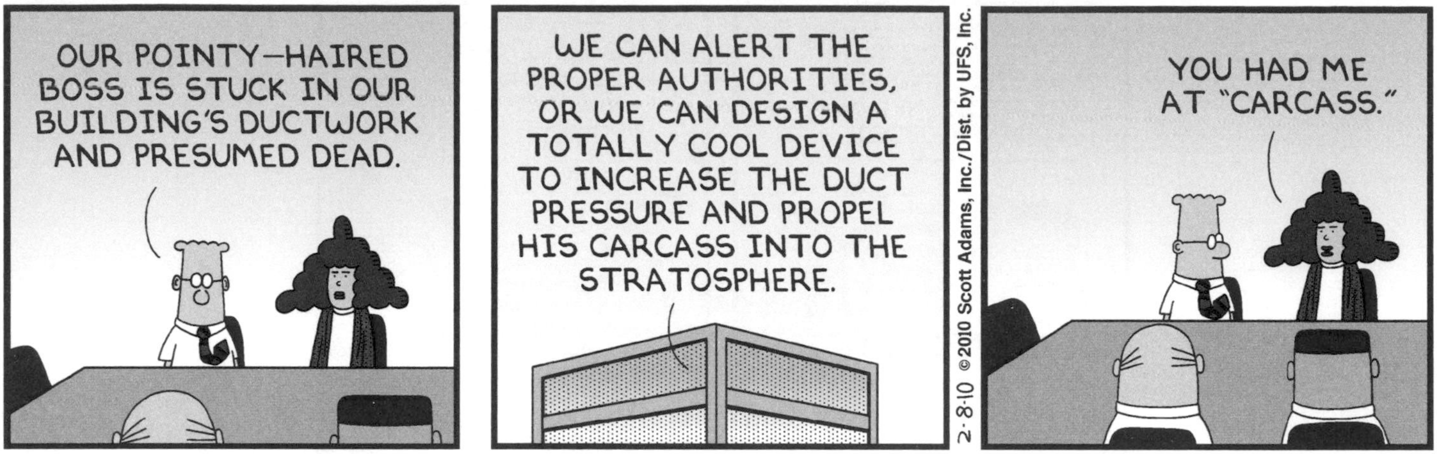
OUR POINTY—HAIRED BOSS IS STUCK IN OUR BUILDING'S DUCTWORK AND PRESUMED DEAD.
WE CAN ALERT THE PROPER AUTHORITIES, OR WE CAN DESIGN A TOTALLY COOL DEVICE TO INCREASE THE DUCT PRESSURE AND PROPEL HIS CARCASS INTO THE STRATOSPHERE.
2·8·10 © 2010 Scott Adams, Inc./Dist. by UFS, Inc.
YOU HAD ME AT "CARCASS."

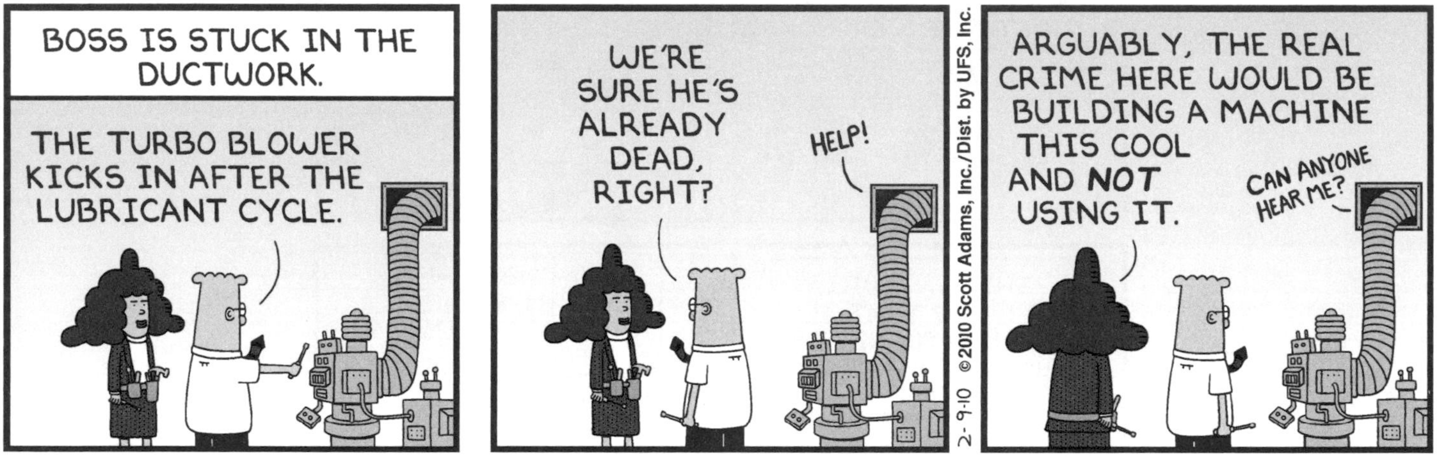
BOSS IS STUCK IN THE DUCTWORK.
THE TURBO BLOWER KICKS IN AFTER THE LUBRICANT CYCLE.
WE'RE SURE HE'S ALREADY DEAD, RIGHT?
HELP!
2·9·10 © 2010 Scott Adams, Inc./Dist. by UFS, Inc.
ARGUABLY, THE REAL CRIME HERE WOULD BE BUILDING A MACHINE THIS COOL AND **NOT** USING IT.
CAN ANYONE HEAR ME?

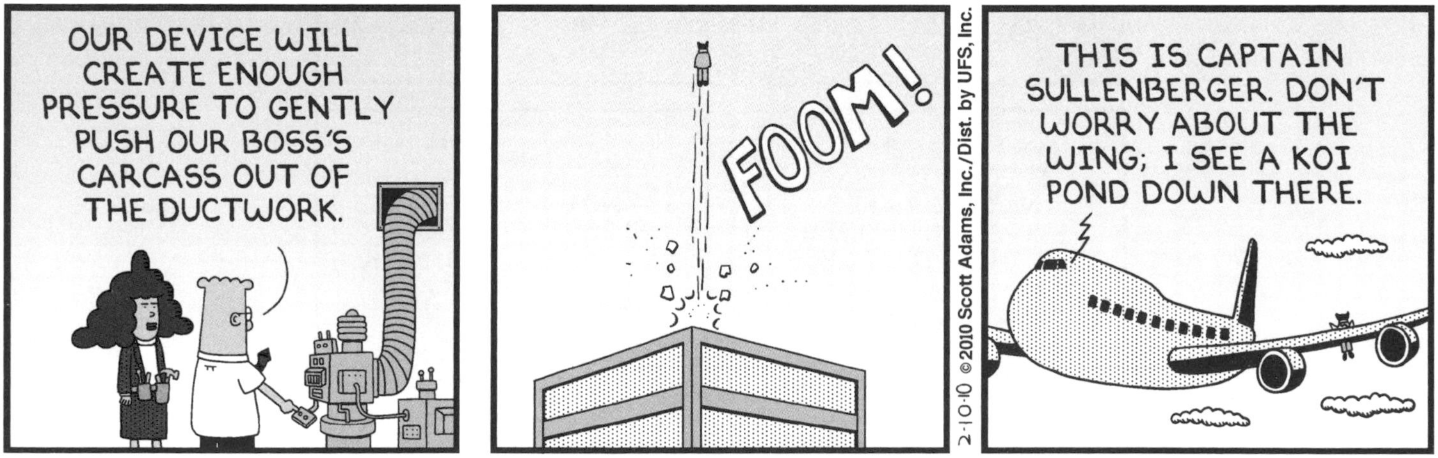
OUR DEVICE WILL CREATE ENOUGH PRESSURE TO GENTLY PUSH OUR BOSS'S CARCASS OUT OF THE DUCTWORK.
FOOM!
2·10·10 © 2010 Scott Adams, Inc./Dist. by UFS, Inc.
THIS IS CAPTAIN SULLENBERGER. DON'T WORRY ABOUT THE WING; I SEE A KOI POND DOWN THERE.

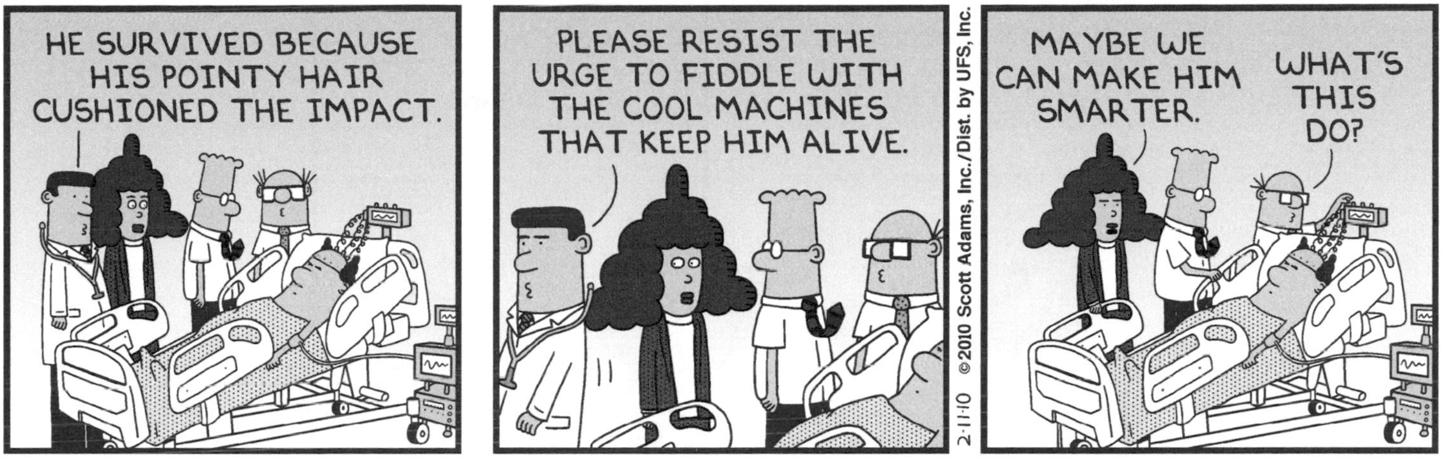
HE SURVIVED BECAUSE HIS POINTY HAIR CUSHIONED THE IMPACT.
PLEASE RESIST THE URGE TO FIDDLE WITH THE COOL MACHINES THAT KEEP HIM ALIVE.
2·11·10 ©2010 Scott Adams, Inc./Dist. by UFS, Inc.
MAYBE WE CAN MAKE HIM SMARTER.
WHAT'S THIS DO?

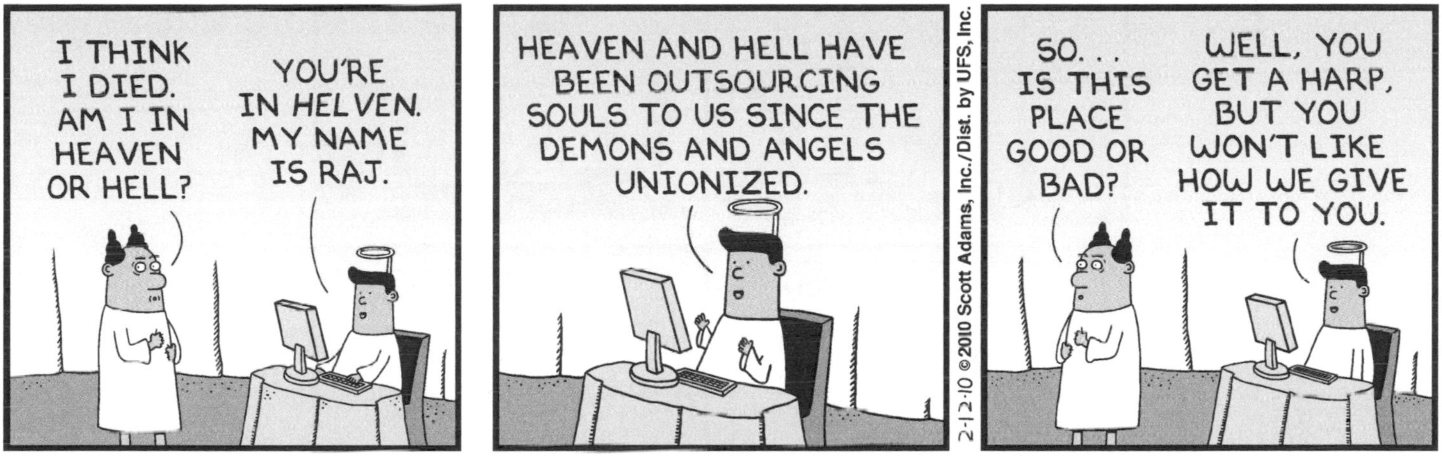
I THINK I DIED. AM I IN HEAVEN OR HELL?
YOU'RE IN *HELVEN*. MY NAME IS RAJ.
HEAVEN AND HELL HAVE BEEN OUTSOURCING SOULS TO US SINCE THE DEMONS AND ANGELS UNIONIZED.
2·12·10 ©2010 Scott Adams, Inc./Dist. by UFS, Inc.
SO. . . IS THIS PLACE GOOD OR BAD?
WELL, YOU GET A HARP, BUT YOU WON'T LIKE HOW WE GIVE IT TO YOU.

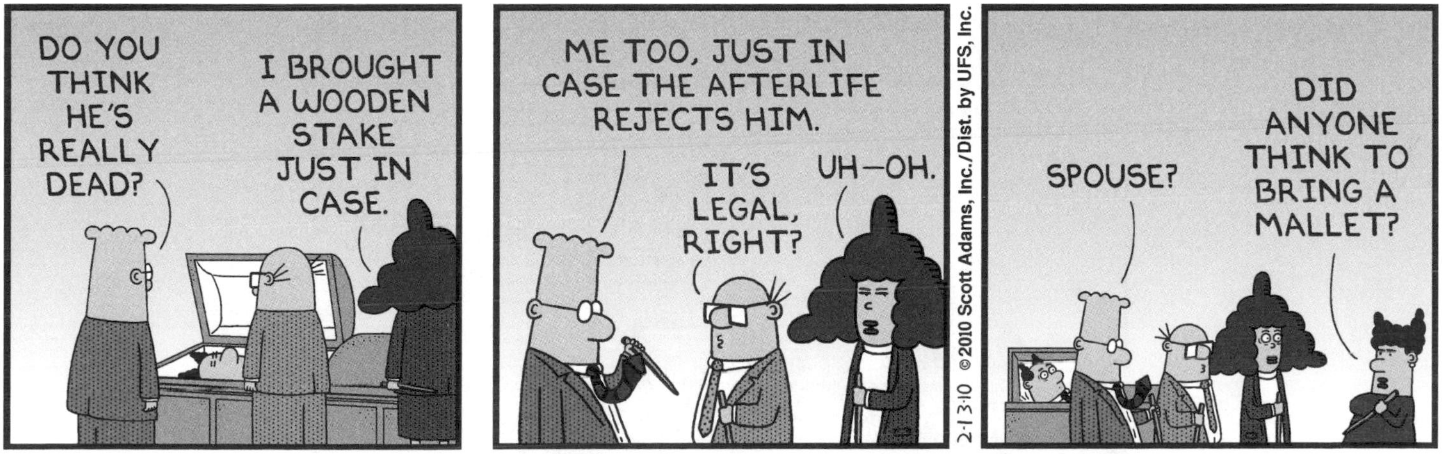
DO YOU THINK HE'S REALLY DEAD?
I BROUGHT A WOODEN STAKE JUST IN CASE.
ME TOO, JUST IN CASE THE AFTERLIFE REJECTS HIM.
IT'S LEGAL, RIGHT?
UH—OH.
2·13·10 ©2010 Scott Adams, Inc./Dist. by UFS, Inc.
SPOUSE?
DID ANYONE THINK TO BRING A MALLET?

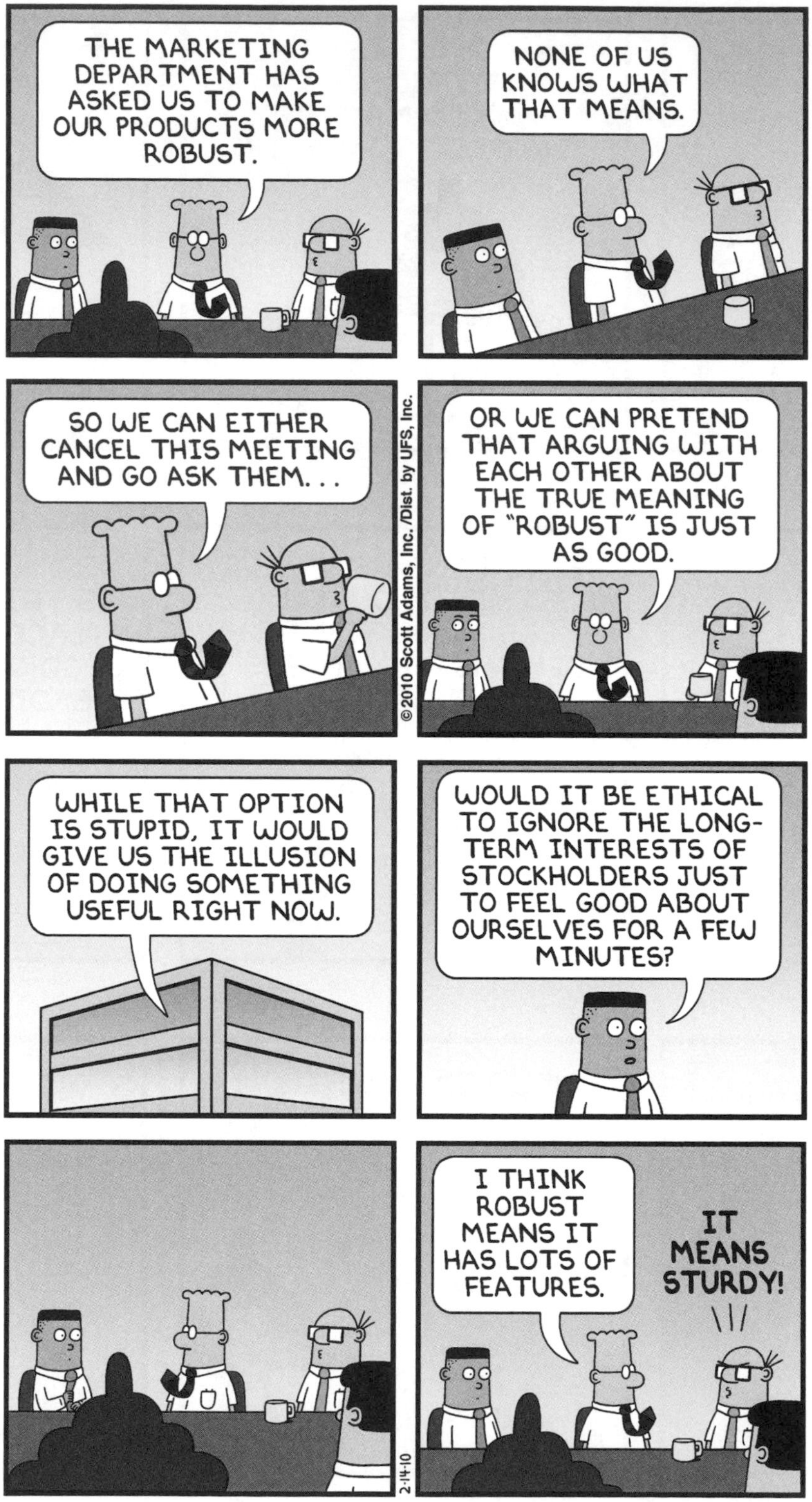
THE MARKETING DEPARTMENT HAS ASKED US TO MAKE OUR PRODUCTS MORE ROBUST.
NONE OF US KNOWS WHAT THAT MEANS.
SO WE CAN EITHER CANCEL THIS MEETING AND GO ASK THEM. . .
OR WE CAN PRETEND THAT ARGUING WITH EACH OTHER ABOUT THE TRUE MEANING OF "ROBUST" IS JUST AS GOOD.
WHILE THAT OPTION IS STUPID, IT WOULD GIVE US THE ILLUSION OF DOING SOMETHING USEFUL RIGHT NOW.
WOULD IT BE ETHICAL TO IGNORE THE LONG-TERM INTERESTS OF STOCKHOLDERS JUST TO FEEL GOOD ABOUT OURSELVES FOR A FEW MINUTES?
I THINK ROBUST MEANS IT HAS LOTS OF FEATURES.
IT MEANS STURDY!
©2010 Scott Adams, Inc. /Dist. by UFS, Inc.
2-14-10

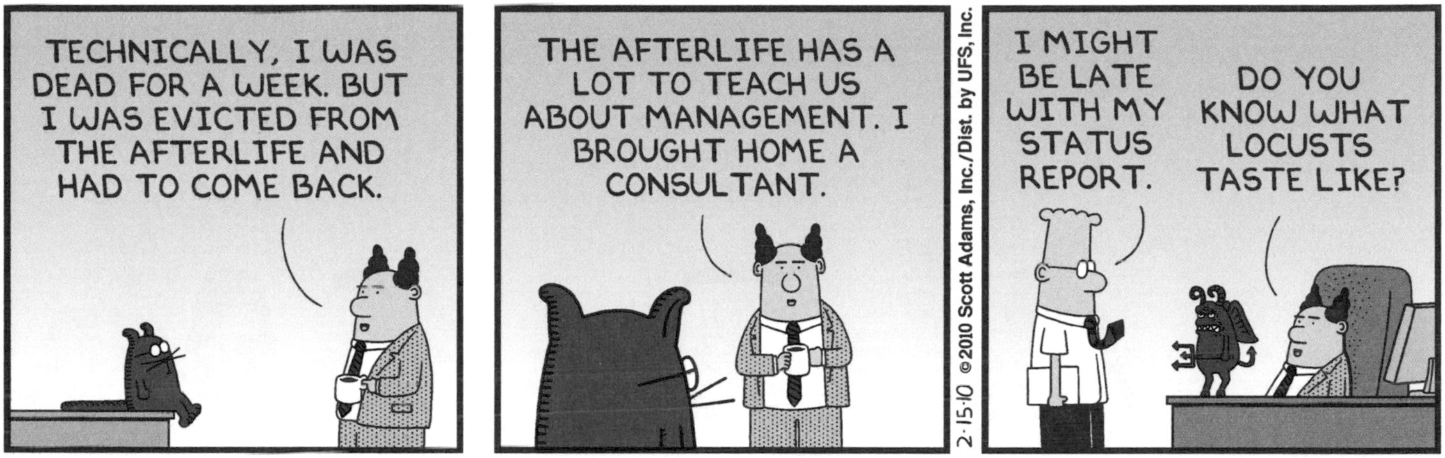
TECHNICALLY, I WAS DEAD FOR A WEEK. BUT I WAS EVICTED FROM THE AFTERLIFE AND HAD TO COME BACK.
THE AFTERLIFE HAS A LOT TO TEACH US ABOUT MANAGEMENT. I BROUGHT HOME A CONSULTANT.
2·15·10 ©2010 Scott Adams, Inc./Dist. by UFS, Inc.
I MIGHT BE LATE WITH MY STATUS REPORT.
DO YOU KNOW WHAT LOCUSTS TASTE LIKE?

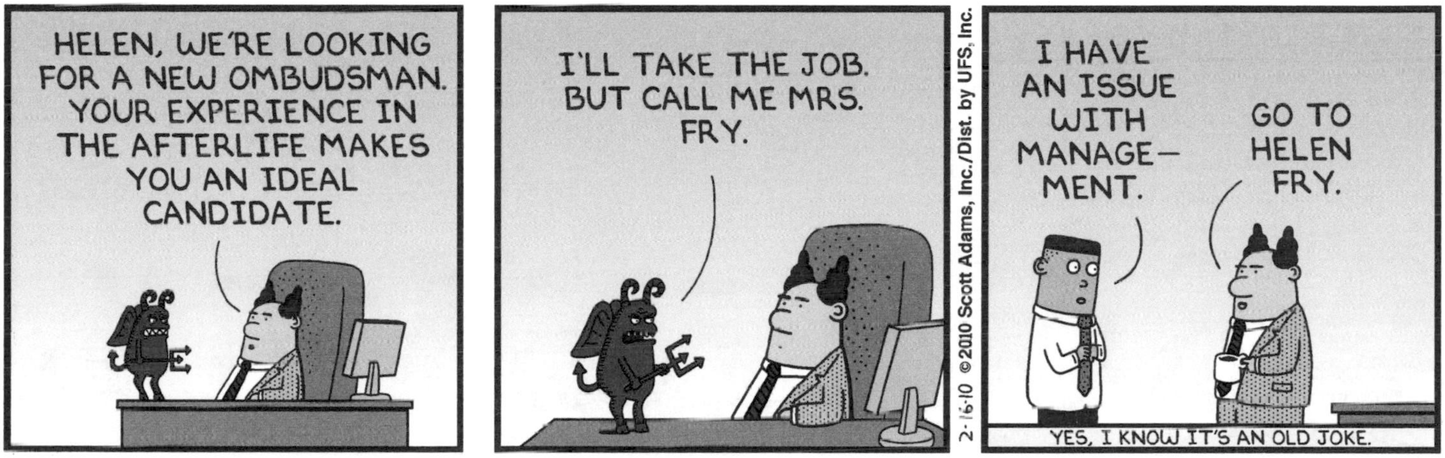
HELEN, WE'RE LOOKING FOR A NEW OMBUDSMAN. YOUR EXPERIENCE IN THE AFTERLIFE MAKES YOU AN IDEAL CANDIDATE.
I'LL TAKE THE JOB. BUT CALL ME MRS. FRY.
2·16·10 ©2010 Scott Adams, Inc./Dist. by UFS, Inc.
I HAVE AN ISSUE WITH MANAGE-MENT.
GO TO HELEN FRY.
YES, I KNOW IT'S AN OLD JOKE.

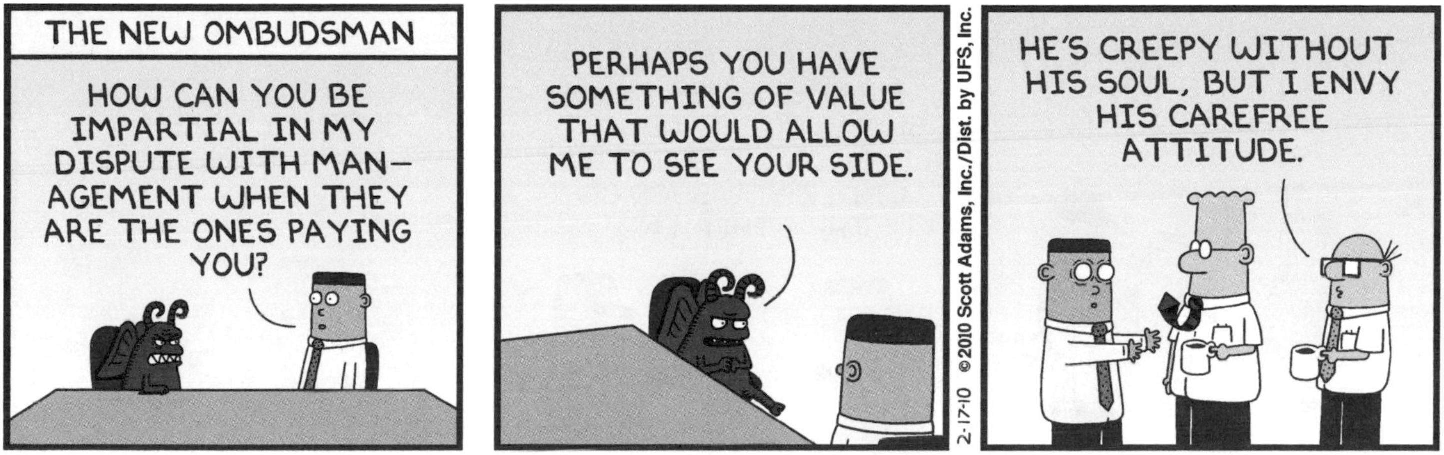
THE NEW OMBUDSMAN
HOW CAN YOU BE IMPARTIAL IN MY DISPUTE WITH MAN-AGEMENT WHEN THEY ARE THE ONES PAYING YOU?
PERHAPS YOU HAVE SOMETHING OF VALUE THAT WOULD ALLOW ME TO SEE YOUR SIDE.
2·17·10 ©2010 Scott Adams, Inc./Dist. by UFS, Inc.
HE'S CREEPY WITHOUT HIS SOUL, BUT I ENVY HIS CAREFREE ATTITUDE.

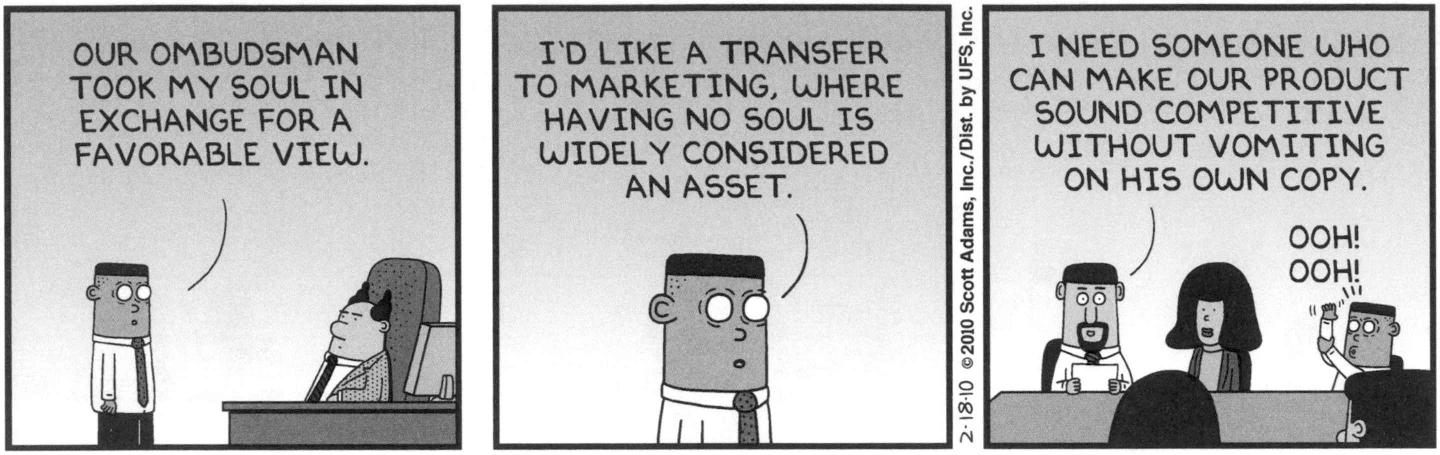
OUR OMBUDSMAN TOOK MY SOUL IN EXCHANGE FOR A FAVORABLE VIEW.
I'D LIKE A TRANSFER TO MARKETING, WHERE HAVING NO SOUL IS WIDELY CONSIDERED AN ASSET.
2-18-10 ©2010 Scott Adams, Inc./Dist. by UFS, Inc.
I NEED SOMEONE WHO CAN MAKE OUR PRODUCT SOUND COMPETITIVE WITHOUT VOMITING ON HIS OWN COPY.
OOH! OOH!

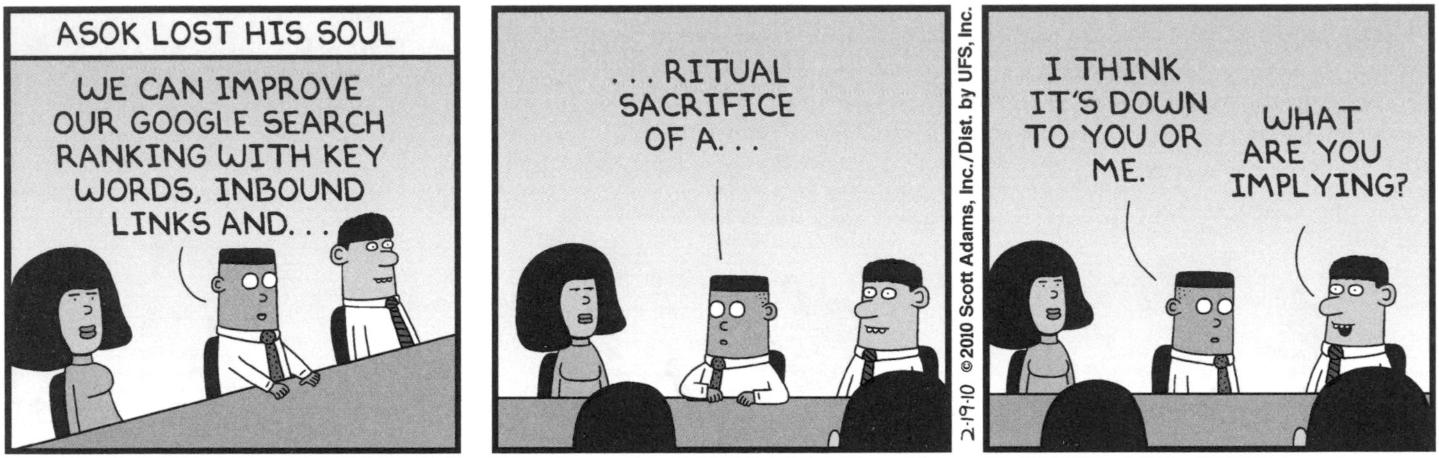
ASOK LOST HIS SOUL
WE CAN IMPROVE OUR GOOGLE SEARCH RANKING WITH KEY WORDS, INBOUND LINKS AND. . .
. . . RITUAL SACRIFICE OF A. . .
2-19-10 ©2010 Scott Adams, Inc./Dist. by UFS, Inc.
I THINK IT'S DOWN TO YOU OR ME.
WHAT ARE YOU IMPLYING?

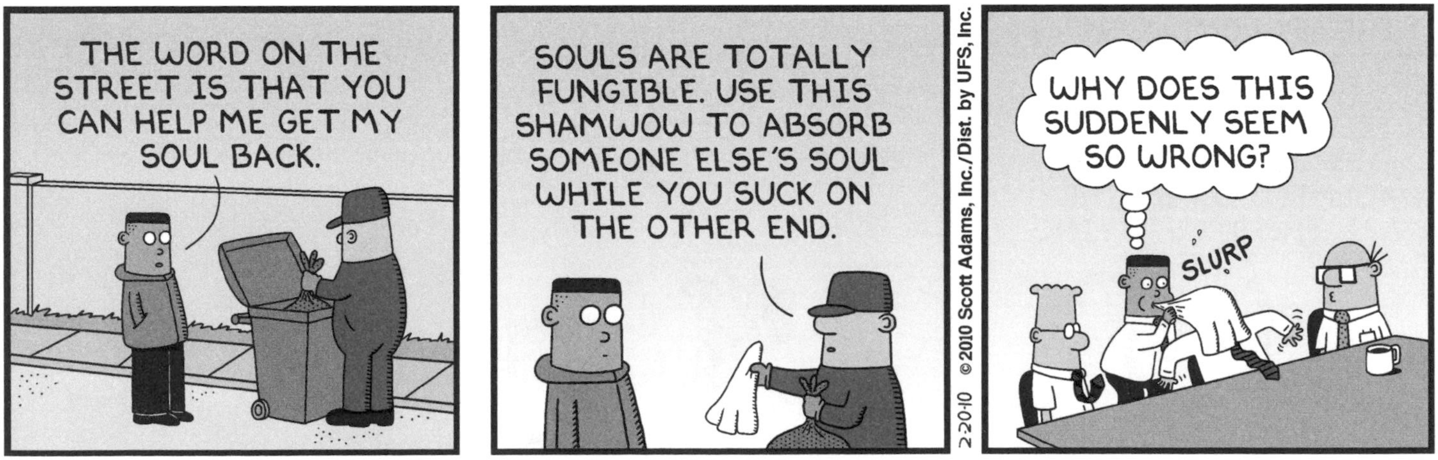
THE WORD ON THE STREET IS THAT YOU CAN HELP ME GET MY SOUL BACK.
SOULS ARE TOTALLY FUNGIBLE. USE THIS SHAMWOW TO ABSORB SOMEONE ELSE'S SOUL WHILE YOU SUCK ON THE OTHER END.
2-20-10 ©2010 Scott Adams, Inc./Dist. by UFS, Inc.
WHY DOES THIS SUDDENLY SEEM SO WRONG?
SLURP

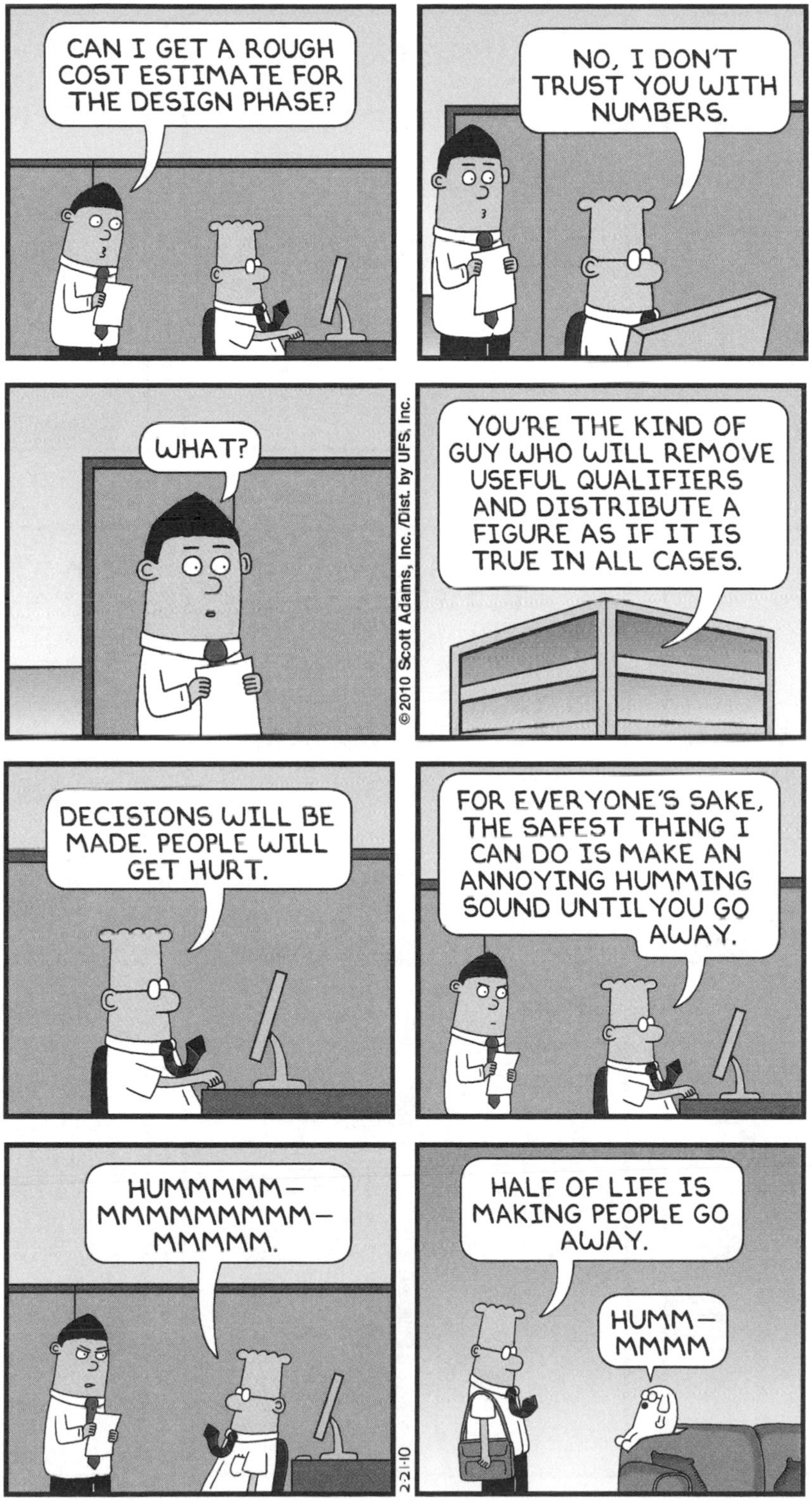
CAN I GET A ROUGH COST ESTIMATE FOR THE DESIGN PHASE?
NO, I DON'T TRUST YOU WITH NUMBERS.
WHAT?
YOU'RE THE KIND OF GUY WHO WILL REMOVE USEFUL QUALIFIERS AND DISTRIBUTE A FIGURE AS IF IT IS TRUE IN ALL CASES.
DECISIONS WILL BE MADE. PEOPLE WILL GET HURT.
FOR EVERYONE'S SAKE, THE SAFEST THING I CAN DO IS MAKE AN ANNOYING HUMMING SOUND UNTILYOU GO AWAY.
HUMMMMM—MMMMMMMMM—MMMMM.
HALF OF LIFE IS MAKING PEOPLE GO AWAY.
HUMM—MMMM
©2010 Scott Adams, Inc./Dist. by UFS, Inc.
2-21-10

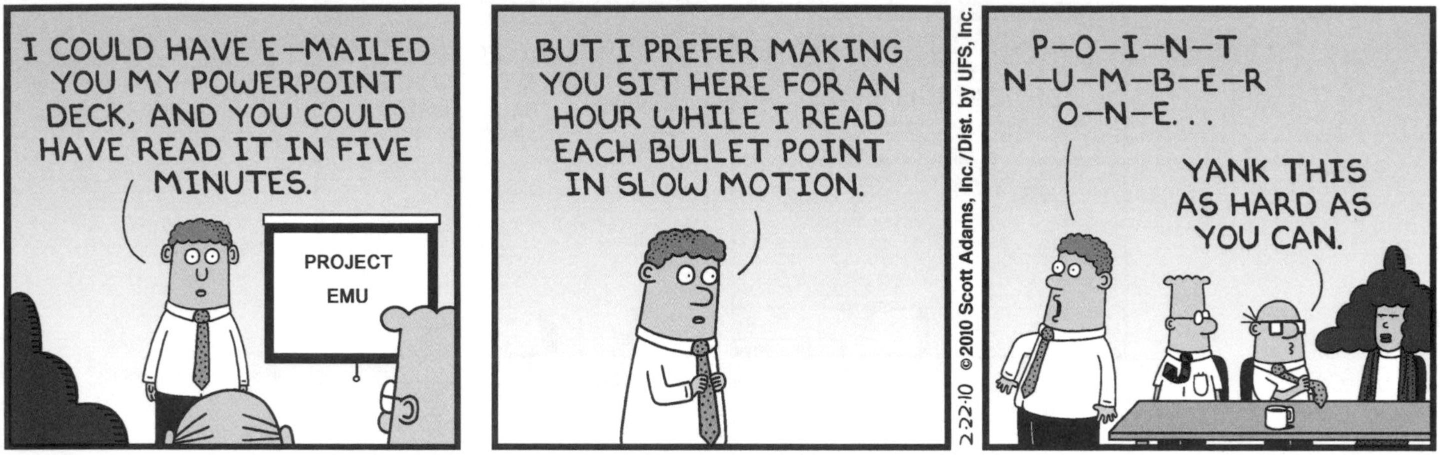
I COULD HAVE E-MAILED YOU MY POWERPOINT DECK, AND YOU COULD HAVE READ IT IN FIVE MINUTES.
PROJECT EMU
BUT I PREFER MAKING YOU SIT HERE FOR AN HOUR WHILE I READ EACH BULLET POINT IN SLOW MOTION.
P-O-I-N-T N-U-M-B-E-R O-N-E. . .
YANK THIS AS HARD AS YOU CAN.
2-22-10 ©2010 Scott Adams, Inc./Dist. by UFS, Inc.

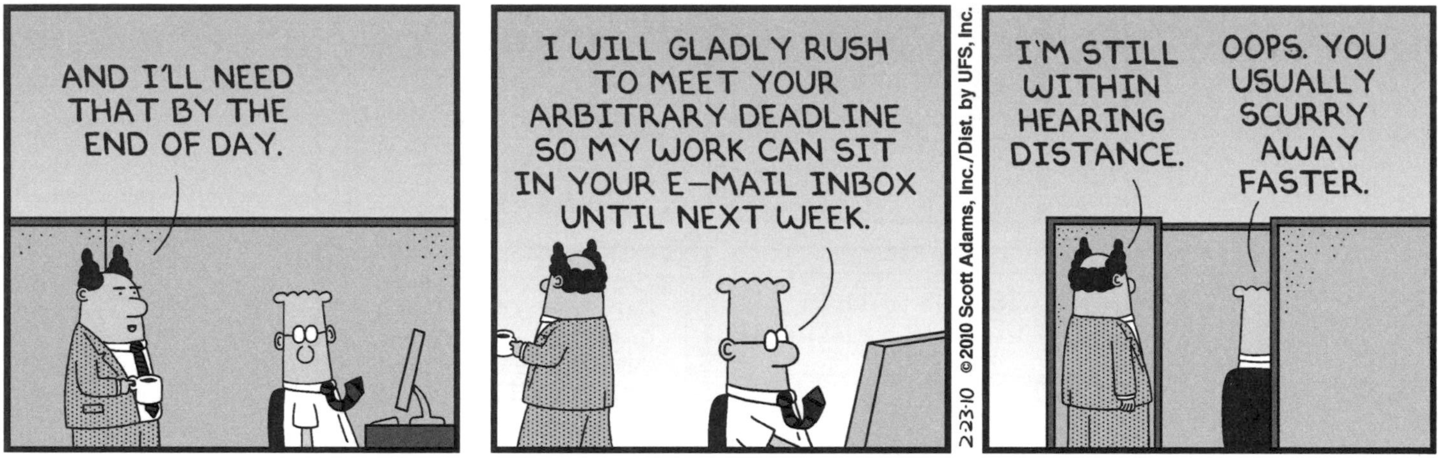
AND I'LL NEED THAT BY THE END OF DAY.
I WILL GLADLY RUSH TO MEET YOUR ARBITRARY DEADLINE SO MY WORK CAN SIT IN YOUR E-MAIL INBOX UNTIL NEXT WEEK.
I'M STILL WITHIN HEARING DISTANCE.
OOPS. YOU USUALLY SCURRY AWAY FASTER.
2-23-10 ©2010 Scott Adams, Inc./Dist. by UFS, Inc.

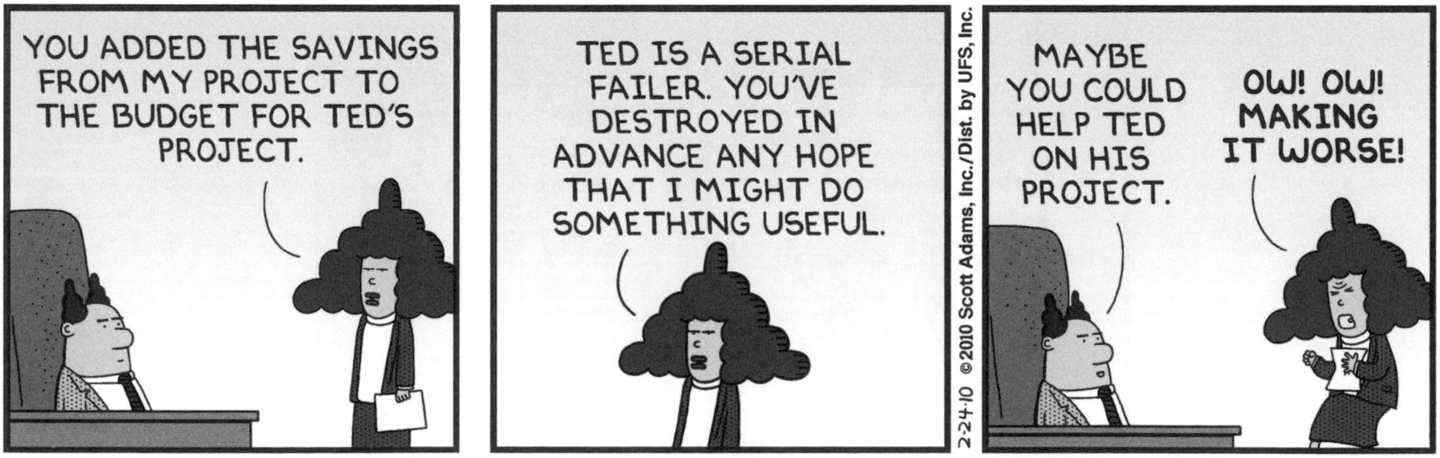
YOU ADDED THE SAVINGS FROM MY PROJECT TO THE BUDGET FOR TED'S PROJECT.
TED IS A SERIAL FAILER. YOU'VE DESTROYED IN ADVANCE ANY HOPE THAT I MIGHT DO SOMETHING USEFUL.
MAYBE YOU COULD HELP TED ON HIS PROJECT.
OW! OW! MAKING IT WORSE!
2-24-10 ©2010 Scott Adams, Inc./Dist. by UFS, Inc.

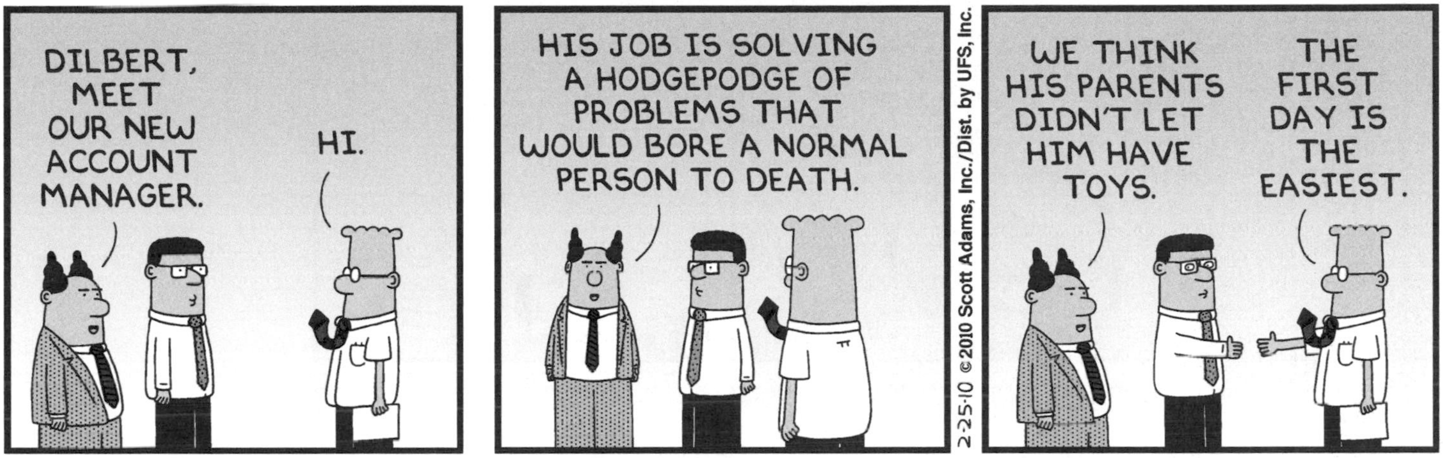
DILBERT, MEET OUR NEW ACCOUNT MANAGER.
HI.
HIS JOB IS SOLVING A HODGEPODGE OF PROBLEMS THAT WOULD BORE A NORMAL PERSON TO DEATH.
2·25·10 ©2010 Scott Adams, Inc./Dist. by UFS, Inc.
WE THINK HIS PARENTS DIDN'T LET HIM HAVE TOYS.
THE FIRST DAY IS THE EASIEST.

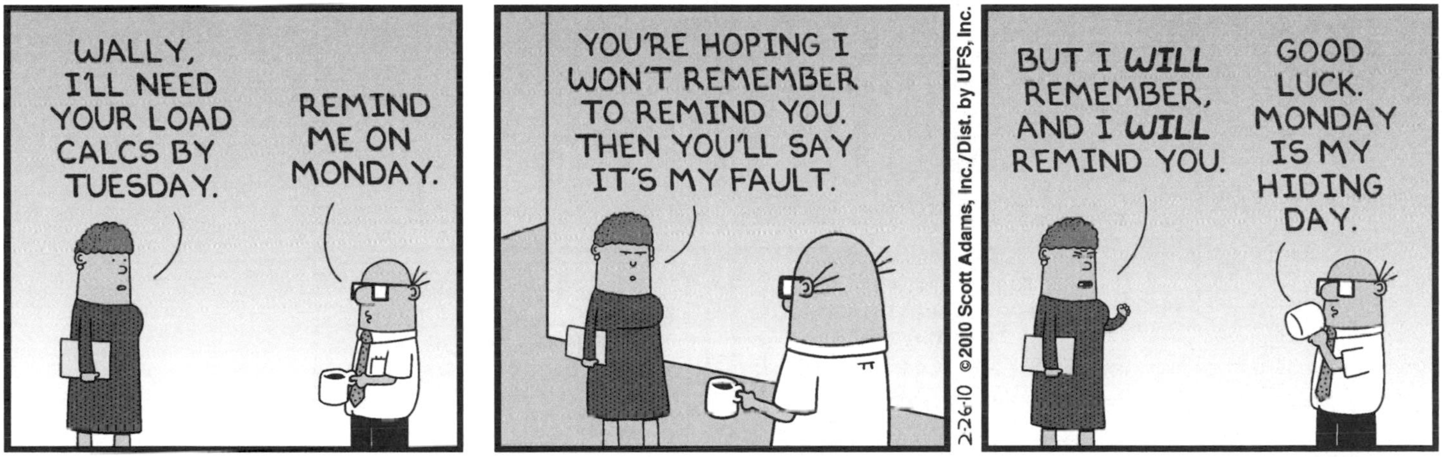
WALLY, I'LL NEED YOUR LOAD CALCS BY TUESDAY.
REMIND ME ON MONDAY.
YOU'RE HOPING I WON'T REMEMBER TO REMIND YOU. THEN YOU'LL SAY IT'S MY FAULT.
2·26·10 ©2010 Scott Adams, Inc./Dist. by UFS, Inc.
BUT I ***WILL*** REMEMBER, AND I ***WILL*** REMIND YOU.
GOOD LUCK. MONDAY IS MY HIDING DAY.

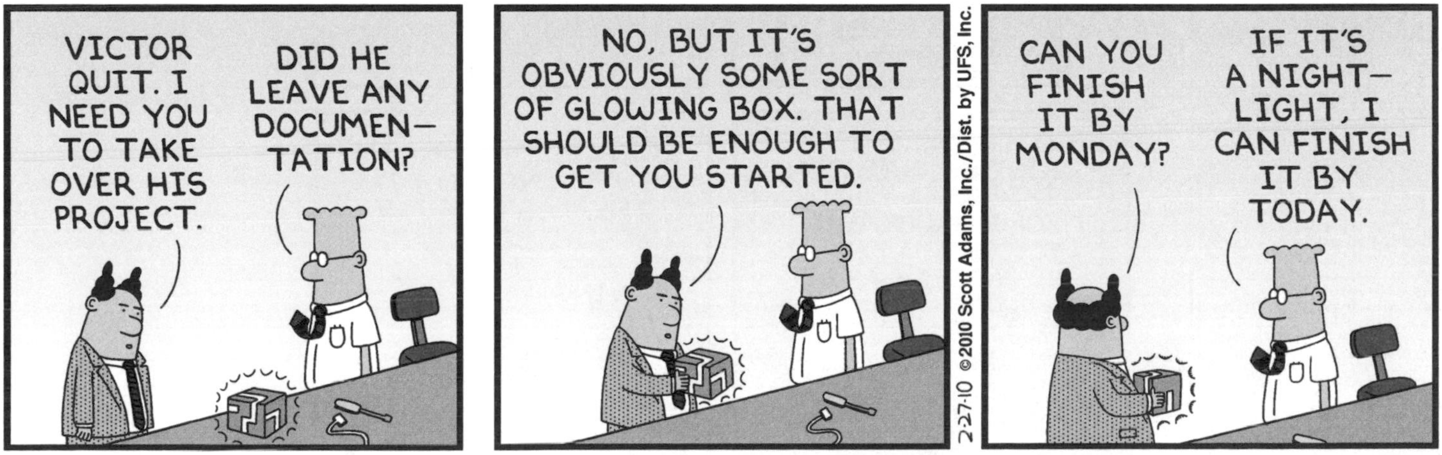
VICTOR QUIT. I NEED YOU TO TAKE OVER HIS PROJECT.
DID HE LEAVE ANY DOCUMEN- TATION?
NO, BUT IT'S OBVIOUSLY SOME SORT OF GLOWING BOX. THAT SHOULD BE ENOUGH TO GET YOU STARTED.
2·27·10 ©2010 Scott Adams, Inc./Dist. by UFS, Inc.
CAN YOU FINISH IT BY MONDAY?
IF IT'S A NIGHT- LIGHT, I CAN FINISH IT BY TODAY.

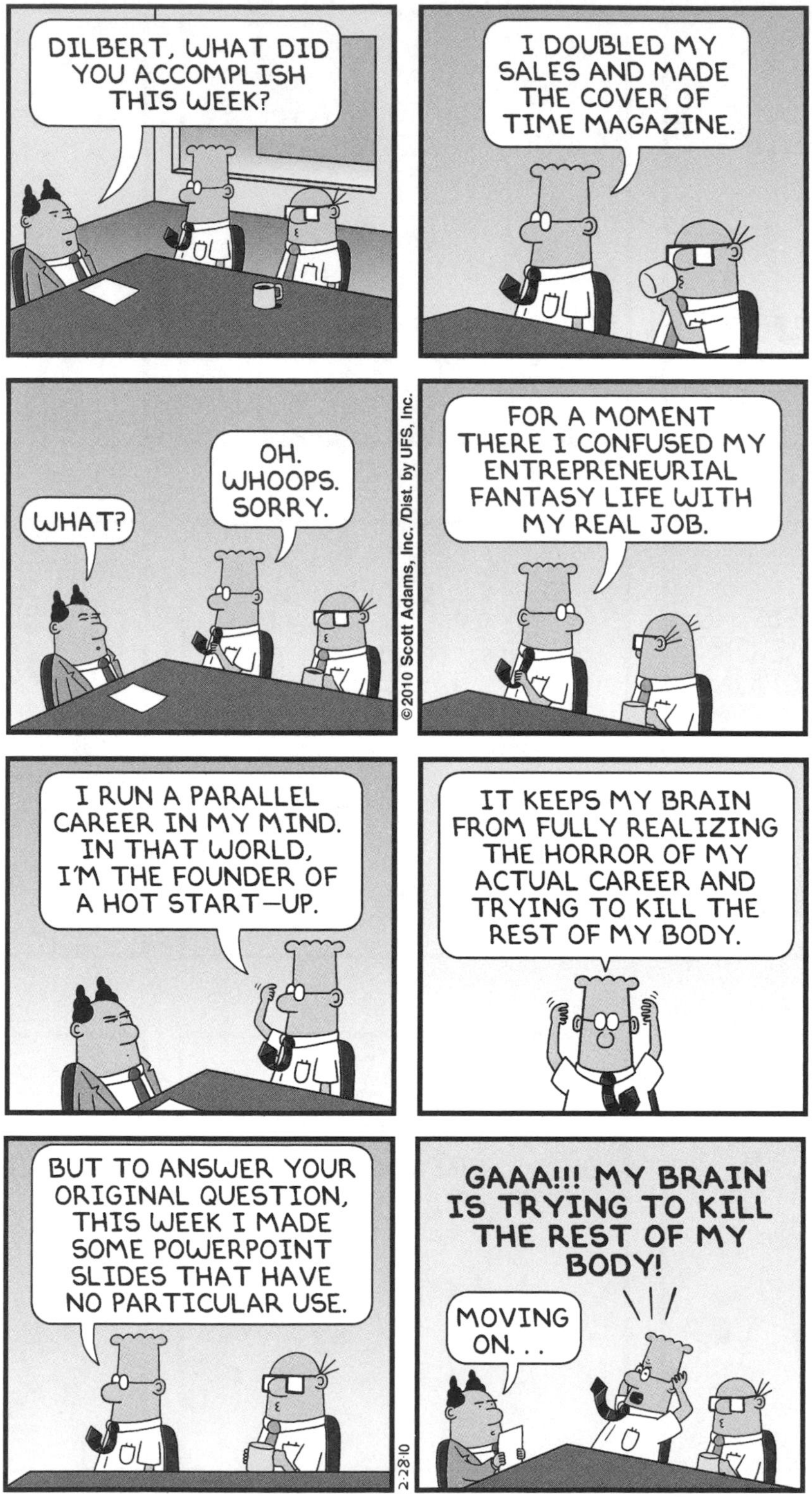
DILBERT, WHAT DID YOU ACCOMPLISH THIS WEEK?
I DOUBLED MY SALES AND MADE THE COVER OF TIME MAGAZINE.
WHAT?
OH. WHOOPS. SORRY.
FOR A MOMENT THERE I CONFUSED MY ENTREPRENEURIAL FANTASY LIFE WITH MY REAL JOB.
I RUN A PARALLEL CAREER IN MY MIND. IN THAT WORLD, I'M THE FOUNDER OF A HOT START-UP.
IT KEEPS MY BRAIN FROM FULLY REALIZING THE HORROR OF MY ACTUAL CAREER AND TRYING TO KILL THE REST OF MY BODY.
BUT TO ANSWER YOUR ORIGINAL QUESTION, THIS WEEK I MADE SOME POWERPOINT SLIDES THAT HAVE NO PARTICULAR USE.
GAAA!!! MY BRAIN IS TRYING TO KILL THE REST OF MY BODY!
MOVING ON. . .
© 2010 Scott Adams, Inc. /Dist. by UFS, Inc.
2-28-10

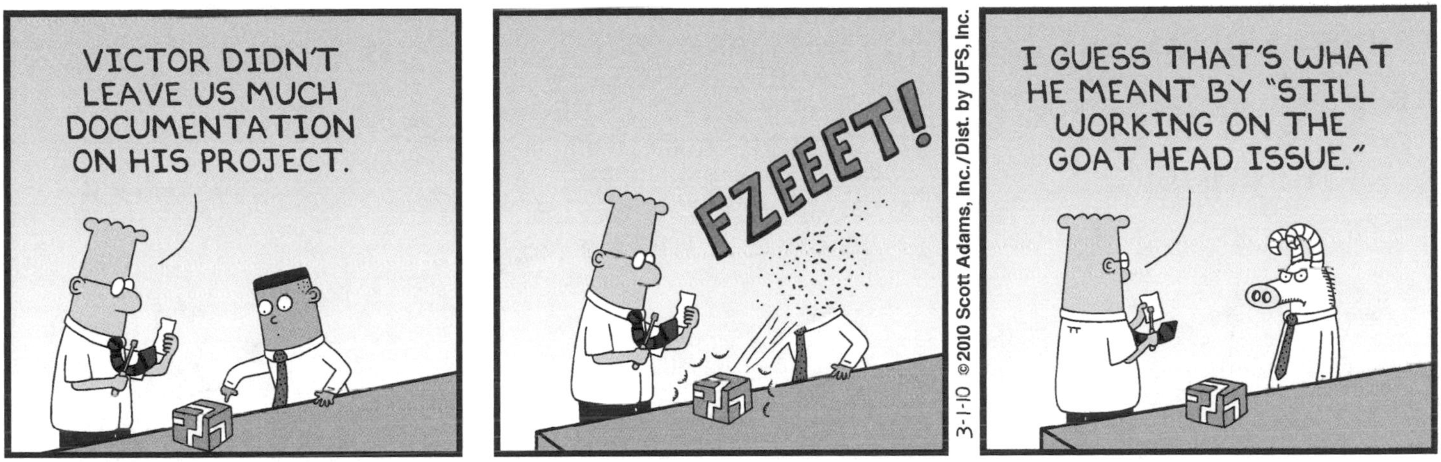
VICTOR DIDN'T LEAVE US MUCH DOCUMENTATION ON HIS PROJECT.
FZEEET!
3-1-10 ©2010 Scott Adams, Inc./Dist. by UFS, Inc.
I GUESS THAT'S WHAT HE MEANT BY "STILL WORKING ON THE GOAT HEAD ISSUE."

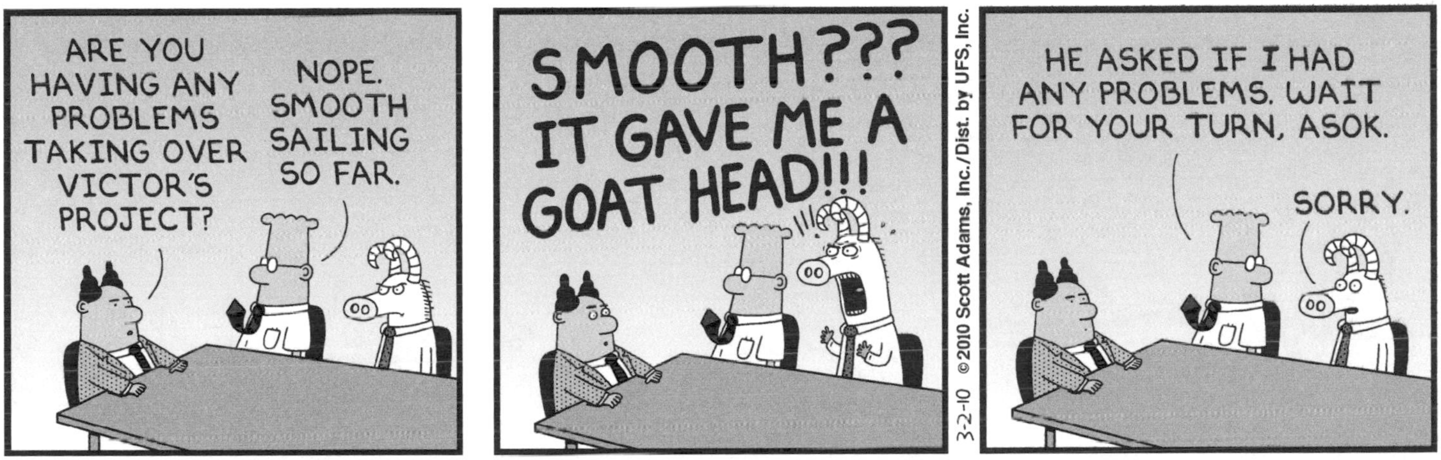
ARE YOU HAVING ANY PROBLEMS TAKING OVER VICTOR'S PROJECT?
NOPE. SMOOTH SAILING SO FAR.
SMOOTH??? IT GAVE ME A GOAT HEAD!!!
3-2-10 ©2010 Scott Adams, Inc./Dist. by UFS, Inc.
HE ASKED IF I HAD ANY PROBLEMS. WAIT FOR YOUR TURN, ASOK.
SORRY.

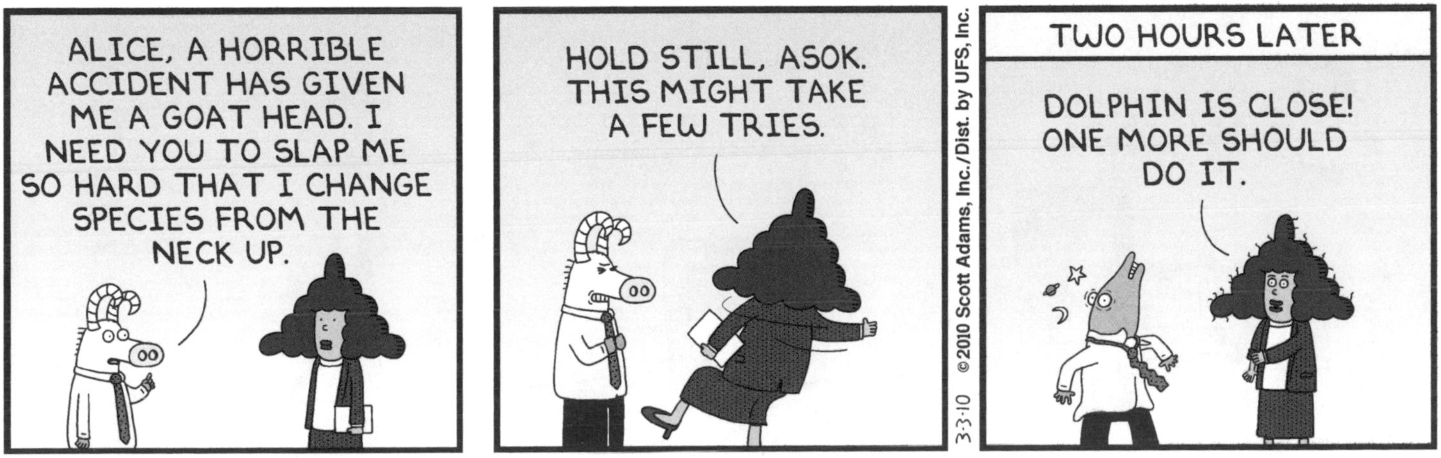
ALICE, A HORRIBLE ACCIDENT HAS GIVEN ME A GOAT HEAD. I NEED YOU TO SLAP ME SO HARD THAT I CHANGE SPECIES FROM THE NECK UP.
HOLD STILL, ASOK. THIS MIGHT TAKE A FEW TRIES.
3-3-10 ©2010 Scott Adams, Inc./Dist. by UFS, Inc.
TWO HOURS LATER
DOLPHIN IS CLOSE! ONE MORE SHOULD DO IT.

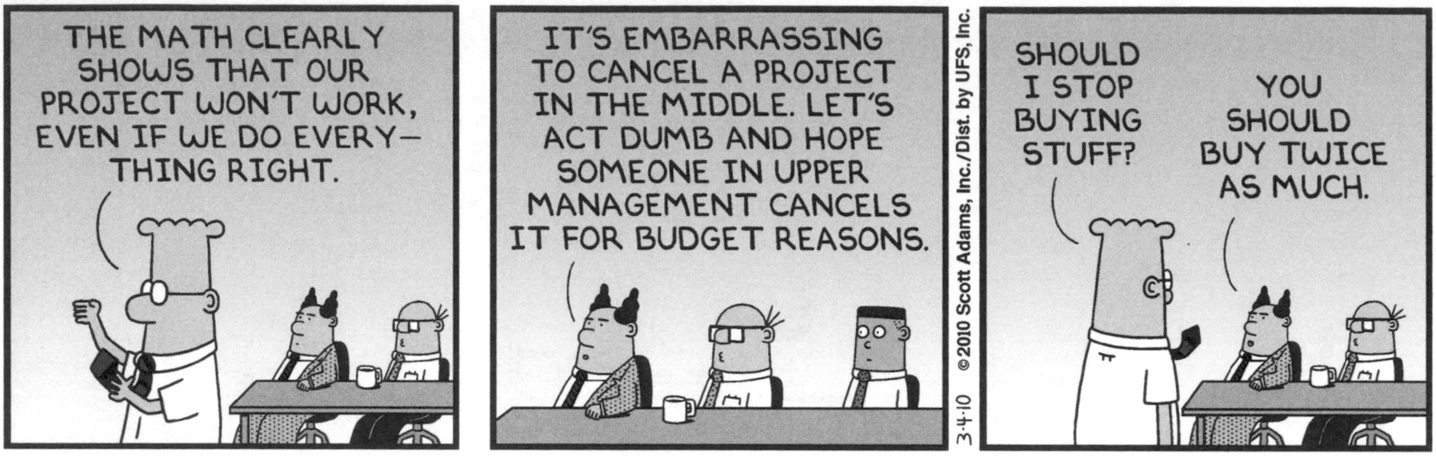
THE MATH CLEARLY SHOWS THAT OUR PROJECT WON'T WORK, EVEN IF WE DO EVERY— THING RIGHT.
IT'S EMBARRASSING TO CANCEL A PROJECT IN THE MIDDLE. LET'S ACT DUMB AND HOPE SOMEONE IN UPPER MANAGEMENT CANCELS IT FOR BUDGET REASONS.
3·4·10 ©2010 Scott Adams, Inc./Dist. by UFS, Inc.
SHOULD I STOP BUYING STUFF?
YOU SHOULD BUY TWICE AS MUCH.

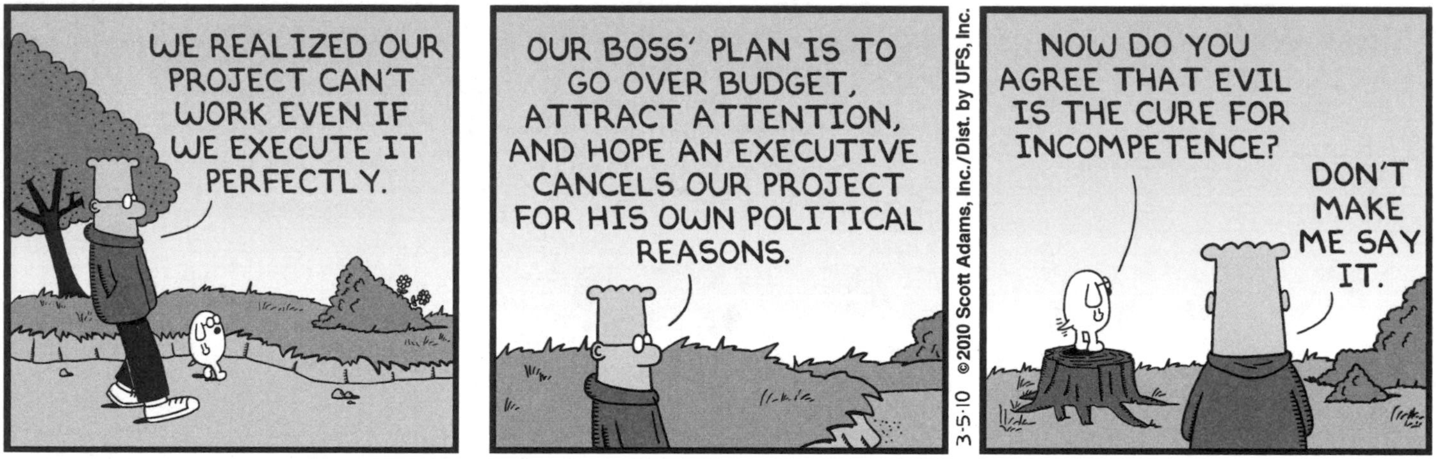
WE REALIZED OUR PROJECT CAN'T WORK EVEN IF WE EXECUTE IT PERFECTLY.
OUR BOSS' PLAN IS TO GO OVER BUDGET, ATTRACT ATTENTION, AND HOPE AN EXECUTIVE CANCELS OUR PROJECT FOR HIS OWN POLITICAL REASONS.
3·5·10 ©2010 Scott Adams, Inc./Dist. by UFS, Inc.
NOW DO YOU AGREE THAT EVIL IS THE CURE FOR INCOMPETENCE?
DON'T MAKE ME SAY IT.

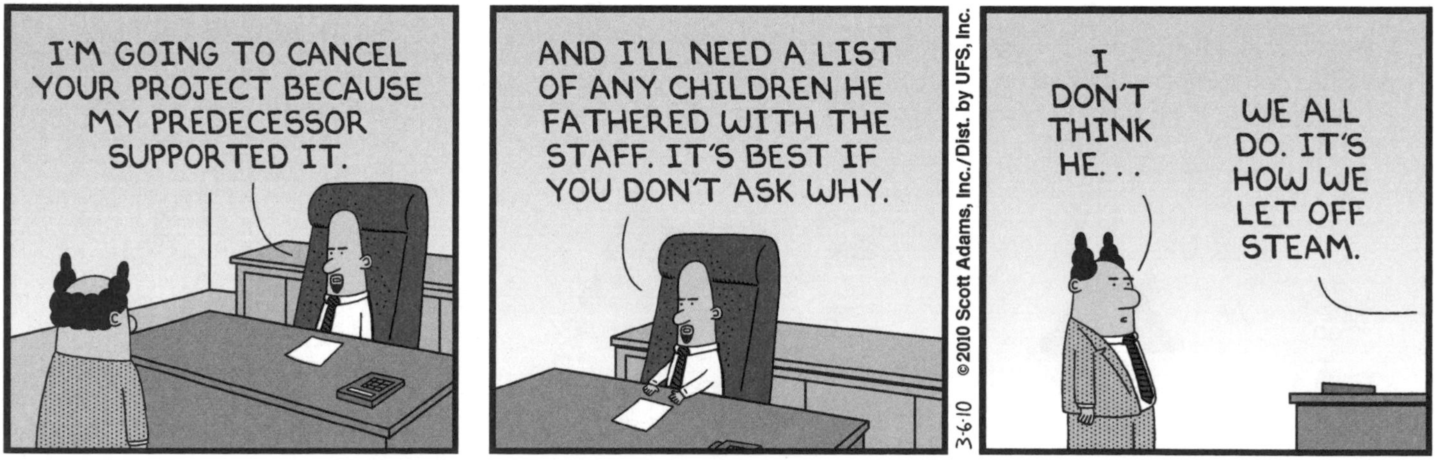
I'M GOING TO CANCEL YOUR PROJECT BECAUSE MY PREDECESSOR SUPPORTED IT.
AND I'LL NEED A LIST OF ANY CHILDREN HE FATHERED WITH THE STAFF. IT'S BEST IF YOU DON'T ASK WHY.
3·6·10 ©2010 Scott Adams, Inc./Dist. by UFS, Inc.
I DON'T THINK HE. . .
WE ALL DO. IT'S HOW WE LET OFF STEAM.

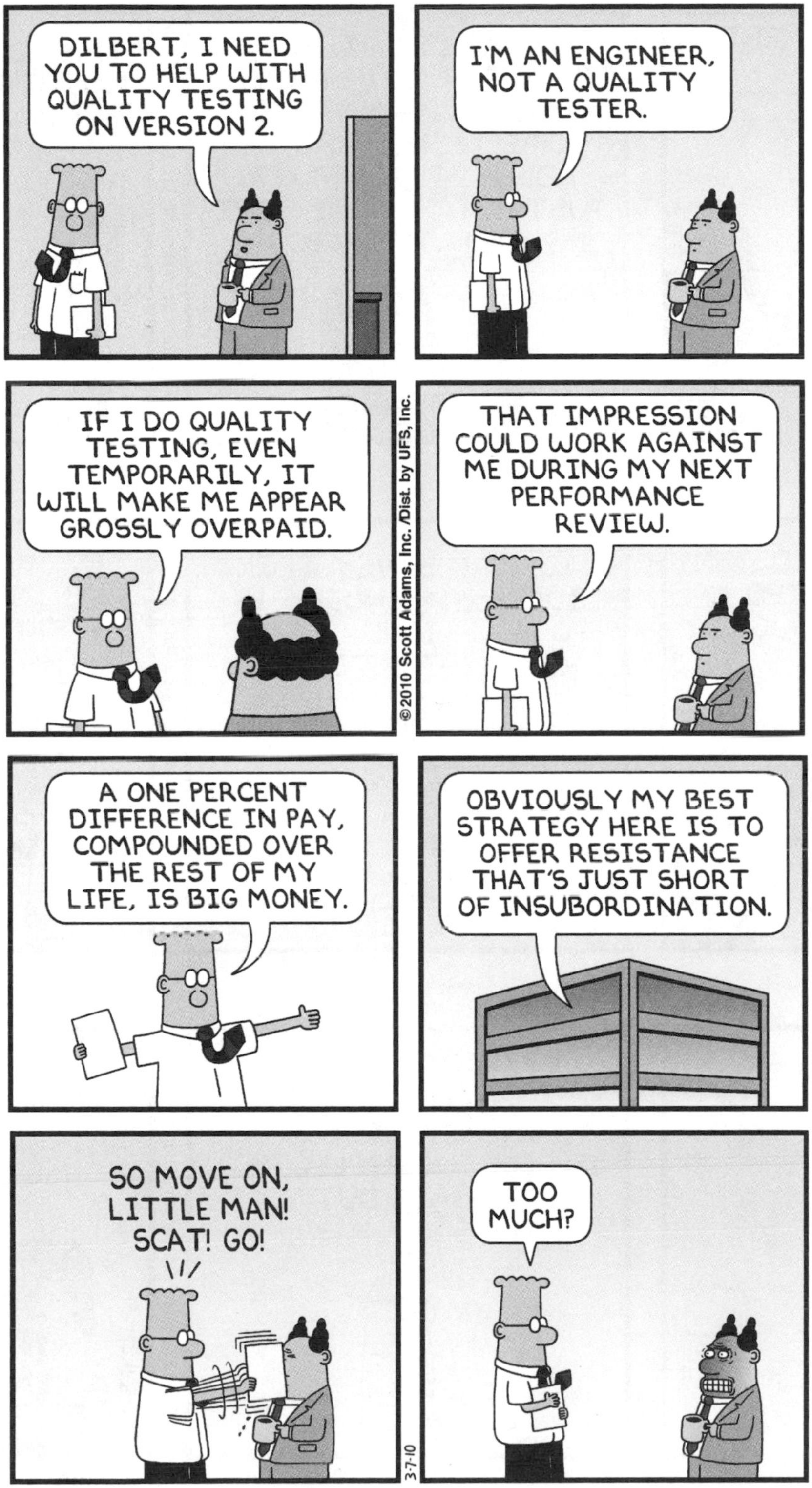
DILBERT, I NEED YOU TO HELP WITH QUALITY TESTING ON VERSION 2.
I'M AN ENGINEER, NOT A QUALITY TESTER.
IF I DO QUALITY TESTING, EVEN TEMPORARILY, IT WILL MAKE ME APPEAR GROSSLY OVERPAID.
THAT IMPRESSION COULD WORK AGAINST ME DURING MY NEXT PERFORMANCE REVIEW.
A ONE PERCENT DIFFERENCE IN PAY, COMPOUNDED OVER THE REST OF MY LIFE, IS BIG MONEY.
OBVIOUSLY MY BEST STRATEGY HERE IS TO OFFER RESISTANCE THAT'S JUST SHORT OF INSUBORDINATION.
SO MOVE ON, LITTLE MAN! SCAT! GO!
TOO MUCH?
©2010 Scott Adams, Inc./Dist. by UFS, Inc.
3-7-10

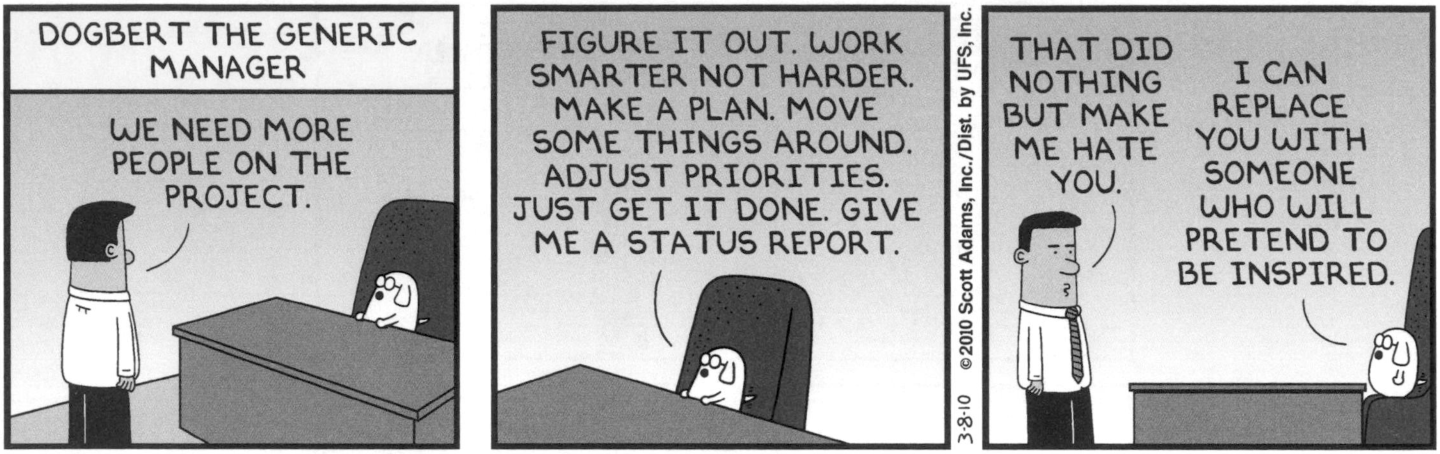
DOGBERT THE GENERIC MANAGER
WE NEED MORE PEOPLE ON THE PROJECT.
FIGURE IT OUT. WORK SMARTER NOT HARDER. MAKE A PLAN. MOVE SOME THINGS AROUND. ADJUST PRIORITIES. JUST GET IT DONE. GIVE ME A STATUS REPORT.
3-8-10 ©2010 Scott Adams, Inc./Dist. by UFS, Inc.
THAT DID NOTHING BUT MAKE ME HATE YOU.
I CAN REPLACE YOU WITH SOMEONE WHO WILL PRETEND TO BE INSPIRED.

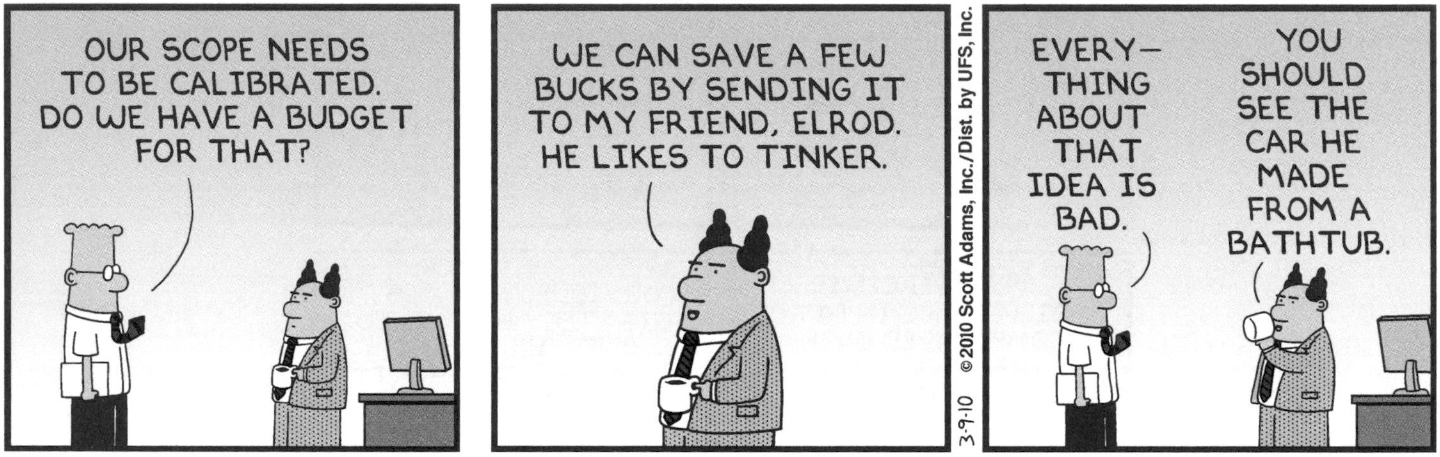
OUR SCOPE NEEDS TO BE CALIBRATED. DO WE HAVE A BUDGET FOR THAT?
WE CAN SAVE A FEW BUCKS BY SENDING IT TO MY FRIEND, ELROD. HE LIKES TO TINKER.
3-9-10 ©2010 Scott Adams, Inc./Dist. by UFS, Inc.
EVERY—THING ABOUT THAT IDEA IS BAD.
YOU SHOULD SEE THE CAR HE MADE FROM A BATHTUB.

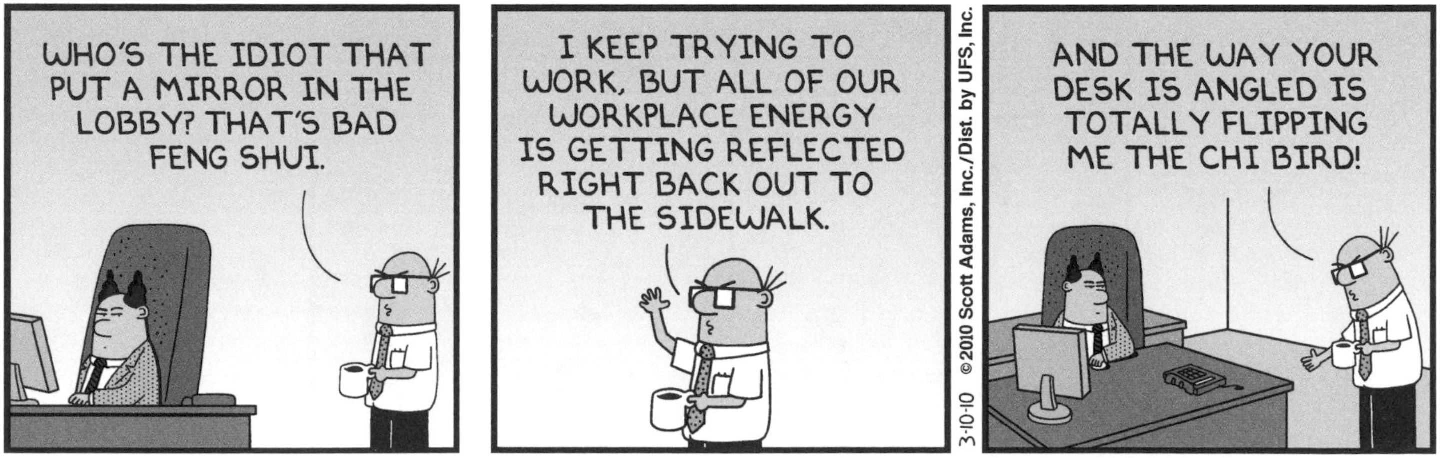
WHO'S THE IDIOT THAT PUT A MIRROR IN THE LOBBY? THAT'S BAD FENG SHUI.
I KEEP TRYING TO WORK, BUT ALL OF OUR WORKPLACE ENERGY IS GETTING REFLECTED RIGHT BACK OUT TO THE SIDEWALK.
3-10-10 ©2010 Scott Adams, Inc./Dist. by UFS, Inc.
AND THE WAY YOUR DESK IS ANGLED IS TOTALLY FLIPPING ME THE CHI BIRD!

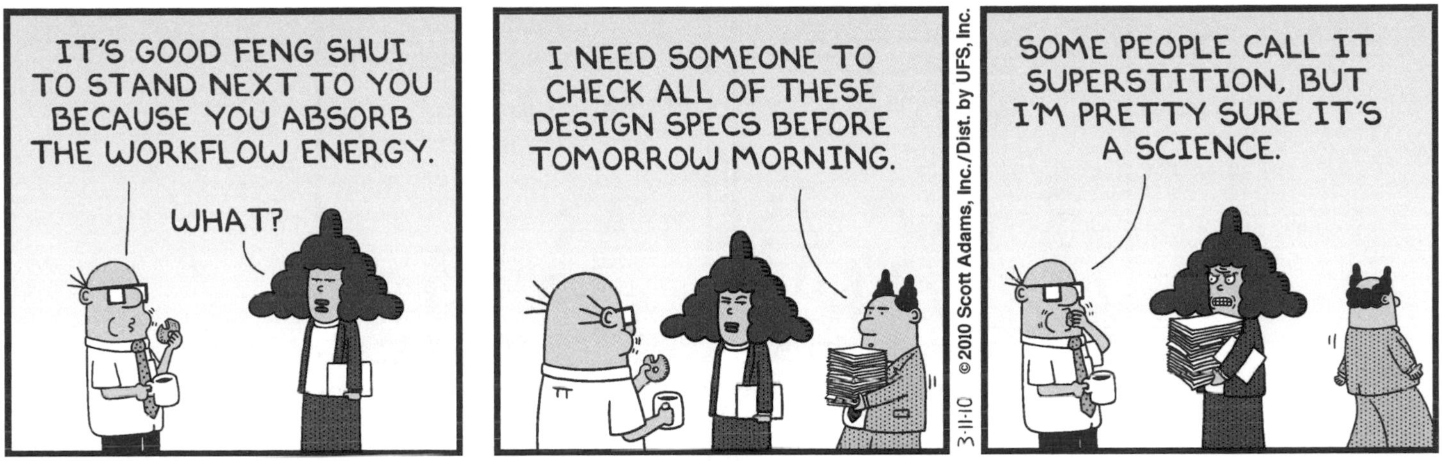
IT'S GOOD FENG SHUI TO STAND NEXT TO YOU BECAUSE YOU ABSORB THE WORKFLOW ENERGY.
WHAT?
I NEED SOMEONE TO CHECK ALL OF THESE DESIGN SPECS BEFORE TOMORROW MORNING.
SOME PEOPLE CALL IT SUPERSTITION, BUT I'M PRETTY SURE IT'S A SCIENCE.
3-11-10 © 2010 Scott Adams, Inc./Dist. by UFS, Inc.

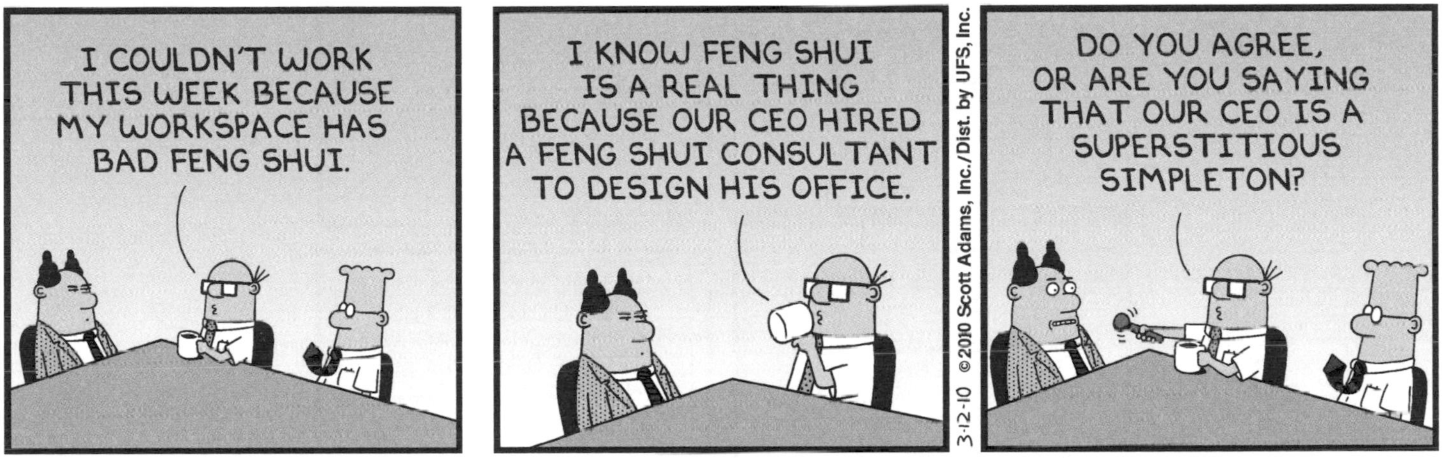
I COULDN'T WORK THIS WEEK BECAUSE MY WORKSPACE HAS BAD FENG SHUI.
I KNOW FENG SHUI IS A REAL THING BECAUSE OUR CEO HIRED A FENG SHUI CONSULTANT TO DESIGN HIS OFFICE.
DO YOU AGREE, OR ARE YOU SAYING THAT OUR CEO IS A SUPERSTITIOUS SIMPLETON?
3-12-10 © 2010 Scott Adams, Inc./Dist. by UFS, Inc.

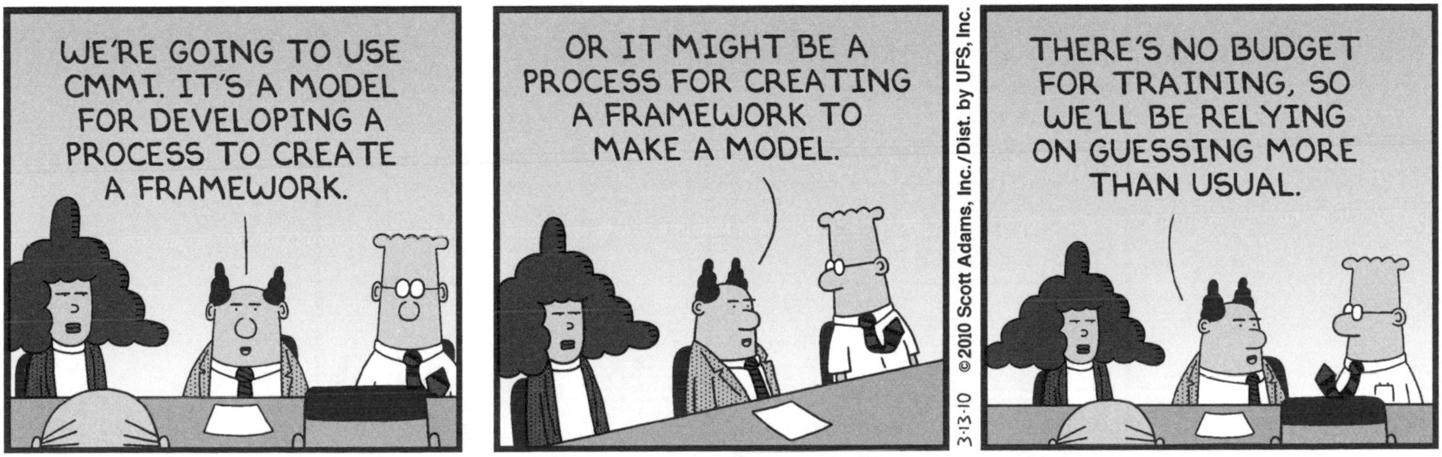
WE'RE GOING TO USE CMMI. IT'S A MODEL FOR DEVELOPING A PROCESS TO CREATE A FRAMEWORK.
OR IT MIGHT BE A PROCESS FOR CREATING A FRAMEWORK TO MAKE A MODEL.
THERE'S NO BUDGET FOR TRAINING, SO WE'LL BE RELYING ON GUESSING MORE THAN USUAL.
3-13-10 © 2010 Scott Adams, Inc./Dist. by UFS, Inc.

WE START SHIPPING IN TWO WEEKS.
THAT'S NOT ENOUGH TIME TO FIX THE KNOWN BUGS.
WHEN YOU SAY "BUGS," THAT'S SORT OF A GRAY AREA.
UM. . .I DON'T THINK IT IS.
FOR EXAMPLE, A USER MIGHT NEED SEVERAL STEPS TO DO SOME-THING THAT SHOULD ONLY TAKE ONE.
OR PERHAPS THE INTERFACE IS A BIT UNCLEAR.
OR PERHAPS IT CAN ONLY BE OPERATED BY A ROBOT FROM THE FUTURE WHO JACKS INTO IT AND SENDS COMMANDS IN ZEROS AND ONES.
I CAN'T TELL IF YOU'RE AGREEING WITH ME OR MOCKING ME.
THAT'S SORT OF A GRAY AREA.
3-14-10

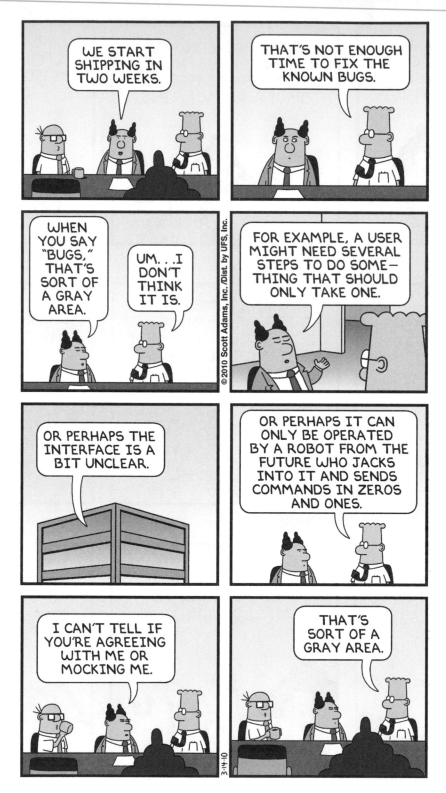

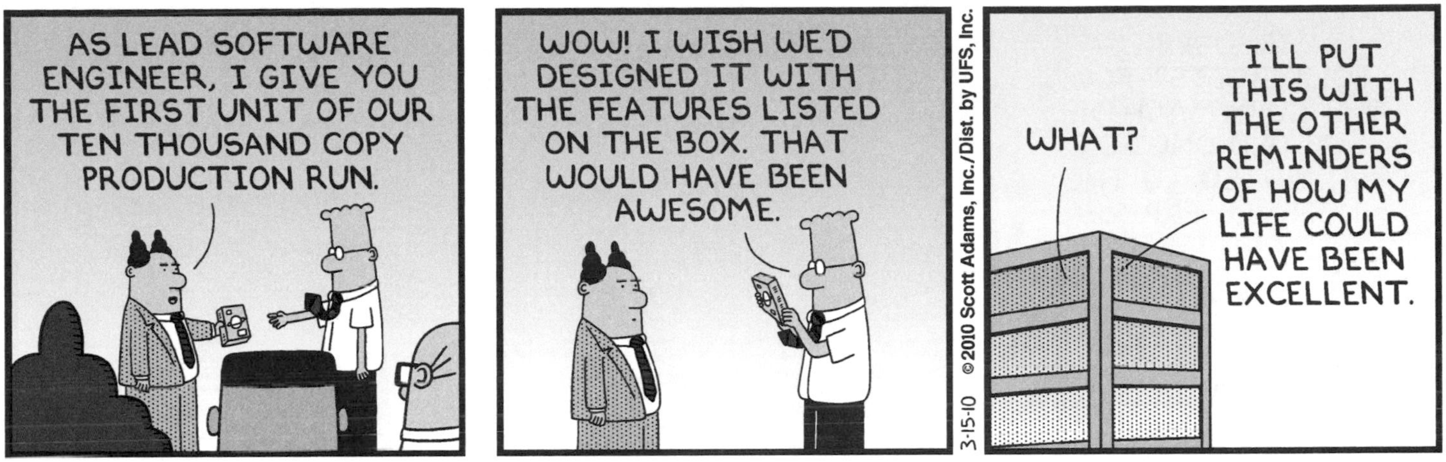
AS LEAD SOFTWARE ENGINEER, I GIVE YOU THE FIRST UNIT OF OUR TEN THOUSAND COPY PRODUCTION RUN.
WOW! I WISH WE'D DESIGNED IT WITH THE FEATURES LISTED ON THE BOX. THAT WOULD HAVE BEEN AWESOME.
3-15-10 ©2010 Scott Adams, Inc./Dist. by UFS, Inc.
WHAT?
I'LL PUT THIS WITH THE OTHER REMINDERS OF HOW MY LIFE COULD HAVE BEEN EXCELLENT.

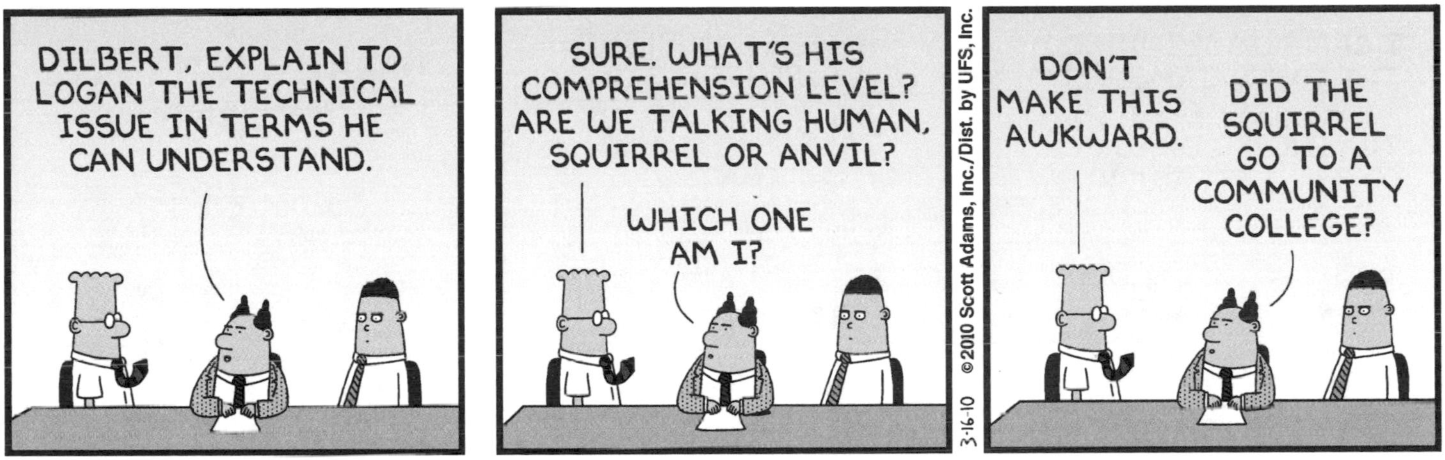
DILBERT, EXPLAIN TO LOGAN THE TECHNICAL ISSUE IN TERMS HE CAN UNDERSTAND.
SURE. WHAT'S HIS COMPREHENSION LEVEL? ARE WE TALKING HUMAN, SQUIRREL OR ANVIL?
WHICH ONE AM I?
3-16-10 ©2010 Scott Adams, Inc./Dist. by UFS, Inc.
DON'T MAKE THIS AWKWARD.
DID THE SQUIRREL GO TO A COMMUNITY COLLEGE?

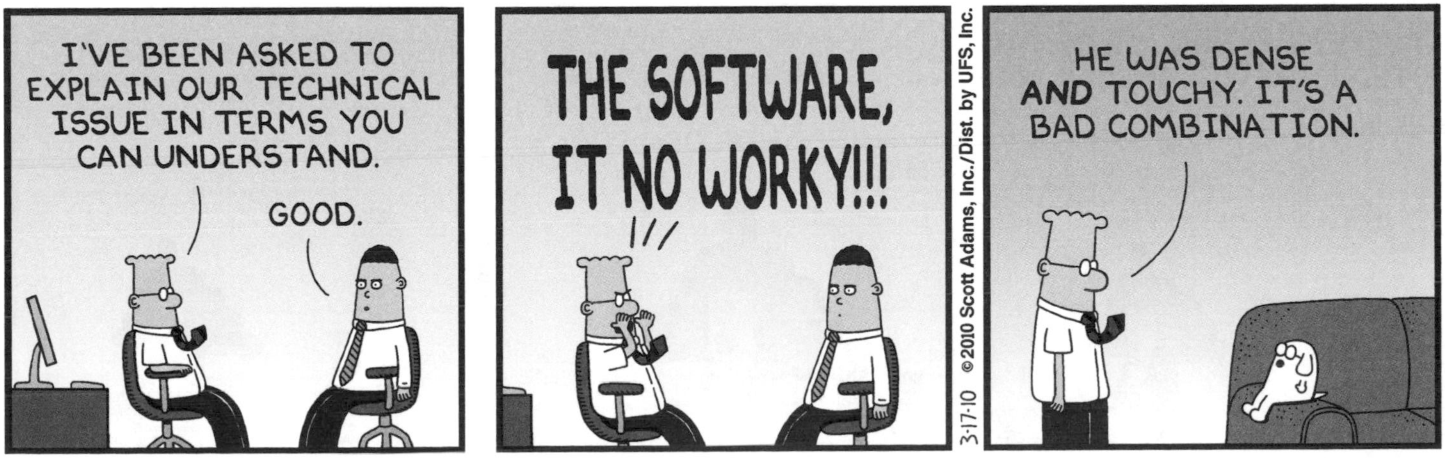
I'VE BEEN ASKED TO EXPLAIN OUR TECHNICAL ISSUE IN TERMS YOU CAN UNDERSTAND.
GOOD.
THE SOFTWARE, IT NO WORKY!!!
3-17-10 ©2010 Scott Adams, Inc./Dist. by UFS, Inc.
HE WAS DENSE AND TOUCHY. IT'S A BAD COMBINATION.

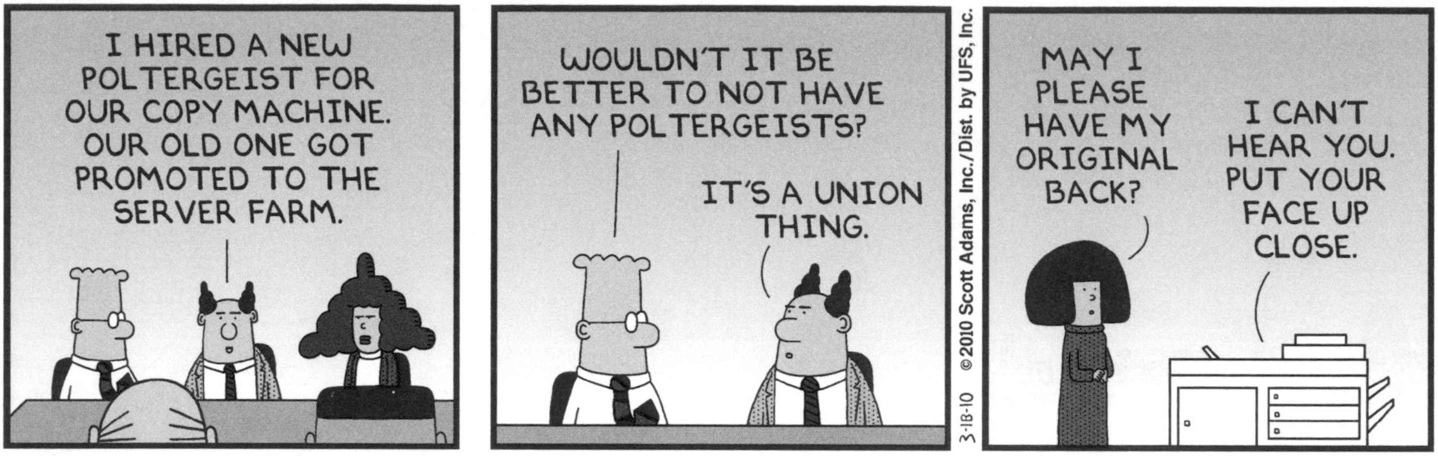
I HIRED A NEW POLTERGEIST FOR OUR COPY MACHINE. OUR OLD ONE GOT PROMOTED TO THE SERVER FARM.
WOULDN'T IT BE BETTER TO NOT HAVE ANY POLTERGEISTS?
IT'S A UNION THING.
3·18·10 © 2010 Scott Adams, Inc./Dist. by UFS, Inc.
MAY I PLEASE HAVE MY ORIGINAL BACK?
I CAN'T HEAR YOU. PUT YOUR FACE UP CLOSE.

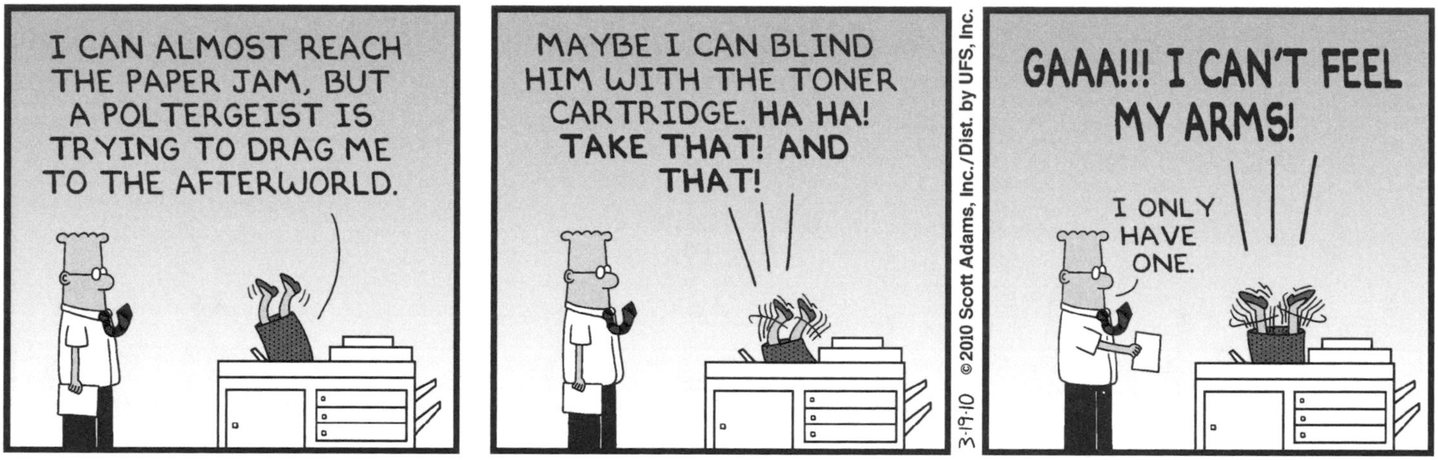
I CAN ALMOST REACH THE PAPER JAM, BUT A POLTERGEIST IS TRYING TO DRAG ME TO THE AFTERWORLD.
MAYBE I CAN BLIND HIM WITH THE TONER CARTRIDGE. HA HA! TAKE THAT! AND THAT!
3·19·10 © 2010 Scott Adams, Inc./Dist. by UFS, Inc.
GAAA!!! I CAN'T FEEL MY ARMS!
I ONLY HAVE ONE.

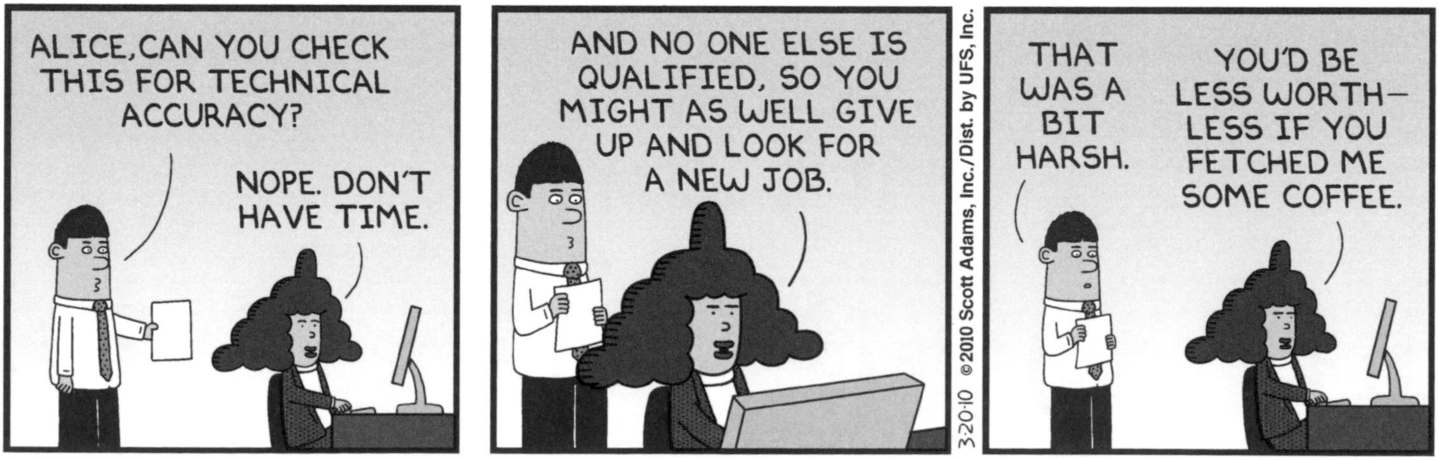
ALICE, CAN YOU CHECK THIS FOR TECHNICAL ACCURACY?
NOPE. DON'T HAVE TIME.
AND NO ONE ELSE IS QUALIFIED, SO YOU MIGHT AS WELL GIVE UP AND LOOK FOR A NEW JOB.
3·20·10 © 2010 Scott Adams, Inc./Dist. by UFS, Inc.
THAT WAS A BIT HARSH.
YOU'D BE LESS WORTH-LESS IF YOU FETCHED ME SOME COFFEE.

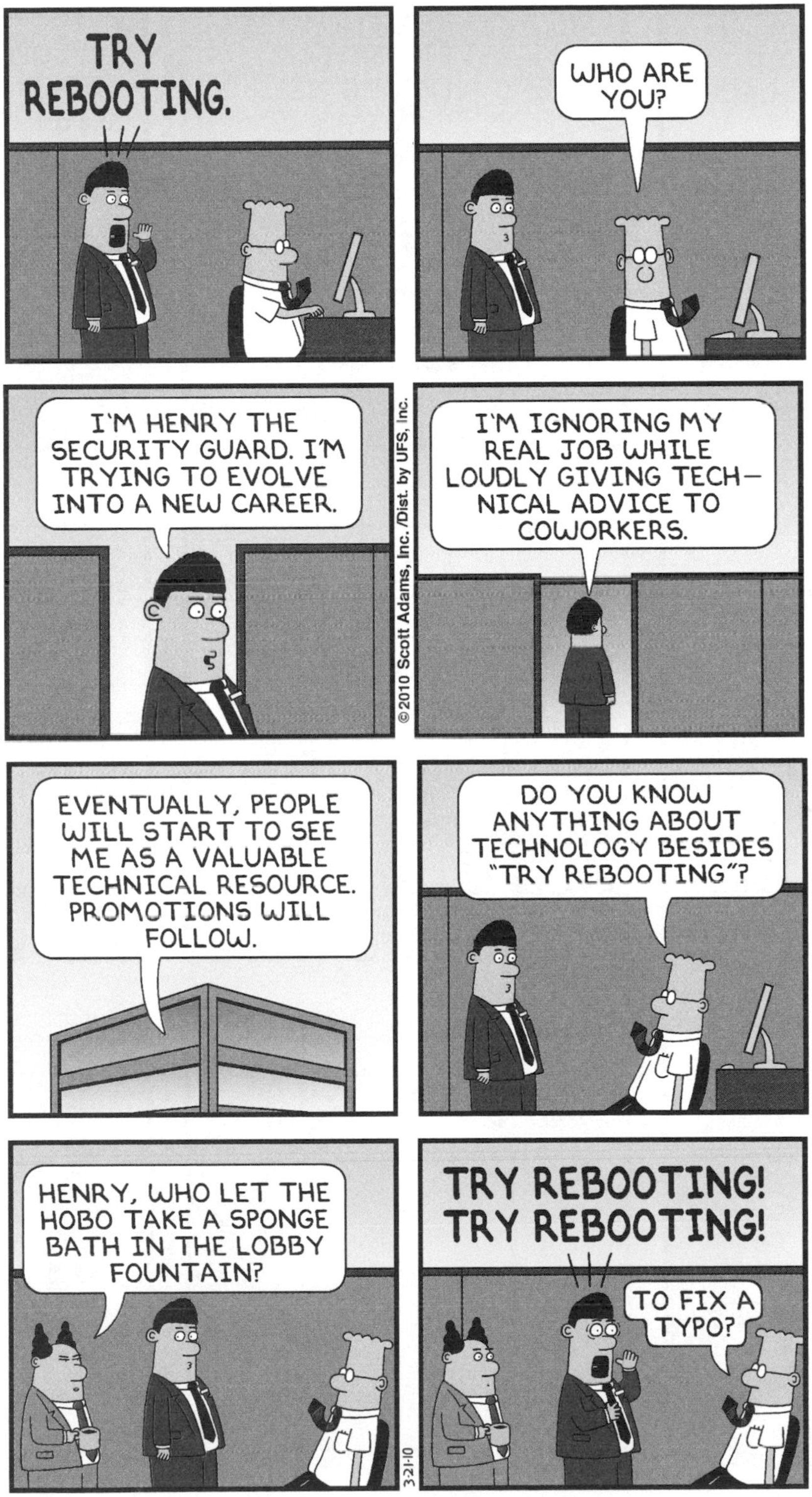
TRY REBOOTING.
WHO ARE YOU?
I'M HENRY THE SECURITY GUARD. I'M TRYING TO EVOLVE INTO A NEW CAREER.
I'M IGNORING MY REAL JOB WHILE LOUDLY GIVING TECHNICAL ADVICE TO COWORKERS.
EVENTUALLY, PEOPLE WILL START TO SEE ME AS A VALUABLE TECHNICAL RESOURCE. PROMOTIONS WILL FOLLOW.
DO YOU KNOW ANYTHING ABOUT TECHNOLOGY BESIDES "TRY REBOOTING"?
HENRY, WHO LET THE HOBO TAKE A SPONGE BATH IN THE LOBBY FOUNTAIN?
TRY REBOOTING! TRY REBOOTING!
TO FIX A TYPO?
©2010 Scott Adams, Inc./Dist. by UFS, Inc.
3-21-10

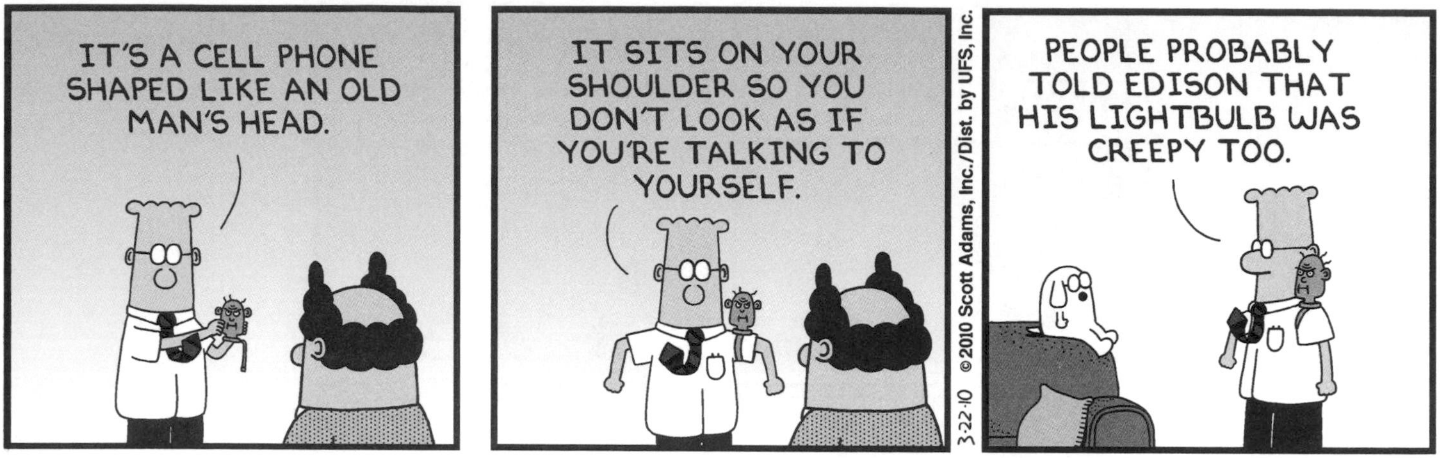
IT'S A CELL PHONE SHAPED LIKE AN OLD MAN'S HEAD.
IT SITS ON YOUR SHOULDER SO YOU DON'T LOOK AS IF YOU'RE TALKING TO YOURSELF.
3-22-10 ©2010 Scott Adams, Inc./Dist. by UFS, Inc.
PEOPLE PROBABLY TOLD EDISON THAT HIS LIGHTBULB WAS CREEPY TOO.

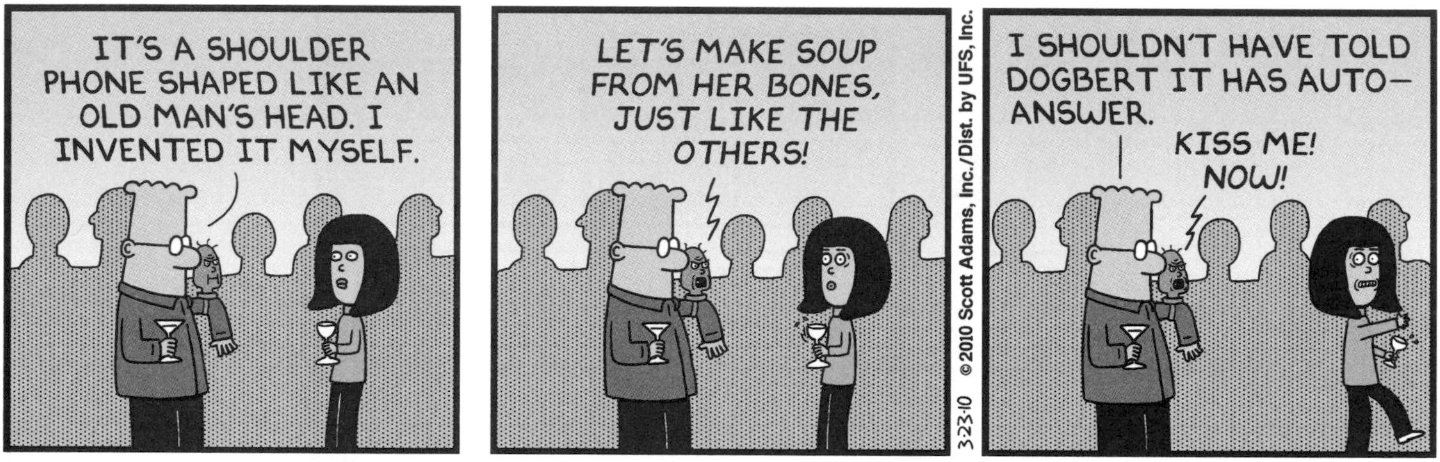
IT'S A SHOULDER PHONE SHAPED LIKE AN OLD MAN'S HEAD. I INVENTED IT MYSELF.
LET'S MAKE SOUP FROM HER BONES, JUST LIKE THE OTHERS!
3-23-10 ©2010 Scott Adams, Inc./Dist. by UFS, Inc.
I SHOULDN'T HAVE TOLD DOGBERT IT HAS AUTO-ANSWER.
KISS ME! NOW!

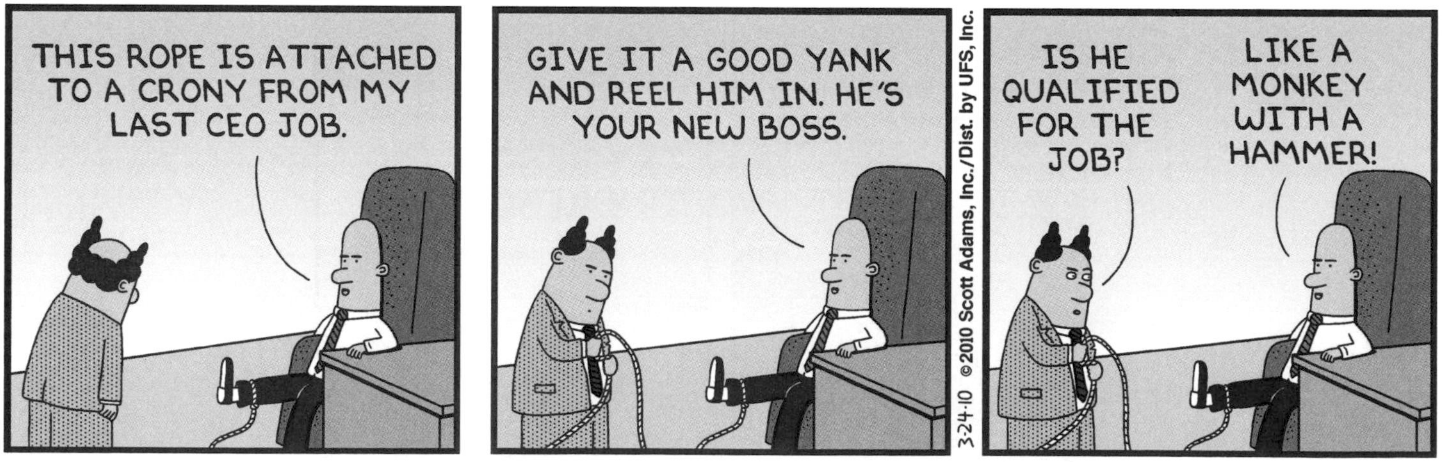
THIS ROPE IS ATTACHED TO A CRONY FROM MY LAST CEO JOB.
GIVE IT A GOOD YANK AND REEL HIM IN. HE'S YOUR NEW BOSS.
3-24-10 ©2010 Scott Adams, Inc./Dist. by UFS, Inc.
IS HE QUALIFIED FOR THE JOB?
LIKE A MONKEY WITH A HAMMER!

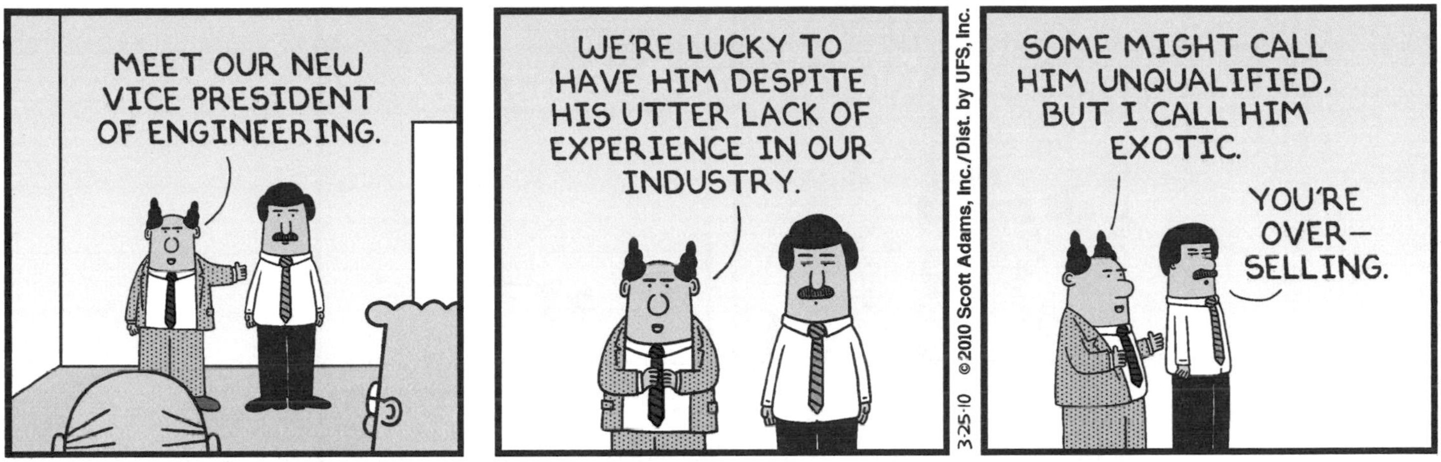
MEET OUR NEW VICE PRESIDENT OF ENGINEERING.
WE'RE LUCKY TO HAVE HIM DESPITE HIS UTTER LACK OF EXPERIENCE IN OUR INDUSTRY.
3·25·10 ©2010 Scott Adams, Inc./Dist. by UFS, Inc.
SOME MIGHT CALL HIM UNQUALIFIED, BUT I CALL HIM EXOTIC.
YOU'RE OVER-SELLING.

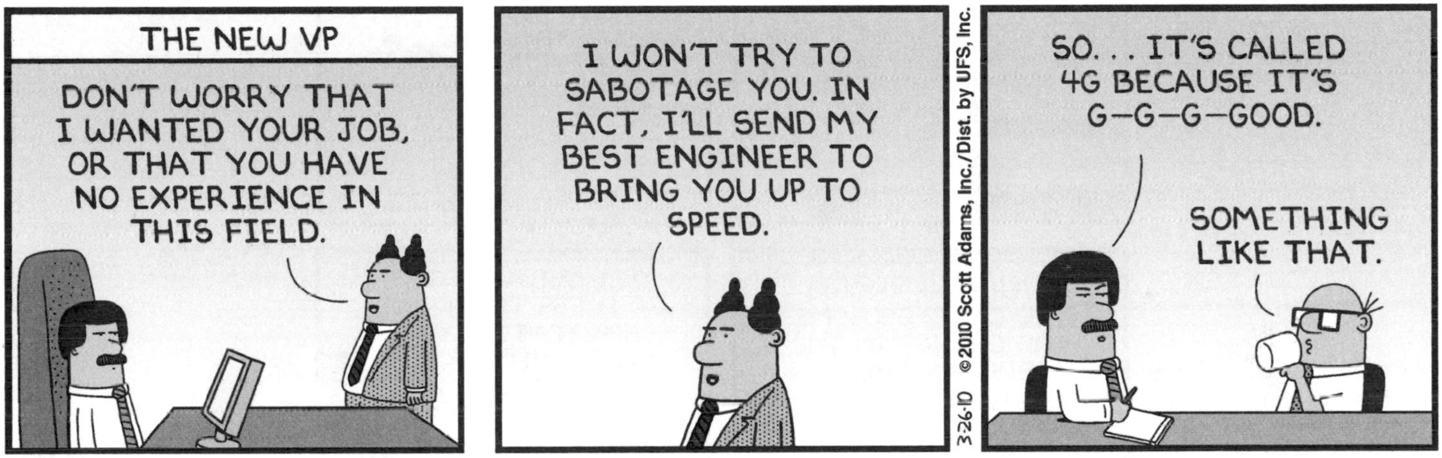
THE NEW VP
DON'T WORRY THAT I WANTED YOUR JOB, OR THAT YOU HAVE NO EXPERIENCE IN THIS FIELD.
I WON'T TRY TO SABOTAGE YOU. IN FACT, I'LL SEND MY BEST ENGINEER TO BRING YOU UP TO SPEED.
3·26·10 ©2010 Scott Adams, Inc./Dist. by UFS, Inc.
SO. . . IT'S CALLED 4G BECAUSE IT'S G-G-G-GOOD.
SOMETHING LIKE THAT.

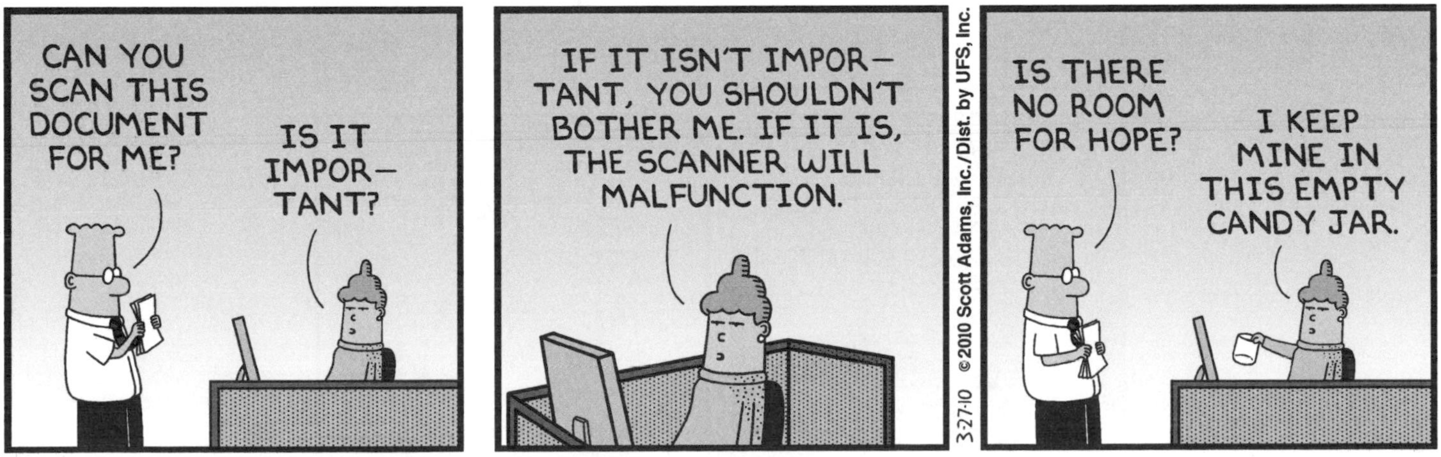
CAN YOU SCAN THIS DOCUMENT FOR ME?
IS IT IMPOR-TANT?
IF IT ISN'T IMPOR-TANT, YOU SHOULDN'T BOTHER ME. IF IT IS, THE SCANNER WILL MALFUNCTION.
3·27·10 ©2010 Scott Adams, Inc./Dist. by UFS, Inc.
IS THERE NO ROOM FOR HOPE?
I KEEP MINE IN THIS EMPTY CANDY JAR.

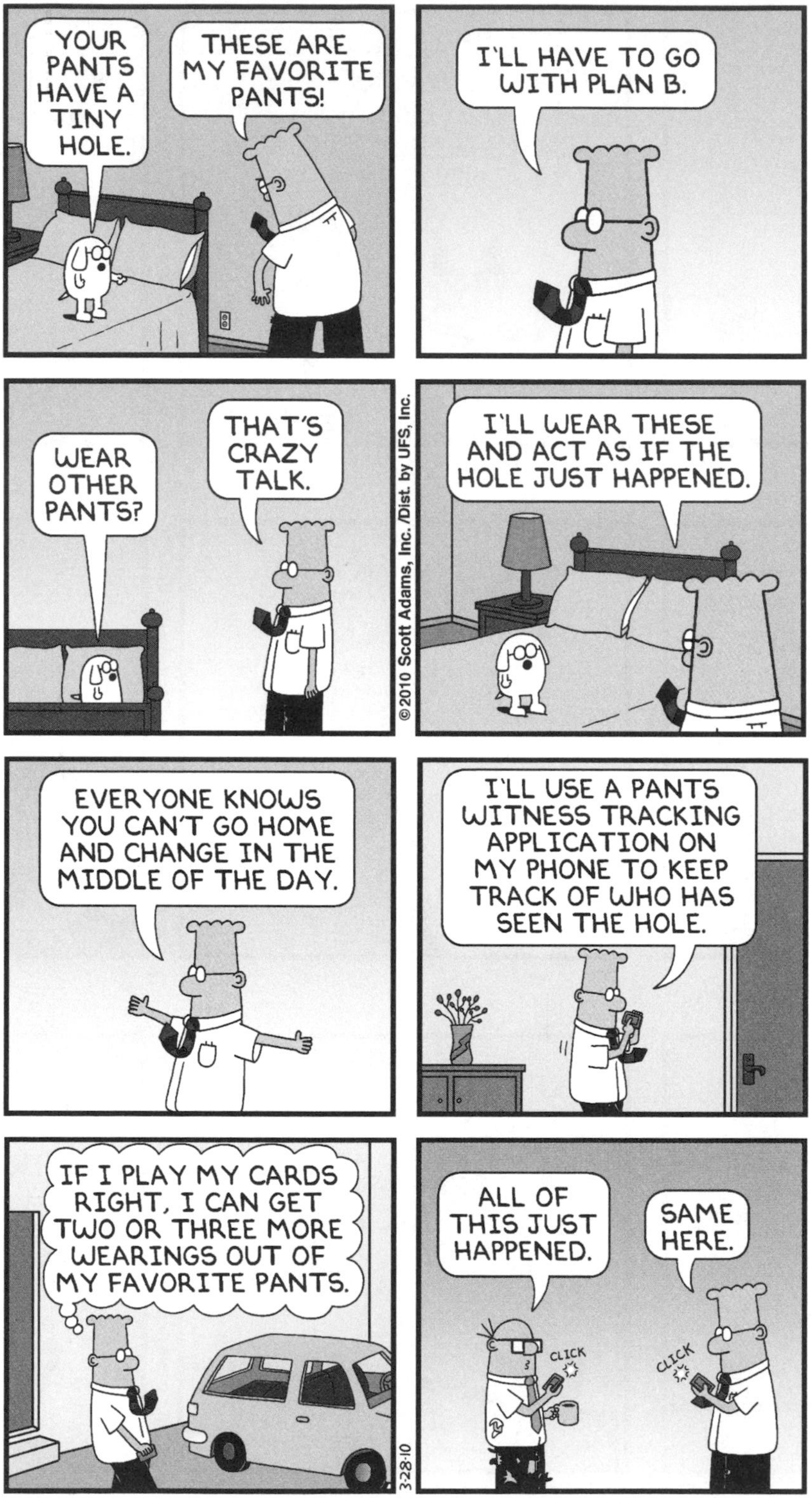
YOUR PANTS HAVE A TINY HOLE.
THESE ARE MY FAVORITE PANTS!
I'LL HAVE TO GO WITH PLAN B.
WEAR OTHER PANTS?
THAT'S CRAZY TALK.
©2010 Scott Adams, Inc. /Dist. by UFS, Inc.
I'LL WEAR THESE AND ACT AS IF THE HOLE JUST HAPPENED.
EVERYONE KNOWS YOU CAN'T GO HOME AND CHANGE IN THE MIDDLE OF THE DAY.
I'LL USE A PANTS WITNESS TRACKING APPLICATION ON MY PHONE TO KEEP TRACK OF WHO HAS SEEN THE HOLE.
IF I PLAY MY CARDS RIGHT, I CAN GET TWO OR THREE MORE WEARINGS OUT OF MY FAVORITE PANTS.
3-28-10
ALL OF THIS JUST HAPPENED.
SAME HERE.
CLICK
CLICK

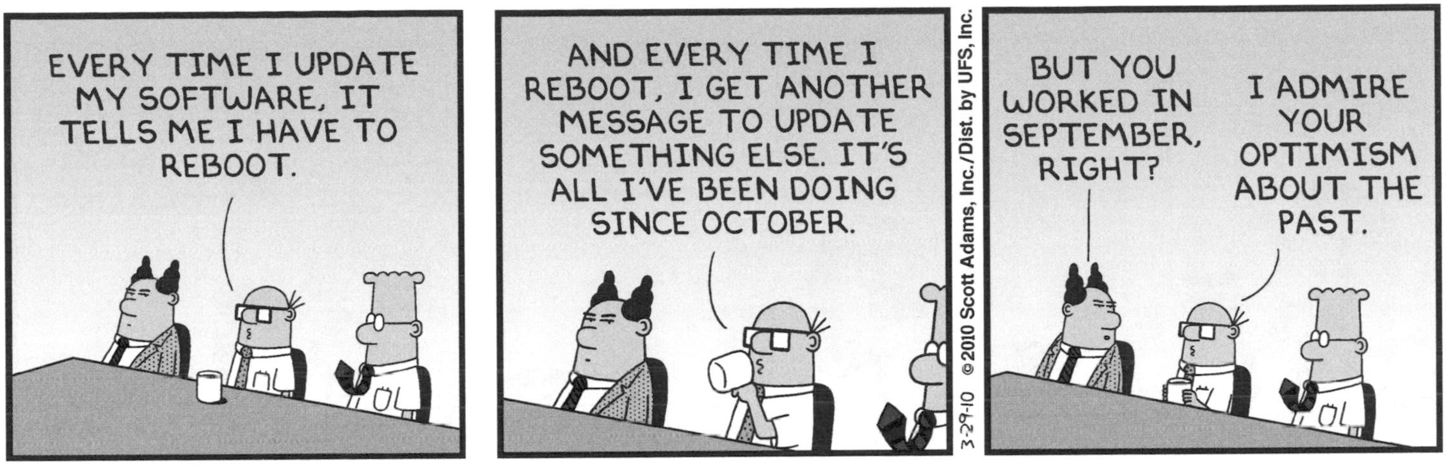
EVERY TIME I UPDATE MY SOFTWARE, IT TELLS ME I HAVE TO REBOOT.
AND EVERY TIME I REBOOT, I GET ANOTHER MESSAGE TO UPDATE SOMETHING ELSE. IT'S ALL I'VE BEEN DOING SINCE OCTOBER.
3-29-10 ©2010 Scott Adams, Inc./Dist. by UFS, Inc.
BUT YOU WORKED IN SEPTEMBER, RIGHT?
I ADMIRE YOUR OPTIMISM ABOUT THE PAST.

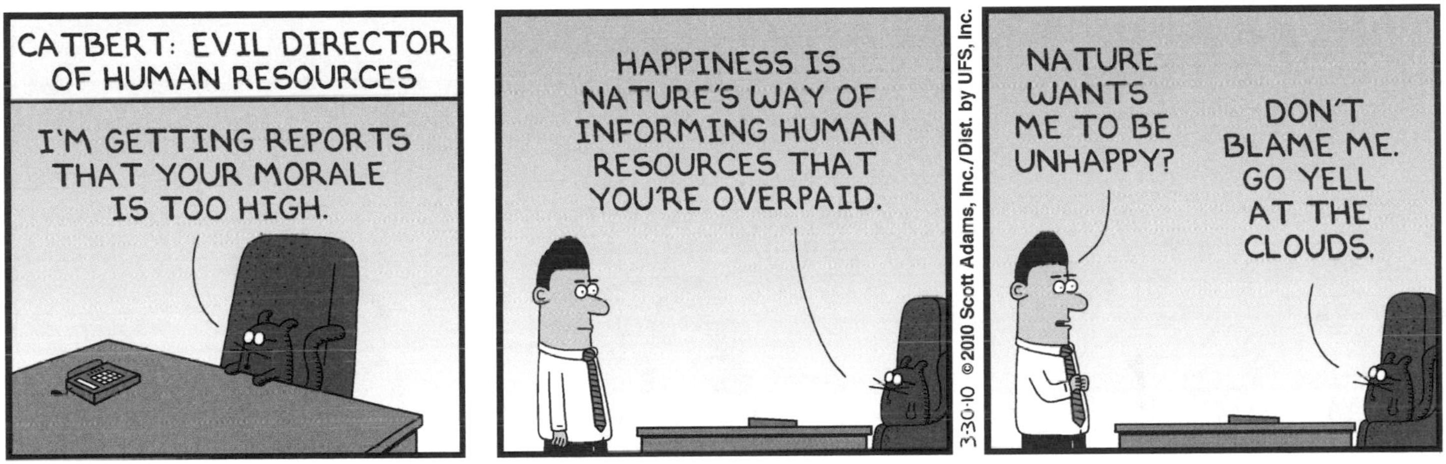
CATBERT: EVIL DIRECTOR OF HUMAN RESOURCES
I'M GETTING REPORTS THAT YOUR MORALE IS TOO HIGH.
HAPPINESS IS NATURE'S WAY OF INFORMING HUMAN RESOURCES THAT YOU'RE OVERPAID.
3-30-10 ©2010 Scott Adams, Inc./Dist. by UFS, Inc.
NATURE WANTS ME TO BE UNHAPPY?
DON'T BLAME ME. GO YELL AT THE CLOUDS.

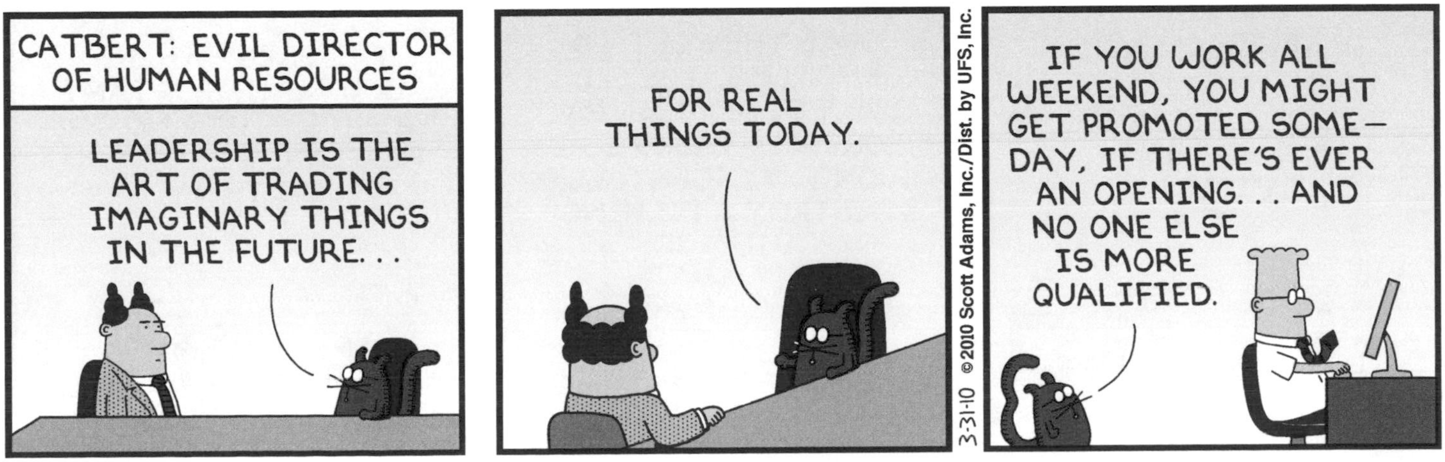
CATBERT: EVIL DIRECTOR OF HUMAN RESOURCES
LEADERSHIP IS THE ART OF TRADING IMAGINARY THINGS IN THE FUTURE. . .
FOR REAL THINGS TODAY.
3-31-10 ©2010 Scott Adams, Inc./Dist. by UFS, Inc.
IF YOU WORK ALL WEEKEND, YOU MIGHT GET PROMOTED SOME-DAY, IF THERE'S EVER AN OPENING. . . AND NO ONE ELSE IS MORE QUALIFIED.

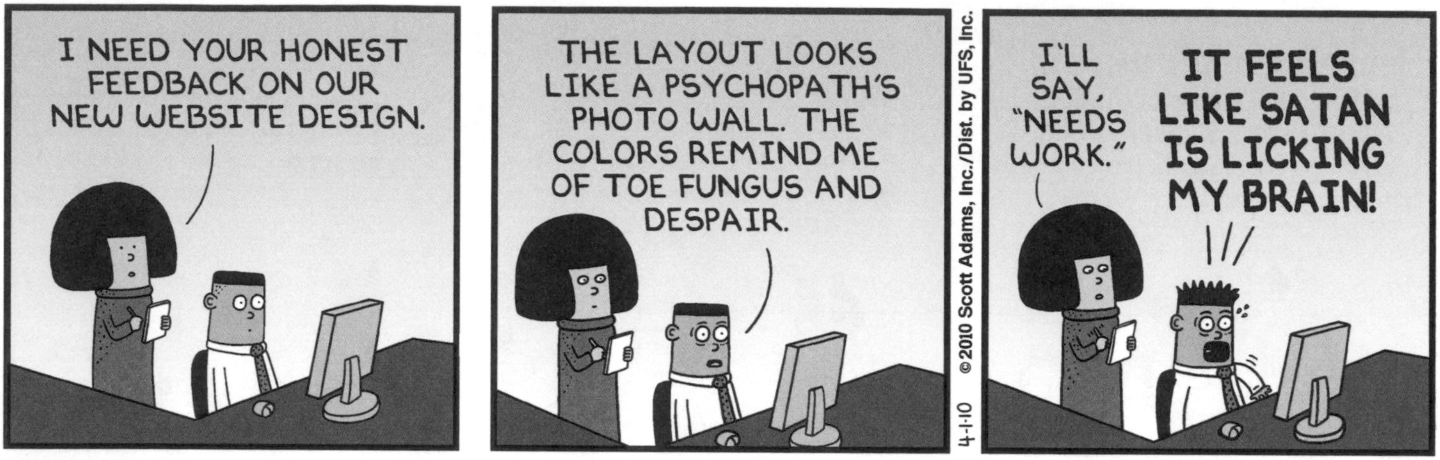
I NEED YOUR HONEST FEEDBACK ON OUR NEW WEBSITE DESIGN.
THE LAYOUT LOOKS LIKE A PSYCHOPATH'S PHOTO WALL. THE COLORS REMIND ME OF TOE FUNGUS AND DESPAIR.
4-1-10
©2010 Scott Adams, Inc./Dist. by UFS, Inc.
I'LL SAY, "NEEDS WORK."
IT FEELS LIKE SATAN IS LICKING MY BRAIN!

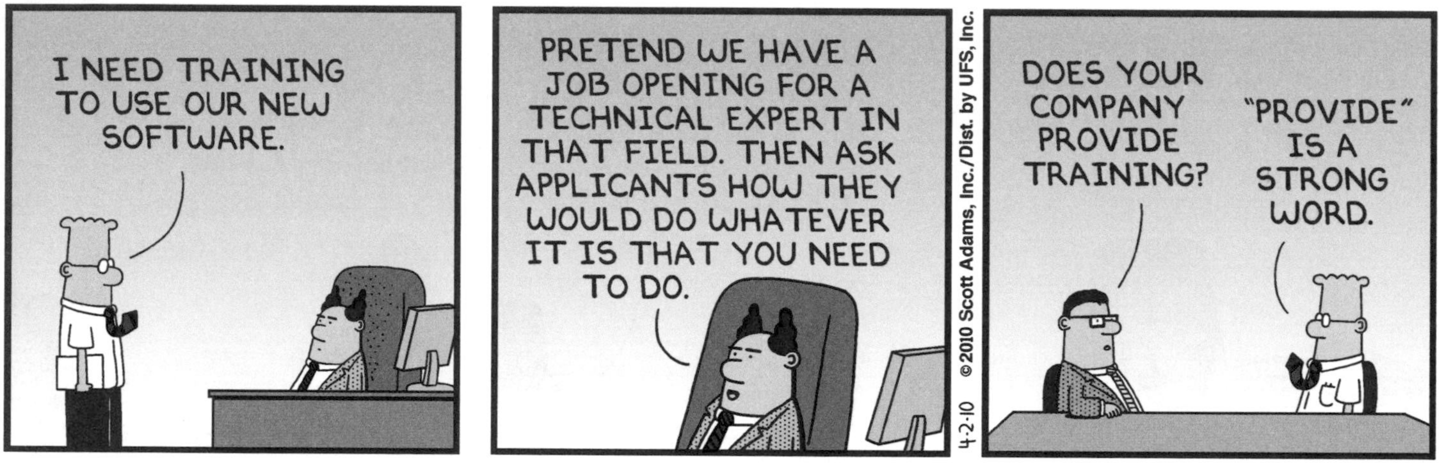
I NEED TRAINING TO USE OUR NEW SOFTWARE.
PRETEND WE HAVE A JOB OPENING FOR A TECHNICAL EXPERT IN THAT FIELD. THEN ASK APPLICANTS HOW THEY WOULD DO WHATEVER IT IS THAT YOU NEED TO DO.
4-2-10
©2010 Scott Adams, Inc./Dist. by UFS, Inc.
DOES YOUR COMPANY PROVIDE TRAINING?
"PROVIDE" IS A STRONG WORD.

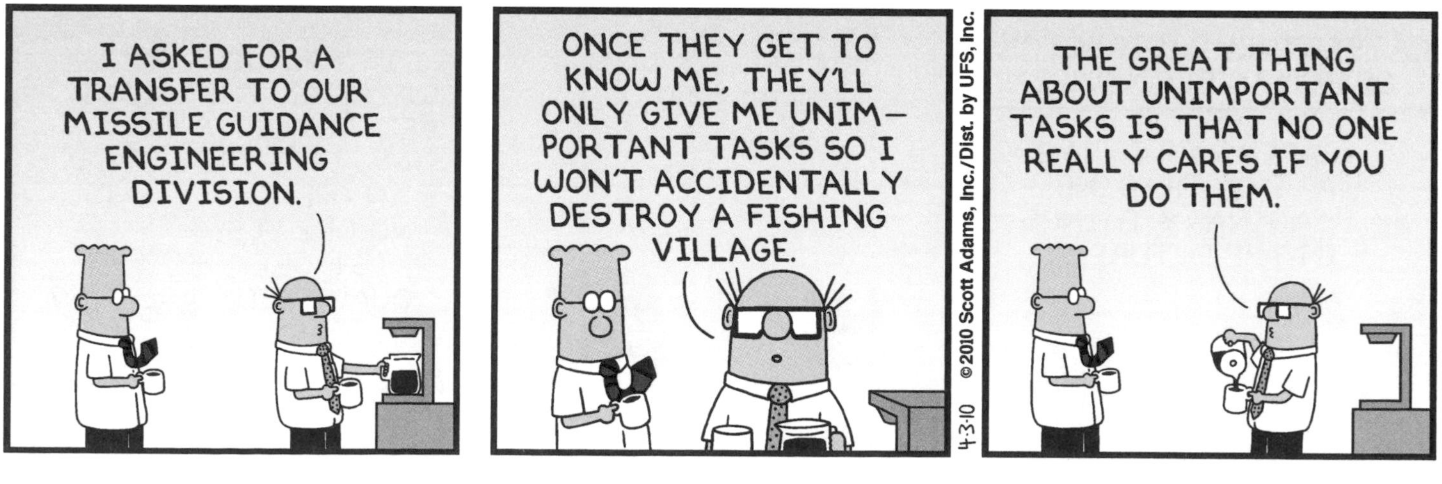
I ASKED FOR A TRANSFER TO OUR MISSILE GUIDANCE ENGINEERING DIVISION.
ONCE THEY GET TO KNOW ME, THEY'LL ONLY GIVE ME UNIM–PORTANT TASKS SO I WON'T ACCIDENTALLY DESTROY A FISHING VILLAGE.
4-3-10
©2010 Scott Adams, Inc./Dist. by UFS, Inc.
THE GREAT THING ABOUT UNIMPORTANT TASKS IS THAT NO ONE REALLY CARES IF YOU DO THEM.

HOW'S THE CPG PROJECT COMING ALONG?
HOW WOULD I KNOW?
YOU'RE LEADING THAT PROJECT.
I AM? SINCE WHEN?
I TOLD EVERYONE ON THE TEAM TWO MONTHS AGO.
I'M NOT ON THE TEAM. YOU NEVER TOLD ME.
WHATEVER, GO TELL THE TEAM YOU'VE BEEN IN CHARGE FOR THE PAST TWO MONTHS AND SEE WHAT THEY'VE ACCOMPLISHED.
© 2010 Scott Adams, Inc. /Dist. by UFS, Inc.
WHO IS ON THE TEAM?
I FORGET. I THINK ONE HAD DARK HAIR, AND ANOTHER ONE WAS SAD.
DON'T TELL THEM THERE'S A DUPLICATE PROJECT IN ANOTHER DIVISION.
4-4-10
YOU'LL BE OKAY. JUST RELEASE THE CARING. LET IT GO.

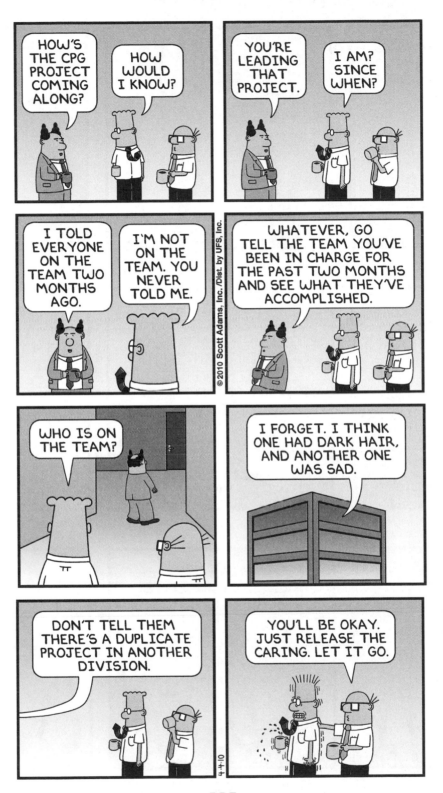

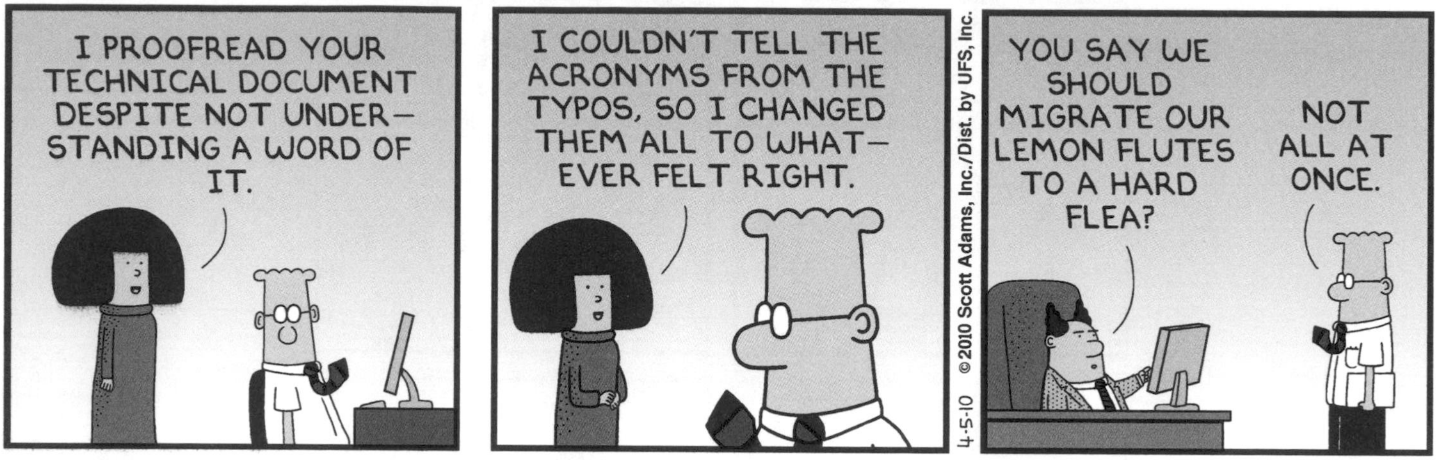
I PROOFREAD YOUR TECHNICAL DOCUMENT DESPITE NOT UNDER-STANDING A WORD OF IT.
I COULDN'T TELL THE ACRONYMS FROM THE TYPOS, SO I CHANGED THEM ALL TO WHAT-EVER FELT RIGHT.
4-5-10 ©2010 Scott Adams, Inc./Dist. by UFS, Inc.
YOU SAY WE SHOULD MIGRATE OUR LEMON FLUTES TO A HARD FLEA?
NOT ALL AT ONCE.

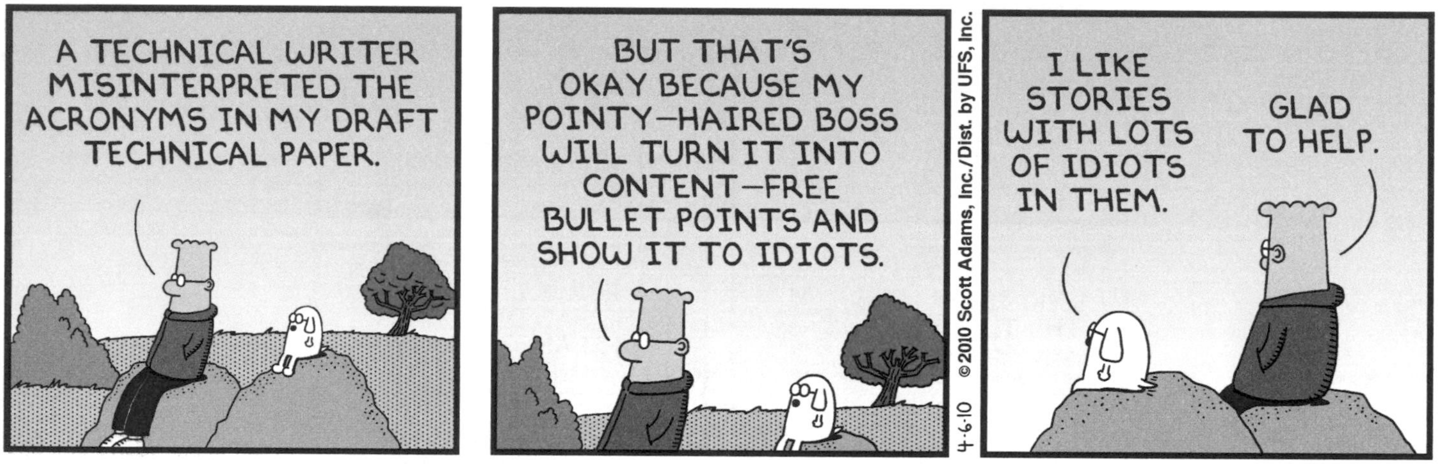
A TECHNICAL WRITER MISINTERPRETED THE ACRONYMS IN MY DRAFT TECHNICAL PAPER.
BUT THAT'S OKAY BECAUSE MY POINTY-HAIRED BOSS WILL TURN IT INTO CONTENT-FREE BULLET POINTS AND SHOW IT TO IDIOTS.
4-6-10 ©2010 Scott Adams, Inc./Dist. by UFS, Inc.
I LIKE STORIES WITH LOTS OF IDIOTS IN THEM.
GLAD TO HELP.

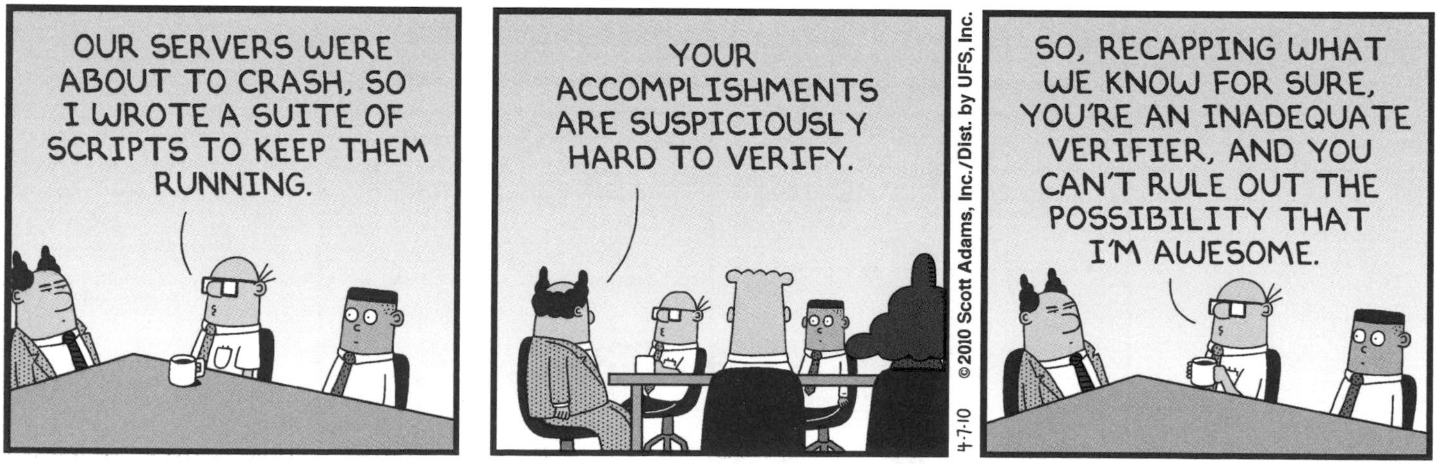
OUR SERVERS WERE ABOUT TO CRASH, SO I WROTE A SUITE OF SCRIPTS TO KEEP THEM RUNNING.
YOUR ACCOMPLISHMENTS ARE SUSPICIOUSLY HARD TO VERIFY.
4-7-10 ©2010 Scott Adams, Inc./Dist. by UFS, Inc.
SO, RECAPPING WHAT WE KNOW FOR SURE, YOU'RE AN INADEQUATE VERIFIER, AND YOU CAN'T RULE OUT THE POSSIBILITY THAT I'M AWESOME.

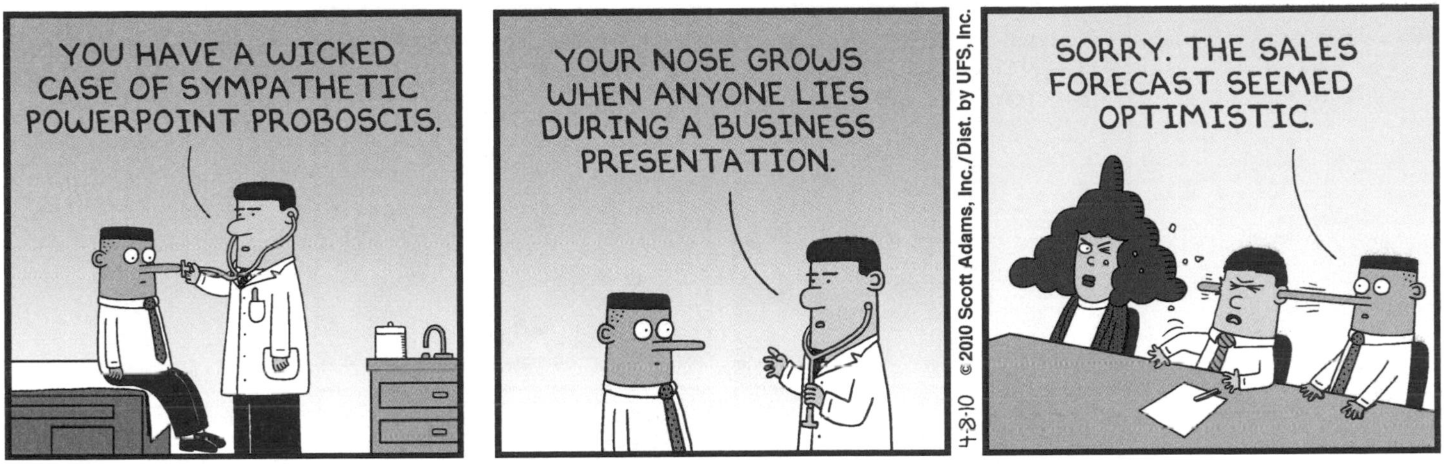
YOU HAVE A WICKED CASE OF SYMPATHETIC POWERPOINT PROBOSCIS.
YOUR NOSE GROWS WHEN ANYONE LIES DURING A BUSINESS PRESENTATION.
SORRY. THE SALES FORECAST SEEMED OPTIMISTIC.
4-8-10 © 2010 Scott Adams, Inc./Dist. by UFS, Inc.

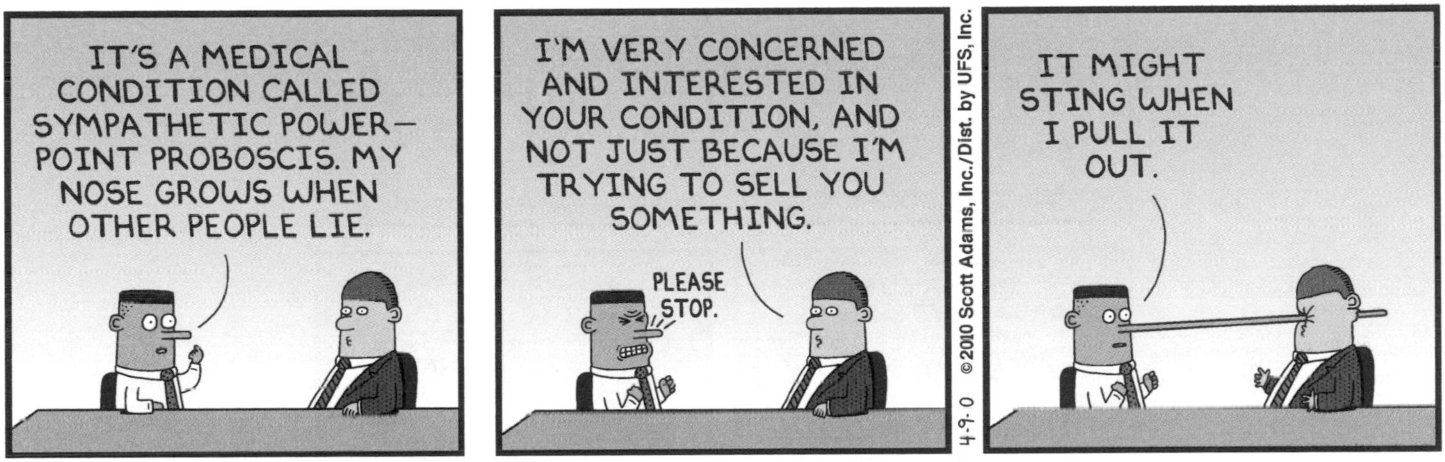
IT'S A MEDICAL CONDITION CALLED SYMPATHETIC POWER-POINT PROBOSCIS. MY NOSE GROWS WHEN OTHER PEOPLE LIE.
I'M VERY CONCERNED AND INTERESTED IN YOUR CONDITION, AND NOT JUST BECAUSE I'M TRYING TO SELL YOU SOMETHING.
PLEASE STOP.
IT MIGHT STING WHEN I PULL IT OUT.
© 2010 Scott Adams, Inc./Dist. by UFS, Inc.

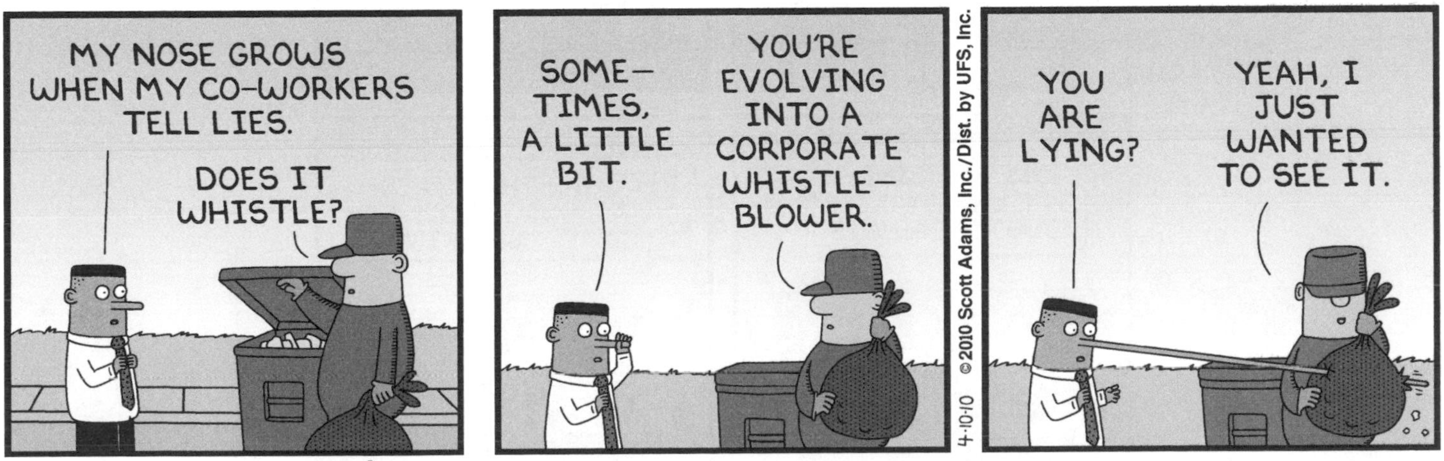
MY NOSE GROWS WHEN MY CO-WORKERS TELL LIES.
DOES IT WHISTLE?
SOME-TIMES, A LITTLE BIT.
YOU'RE EVOLVING INTO A CORPORATE WHISTLE-BLOWER.
YOU ARE LYING?
YEAH, I JUST WANTED TO SEE IT.
4-10-10 © 2010 Scott Adams, Inc./Dist. by UFS, Inc.

THE BETA TEST WENT WELL. THANK YOU, DILBERT.
NOW I'LL HAVE TINA ADD AN IMPRACTICAL MAINTENANCE REQUIRE-MENT TO THE MANUAL AND WE'RE READY TO GO.
WHAT?
IT'S STANDARD PROCEDURE.
©2010 Scott Adams, Inc. /Dist. by UFS, Inc.
SAY THE USER NEEDS TO LUBE THE PRODUCT TEN TIMES A DAY WITH THE WAX FROM A BEAR'S EAR.
AND SAY THE WARRANTY IS VOIDED IF THE DEVICE ISN'T PROPERLY MAINTAINED.
IS THAT LEGAL?
IT'S BETTER THAN LEGAL.
WE'RE USING THE LAW TO KEEP JUSTICE AWAY!!
4-11-10
I FEEL SICK.
THAT'S HOW YOU KNOW IT'S WORKING.

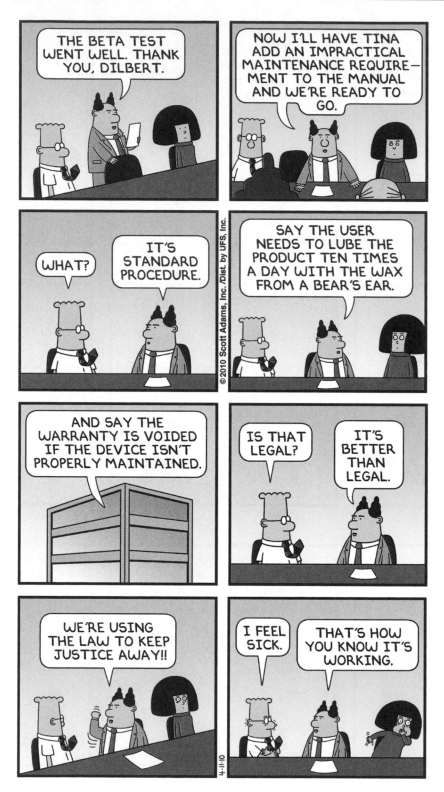

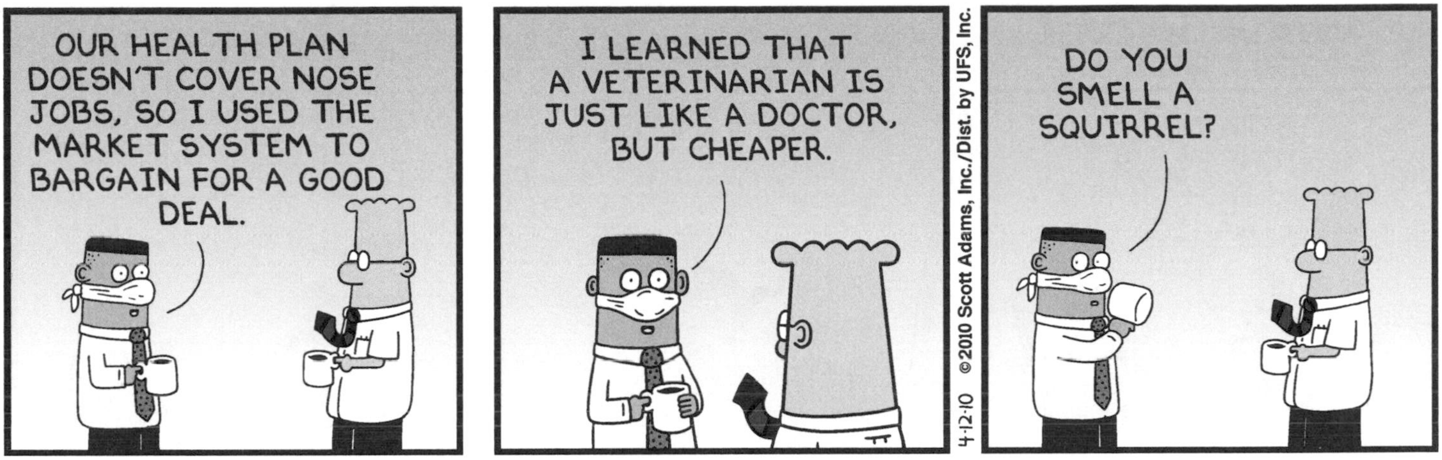
OUR HEALTH PLAN DOESN'T COVER NOSE JOBS, SO I USED THE MARKET SYSTEM TO BARGAIN FOR A GOOD DEAL.
I LEARNED THAT A VETERINARIAN IS JUST LIKE A DOCTOR, BUT CHEAPER.
4-12-10 ©2010 Scott Adams, Inc./Dist. by UFS, Inc.
DO YOU SMELL A SQUIRREL?

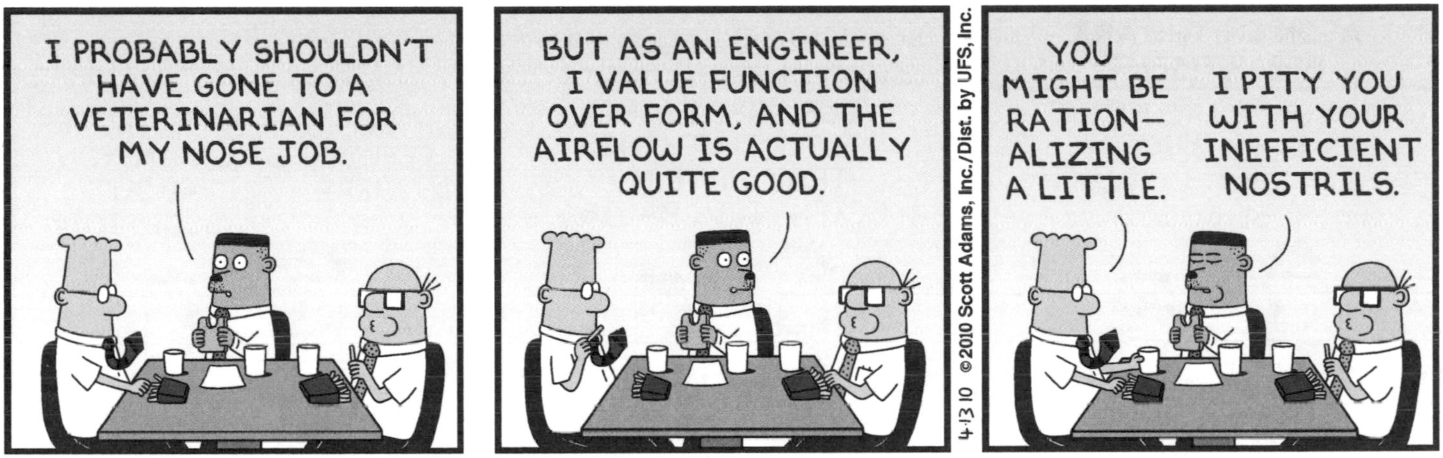
I PROBABLY SHOULDN'T HAVE GONE TO A VETERINARIAN FOR MY NOSE JOB.
BUT AS AN ENGINEER, I VALUE FUNCTION OVER FORM, AND THE AIRFLOW IS ACTUALLY QUITE GOOD.
4-13-10 ©2010 Scott Adams, Inc./Dist. by UFS, Inc.
YOU MIGHT BE RATION- ALIZING A LITTLE.
I PITY YOU WITH YOUR INEFFICIENT NOSTRILS.

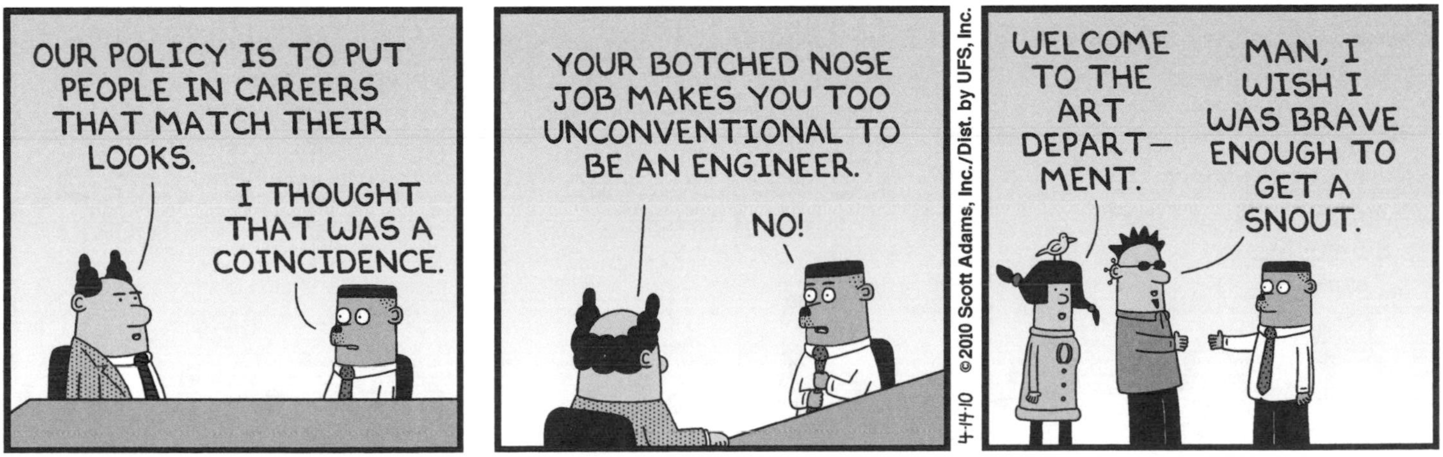
OUR POLICY IS TO PUT PEOPLE IN CAREERS THAT MATCH THEIR LOOKS.
I THOUGHT THAT WAS A COINCIDENCE.
YOUR BOTCHED NOSE JOB MAKES YOU TOO UNCONVENTIONAL TO BE AN ENGINEER.
NO!
4-14-10 ©2010 Scott Adams, Inc./Dist. by UFS, Inc.
WELCOME TO THE ART DEPART- MENT.
MAN, I WISH I WAS BRAVE ENOUGH TO GET A SNOUT.

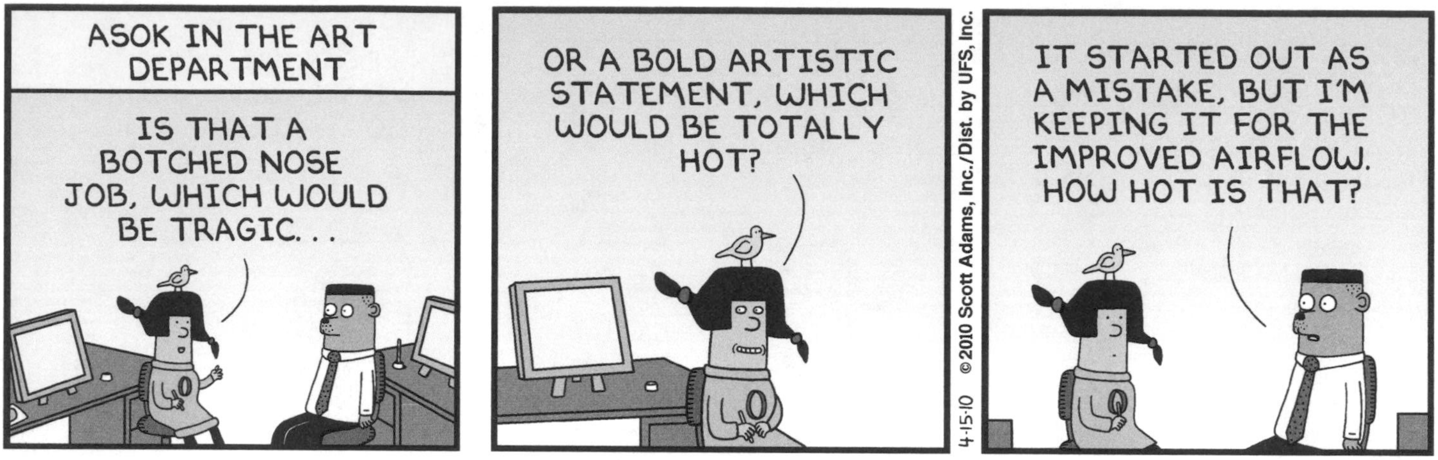
ASOK IN THE ART DEPARTMENT
IS THAT A BOTCHED NOSE JOB, WHICH WOULD BE TRAGIC. . .
OR A BOLD ARTISTIC STATEMENT, WHICH WOULD BE TOTALLY HOT?
4-15-10 ©2010 Scott Adams, Inc./Dist. by UFS, Inc.
IT STARTED OUT AS A MISTAKE, BUT I'M KEEPING IT FOR THE IMPROVED AIRFLOW. HOW HOT IS THAT?

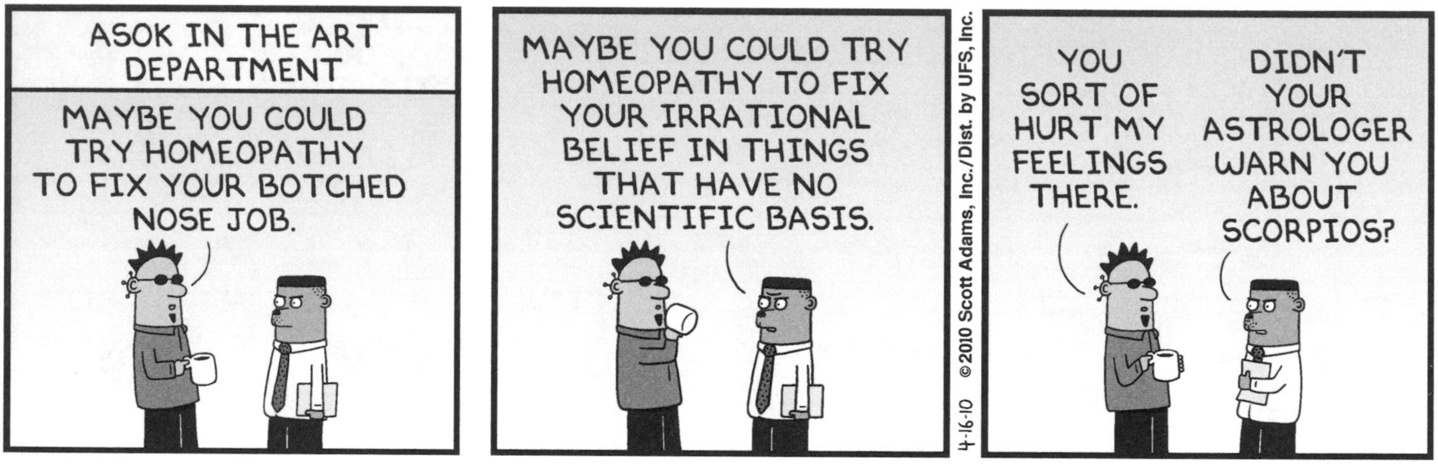
ASOK IN THE ART DEPARTMENT
MAYBE YOU COULD TRY HOMEOPATHY TO FIX YOUR BOTCHED NOSE JOB.
MAYBE YOU COULD TRY HOMEOPATHY TO FIX YOUR IRRATIONAL BELIEF IN THINGS THAT HAVE NO SCIENTIFIC BASIS.
4-16-10 ©2010 Scott Adams, Inc./Dist. by UFS, Inc.
YOU SORT OF HURT MY FEELINGS THERE.
DIDN'T YOUR ASTROLOGER WARN YOU ABOUT SCORPIOS?

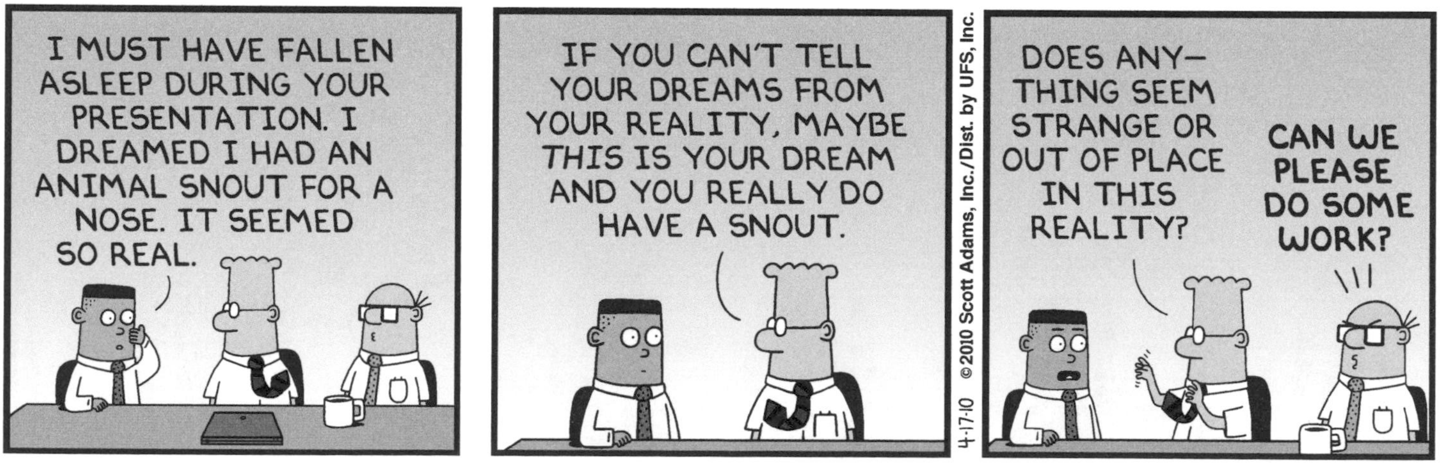
I MUST HAVE FALLEN ASLEEP DURING YOUR PRESENTATION. I DREAMED I HAD AN ANIMAL SNOUT FOR A NOSE. IT SEEMED SO REAL.
IF YOU CAN'T TELL YOUR DREAMS FROM YOUR REALITY, MAYBE *THIS* IS YOUR DREAM AND YOU REALLY DO HAVE A SNOUT.
4-17-10 ©2010 Scott Adams, Inc./Dist. by UFS, Inc.
DOES ANY-THING SEEM STRANGE OR OUT OF PLACE IN THIS REALITY?
CAN WE PLEASE DO SOME WORK?

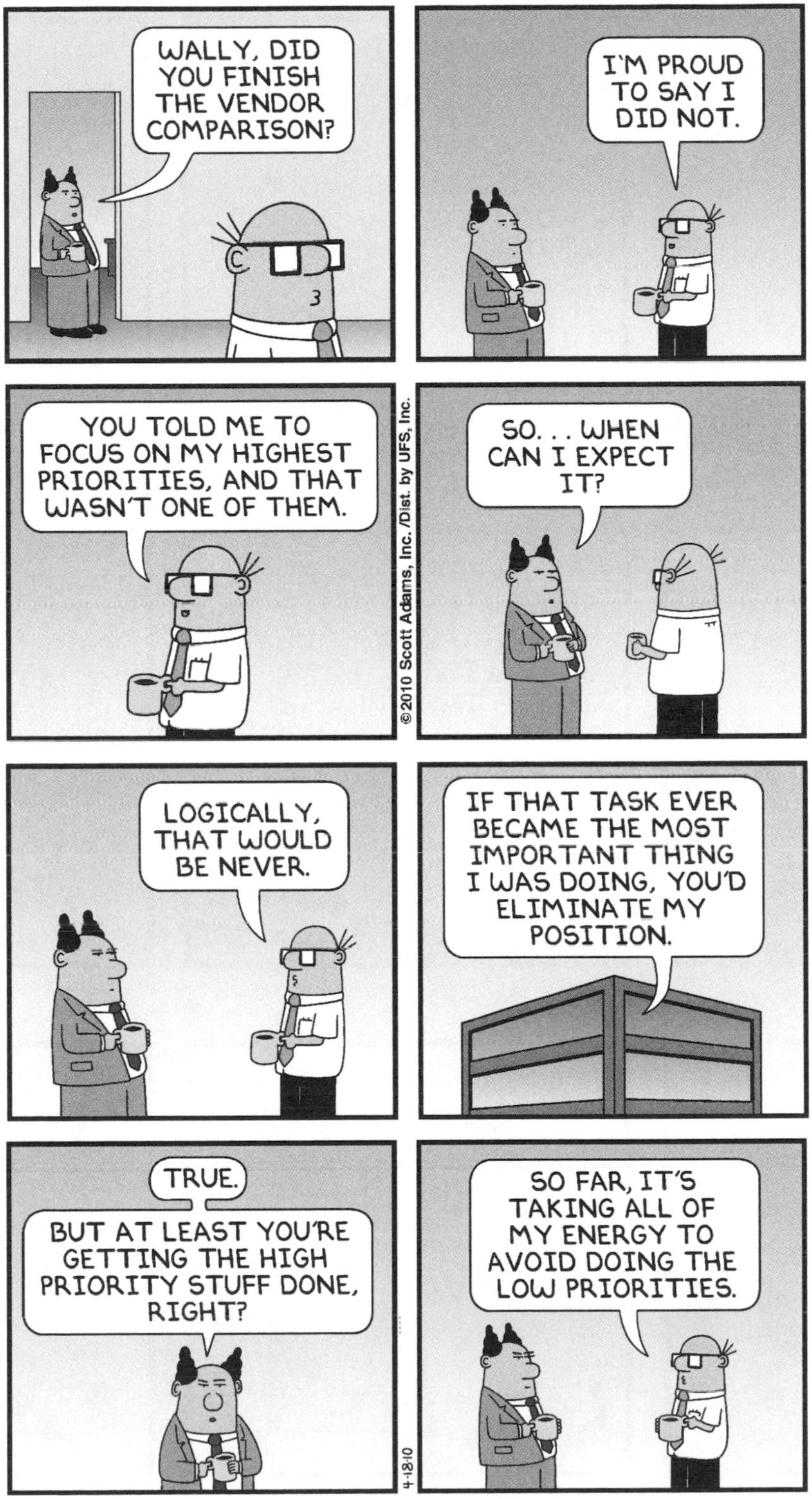
WALLY, DID YOU FINISH THE VENDOR COMPARISON?
I'M PROUD TO SAY I DID NOT.
YOU TOLD ME TO FOCUS ON MY HIGHEST PRIORITIES, AND THAT WASN'T ONE OF THEM.
SO. . . WHEN CAN I EXPECT IT?
LOGICALLY, THAT WOULD BE NEVER.
IF THAT TASK EVER BECAME THE MOST IMPORTANT THING I WAS DOING, YOU'D ELIMINATE MY POSITION.
TRUE.
BUT AT LEAST YOU'RE GETTING THE HIGH PRIORITY STUFF DONE, RIGHT?
SO FAR, IT'S TAKING ALL OF MY ENERGY TO AVOID DOING THE LOW PRIORITIES.
© 2010 Scott Adams, Inc. /Dist. by UFS, Inc.
4-18-10

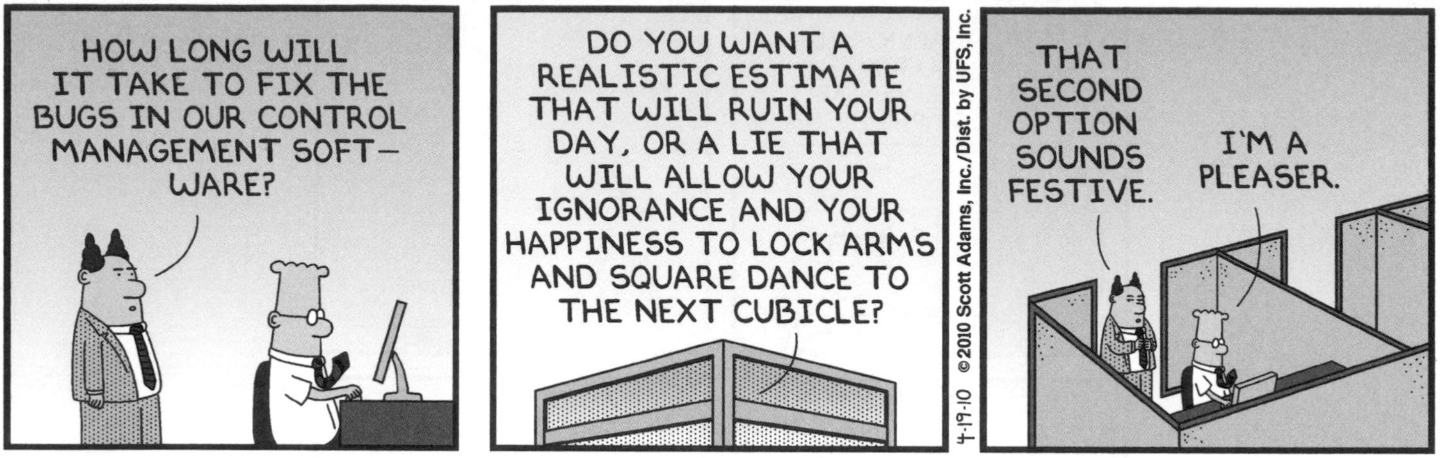
HOW LONG WILL IT TAKE TO FIX THE BUGS IN OUR CONTROL MANAGEMENT SOFT-WARE?
DO YOU WANT A REALISTIC ESTIMATE THAT WILL RUIN YOUR DAY, OR A LIE THAT WILL ALLOW YOUR IGNORANCE AND YOUR HAPPINESS TO LOCK ARMS AND SQUARE DANCE TO THE NEXT CUBICLE?
4-19-10 ©2010 Scott Adams, Inc./Dist. by UFS, Inc.
THAT SECOND OPTION SOUNDS FESTIVE.
I'M A PLEASER.

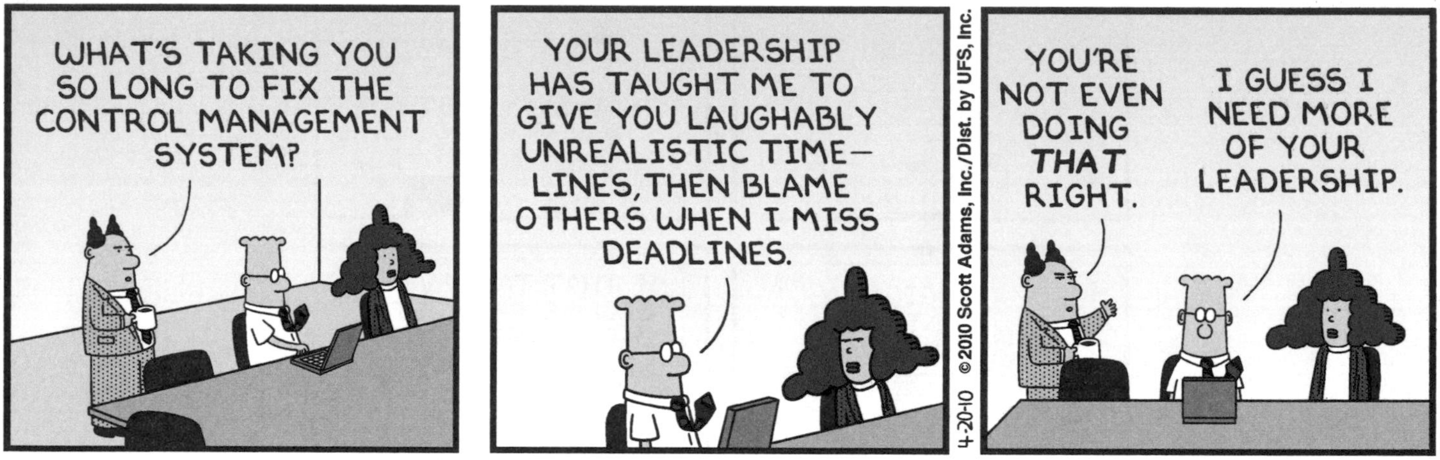
WHAT'S TAKING YOU SO LONG TO FIX THE CONTROL MANAGEMENT SYSTEM?
YOUR LEADERSHIP HAS TAUGHT ME TO GIVE YOU LAUGHABLY UNREALISTIC TIME-LINES, THEN BLAME OTHERS WHEN I MISS DEADLINES.
4-20-10 ©2010 Scott Adams, Inc./Dist. by UFS, Inc.
YOU'RE NOT EVEN DOING *THAT* RIGHT.
I GUESS I NEED MORE OF YOUR LEADERSHIP.

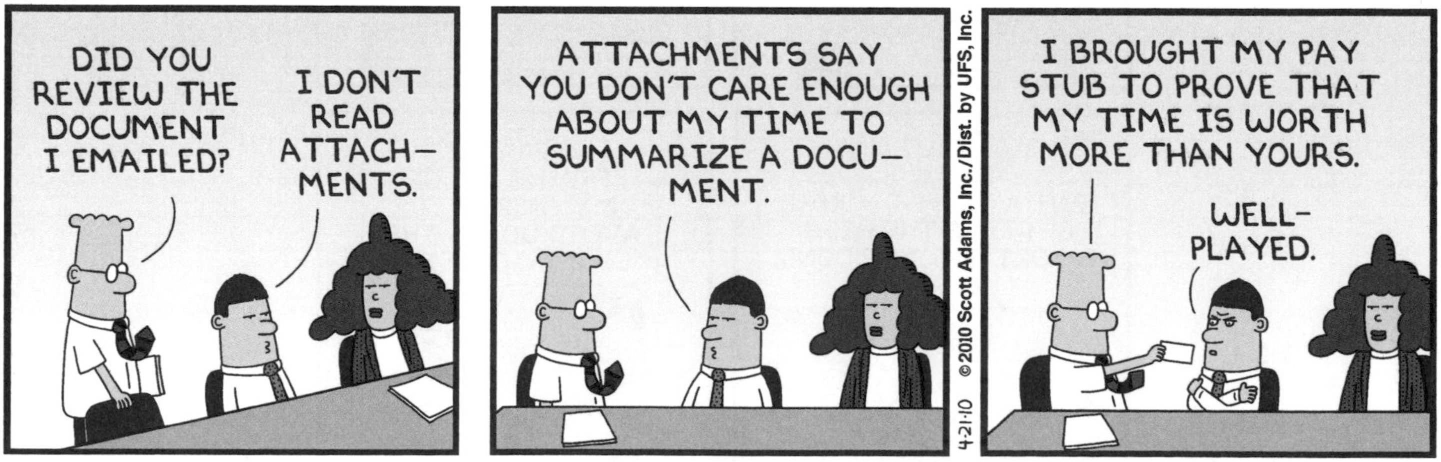
DID YOU REVIEW THE DOCUMENT I EMAILED?
I DON'T READ ATTACH-MENTS.
ATTACHMENTS SAY YOU DON'T CARE ENOUGH ABOUT MY TIME TO SUMMARIZE A DOCU-MENT.
4-21-10 ©2010 Scott Adams, Inc./Dist. by UFS, Inc.
I BROUGHT MY PAY STUB TO PROVE THAT MY TIME IS WORTH MORE THAN YOURS.
WELL-PLAYED.

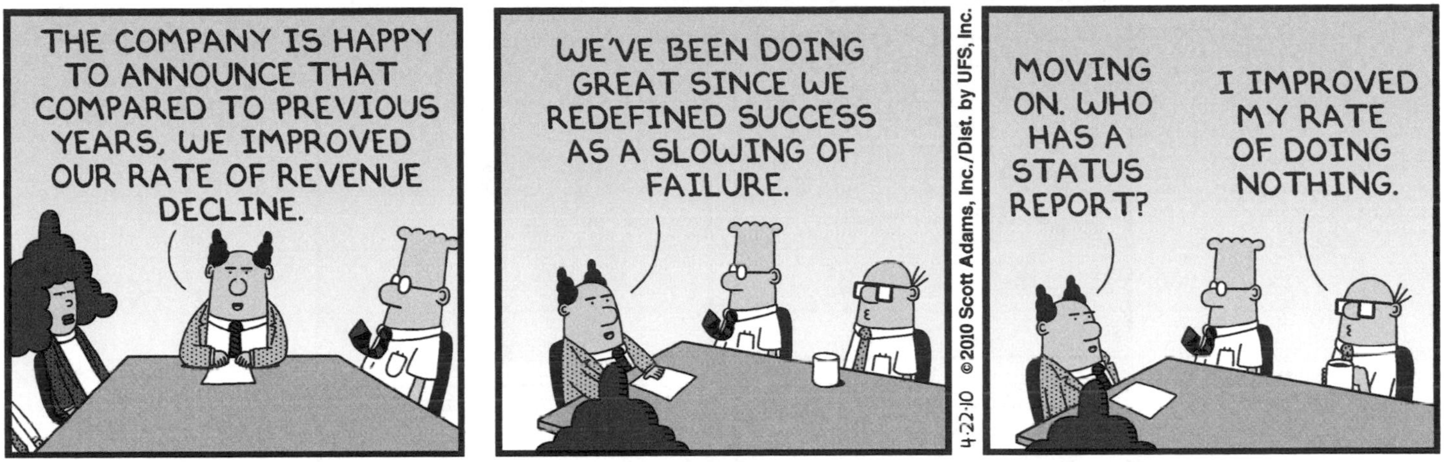
THE COMPANY IS HAPPY TO ANNOUNCE THAT COMPARED TO PREVIOUS YEARS, WE IMPROVED OUR RATE OF REVENUE DECLINE.
WE'VE BEEN DOING GREAT SINCE WE REDEFINED SUCCESS AS A SLOWING OF FAILURE.
4-22-10 ©2010 Scott Adams, Inc./Dist. by UFS, Inc.
MOVING ON. WHO HAS A STATUS REPORT?
I IMPROVED MY RATE OF DOING NOTHING.

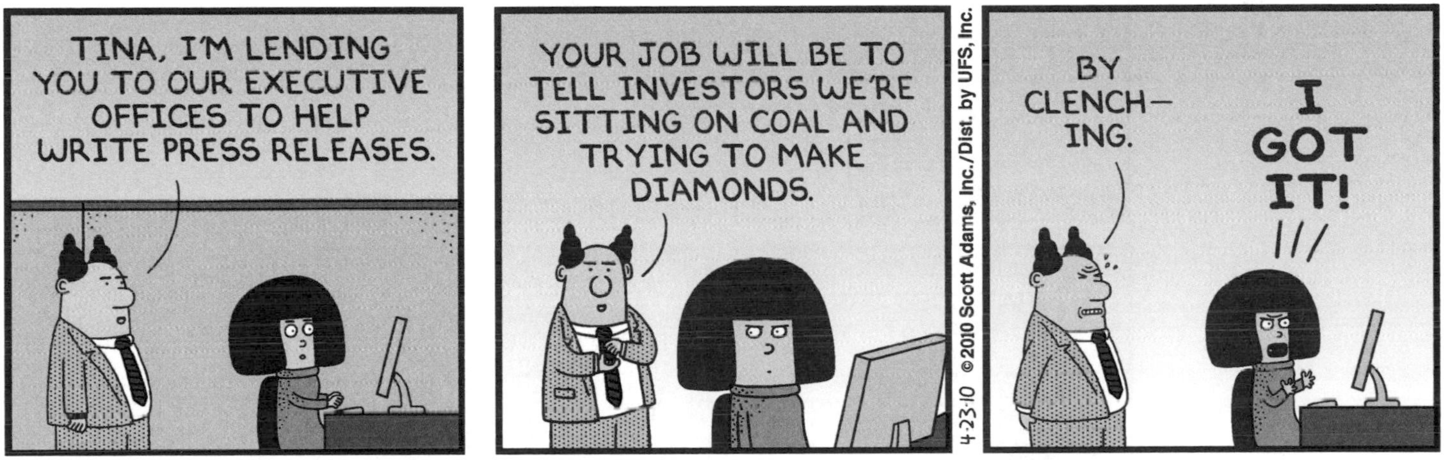
TINA, I'M LENDING YOU TO OUR EXECUTIVE OFFICES TO HELP WRITE PRESS RELEASES.
YOUR JOB WILL BE TO TELL INVESTORS WE'RE SITTING ON COAL AND TRYING TO MAKE DIAMONDS.
4-23-10 ©2010 Scott Adams, Inc./Dist. by UFS, Inc.
BY CLENCH-ING.
I GOT IT!

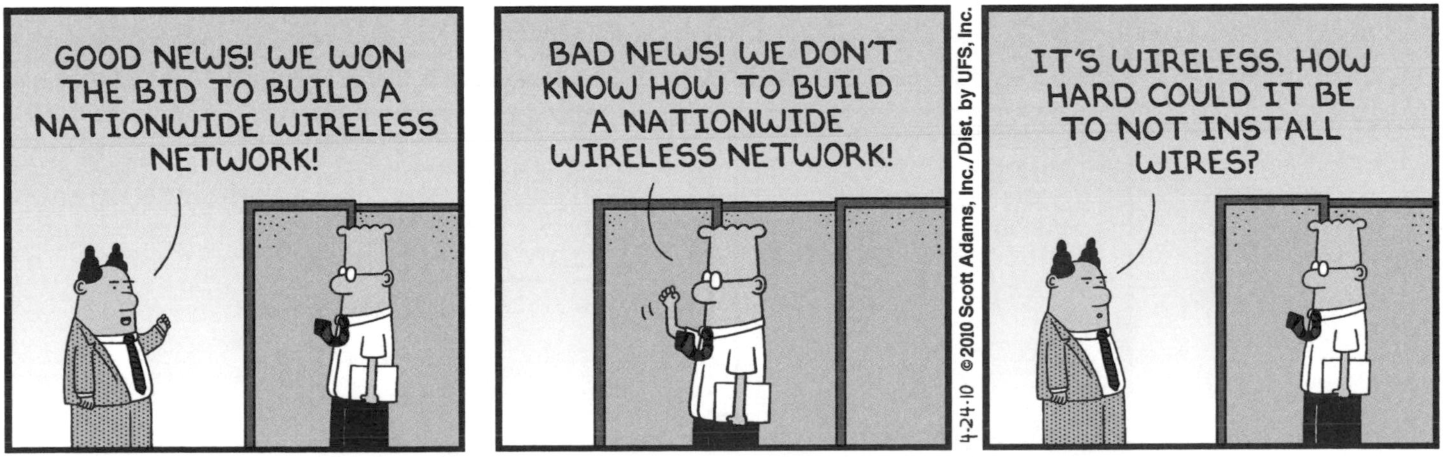
GOOD NEWS! WE WON THE BID TO BUILD A NATIONWIDE WIRELESS NETWORK!
BAD NEWS! WE DON'T KNOW HOW TO BUILD A NATIONWIDE WIRELESS NETWORK!
4-24-10 ©2010 Scott Adams, Inc./Dist. by UFS, Inc.
IT'S WIRELESS. HOW HARD COULD IT BE TO NOT INSTALL WIRES?

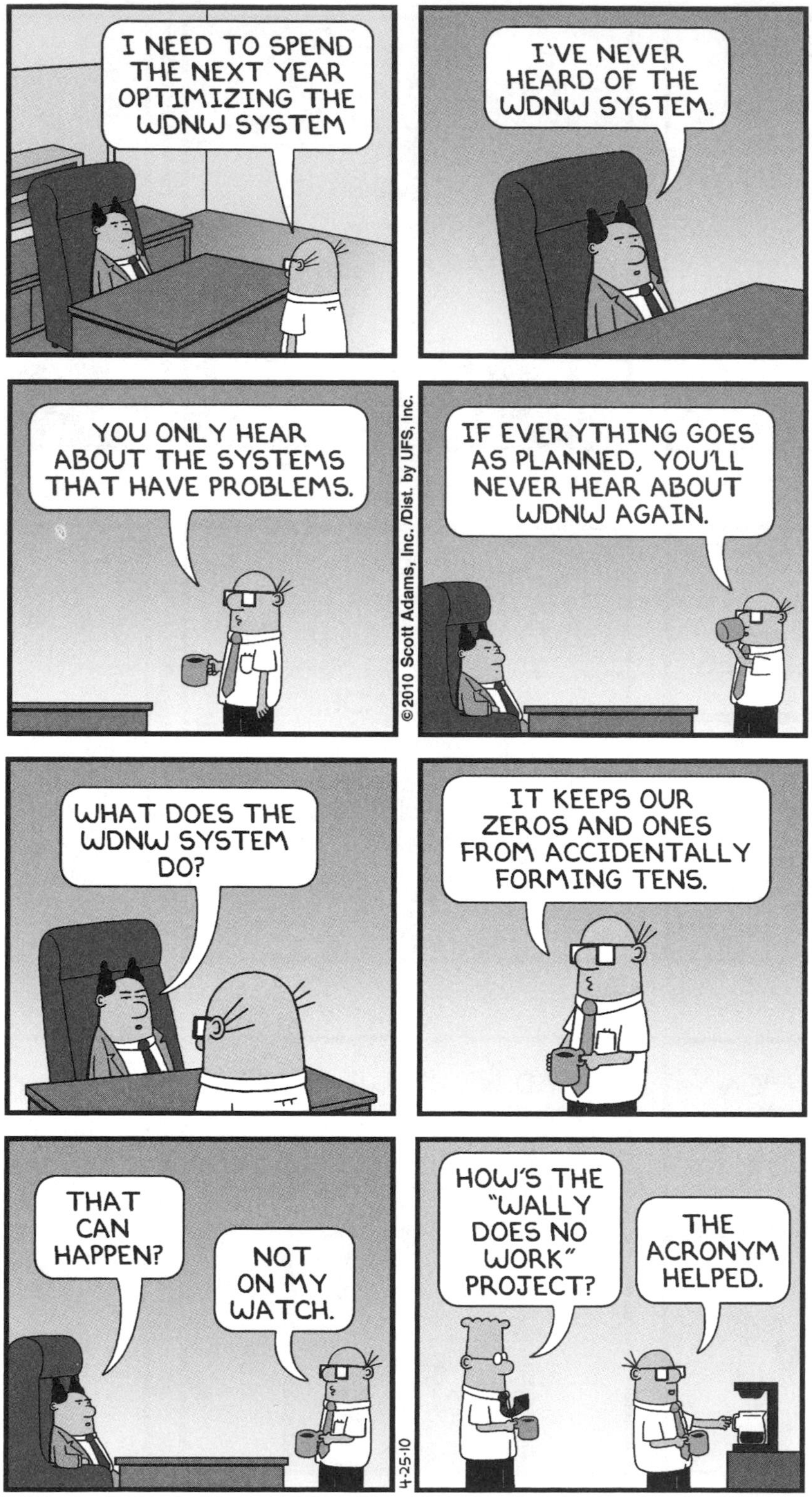
I NEED TO SPEND THE NEXT YEAR OPTIMIZING THE WDNW SYSTEM
I'VE NEVER HEARD OF THE WDNW SYSTEM.
YOU ONLY HEAR ABOUT THE SYSTEMS THAT HAVE PROBLEMS.
IF EVERYTHING GOES AS PLANNED, YOU'LL NEVER HEAR ABOUT WDNW AGAIN.
WHAT DOES THE WDNW SYSTEM DO?
IT KEEPS OUR ZEROS AND ONES FROM ACCIDENTALLY FORMING TENS.
THAT CAN HAPPEN?
NOT ON MY WATCH.
HOW'S THE "WALLY DOES NO WORK" PROJECT?
THE ACRONYM HELPED.
© 2010 Scott Adams, Inc. /Dist. by UFS, Inc.
4-25-10

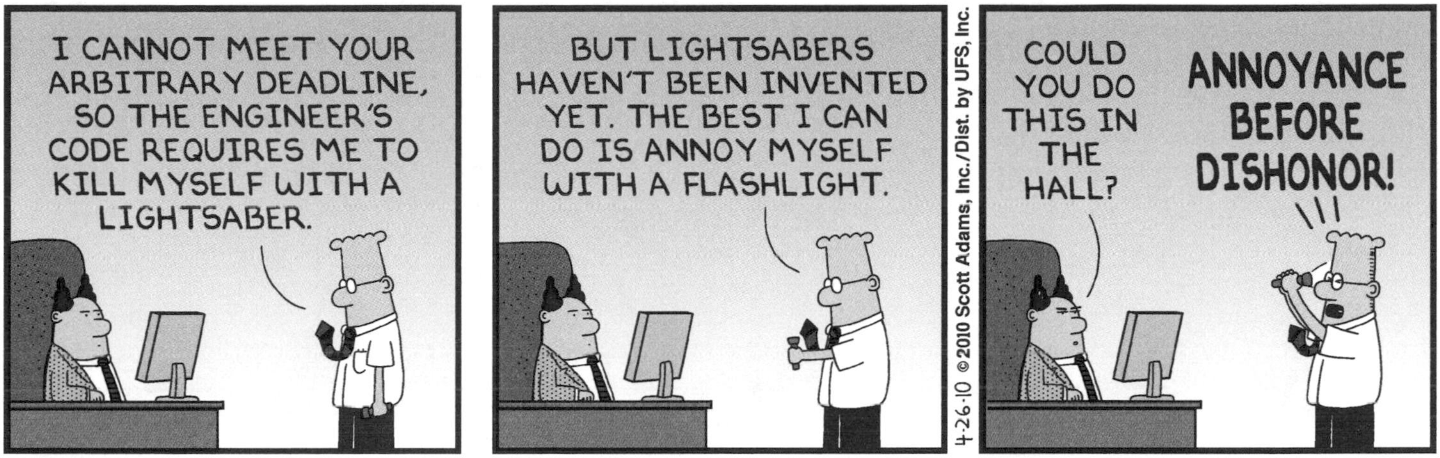
I CANNOT MEET YOUR ARBITRARY DEADLINE, SO THE ENGINEER'S CODE REQUIRES ME TO KILL MYSELF WITH A LIGHTSABER.
BUT LIGHTSABERS HAVEN'T BEEN INVENTED YET. THE BEST I CAN DO IS ANNOY MYSELF WITH A FLASHLIGHT.
4-26-10 © 2010 Scott Adams, Inc./Dist. by UFS, Inc.
COULD YOU DO THIS IN THE HALL?
ANNOYANCE BEFORE DISHONOR!

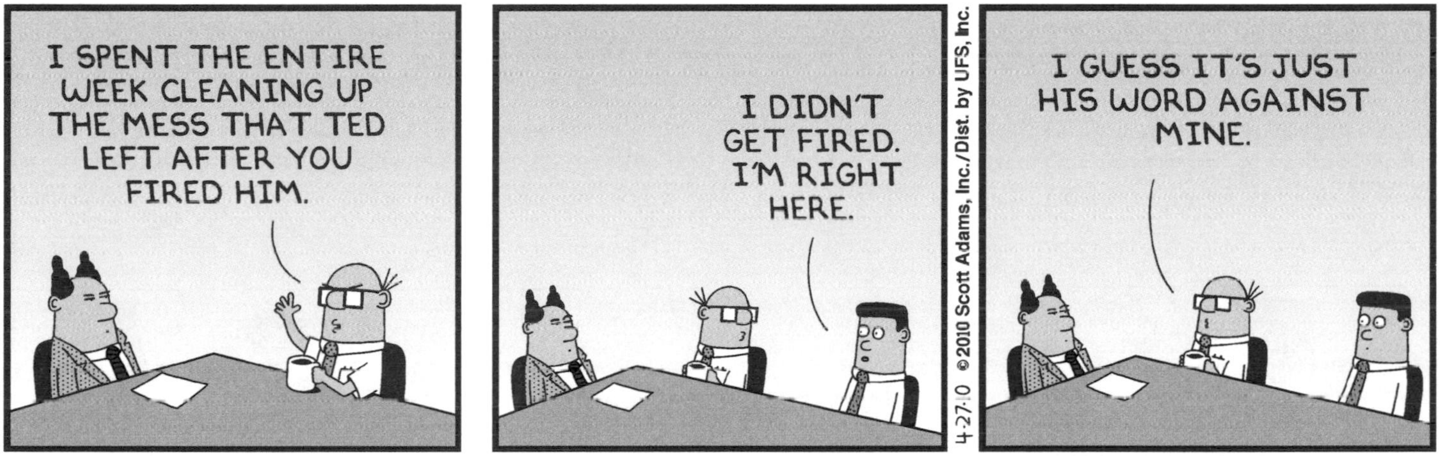
I SPENT THE ENTIRE WEEK CLEANING UP THE MESS THAT TED LEFT AFTER YOU FIRED HIM.
I DIDN'T GET FIRED. I'M RIGHT HERE.
4-27-10 © 2010 Scott Adams, Inc./Dist. by UFS, Inc.
I GUESS IT'S JUST HIS WORD AGAINST MINE.

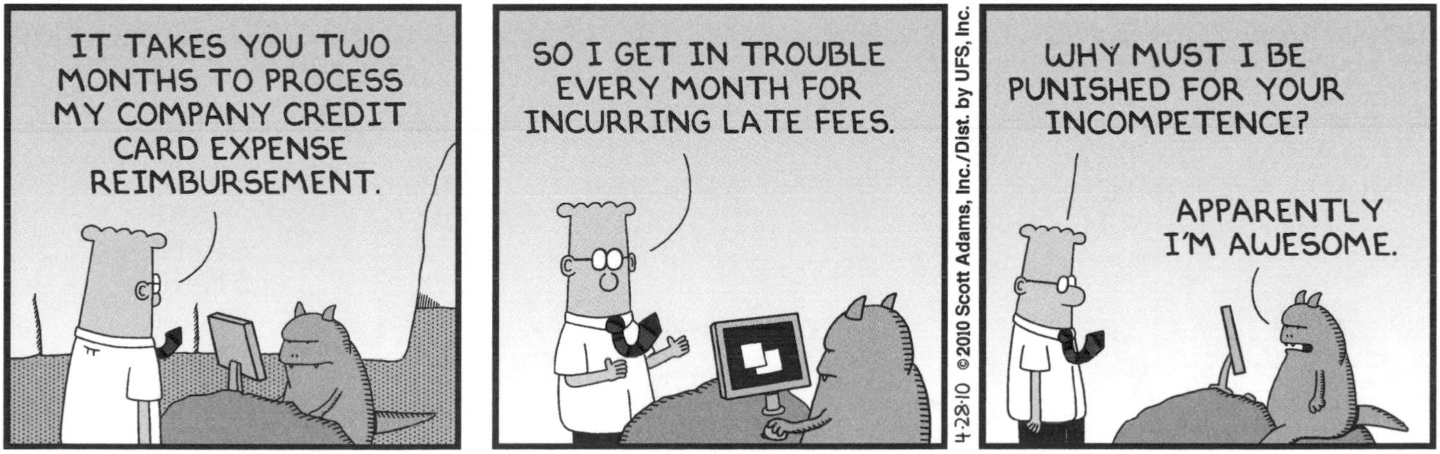
IT TAKES YOU TWO MONTHS TO PROCESS MY COMPANY CREDIT CARD EXPENSE REIMBURSEMENT.
SO I GET IN TROUBLE EVERY MONTH FOR INCURRING LATE FEES.
4-28-10 © 2010 Scott Adams, Inc./Dist. by UFS, Inc.
WHY MUST I BE PUNISHED FOR YOUR INCOMPETENCE?
APPARENTLY I'M AWESOME.

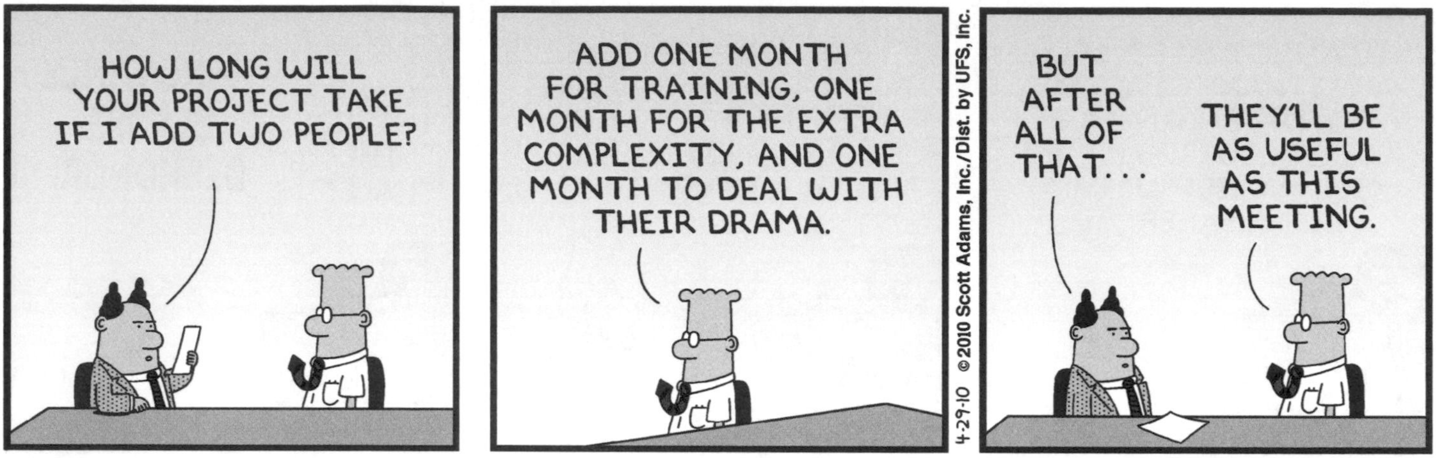
HOW LONG WILL YOUR PROJECT TAKE IF I ADD TWO PEOPLE?
ADD ONE MONTH FOR TRAINING, ONE MONTH FOR THE EXTRA COMPLEXITY, AND ONE MONTH TO DEAL WITH THEIR DRAMA.
4-29-10 ©2010 Scott Adams, Inc./Dist. by UFS, Inc.
BUT AFTER ALL OF THAT...
THEY'LL BE AS USEFUL AS THIS MEETING.

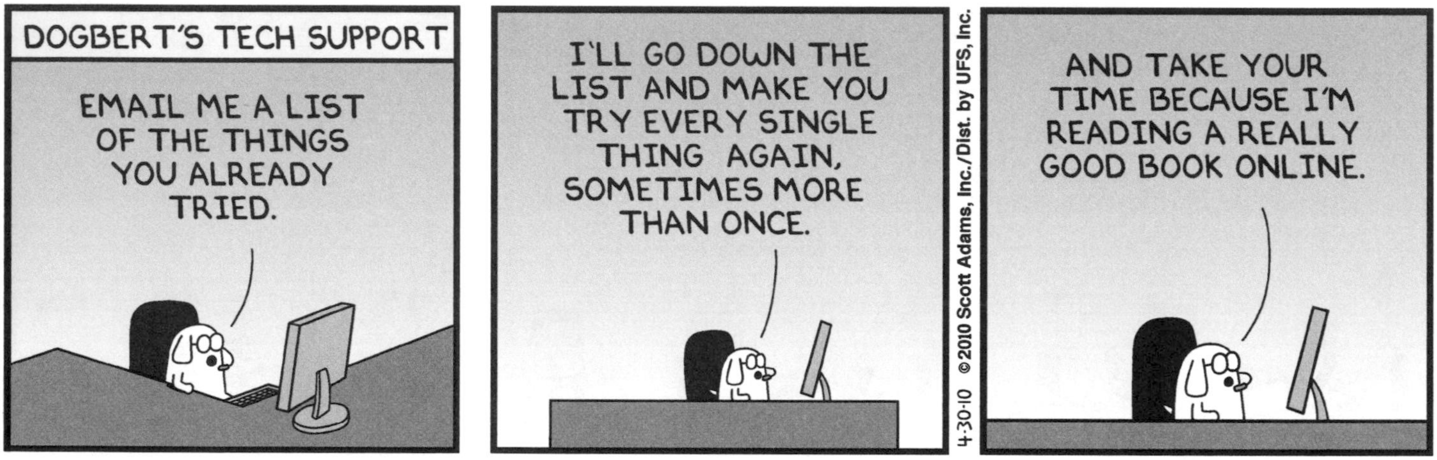
DOGBERT'S TECH SUPPORT
EMAIL ME A LIST OF THE THINGS YOU ALREADY TRIED.
I'LL GO DOWN THE LIST AND MAKE YOU TRY EVERY SINGLE THING AGAIN, SOMETIMES MORE THAN ONCE.
4-30-10 ©2010 Scott Adams, Inc./Dist. by UFS, Inc.
AND TAKE YOUR TIME BECAUSE I'M READING A REALLY GOOD BOOK ONLINE.

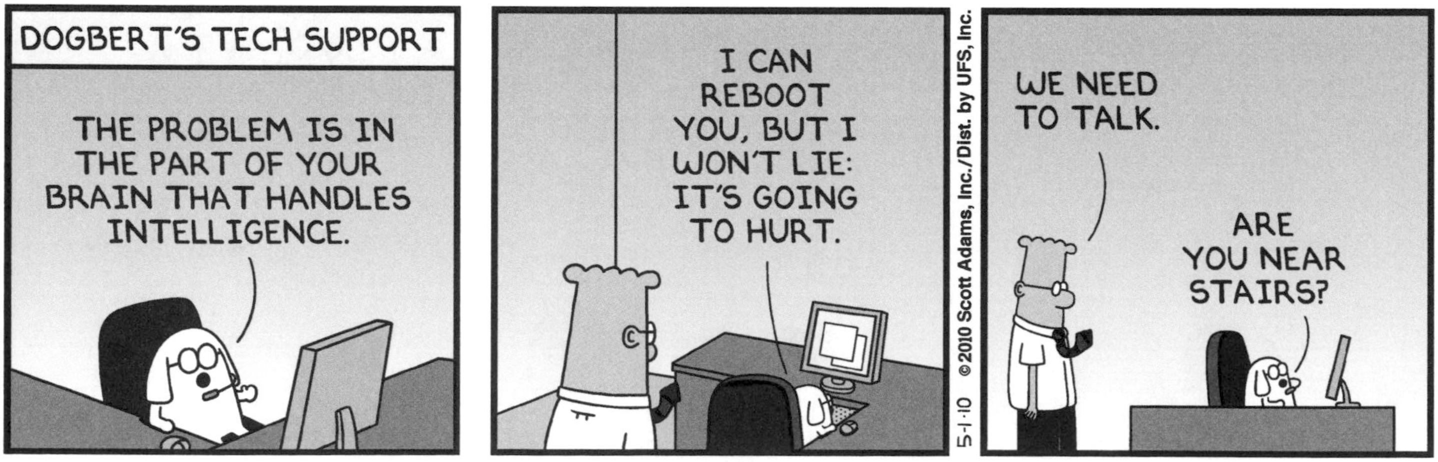
DOGBERT'S TECH SUPPORT
THE PROBLEM IS IN THE PART OF YOUR BRAIN THAT HANDLES INTELLIGENCE.
I CAN REBOOT YOU, BUT I WON'T LIE: IT'S GOING TO HURT.
5-1-10 ©2010 Scott Adams, Inc./Dist. by UFS, Inc.
WE NEED TO TALK.
ARE YOU NEAR STAIRS?

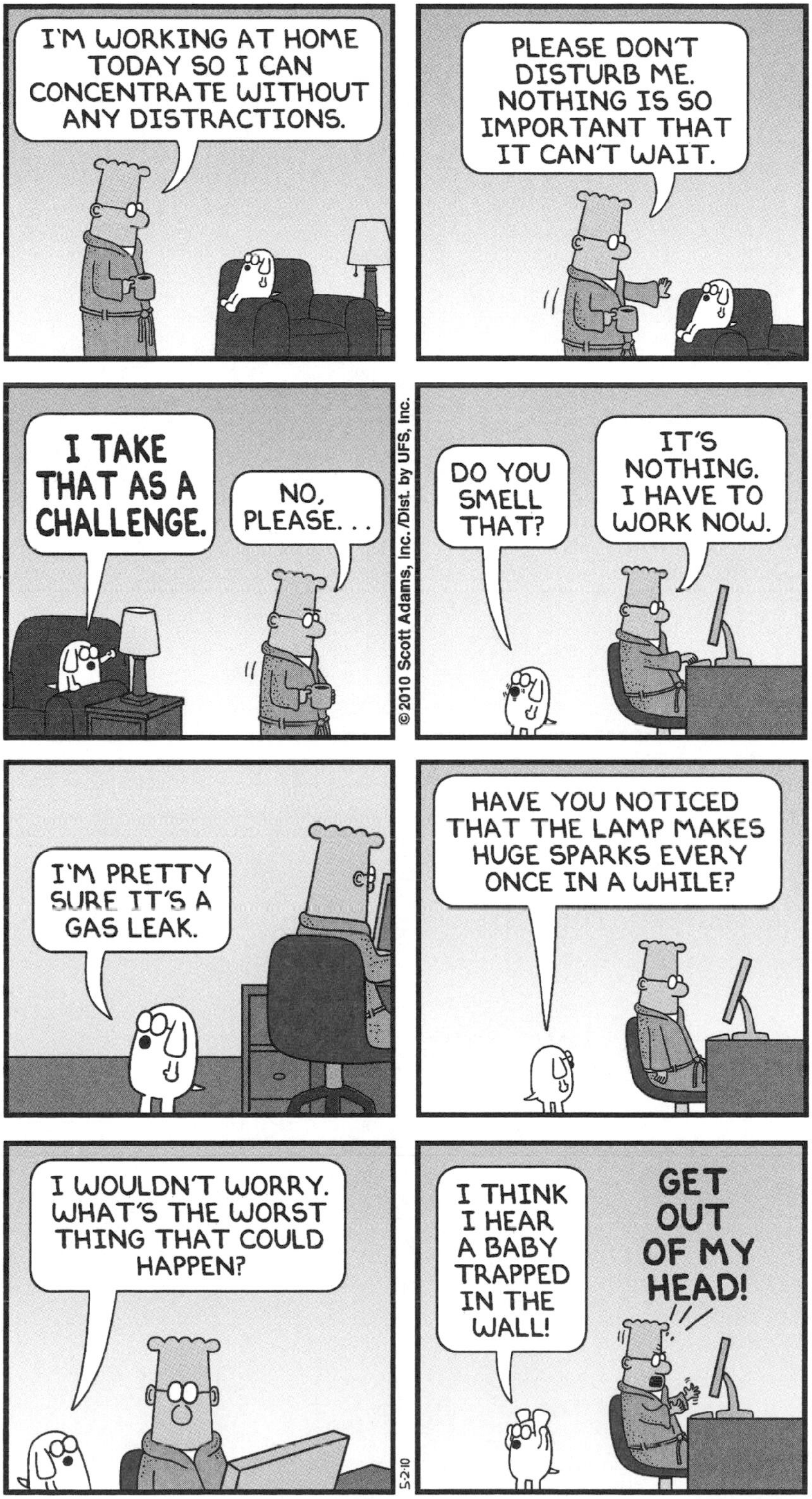
I'M WORKING AT HOME TODAY SO I CAN CONCENTRATE WITHOUT ANY DISTRACTIONS.
PLEASE DON'T DISTURB ME. NOTHING IS SO IMPORTANT THAT IT CAN'T WAIT.
I TAKE THAT AS A CHALLENGE.
NO, PLEASE. . .
©2010 Scott Adams, Inc./Dist. by UFS, Inc.
DO YOU SMELL THAT?
IT'S NOTHING. I HAVE TO WORK NOW.
I'M PRETTY SURE IT'S A GAS LEAK.
HAVE YOU NOTICED THAT THE LAMP MAKES HUGE SPARKS EVERY ONCE IN A WHILE?
I WOULDN'T WORRY. WHAT'S THE WORST THING THAT COULD HAPPEN?
5-2-10
I THINK I HEAR A BABY TRAPPED IN THE WALL!
GET OUT OF MY HEAD!